The UCAS Guide to getting into
NURSING, HEALTHCARE AND SOCIAL WORK

For entry to university and college in 2013

378.41

Published by: UCAS Rosehill New Barn Lane Cheltenham GL52 3LZ

Produced in conjunction with GTI Media Ltd

© UCAS 2012

UCAS is a registered trade mark.

UCAS, a company limited by guarantee, is registered in England and Wales number: 2839815
Registered charity number: 1024741 (England and Wales) and SC038598 (Scotland)

UCAS reference number: PU034013
Publication reference: 12_048
ISBN: 978-1-908077-14-1
Price £15.99

We have made all reasonable efforts to ensure that the information in this publication was correct at time of publication. We will not, however, accept any liability for errors, omissions or changes to information since publication. Wherever possible any changes will be updated on the UCAS website (www.ucas.com).

UCAS and its trading subsidiary, UCAS Media Limited, accept advertising for publications that promote products and services relating to higher education and career progression. Revenue generated by advertising is invested by UCAS in order to enhance our applications services and to keep the cost to applicants as low as possible. Neither UCAS nor UCAS Media Limited endorse the products and services of other organisations that appear in this publication.

Further copies available from UCAS (p&p charges apply):

Contact Publication Services PO Box 130 Cheltenham GL52 3ZF

email: publicationservices@ucas.ac.uk or fax: 01242 544806

For further information about the UCAS application process go to www.ucas.com.

If you need to contact us, details can be found at www.ucas.com/about_us/contact_us

UCAS QUALITY AWARDS

Foreword

THINKING ABOUT NURSING, HEALTHCARE OR SOCIAL WORK?

Finding the course that's right for you at the right university or college can take time and it's important that you use all the resources available to you in making this key decision. We at UCAS have teamed up with TARGETjobs.co.uk to provide you with *The UCAS Guide to getting into Nursing, Healthcare and Social Work* to show you how you can progress from being a student to careers in nursing, healthcare and social work. You will find information on what the subjects include, entry routes and real-life case studies showing how it worked out for others.

Once you know which subject area you might be interested in, you can use the listings of all the full-time higher education courses in nursing, healthcare and social work to see where you can study your subject. The course entry requirements are listed so you can check if getting in would be achievable for you. There's also advice on applying through UCAS, telling you what you need to know at each stage of the application process in just six easy steps to starting university or college.

We hope you find this publication helps you to choose and make your application to a course and university or college that is right for you.

On behalf of UCAS and TARGETjobs.co.uk, I wish you every success in your research.

Mary Curnock Cook, Chief Executive, UCAS

At TARGETjobs we champion paid work experience for UK university students. Find internships and placements across all sectors, plus take part in the TARGETjobs Undergraduate of the Year awards.

TARGETjobs.co.uk

the best possible start to your career

Introducing nursing, health and social care

It could be you…

... empowering someone with a mental illness to take responsibility for their life

— mental health social worker

... building a rapport with patients and making their stay in hospital as comfortable as possible

— adult nurse

... teaching a stroke sufferer a new way to get dressed so that they can be more independent

— occupational therapist

... giving a woman the right information so that she can decide where to give birth to her baby

— midwife

... offering advice to a woman in an abusive relationship about how best to protect her children

— domestic violence social worker

... and lots more besides. Could a career in nursing, health or social care be for you? The aim of this guide is to help you decide.

A CAREER IN NURSING, HEALTH OR SOCIAL CARE?

- The Health Professions Council has 219,000 allied health professionals registered from 15 different professions – see **A career in nursing and healthcare** on page 14
- There are over 1 million social care workers in the UK, making up 5% of the workforce. Qualified social workers are in demand – see **A career in social care** on page 24
- Social workers can work with children or adults in a range of different specialisms such as mental health, learning disabilities and asylum seekers – see **Which area?** on page 27
- Admissions tutors and recruiters look for good interpersonal and communication skills, as well as leadership and problem-solving ability – see **The career for you?** on page 31

NURSING AND HEALTHCARE

Healthcare encompasses a range of different careers from nursing and midwifery to complementary medicine and the allied health professions. People enter these professions for a number of reasons, often combining an existing interest with a desire to make a difference to people's lives. Whatever the reason for joining, it's an exciting time to enter the healthcare workforce in the UK. Changes to the provision of NHS services will create further opportunities for practitioners to work in the community, while it is likely that healthcare services will, in the future, be delivered by a range of different service providers rather than just the NHS.

SOCIAL CARE

A career in social services is a job like no other; in fact it's much more than just a job. It's a career that can give you a pivotal role in another person's life. Social service workers provide practical help and support to individuals and families in times of crisis. They may be needed in the early or final stages of life, or in response to specific obstacles faced as a result of physical make-up, environment or lifestyle (for example, physical handicaps, mental health problems or substance misuse).

Recent changes to the professional status of social workers means that there are now codes of practice for social workers and their employers. The codes of practice set down the standards of conduct and practice that people can expect from social service workers and their employers.

The degree in social work introduced in 2004 and the register of qualified social workers have also put social workers on a similar footing to other registered professionals, such as doctors, nurses and teachers. The Care Council for Wales (CCW), the General Social Care Council (GSCC) (subject to parliamentary approval, the GSCC will cease to exist after 31 July 2012, and its functions will be taken over by the Health Professions Council), the Northern Ireland Social Care Council (NISCC) and the Scottish Social Services Council (SSSC) are responsible for registering people who work in social services and regulating their education and training. The four councils do this by registering qualified social workers and key groups of social service workers. The aim of registering social service workers and social work students is to ensure that people who use services and carers can rely on a workforce that is properly trained, appropriately qualified and effectively regulated.

YOUR PART IN NURSING, HEALTH AND SOCIAL CARE

Are you good at problem solving? Are you a team player? Are you good with people? Great. By joining the health and social care sector you could put these skills to good use and make a real difference to people's lives.

Inside this guide you'll find help and guidance to choose the course that's right for you at the institution that suits you best. You'll find examples of the great jobs you can do in health and social care, and personal stories from the people doing them. You'll also find information on how much you can expect to be paid. Read on to discover:

- the main areas of work and roles on offer
- what it takes to work in health and social care
- how to get in and the paths to qualification
- advice from people working in the sector.

Why nursing, health and social care?

Choose a career that is...

VARIED

There is such a wide variety of careers on offer within the health and social care professions that you're sure to find something to suit your skills and interests. Those working in healthcare include nurses, midwives, prosthetists, arts therapists, dieticians and occupational therapists, among others. Each in turn will work across a range of different areas, such as in research or dealing directly with patients. Once you are a qualified social worker there are many different options including working in general frontline services or choosing to specialise in areas such as child protection, criminal justice, forensic social work, asylum seekers, children and families, community care or mental health.

But it isn't just the career options that are varied. Health and social workers work in a number of different settings as well, such as hospitals, clinics or schools – and you can be sure that even if you are

treating the same problems, the people you meet every day will ensure that no two days are ever the same.

CHALLENGING AND REWARDING

Social workers are professionals who help support and protect people who are vulnerable and at risk. They work with people who are experiencing social and emotional problems, as well as their families if they are affected. Health professionals work with people suffering from illness or injury who are in need of medical support that could save their life or improve their day-to-day living. However, if you take a look at what those working in the profession say (see box on the following page), you'll see that the ability to make a difference is a common theme. Being able to see the direct effects of your work in the well-being of your patients is pretty hard to beat in terms of job satisfaction.

SECURE IN THE LONG TERM

Most people will come into contact with social services in their lifetime. Whether you are using a service yourself or if it's a friend or relative, you'll know how important a quality care service can be. People will always fall ill, be involved in accidents and need help recovering from operations or integrating into society, so your skills, knowledge and expertise will always be in demand. Changes to the organisation of services in the NHS mean that you won't necessarily be tied to one workplace or location, and working in health or social care means that you could find a job anywhere in the country – or even take your skills overseas.

HIGHLY SKILLED

Both social workers and healthcare professionals work with vulnerable people every day who are in need of care and support. They must make decisions and recommendations, based on their knowledge and skills, that could affect the rest of a person's life. Because of this, they need to be highly trained and must keep their skills up-to-date to ensure that they have the right tools for the job. From nursing to acupuncture, dietetics to radiography, healthcare professionals constantly update their skills and learn new techniques so that they can treat and care for patients better. Social workers are required to renew their registration with the General Social Care Council every three years and to do so must demonstrate that they have met the requirements of the Post Registration Training and Learning (PRTL) scheme by completing activities that contribute to their professional development.

WHAT DO THOSE IN THE PROFESSIONS SAY?

'Gain as much practical experience as you can so you can apply your knowledge in a fitness or health setting. Focus on understanding why people behave as they do – health psychology is an important part of this job. Walk the talk. If you want your clients to live healthily you need to do so yourself!'
Chris Jones, professional head of physiology, page 44

'I like the sheer variety of tasks that I deal with daily. It's also fantastic to feel that the work I do is useful to someone and can make a difference to their life.'
Katherine Fincham, specialist support officer, page 46

'Anyone from any area of work is welcome, as the most important criteria is a drive and commitment to working with partners to make a difference to people's lives, particularly those who are most disadvantaged or vulnerable.'
Madeline Heaney, head of health and social wellbeing improvement, page 48

'The best thing is meeting lots of new people, who usually come to the clinic feeling miserable and vulnerable – in pain and sometimes unable to walk – and watching these patients flourish under osteopathic care. Hearing stories of how their treatment has positively changed their lives is very rewarding.'
Amy Hope, osteopath, page 50

'Don't be scared of things like blood or bodily fluid – you get used to them! You need to work hard and have good time-management skills. Keep your friends close – tell them you will be less available but keep in touch and do take some time off to have fun.'
Valerian Delagarde, second year, pre-registration adult nursing diploma, page 52

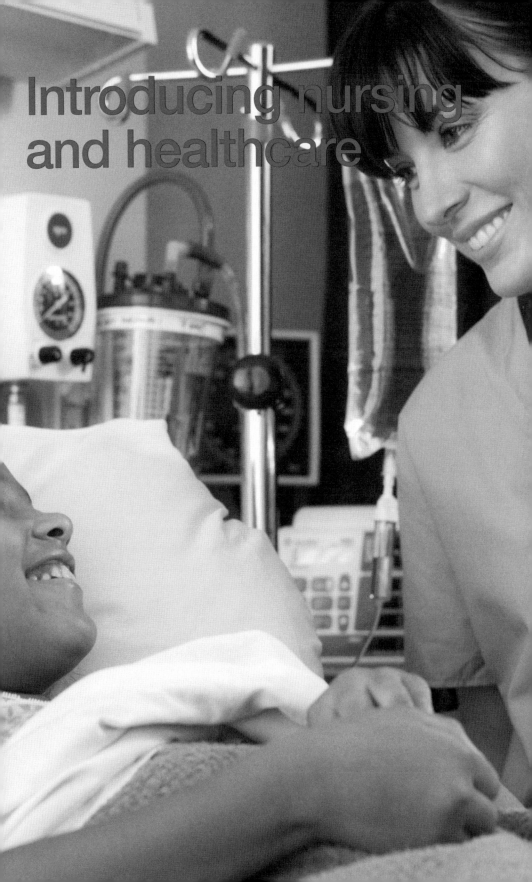

Introducing nursing and healthcare

A career in nursing and healthcare

The healthcare sector is huge and although dominated by the National Health Service (NHS) in the UK, it encompasses a wide variety of professions and employers. Private healthcare organisations offer services such as hospital treatments, cosmetic surgery, dentistry, and laser eye surgery, and there has also been a significant increase in the range of complementary and alternative therapies to which patients have access, both within the NHS and privately.

The health sector is traditionally split into primary and secondary care. Primary care is your first port of call when you have a health problem and includes general practitioners (GPs), dentists, opticians and pharmacists. Secondary care is treatment that is normally carried out in a hospital and which cannot be dealt with by a primary care specialist.

WHICH PROFESSION?

The NHS is one of the world's largest employers, so there is no lack of opportunity to get involved. You could work in any one of a number of different professions from nursing, midwifery and the allied health professions to healthcare science and health informatics. In fact, the range of professions is so large that the NHS has split them into ten different areas – see **Which area?** on page 17 for more information. Which area and career you choose will depend entirely on your skills, preferences and what you want to get from your career, but all will require the ability to work in a team and to communicate with people from a diverse range of backgrounds.

WORKING CONDITIONS

Depending on which career you choose, working in healthcare can be stressful due to the large number of patients to be seen and limited resources. However, the satisfaction that health practitioners receive from being able to see the direct effects of their work on their patients' well-being is immense and, for most, far outweighs the downsides.

Allied health practitioners, particularly those working in the NHS, can often be flexible in terms of their place and hours of work. The NHS actively promotes a good work/life balance for its entire staff, usually offering flexi-time working and career breaks among other benefits. This is more readily available in some areas than others, but the NHS also provides continuous training and development opportunities to help you progress throughout your career.

Plans to increase the range of healthcare services provided in the community, and an increase in the number and range of services being contracted out to private companies, does mean that some healthcare professionals (such as those in the allied health professions, for example) may not be employed directly by the NHS in the future. Instead, private organisations will be contracted to provide certain NHS services and will employ healthcare practitioners to provide them.

PAY

If you work in the NHS you will be subject to the Agenda for Change (AfC) pay scale, which covers all staff except doctors, dentists and the most senior managers. Jobs are matched to one of nine pay bands that determine the level of basic salary. Each band is again split into 'points', which staff progress through in order to reach the next band. For example, an entry-level midwife will usually start on band 5, which is broken down into 9 points from point 16 at £21,176 to point 23 at £27,625. See the NHS careers website **www.nhscareers.nhs.uk** for more information about the different bands and salary levels. Salaries in the private sector will vary so you will need to check details with individual employers.

NHS STATISTICS

- The NHS is one of the largest employers in the world, employing approximately 1.4 million staff.
- NHS staff are in contact with over one million patients and their families every day.
- Men and women live an average of 10 years longer than before the NHS was created in 1948.

STAFF STATISTICS

Staff in the NHS in 2011

- Overall staff total: 1,350,377
- Professionally qualified clinical staff: 685,066
- GPs: 39,780
- Nurses: 348,693
- Qualified scientific, therapeutic and technical staff: 152,216
- Support to clinical staff: 219,624

Which area?

Choosing which area you want to enter is an important decision.

If you are thinking about healthcare you might be forgiven for thinking that you have a straight choice between doctor, dentist, nurse or midwife. In reality, the range of different careers on offer in the healthcare sector is simply staggering. In order to make things easier to understand, the NHS has split the professions into 12 areas. Over the next few pages you can explore some of these areas to learn about the careers on offer and find out which one is right for you.

ALLIED HEALTH PROFESSIONS

The allied health professions encompass a range of careers whose main aim is to offer care and support to patients. They are a very hands-on group and often work with patients independently, offering treatment options and long-term care in a lot of cases. There are 12 different allied healthcare professions that you could join, outlined below.

Arts therapies

Using music, art and drama, arts therapists work with clients with emotional and/or developmental needs, who can find it difficult to put their thoughts and feelings into words. Therapy provides a non-threatening atmosphere in which clients can express difficulties that are affecting their well-being and create non-verbal images or objects that become a form of communication and self-expression.

Chiropody and podiatry

Chiropodists and podiatrists diagnose and treat abnormalities of the foot and lower limb. Specialist areas can include anything from homeopathic treatment to rheumatic care, podopaediatrics (treating children's feet), podiatric dermatology or treating diabetics' feet. Many patients will refer themselves or they can be referred by their GP or hospital consultant. For more information please see *The UCAS Guide to getting into Sports Science and Physiotherapy*.

Dietetics

Dieticians are highly trained healthcare professionals who work in the field of diet and nutrition. They are based in hospitals or work as part of a community-based health team, advising patients on issues including weight management, manipulating diet or devising feeding regimes (if a patient is experiencing difficulty swallowing following a stroke, for example). Everything a dietician does is focused around communicating with patients and educating them about diet and nutrition.

Occupational therapy

Working with people experiencing physical, psychological or social difficulties, occupational therapists (OTs) help clients to achieve the things they want to do in their daily lives. OTs do not provide 'care' for their clients but rather act as a facilitator, offering advice about how to do things differently, using specialist equipment perhaps, to allow their clients to lead as independent a life as possible.

Operating department practice

Caring for patients who may be vulnerable, nervous or in pain, operating department practitioners (ODPs) are part of a team that monitors and reassures patients during their stay in hospital at all stages of surgery. They will work with anaesthetists, surgeons and nurses to prepare and monitor anaesthetic and surgical equipment, and provide care and expertise for patients in recovery.

Orthoptics

Orthoptists are responsible for the diagnosis and treatment of eye problems, particularly abnormal eye movements. Their role is to ensure that patients have the best possible vision in each eye, as well as good 3D vision when they use their eyes together as a pair. The majority of an orthoptist's work will be with children, who could have a lazy eye and need to wear a patch for example, or with very old people, who could have difficulty controlling their eye movements. Most orthoptists are hospital-based, so patients will be referred to them by other members of the healthcare team. For more information on orthoptics please see *The UCAS Guide to getting into Medicine, Dentistry and Optometry*.

Physiotherapy

Physiotherapists treat the physical problems patients face caused by accident, injury or age. They can work in a range of areas, including respiratory therapy on wards and intensive care units, neurological physiotherapy, musculoskeletal outpatients, orthopaedics, paediatrics, ergonomics or sports physiotherapy with elite athletes. They are responsible for the care and management of patients' rehabilitation, liaising with other health professionals, the patient's family and the patients themselves. For more information please see *The UCAS Guide to getting into Sports Science and Physiotherapy*.

Prosthetics and orthotics

Prosthetists provide care for people who require an artificial limb (called a prosthesis) while orthotists provide aids such as braces, callipers or splints (called orthoses) for people needing physical support or protection. The aim of treatment in both cases is to facilitate everyday life. Most prosthetists and orthotists work in rehabilitation centres, hospitals or clinics, often in close consultation with other members of the healthcare team.

Psychology

Most psychologists working in healthcare are clinical psychologists, which means they apply the principles of psychology to healthcare issues – for example, working with people struggling to come to terms with mental health problems or people who have experienced a severe trauma. Patients will see a psychologist for group or individual therapy and will often need several appointments, although treatment can sometimes take several months to complete. For more information please see *The UCAS Guide to getting into Psychology*.

Psychotherapy

Using a range of techniques based on dialogue, communication and behavioural change, psychotherapists aim to improve the mental or emotional health of a client, or to improve group relationships such as in a family. The length of therapy can vary, but the client and therapist will meet for an assessment session to map out the territory they are going to cover and the client will then be asked to commit to a minimum number of sessions.

Radiography

There are two sorts of radiographer: diagnostic and therapeutic. Diagnostic radiographers produce high-quality images to diagnose an injury or disease using a range of techniques including x-rays, computer tomography, magnetic resonance imaging and ultrasound. Therapeutic radiographers are part of an oncology team who treat patients suffering from cancer, using ionising radiation to deliver doses of radiation to a tumour while minimising the amount of exposure to the surrounding healthy tissue.

Speech and language therapy

Speech and language therapists offer a service for managing difficulties with communication, speech and language, and eating, drinking and swallowing (EDS). Therapists can choose to specialise in early years, childhood or adult disorders and provide direct intervention, working with a client either one-to-one or in a small group. Cases are then closely monitored to see if there has been any improvement, or if it will be necessary for a client to have ongoing support.

HEALTHCARE SCIENCE

Healthcare scientists are involved in the prevention, diagnosis and treatment of medical conditions. They are valued members of the healthcare team and will work with doctors, nurses and allied health professionals to assist in the treatment and diagnosis of patients. There are four career options.

- **Pharmacy**
  Pharmacists evaluate new medicines and work with the wider healthcare team to ensure their cost-effective use, as well as supervising staff involved in medicine distribution. Please see the *Progression to Medicine, Dentistry and Optometry* title for courses.
- **Life sciences and pathology**
  Scientists in this area investigate the cause and progression of illnesses, increase understanding of the genetic components of illnesses or provide solutions to infertility. They can work in hospital laboratories, in the community or in other health protection and organ transplant agencies.
- **Physiological sciences**
  Physiological scientists investigate how organs and body systems function to diagnose and treat abnormalities, restoring function or reducing the consequences of an abnormality for a patient. Scientists in this area have direct contact with patients and use specialist equipment.

- **Clinical engineering and physical sciences**
  Work in this area centres around developing new ways to measure what is happening in the body. This enables scientists to devise new diagnosis methods or treatments and to ensure that equipment functions correctly.

NURSING

Nursing is a demanding but hugely satisfying profession that allows you to work with a wide range of people, helping them to recover from an operation or enabling them to lead an independent life as part of the community. The nursing profession is separated into four branches and you'll need to choose which area appeals to you during your training.

- **Adult nursing**
  Adult nurses care for the physical aspects of adults, which involves monitoring their blood pressure, heart rate and bodily functions as well as helping patients to wash, dress and get about. Adult nurses need to be able to assess how sick patients are and respond to changes quickly.

- **Children's nursing**
  Children's nurses can work with children who have relatively minor illnesses right through to those who have serious, chronic and/or life-threatening conditions. Their work is as much about providing reassurance to the child's family as it is about providing care for the child.

- **Mental health nursing**
  Mental health nurses work with service users (see page 25 to find out what we mean by service user), their carers and their families in a range of settings and help the recovery of people whose mental health problems require a period of hospital care. Nurses also work in community teams to help people in their homes or in the local community.

- **Learning disability nursing**
  Learning disability nurses work with people who have a learning disability that presents a significant impairment to intellectual and social functions. These impairments are present from childhood and are not the result of an accident or illness in adulthood. People with a learning disability (also known as a learning difficulty) often experience physical, sensory and/or mental health problems.

Qualified nurses who have gained relevant experience can go on to a number of specialist roles such as: a **practice nurse** who works in a GP's surgery or in the community; a **district nurse** visiting people in their own homes or in residential care homes to provide care and support for patients and their families; a **school nurse** visiting schools to carry out screening programmes to check that children are developing healthily; or a **health visitor** focusing on promoting health and the prevention of illness rather than treatment.

MIDWIFERY

Midwives are multi-skilled professionals who offer support to women, their partners and their families through each stage of pregnancy, labour and delivery, and the first phase of postnatal care. Their tasks can include carrying out clinical examinations, providing advice on parenting and breastfeeding, running antenatal classes and administering pain-relief drugs. Midwives enjoy a high level of independence and responsibility, usually working in shifts to ensure that continual support is available for women throughout the day and night. It's essential that midwives are able to put people at ease and reassure patients, so interpersonal skills and a caring attitude are a must.

COMPLEMENTARY AND ALTERNATIVE MEDICINE

Complementary and alternative medicine (CAM) is a recognised area of healthcare practice that covers a range of different therapies including acupuncture, aromatherapy, homeopathy, massage and osteopathy. For example, acupuncture is used in some NHS hospitals to assist with childbirth while other CAM therapies are used in the palliative care of cancer patients.

Be aware that CAM therapies in the NHS are usually provided by an NHS professional (eg doctor, nurse or physiotherapist) who has had additional training, or by a suitably qualified external contractor who has been brought in to provide the service instead. Full-time NHS appointments are not widely available, but when they are they will usually involve working at more than one site.

ADDITIONAL OPPORTUNITIES

There are also opportunities in the ambulance service, as a dentist or doctor, in health informatics, management and the wider healthcare team. See the NHS careers website at **www.nhscareers.nhs.uk** for more information.

Focus your career with the TARGETjobs Careers Report. Using biographical data, information about your interests and insightful psychometric testing, the Careers Report gives you a clear picture of jobs that match your skills and personality.

TARGETjobs.co.uk

the best possible start to your career

Introducing social care

A career in social care

If you are interested in a challenging career with enormous potential for personal and professional growth, then social care could be for you.

Social care is one of the major public service areas. It includes almost any occupation that helps people to overcome obstacles in their lives, from protecting a child from a violent home to promoting the independence of a mentally ill service user (see page 25 to find out what we mean by service user). Whatever area of specialism you choose, you'll be helping to make people's lives better. The work can be challenging but, as you'll see from the **Case studies** of people working in social care (see page 43), it's incredibly rewarding to feel that your work is making a positive difference to people's lives.

Social work is at the heart of social care but there is also a variety of other roles within the sector – and there is an increasing emphasis on continuing to train and develop while on the job. As you discover what interests you most, there may also be scope to move into other areas of social care or different types of work. The sector employs a variety of people in allied professions such as probation, special needs support, and youth and community work. These allied professions often overlap with social work, although only those people with a formal social work qualification can call themselves social workers.

WHO COULD YOU WORK WITH?

The people who are in need of social care services are called **service users**. For example, service users could be older people or those with HIV/AIDS who need support. Some of the main groups include children or families who are under stress, people with disabilities and people with problems relating to drugs or alcohol. Increasingly, service users play an active role in the development of social care policy and training, developing and hiring the people who will work with them in the social care sector.

SOCIAL WORK OR SOCIAL CARE WORK?

Social work and social care work – the two types of work sound confusingly similar and make up a large proportion of the social care sector. So, what's the difference?

Social workers are involved with service users at a high level, for example working with users to assess their care requirements and then liaising with other professionals (such as doctors) to provide a 'care package' that gives each user the support that they need. They will usually specialise in a particular area of service – see page 27 for more information. Social workers are required to hold a recognised professional qualification, gained through an undergraduate degree programme or postgraduate qualification.

In contrast, **social care workers** tend to offer more personal care, often supporting a single user or several users in the tasks of daily living. They do not usually need any qualifications to find a job, but will then be expected to work towards a qualification as they work and will receive training through their employers.

WHERE COULD YOU WORK?

Since social care deals with so many issues, it operates in many different contexts: hospitals and health centres, educational and community settings, residential homes, advice centres and people's homes.

There are also a number of different types of employer. People who work in social care will usually decide (through research or direct experience) which service user group they want to work with, and then consider the type of employer that would suit them best. In this sector there are a number of substantially different organisations and it's important to understand the range of employers you could work for.

PAY

Salaries vary according to the type of job, specific employer and area where you are working: there are no fixed salaries as each employer negotiates these. As a newly qualified social worker you could start at around £20,000, rising to £35,000 with several years' experience. Once you have the capacity to take on a management role you could earn considerably more – over £40,000. Social workers at senior management level can earn £60,000 plus.

TYPES OF EMPLOYER

Local authorities hold statutory responsibilities for providing social care to the populations they serve. People working in social care in this setting (called the **statutory sector**) work within a detailed policy and legislative framework. Social workers employed by local authorities often function as 'gatekeepers': they assess the needs of service users and manage the process of meeting those needs in the best way possible. In practice, this could mean working as part of a reception team that is the entry point to children's services or arranging support for elderly people on discharge from hospital. A large portion of the job is to make the best use of often scarce resources and to liaise with other professionals and service providers.

There are also opportunities to work in the **voluntary sector**. A voluntary organisation usually has a clearly defined role, which is to advocate on behalf of particular service user groups, promoting the welfare and rights of that group. The core tasks of social work remain the same but there are greater opportunities to be innovative about meeting the needs of service users and their families, and to build up close working relationships with them. There is a significant difference between the culture and organisation of the statutory and voluntary sectors.

Private social care is a rapidly expanding sector offering primarily residential provision, housing, and fostering and adoption services. Many private organisations specialise in crisis provision and hard-to-place children. The pay, conditions, training and support offered in this sector vary enormously and particular care is needed to research the ethos and reputation of the company.

Another type of work in the social care sector is **agency supply work**. This has become more common over the last few years. Agency workers may cover unfilled vacancies or stand in for employees who are absent through illness, maternity leave, secondment or training. The opportunity to work with different service users in different settings can be a valuable way to experience a variety of work. Agency work can also offer a more flexible way of working.

It is also possible to do **independent social work** and social work consultancy – areas which have grown very quickly in the last decade. Most independent social workers gain experience elsewhere before they make the move to become independent. They are generally self-employed.

Which area?

The social care sector is one of the most diverse in terms of the people you can work alongside and the service users you will be helping. Over the next few pages, you can find out more about the areas that you could work in.

ADOPTION AND FOSTERING

This area primarily involves working with and supporting adults who would like to adopt a child or become foster parents. A social worker will meet with prospective adoptive or foster parents, assess their suitability, provide them with training if necessary and make recommendations about their suitability to an independent panel. If the family is accepted, the social worker will provide them with the relevant support to get them through the process.

Work in this area may occur in a variety of settings and could include conducting home visits to train and assess potential adopters and fosterers. This can involve travelling around the country at unsociable hours in order to secure the most suitable family setting for a child.

ASYLUM SEEKERS

Asylum seekers often face issues that revolve around work, access to healthcare and education, and financial problems. Working in this area may involve helping service users to gain access to accommodation, healthcare, education and employment, as well as attending screening interviews and tribunals. The majority of social work in this area involves unaccompanied children. Contact begins with a screening interview, where the service user's needs are assessed and the best course of action is decided upon. A lot of time will be spent travelling to tribunals, visiting asylum seekers or liaising with agencies such as the local authority to ensure the entire process runs smoothly. This is not the sort of job you can switch off from at 5pm as there may be issues to deal with outside office hours.

CHILDREN AND FAMILIES

People working in this area of service have wide-ranging responsibilities to promote the welfare of children in need and ensure that they are properly safeguarded from harm. The main aim is to support service users by assessing needs and risks and arranging appropriate services. Problems that service users face can include one or more of the following: social isolation, low income, drug and alcohol abuse, teenage pregnancy and domestic violence. Many service users have had poor experiences of being parented themselves, which in turn impacts on their ability to parent their own children adequately.

The work usually involves direct contact with children, young people and families, and liaison with other agencies such as the police and education and health professionals. Services provided include family support, positive parenting, respite foster care, outreach support, child protection, packages of multidisciplinary support and referring children and families to appropriate services and agencies.

DOMESTIC VIOLENCE

People often associate domestic violence with physical abuse but it can occur in many different forms, including emotional and financial. Men are the usual perpetrators, but women can also be abusers. A support worker will carry out needs and risk assessments and will arrange help for any other issues, such as alcohol or drug dependencies or mental health problems. It is normal for service users to need emotional support, as many suffer from guilt, self-blame and low self-esteem.

Social care workers are usually based either in refuges or in outreach work. They provide whatever help is needed, from emergency accommodation to safety plans for people still living with an abusive family member. It is important to have a non-directive approach, to enable service users to make their own decisions.

HOUSING AND HOMELESSNESS

Working in this area will involve assessing housing needs, finding solutions, offering advice and working to prevent homelessness. People who have inadequate housing are also a risk to the economy as they are often unemployed and can be involved in street crime – assessing and meeting their needs can therefore contribute to society as a whole and to the economic well-being of an area. Typical cases will involve people who have been made homeless due to a family or relationship breakdown, because they are unemployed or on a low income, or because they have been evicted from their home. Other people may be referred because they lack a suitable home due to a medical condition, for example.

The work will depend on the case and the underlying causes of that person's homelessness or housing need. Social workers work closely with community care services and other organisations where necessary (such as specialist debt agencies, for example) to resolve issues and help people find suitable housing.

LEARNING DISABILITIES

Service users with learning disabilities (sometimes referred to as learning difficulties) may have a variety of conditions, such as Down's syndrome or autism, which cause impairment or delay intellectual development, resulting in difficulties associated with daily living. A social worker's role in this field is to help service users live as independently as possible in the community. A care plan might be structured around obtaining support for the user to access leisure services or to attend college, or providing support at home. It might also entail helping the individual to find a job or gain a tenancy.

Approximately 60% of a social worker's time is spent out in the community visiting service users and their carers, assessing new referrals and developing care plans to meet service users' needs.

MENTAL HEALTH

Social workers in mental health support and empower people with mental illness to take responsibility for their own lives, protect them from unrealistic societal expectations and ensure that their illness does not put them or the wider community at risk. Care packages could include medication, therapy and attendance at day-care facilities, enabling the service user to cope and be involved in the community. Involvement with a service user could last from a few days to several years. Mental health work can be pressured, often involving working one-to-one with severely distressed individuals, so social workers need to be able to set boundaries and separate work from their personal lives.

OLDER PEOPLE

Social workers in this area promote independence, choice and inclusion, helping combat age discrimination as well as prevent abuse. When working with older people, support workers need to focus on the individual and take into account their changing expectations and needs. Older people often face distressing situations relating to bereavement, isolation and loss. This could be loss of income, status, dignity or motivation.

Social workers will usually assess a service user's case, discuss the outcomes of the assessment and then ensure that the service user receives the help that he or she needs. The service user's situation is then monitored and reviewed periodically. Other professionals you may work with include occupational therapists, geriatricians (physicians who specialise in the care of older people), district nurses and general practitioners.

SUBSTANCE AND DRUG MISUSE

This area of service involves offering support to people who use drugs or alcohol problematically or who have addiction-related needs. The key issues faced by many service users include loss of employment, marriage or family breakdown, poor health, social isolation, poor or insecure accommodation and criminal justice involvement. By the time clients are referred to a social worker they have often experienced many 'losses', which some describe as 'hitting rock bottom'.

A social worker's role is to identify service users' needs and to establish motivations for becoming abstinent from drugs or alcohol. Individuals' needs are reviewed through their treatment programmes and aftercare support is set up to help them in recovery. Social workers will also work closely with the carers and families of service users, offering them support where necessary.

YOUTH JUSTICE

The primary aim of youth justice work is to prevent offending, and this is achieved through a multi-agency partnership approach to tackle the factors that contribute to youth crime. These factors include: disengagement from education, training or employment; problems with parenting; mental health issues; and substance or drug misuse. The teams also offer services to young people who have been arrested and charged, by undertaking assessments, writing court reports and supervising sentences. Work with service users may include reparation schemes, such as community work and environmental projects, to ensure that young offenders repay the community for their offences.

Youth offending teams are made up of social workers and other professionals such as probation officers, police officers and teachers. To prevent youth crime, activities such as sports and drama groups are set up to engage young people and make it easier to re-engage them in education or employment.

The career
for you?

Is health or social care for you?

To become a successful professional in health or social care requires more than just an in-depth understanding of the relevant area. It also requires certain skills and personal qualities or attributes.

To help you decide if a career in health or social care is for you, we suggest that you consider the following questions.

- What do you want from your future work?
- What does the course typically involve?
- Which skills are needed by people who work in health and social care?

WHAT DO YOU WANT FROM YOUR FUTURE WORK?

You may not have an answer for this right now, but your current studies, work experience to date and even your hobbies can help give you clues about the kind of work that you will enjoy and the skills that you have already started to develop. Start with a blank sheet of paper and note down the answers to the questions we've provided on the next page to help get you thinking. Be as brutally honest with yourself as you can. Don't write what you think will impress your teachers or parents; write what really matters to you and you'll start to see a pattern emerge.

WHAT REALLY MATTERS TO YOU?

- When you think of your future, what kind of environment do you see yourself working in? For example an office, outdoors, nine-to-five, relaxed or high-pressured?
- What are your favourite hobbies outside school?
- What is it about them that you enjoy? For example, working with people, finding out how things work?
- What are your favourite subjects at school?
- What is it about those subjects that you enjoy the most? For example, working with other people to arrive at solutions, being able to create something, debating, problem-solving, practical hands-on work?
- What do you dislike about the other subjects you're studying?
- If you've had any work experience, which aspects did you enjoy the most?

WHAT DO HEALTH AND SOCIAL CARE COURSES INVOLVE?

Unsurprisingly, the skills you'll require as a successful healthcare or social care professional will also be required at various stages of your studies. So it's important to know what a typical course entails before you apply so you are sure it's the kind of work that you'll enjoy. For example, most university and college courses will involve a mixture of theoretical knowledge and practical experience – you might want to think about what these include, and what sort of balance you'd like between learning the theory and putting it into practice.

Theoretical study will often include learning about the ethics and theories of healthcare and social care, plus related subjects such as sociology. If you know that you are interested in a particular type of work or area of service, make sure that the courses you apply to cover the relevant material. Some courses (especially in social work) may include a 'reflective' element, designed to help you think about your own practice and deal with any emotions which may arise as a result of the work you do.

Most courses will also include a **practical** element. Vocational courses in particular will often include work placements built into the course where you'll get hands-on experience. If this is the case, you may want to ask questions about the practical element in order to make sure that it is suitable for your needs. Where will the work placements be based and how will you travel there? Will there be opportunities to specialise in the types of work you're interested in and, if so, what are your options?

WHAT SKILLS DO HEALTH AND SOCIAL CARE PRACTITIONERS NEED?

For many roles in health and social care, you'll need to develop specific practical skills. You'll learn these either through your course, work placements or working on the job. You'll also typically need some (if not all) of the following:

- **excellent communication skills** – speaking *and* listening – to be able to draw out crucial information from patients or service users, often when they're under stress, and to put them at their ease
- **empathy** – a high level of sensitivity and an understanding of each client's situation and feelings. Social workers, in particular, need to have strong 'people skills' as you'll be providing support for people of all ages and backgrounds on an ongoing basis
- **confidentiality** – knowing what to communicate, when and to whom
- **calmness under fire** – especially for nurses and others who work in a hospital setting. Given the combination of shift work and the unpredictability of cases, you need to be able to cope under pressure
- **interpersonal skills** – since most, if not all, roles in this sector involve working in teams and dealing with members of the public, you need to be comfortable working with, and relating to, other people
- **problem-solving** – finding appropriate solutions to problems using the information and resources available
- **open-mindedness** – when dealing with patients or service users it's important to understand different points of view and to take an empathic, non-judgmental approach
- **patience** – for example, a domestic violence social worker must be able to work at the service user's pace, without getting frustrated, in order to empower them to make their own decisions
- **compassion** – a deep awareness of the suffering of others, coupled with the desire to relieve it.

Alternative careers

Want to work in health or social care, but not sure that any of the traditional options are right for you? You can take your pick from a variety of alternative careers – it's just a matter of researching what's out there. To start you off, here's a selection of related professions that you could consider.

PROBATION WORK

The National Offender Management Service (NOMS) helps to reduce crime. A probation officer's role is to help rehabilitate offenders given community sentences and those released from prison; to enforce the conditions of their court orders and release licences; and to take whatever steps are in their power to protect the public.

For more information, visit **www.justice.gov.uk/about/ noms**

COUNSELLING

Counsellors help people to examine behaviour or situations that are proving troublesome – and then find an area where it would be possible to initiate some change as a start. Counsellors can work in a variety of settings including schools, further and higher education establishments, organisations for people with disabilities, youth work, alcohol and drugs agencies, AIDS agencies, general practice and other general counselling services. Many telephone lines are also staffed by people trained in listening and counselling skills.

To find out more about how to become accredited, visit **www.bacp.co.uk**

YOUTH AND COMMUNITY WORK

Youth and community workers are employed by a local authority's education department or by leisure, recreation or social services departments. The National Youth Agency (NYA) supports those involved in young people's personal and social development and works to enable all young people to fulfil their potential. There are a number of routes in youth work but full-time youth workers will need to undertake recognised training, which could be a diploma, degree or postgraduate course.

For more information, visit **www.nya.org.uk**

SPECIAL NEEDS SUPPORT IN SCHOOLS

Approximately 20% of students are defined as having special educational needs – caused by physical disability, learning difficulty or problems with speech, behaviours or language. Special needs officers work for county, unitary and metropolitan councils. They are also known as special education needs assistant officers.

For more information, visit **www.nasen.org.uk**

WELFARE RIGHTS

Those who work in welfare rights help individuals with a range of issues including housing benefit, disabled living allowance, help for single parents with child benefits, council tax, employment benefit, sick pay, rent support, bereavement benefits, industrial claims and more. There are many ways to get involved in this area. You could train with an organisation to be an adviser, use your IT skills, language skills or knowledge of local communities, or sit on the management committee and help with fundraising, publicity or social policy work. Voluntary work with organisations such as the Citizens Advice Bureau gives good experience.

For more information, visit **www.citizensadvice.org.uk**

POLICY, STRATEGY, AUDIT AND PLANNING

Within a local authority's social services department, a policy development officer's job is to take a leading role in planning and developing services for the users they are responsible for. Officers can specialise in adult, children or family services and they can also advise elected council members and senior management on their options relating to policy, planning and development.

For more information, visit **www.lgcareers.com**

MANAGEMENT

Managers in healthcare make sure that all parts of the organisation work well together, control finances and work to provide the equipment and buildings needed to offer effective care to patients. Types of work include strategic management, performance and quality management, purchasing and contract management, and facilities management.

For more information, visit **www.nhscareers.nhs.uk/details/Default.aspx?id=796**

HEALTH INFORMATICS

Information management and technology is known as 'health informatics' within the NHS. This is a fast-growing area of the health sector. Health informatics often involves creative uses of IT to help improve patient care, for example a project to help GPs send images electronically to hospital specialists based on the other side of the country. Health informatics includes work in areas such as data analysis, data protection and confidentiality, systems development and records management.

For more information, visit
www.nhscareers.nhs.uk/hinfo.shtml

CLINICAL SUPPORT

The role of clinical support staff is to assist healthcare professionals, sometimes working alongside them. Clinical support roles can be found in a huge number of different healthcare settings, many in the NHS. For example, you could work in a laboratory helping to diagnose different conditions or in a hospital or clinic assisting with treatment or providing general care. Roles in this area include phlebotomists (who take blood samples), healthcare assistants, cardiographers and medical laboratory assistants.

For more information, visit
www.nhscareers.nhs.uk/widerClinic_opt.shtml

AMBULANCE

Ambulance services are made up of a whole range of people working in different roles – not just paramedics who are sent out as part of the emergency response crew to assess the patient's condition and give essential treatment. There are also ambulance technicians and assistants, call handlers who answer 999 calls in a control room and non-emergency patient transport services.

For more information, visit
www.nhscareers.nhs.uk/amb.shtml

Professional bodies

Professional bodies are responsible for overseeing a particular profession or career area, ensuring that people who work in the area are fully trained and meet ethical guidelines. Professional bodies may be known as institutions, societies and associations. They generally have regulatory roles: they make sure that members of the profession are able to work successfully in their jobs without endangering lives or abusing their position.

Professional bodies are often involved in training and career development, so courses and workplace training may have to follow the body's guidelines. In order to be fully qualified and licensed to work in your profession of choice, you will have to follow the professional training route. In many areas of work, completion of the professional training results in gaining chartered status – and the addition of some extra letters after your name. Other institutions may award other types of certification once certain criteria have been met. Chartered or certified members will usually need to take further courses and training to ensure their skills are kept up-to-date.

WHAT PROFESSIONAL BODIES ARE THERE?

Not all career areas have professional bodies. Those jobs that require extensive learning and training are likely to have bodies with a regulatory focus. This includes careers such as engineering, law, construction, health and finance. If you want to work in one of these areas, it's important to make sure your degree course is accredited by the professional body – otherwise you may have to undertake further study or training later on.

Other bodies may play more of a supportive role, looking after the interests of people who work in the sector. This includes journalism, management and arts-based careers. Professional bodies may also be learned bodies, providing opportunities for further learning and promoting the development of knowledge in the field.

CAN I JOIN AS A STUDENT?

Many professional bodies offer student membership – sometimes free or for reduced fees. Membership can be extremely valuable as a source of advice, information and resources. You'll have the opportunity to meet other students in the field, as well as experienced professionals. It will also look good on your CV, when you come to apply for jobs.

See below for a list of professional bodies in health and social care.

General Social Care Council (until 31 July 2012 – see page 9)
www.gscc.org.uk

Care Council for Wales
www.ccwales.org.uk

Scottish Social Services Council
www.sssc.uk.com

Northern Ireland Social Care Council
www.niscc.info

Health Professions Council (HPC)
www.hpc-uk.org

Royal College of Nursing
www.rcn.org.uk

Nursing & Midwifery Council
www.nmc-uk.org

The General Chiropractic Council
www.gcc-uk.org

The General Osteopathic Council
www.osteopathy.org.uk

Complementary & Natural Healthcare Council
www.cnhc.org.uk

National Youth Agency
www.nya.org.uk

The Trade Union and Professional Association for Family Court and Probation Staff
www.napo.org.uk

Graduate destinations

Health and Social Care
HESA Destination of Leavers of Higher Education Survey

Each year, comprehensive statistics are collected on what graduates are doing six months after they complete their course. The survey is co-ordinated by the Higher Education Statistics Agency (HESA) and provides information about how many graduates move into employment (and what type of career) or further study and how many are believed to be unemployed.

The full results across all subject areas are published by the Higher Education Careers Service Unit (HECSU) and the Association of Graduate Careers Advisory Services (AGCAS) in *What Do Graduates Do?*, which is available from **www.ucasbooks.com**.

	Health & Social Care
In UK employment	76.3%
In overseas employment	0.6%
Working and studying	7.3%
Studying in the UK for a higher degree	1.8%
Studying in the UK for a teaching qualification	0.7%
Undertaking other further study or training in the UK	1.5%
Studying overseas	0.1%
Not available for employment, study or training	1.8%
Assumed to be unemployed	5.4%
Other	4.6%

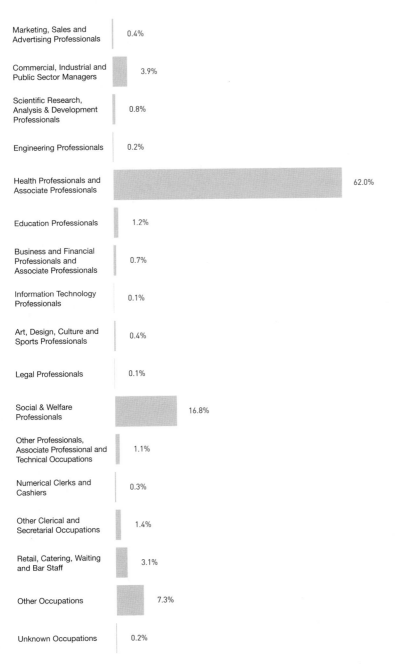

Marketing, Sales and Advertising Professionals — 0.4%

Commercial, Industrial and Public Sector Managers — 3.9%

Scientific Research, Analysis & Development Professionals — 0.8%

Engineering Professionals — 0.2%

Health Professionals and Associate Professionals — 62.0%

Education Professionals — 1.2%

Business and Financial Professionals and Associate Professionals — 0.7%

Information Technology Professionals — 0.1%

Art, Design, Culture and Sports Professionals — 0.4%

Legal Professionals — 0.1%

Social & Welfare Professionals — 16.8%

Other Professionals, Associate Professional and Technical Occupations — 1.1%

Numerical Clerks and Cashiers — 0.3%

Other Clerical and Secretarial Occupations — 1.4%

Retail, Catering, Waiting and Bar Staff — 3.1%

Other Occupations — 7.3%

Unknown Occupations — 0.2%

Owing to rounding, total might not equal 100%

Reproduced with the kind permission of HECSU/AGCAS *What Do Graduates Do? 2011.*
Data from the HESA *Destinations of Leavers from Higher Education Survey 09/10.*

Connect with us...

 www.facebook.com/ucasonline

 www.twitter.com/ucas_online

 www.youtube.com/ucasonline

Case studies

Professional head of physiology

Nuffield Health

CHRIS JONES

Route into physiology:
A levels – sports studies, history, sociology, general studies (2001); BA health and fitness management, Southampton Solent University (2005); MSc exercise and nutrition science, University of Chester (2007)

WHY PHYSIOLOGY?

I've always enjoyed sports and wanted to extend that into a role that would encompass helping other people become fitter and healthier, not just through exercise but also through related fields.

HOW DID YOU GET TO WHERE YOU ARE TODAY?

What attracted me to the course at Southampton Solent was that the practical element was encouraged as much as the academic – advisers told me that I could qualify as a personal trainer within months of starting

my degree, whereas friends on other courses had to wait until graduation.

This was certainly true. From year one, I spent a number of hours in the university gym, learning how to deliver sessions and classes to clients, some of whom had particular medical conditions. This led to me being offered a job working in the gym for up to 30 hours a week throughout my degree, which was great as I got excellent experience at the same time as studying.

My master's degree was noticeably harder in that it took subjects I already knew well and analysed them in much greater detail, but it led on well from my BSc. At the end of the year, I was offered one of the 45 physiology places Nuffield Health was offering to reinvigorate their health assessment services. An extra bonus was being taken on as a regional lead, heading up a team of newcomers like myself in a small hospital.

There was a lot to learn on the job – looking in more detail into all aspects that affect health such as diet, exercise, psychology and stress. I was trained to perform tests on clients, such as ECGs, and to take blood, so my role developed quite a clinical slant.

WHAT DOES YOUR JOB INVOLVE?

One of the reasons I enjoy my job so much is that it's very broad. I sit on the Wellbeing Medical Directorate, reporting to the Medical Director, and am responsible for ensuring that all our teams work safely, effectively and according to current legislation.

I also undertake public relations activities, such as giving guest lectures at universities, talking to the media, and giving health talks on managing stress in the workplace. Additionally, when a company identifies a gap in the market for our health services, I work to come up with products that meet the demand.

Contractually I work a 40-hour week but in reality it tends to be longer. However, a good work/life balance is naturally recognised in this profession and I always ensure I go running most days!

WHAT HAS BEEN YOUR BIGGEST CHALLENGE?

My professional progression has proved to be the most challenging aspect I have faced. Nearly three years ago I was promoted from deputy head of physiology to professional head, and moved from overseeing a group of eight people to leading 70 plus. However, I received great support from my colleagues and adapted as I went along.

AND THE BEST BITS?

I am lucky as I enjoy every aspect of my job – I get to work in what I am most passionate about!

CHRIS' TOP TIPS

Gain as much practical experience as you can so you can apply your knowledge in a fitness or health setting. Focus on understanding why people behave as they do – health psychology is an important part of this job. Walk the talk. If you want your clients to live healthily you need to do so yourself!

Specialist support officer (benefits)

Citizens' Advice Bureau

KATHERINE FINCHAM

Route into welfare rights:
BA social policy, Leeds Polytechnic (1992); MA social legal studies, Leicester University (1994)

WHY WELFARE RIGHTS?

What attracted me to a career in this field was a desire to work in an area involving direct contact with service users and clients.

HOW DID YOU GET TO WHERE YOU ARE TODAY?

My degree included specialisms in social policy and socio-legal studies, which sparked my interest in welfare rights. I also did some voluntary and paid work experience in Citizens' Advice Bureaux, local authority homelessness teams and community centres, which helped me gain more knowledge and skills to make working in welfare rights a natural and appropriate career choice.

WHAT DOES YOUR JOB INVOLVE?

The main area of responsibility in my job is to support CAB advisers through consultancy, training and information. The consultancy side involves about two days a week; otherwise I am busy delivering and maintaining training courses to staff, producing information for staff and clients and working and liaising with other departments and agencies.

Our consultancy service is available to advisers within the CAB service, and some other voluntary-sector agencies, and is shared between our small team of four benefits specialists. Since queries vary in complexity, I have to be able to explain basic benefit rules clearly, as well as being able to research and advise on more complex cases. As part of a small benefits team, I am usually able to call on colleagues for a second opinion. Teamwork is a very important part of what I do.

I work approximately 38 hours per week, mainly in an office, but I do go out to deliver training at various other venues. Occasionally I work from home. I work alongside colleagues in similar roles, as well as staff in different jobs through the Citizens' Advice Service and other voluntary sector agencies.

The training we deliver is across a range of benefit areas, depending on demand. We train up to 20 people on each course, with a minimum of six. I particularly enjoy delivering training as it gives me the opportunity to meet advisers and hear about the experiences of their clients. It can be challenging at times but I have found that I have developed more confidence as my ability to deal with difficult questions has increased over time. I also facilitate a regional welfare rights workers' group, which also involves contact with benefit advisers.

In this sort of work you need to develop a systematic approach to work, learn how to juggle competing priorities, and hone your teamworking skills. Another important area is the capacity to identify and recognise issues that affect benefit claimants, especially as I do not have direct contact with them, as well as making sense of complex legislation and case law.

WHAT HAS BEEN YOUR BIGGEST CHALLENGE SO FAR?

Managing a heavy workload and keeping up to date with my specialist subject has been challenging, mainly because of time pressures.

AND THE BEST BITS?

I like the sheer variety of tasks that I deal with daily. Although I miss direct contact with clients, I enjoy the range of issues and different tasks involved in my role, which might otherwise be more limited as a casework adviser. It's also fantastic to feel that the work I do is useful to someone and can make a difference to their life.

KATHERINE'S TOP TIPS

It is hard to overestimate the value of work experience in this or a related area in order to get a feel for the responsibilities you will have to take on and what is involved.

Head of health and social wellbeing improvement

Public Health Agency, Northern Ireland

MADELINE HEANEY

Route into health and social wellbeing improvement:
A levels – history, English, social & economic history (1980); BA youth and community work, Ulster Polytechnic Jordanstown (1984)

WHY THIS FIELD?

My degree was a generic social sciences course but within this I could choose specific professional options after the first year. I chose youth and community work as I felt it would qualify me for a flexible job with opportunities to work in different settings.

HOW DID YOU GET TO WHERE YOU ARE TODAY?

After graduating I worked in a number of inner-city youth centres in Belfast, which gave me a good grounding in working with young people with health and wellbeing issues, as well as with marginalised and disadvantaged communities.

I then studied for a Diploma in Advanced Study of Education (DASE) in Guidance and Counselling at Queen's University, which developed my skills in understanding and supporting individuals, families, and groups in emotional distress. I also worked in a youth and family counselling service in a very disadvantaged area of Belfast before being appointed as a senior health promotion officer for young people within a health and social care trust, while undertaking an MSc in health promotion at the same time. I then became a commissioner of health promotion services, identifying needs and priorities across all age groups and settings and commissioning services to address these needs.

WHAT DOES YOUR JOB INVOLVE?

As a head of health and social wellbeing improvement with the Public Health Agency, I have both local and regional responsibilities. Locally, I lead a team of health and social wellbeing improvement staff working across one HSC Trust area. Regionally, I am strategic lead for mental and emotional wellbeing and suicide prevention.

My role is to influence planning, policy and decision-making within various groups, including local government, education, housing, community, the voluntary sector, and the private and independent sectors in order to improve the health and social wellbeing of the local population.

My working hours are 9am to 5pm but there is occasional evening work. Key duties include meeting with other health and social care staff, engaging with voluntary and community organisations and other statutory groups, overseeing the work of the health and social wellbeing improvement team, participating in local and regional planning and policy meetings, and responding to requests from our minister or elected representatives. I also have budgetary responsibility and lead the commissioning of local health improvement services.

WHAT HAS BEEN YOUR BIGGEST CHALLENGE TO DATE?

To build relationships with stakeholders – who might not realise the important contribution they make – and work on a longer-term basis to establish trust, understanding and commitment. While the very nature of this work is ongoing, we have been very successful in getting joint working with a number of significant stakeholders, including local government, education and local communities.

WHAT DO YOU MOST ENJOY ABOUT YOUR JOB?

Opportunities to meet and work with so many different organisations and individuals. The real benefits from this work tend to be longer-term but I frequently see improved outcomes in the short term for individuals and communities, which makes it even more enjoyable.

MADELINE'S TOP TIPS

One of health improvement's greatest strengths is that people come to it from very diverse backgrounds and experiences. While there are now graduate and postgraduate training courses, anyone from any area of work is welcome, as the most important criterion is a drive and commitment to working with partners to make a difference to people's lives, particularly those who are most disadvantaged or vulnerable.

Osteopath

Eltham Health Clinic

AMY HOPE

Route into osteopathy:
A levels – biology, chemistry, maths; AS levels – English literature, Christian theology (2006); Masters in osteopathic medicine at the British College of Osteopathic Medicine (2001)

WHY OSTEOPATHY?

I wanted to combine my previous dancing background with working within a caring profession, and wanted to work in private practice immediately after university.

HOW DID YOU GET TO WHERE YOU ARE TODAY?

After considering training as a physiotherapist, I was lucky to meet a third-year osteopathic student while dancing. She told me the basics and it stuck in my mind during the UCAS application process. I secured four places for physiotherapy but by the time I had visited the British College of Osteopathic Medicine I was certain it was the right choice, and haven't changed my mind since.

During my time at university, I undertook work experience at an osteopathic clinic and as a sports massage therapist for a premiership rugby team, which provided me with the contacts I needed to start work in a non-specialist osteopathic clinic, to get the broadest experience base as possible. I can always choose to specialise in a particular field in the future if I want to.

WHAT DOES YOUR JOB INVOLVE?

Osteopathy is a system of diagnosis and treatment. When a patient arrives at the clinic, I take a full case history, including their medical and family histories, as this gives a good indication of whether the patient is suitable for osteopathic care. If they are, I carry out a full examination of orthopaedic, neurological and osteopathic tests. Then I'll explain the problem to the patient, including how I will treat them, and if they are happy we will proceed. As an osteopath, I use a wide range of treatment techniques, including joint manipulation (commonly recognised by the 'clicking' noise!), joint mobilisation, massage, exercise prescription and nutritional advice.

I see up to 25 patients a day in the private osteopathic clinic I work in. I don't work a normal nine-to-five day, as patients often need to come to the clinic outside of working hours, so I work until 8pm three evenings a week. However, hours of work can be very flexible and I have Monday mornings and Wednesdays off. Other responsibilities include writing letters to doctors to request relevant tests to aid diagnosis, or to refer the patient if they are not suitable for treatment.

WHAT HAS BEEN YOUR BIGGEST CHALLENGE?

As osteopathy is a very physical job, my biggest challenge has been building my stamina to last a nine-hour day, as well as remaining aware of patients' new, or moving, symptoms which may affect the diagnosis. It can also be challenging working alone but there are three other osteopaths working in the clinic, so there is always somebody on hand for a second opinion.

AND THE BEST BITS?

The best thing is meeting lots of new people, who usually come to the clinic feeling miserable and vulnerable – in pain and sometimes unable to walk – and watching these patients flourish under osteopathic care. Hearing stories of how their treatment has positively changed their lives is very rewarding.

AMY'S TOP TIPS

Go and watch an osteopath work, or book in for a treatment. Take your time to visit the universities, and try to get an idea of whether osteopathy is the career for you, as it is the only career that the degree equips you for. Get ready for four years of hard work, and a lot of exams!

Second-year, pre-registration adult nursing diploma

City University London

VALERIAN DELAGARDE

Route into nursing:
French Baccalaureate: scientific, major in biology (2002); pre-registration adult nursing diploma, City University London (current)

WHY NURSING?

Despite having an interest in studying biological sciences, I chose to study law at university. However, while it was an interesting subject, I left after six months as I knew that working in a law-oriented environment wasn't for me. I travelled around Asia for a year, lived in Australia for two more years, and then came to London to work in an office.

I decided to study international development and anthropology for a year at Birkbeck University. It was during this time that I first decided I wanted to study nursing, as it was the perfect way to combine all the things I wanted: sciences, a human approach to medicine, people, caring, teamwork and the possibility to work anywhere and in an endless variety of settings. After researching different nursing degrees, I discovered I particularly wanted to specialise in adults, so City's speciality in this area was ideal.

WHAT DOES YOUR COURSE INVOLVE?

My degree involves an almost equal mixture of practice and theory. Theory is taught in lectures and covers big themes and ideas in nursing knowledge, biology, sociology, psychology and so on. Smaller group sessions focus on more practical issues, with some practical tutorials on technical skills. The lecturers are mostly nurses, which is great as they all have different fields of expertise and are truly passionate about nursing and patient care.

TELL US ABOUT YOUR WORK PLACEMENT

I completed an acute-ward placement on a day-surgery unit, where patients come in for surgery in the morning and leave in the afternoon or early evening. The team's job is to get them ready for theatre by carrying out assessments and checklists, and taking vital signs (eg pulse and temperature). After surgery, the nurses take the patients back to the recovery ward and monitor their recovery before they can go home. During the placement I helped out with these tasks and had a mentor who taught me the relevant practical skills. I was also able to see operations and attend patient examinations.

It was a life-changing experience for me because even though I enjoyed the training, it was hard to know whether I was really suited to being a nurse. But my first day confirmed I had made the right decision. Being in a hospital environment, surrounded by medical professionals, caring for people who are in a strange environment and feeling worried, and learning so much was very rewarding.

WHAT WAS THE TOUGHEST CHALLENGE YOU HAVE FACED ON YOUR COURSE?

Essay writing and the lead-up to exams can become very stressful but there are a number of support services to help students. Also, finding yourself in a busy environment with patients requiring your attention can be demanding. You quickly realise the huge responsibility you have as a health professional and it can be daunting. But it is a reality of this career and it is thrilling.

AND THE BEST BITS?

I think most of my colleagues would agree that the best part is when you get to be a 'nurse' on placement. Caring for others and helping them get better and back to their normal life is the best feeling ever.

VALERIAN'S TOP TIPS

Don't be scared of things like blood or bodily fluid – you get used to them! You need to work hard and have good time-management skills. Keep your friends close – tell them you will be less available but keep in touch and do take some time off to have fun.

Entry routes

Routes to qualification – health

ALLIED HEALTH PROFESSIONALS

Allied health professionals are entrusted with a large amount of responsibility for their patients' well-being and will often spend time working on their own in patients' homes or in clinics, for example, as well as in a range of other healthcare settings. Because of this level of independence, allied health professionals need to be highly trained. Entry into most areas will require an extended period of study at degree or diploma level or above, which means that you will need good A level grades or equivalent to secure a place on a university or college course.

Be aware that, to practise, most allied health professionals need to register with the appropriate regulatory body. Registration is usually through the Health Professions Council (HPC) but you will only be eligible for registration if you have completed an accredited training course and have been awarded an approved qualification. Visit the HPC website for more information: **www.hpc-uk.org**.

NURSING AND MIDWIFERY

Qualifying as a nurse or midwife will require at least three years' study at a college or university leading to a diploma or degree-level qualification. Courses involve practical placements in hospitals and in the community, both of which are designed to develop practical skills and experience under supervision. Once qualified, students will need to register with the Nursing & Midwifery Council (NMC). Learn more at **www.nmc-uk.org**.

Nursing students can choose to do a shortened midwifery course after qualifying as a registered nurse. These courses take 18 months to complete and generally lead to a degree qualification.

HEALTHCARE SCIENCE

To enter certain areas of healthcare science, you will need to study for a degree course that is accredited by the relevant regulatory body, which will enable you to become a registered practitioner on completion of the degree.

Another option is to complete a science degree and then undertake further training in your area of interest to increase your specialist knowledge. Courses usually last between 18 and 24 months and lead to a postgraduate diploma or MSc qualification and professional registration. Most courses will involve practical placements, although some will allow you to work under supervision as a paid trainee.

COMPLEMENTARY AND ALTERNATIVE MEDICINE

Entry requirements for the complementary and alternative medicine (CAM) professions vary depending on the area that you want to enter. So the best advice is to research your chosen career carefully, contacting the relevant society or council for further information.

Only two professions currently require registration: students wanting to practise as a chiropractor or osteopath in the UK must have a recognised qualification and be registered with either the General Chiropractic Council (see **www.gcc-uk.org**) or the General Osteopathic Council (see **www.osteopathy.org.uk**). In 2008, the Department of Health reaffirmed proposals to regulate CAM practitioners, stating that regulation would improve public protection and set clear standards of training and competence. As a result of this, the Complementary and Natural Healthcare Council (CNHC) has been formed as a voluntary regulatory body. Practitioners of some CAM disciplines can register with the CNHC, and additional disciplines are being added.

However, be aware that, unlike other healthcare professions, the Department of Health does not provide funding for students who want to undertake courses in complementary and alternative medicine.

For more information visit the CNHC website, **www.cnhc.org.uk**.

To research and apply for postgraduate courses, go to **www.ukpass.ac.uk**.

Routes to qualification – social care

There are many different types of work within social care so you should check carefully to find out which qualifications are required for each specialisation. Many universities and colleges will insist that applicants have some knowledge of social care, what it is and how it works – so paid or voluntary experience that you've gained in the sector will be essential.

Some social care roles don't require specific accredited qualifications, although related work experience and a relevant qualification will help your chances of application success. In these social care roles you will be given on-the-job training that is specific to the role and will usually be encouraged to gain further qualifications as you work.

For many other roles you will need to make sure that your degree course has been accredited by a relevant organisation or council. A recognised professional qualification is now essential for gaining employment in social work, which is at the heart of social care and makes up a large proportion of the sector. Since 2003, only those with a recognised qualification can be registered as, or call themselves, a social worker.

SOCIAL WORK

So how do you get into social work? The introduction of new professional qualifications in social work in 2003 has improved the status of this career area, placing it on a par with those of other public service professionals. Degree courses are accredited by the relevant regional body (see page 61) and work training is now provided jointly by social services and course providers working together. As a social work student you'll receive thorough training to enable you to deliver effective services and to protect service users and carers.

The course

Undergraduate degrees usually take three to four years to complete (if studied full-time) and the new training ensures that academic theory and practice skills are effectively integrated. Much of the course is devoted to academic study, which includes the teaching of key areas such as human growth and development, mental health, disability, assessments, communication skills, law and partnership working. A minimum of 200 days are spent on placements in at least two contrasting settings, and students must gain some experience with a statutory body. Course providers facilitate placements and make sure that support mechanisms such as appropriate training and assessment are in place. Most courses will have a system of continuous assessment, which could include written work, assessment of social work knowledge or values and assessment of how you apply practice skills while on work placements.

A range of experience

Social work courses cover all areas of social work and aim to prepare students to work with a range of service user groups. Before deciding on a course, find out what your choices will be.

As a student on an accredited course, you will be given the opportunity to experience working in at least two practice settings with two or more different user groups. You'll also experience statutory social work tasks involving legal interventions – this does not mean that you will have to do a placement in the statutory sector but your course must offer you the chance to gain experience of statutory work.

After qualification

Employment prospects for qualified social workers are excellent. Devolution in the UK has led to the establishment of four regulatory bodies for social workers but social work training is broadly similar throughout the UK and official regulation of courses means that social workers can, for example, qualify in England but register and work in Northern Ireland, Wales or Scotland. Once qualified, social workers must renew their registration every three years to make sure that they have kept their training and learning up to date, which includes reading and attending conferences and training courses.

Social workers can undertake further training under the post-qualifying framework and there are awards available at three levels: specialist, higher specialist and advanced. These let you progress in a logical way as you carry on studying. You can also choose courses from five areas of practice:

- children and young people, their families and carers
- leadership and management
- practice education
- social work in mental health services
- social work with adults.

Most of the new courses began in autumn 2007 and more are being approved all the time.

PROBATION AND CRIMINAL JUSTICE

In 2010 changes to training to become a probation officer were introduced. In order to apply for probation officer posts applicants will need an honours degree in community justice as well as the vocational qualification diploma in probation practice, level 5. The primary route to becoming a probation officer is through employment and study within a probation trust as a probation services officer.

Those with honours degrees in criminology, community justice, criminal justice and police studies will also be able to apply to a probation trust to work as a probation services officer and undertake the relevant qualifications in order to work as a probation officer.

For further information visit **www.justice.gov.uk**.

YOUTH WORK

To work in this area you will usually need to have a formal, nationally recognised qualification in youth work and would be expected to be working towards one if you do not already have a qualification. All qualifications are based on national occupational standards for youth work. There are two types of qualification – youth support worker (pre-professional/vocational qualifications) and professional qualifications. For work at higher levels of responsibility, you will be expected to hold a professional qualification.

Visit **www.nya.org.uk** for further information.

To research and apply for postgraduate courses, go to **www.ukpass.ac.uk**.

Northern Ireland, Scotland and Wales

SOCIAL WORK

A degree in social work gained in any part of the country will be recognised throughout the United Kingdom. For example, if you qualify in Northern Ireland you will be able to work in England and vice versa. Seek further information from the relevant council, however, as their course content and funding arrangements can vary. The councils set standards, regulate social work education and training, and are responsible for registration of the social work and social care workforce.

Northern Ireland
Northern Ireland Social Care Council (NISCC)
www.niscc.info

Scotland
Scottish Social Services Council (SSSC)
www.sssc.uk.com

Wales
Care Council for Wales (CCW)
www.ccwales.org.uk

Social work in Northern Ireland

Following successful completion of a recognised degree in social work, graduates entering social work employment in Northern Ireland are required to complete an assessed year in employment (AYE) as part of the registration requirements. During this year all newly qualified social workers will be supervised by a registered social worker.

HEALTHCARE

Healthcare qualifications will generally be recognised throughout the UK although you may want to check this with your course provider. Northern Ireland, Scotland and Wales have separate National Health Service organisations. Find out more by visiting their websites, listed below.

Northern Ireland

Health and Social Care in Northern Ireland:

www.n-i.nhs.uk

Northern Ireland HSC Recruit:

www.hscrecruit.com

Scotland

NHS Scotland:

www.scot.nhs.uk

NHS Careers Scotland:

http://nhsrecruitment.scotland.gov.uk/

Wales

NHS Wales:

www.wales.nhs.uk

NHS Wales Careers:

www.nhswalescareers.com

What others say...

What others say…

These are extracts from case studies in previous editions of this book. They give some insights into the experiences and thoughts of people who were once in the same position as you.

SARAH ROYLE – COUNSELLOR AND PSYCHOTHERAPIST

Part of my previous job was being responsible for the people in theatre companies; I was the one people would come to if they had a problem. I found this aspect of my work very rewarding, so I decided to become a counsellor.

My job involves helping people to learn how best to deal with their problems and to hopefully prevent them feeling worse. On a daily basis, I see clients and talk through their issues with them, before working with them – either through just talking or using different exercises – to decide how they can best cope with their situation. Skills such as active listening, communication, empathy and being able to have a genuine respect for others are all important to my job, and they are all skills that can always be improved!

I find it very satisfying when someone has had their final session and I have made an improvement to their life. Any struggles we may have had along the way are more than worthwhile – these are very rewarding moments.

If you would like to become a councellor or psychotherapist, start doing some volunteer work as soon as possible – finding placements during a course can be very difficult. Be prepared to work hard, both on seeing clients and on the theories of the therapists who developed your chosen approach (there are many different schools of psychotherapy). And don't expect to be able to actually find 20 private clients per week – three or four is more realistic. You will not, unfortunately, become rich doing counselling work unless you are very lucky!

MOOSE BAXTER - PROSTHETIST

What I like most about prosthetics is that every day can be a challenge. One day there may be an unusual case that requires input from many members of the clinical team. The next day all the patients attending could be in the department for hours, needing lots done to their artificial limbs and I'm rushing round all day. Other days, newly available components and products may be demonstrated, or I'm fitting one of them for the first time. Some days are less exciting than others, but helping people to walk again is something that I expect to continue to enjoy for a long time!

FIONA BROOKE-VINCENT - MIDWIFE

I developed my interest in healing from a mother who was into alternative therapies, and this led me into nursing in accident and emergency departments. Then, one day, I had to deliver a baby in a hospital corridor and became hooked on midwifery. Since I already had a nursing degree, I was able to do the BSc in midwifery in 18 months instead of three years.

I am currently employed as a midwife in the award-winning NICU at Bristol's Southmead Hospital, but I will shortly be leaving to deliver babies at St Michael's Hospital in Bristol.

Midwifery normally involves antenatal care (looking after women when they are pregnant) right through to delivering babies and offering postnatal care once the baby has been born. Hospital midwives tend to rotate between the wards and the delivery suites, and also work in the community in patients' homes. Additionally, we are responsible for providing breast-feeding support for mothers and care for infants until they are 28 days old.

KAREN BROOKER - ADULT SOCIAL WORKER

My son was born severely disabled and I became his full-time carer until he died in February 1999. This experience influenced my decision to go into social work and definitely helped me in my studies.

My job focuses on assessing adults' social care needs, mainly those aged over 65, so they can get a personal budget that gives them a choice on how to meet their needs. I liaise with brokers, set up support plans, review cases, and carry out safeguarding adults' activities, as well as sharing the weekly duty rota with my colleagues. This involves responding to emergency calls, for example from people not coping in their current living situation, or representing someone who has been taken into police custody and has no one else to represent them.

Being a social worker means working as part of a multidisciplinary team: I regularly work with families, district nurses, GPs, care home managers, physiotherapists and occupational therapists, amongst others.

A career in social work requires some sort of previous experience, be it in a voluntary or statutory capacity. You will need good people skills, not only to deal with the clients but also with the multidisciplinary teams you work within. Organisational skills are a must, as is a knowledge of the legal and policy framework for the area of social work that you are working in.

LUBNA BEGUM – DEVELOPMENTAL DRUG WORKER

Try to get some voluntary experience as this will not only help you to develop your skills, it's also a great way of making contacts, which can help you later on. It's also worth trying to get a background in substance misuse and reading up on the subject before any interviews. It's important to take advantage of any opportunity that presents itself in order to succeed
in this sector.

During my degree [in biology and psychology] I did a one-year placement as a psychology assistant. This gave me valuable experience of client contact and working within the NHS. After graduating, I spent six months working as an assistant genetic counsellor at a genetics clinic before applying for my current role. The job description asked for two years' previous experience so my placement and previous work experience proved useful.

CHRIS PYKE – POLICE CONSTABLE

My job involves responding to emergency calls and dealing with crime. This can entail speaking to and interacting with members of the public, assessing crime scenes, identifying crimes that have been committed, making arrests and interviewing suspects. There is also paperwork to complete for assessment by the Crown Prosecution Service, as well as attending court and giving evidence on cases. The job provides opportunities to specialise in different areas of policing, such as firearms, road policing, dog handling and air operations. Make a note or record of any significant life experiences you have so that you can draw on them when interviewed. This will provide you with the necessary evidence to prove that you are a strong candidate when applying for the police force. There is a lot of competition to become a police officer so be patient, make sure you do your research before going to the assessment day, and stay fit.

LAURA BOOTHROYD – MENTAL HEALTH NURSE

Before your university interview, make sure that you research and are up-to-date with literature from the Department of Health and the National Institute of Mental Health. While at university use all resources available such as supervision from your tutors – they are there to help. Finally, when on placements try to get involved in everything you can. There more you do something, the more confident you will be.

ANNA COLLINS – 'PLUM' (SOCIAL HOUSING) OPERATIONAL OFFICER

Get as broad knowledge as possible, not only within social housing, but also sociology, politics and some history, as they all affect each other.

Don't think any post is too low down the rung: an administrative position can be excellent in terms of gaining knowledge, skills and experience, and working within the public sector often means managers are positively encouraging you to develop.

JOANNA – SELF-EMPLOYED MASSEUSE AND SHIATSU PRACTITIONER

I enjoy both massage and shiatsu: massage is more tactile and immediate, while shiatsu is a subtler treatment that goes deeper. It's very satisfying when I feel a clear connection with a client, and I know that I'm giving a really good treatment. I work around 20 hours a week for which I get paid well – and I'm doing something I love in a beautiful environment. Ongoing professional training keeps you inspired and motivated, and gives you fresh input and new ways of working with patients. Building up a practice doesn't happen overnight though. You may need to do other work to make ends meet, but make sure you're not too exhausted to treat patients effectively. It's also really important to receive lots of treatments yourself.

ALICE EMERTON - RECENT GRADUATE IN OCCUPATIONAL THERAPY

The course was fascinating and everyone there – lecturers and other students – were amazingly supportive and friendly.

My course became harder with each passing year, and it was often difficult finding time to conduct research alongside completing assignments. I think the hardest time was when I was on a placement and also had to finish and submit three assignments with very close deadlines. It certainly taught me how to prioritise my time. Despite the hefty workload I still had time to play sports and enjoy everything Canterbury as a town had to offer.

Occupational therapy isn't just about rehabilitating people physically. There is that side, of course, which looks at how to help people adapt to daily life after accidents or illness. But it's also about assisting people who have mental health difficulties. For example, in my placement in the mental health unit I helped a wide range of patients, from those with Alzheimer's to eating disorders, by playing memory games with them, doing puzzles and taking them out on day trips. On my prison placement, my friend and I ran a music group in order to explore how music made the offenders feel. At the end they did a performance, reading out poetry and playing instruments, to express the anxiety and stress that they sometimes suffered from.

If possible, get some work experience in an occupational therapy setting so you know what it's about and whether it suits you. If it does then go for it with open arms!

EMMA GAYER – COMMUNITY NURSE

I see people in their own homes and, sometimes, I can have quite an impact on their lives. This can include anything from explaining to patients how to live more healthily to organising more social input if people are not coping alone. Although I work to deadlines I am still able to spend more quality time with my patients than would be possible in a hospital setting with the distractions that come with working on a ward.

NEIL COULL - SPEECH AND LANGUAGE THERAPIST

TI became a speech therapist because I wanted to pursue my interest in language while working closely with people.

I work with adults who have speech, language, voice or swallowing difficulties, acquired through strokes, head injuries or neurological conditions. Very often, my role is to help individuals adapt to big life changes or to aid their rehabilitation back into everyday life, which involves working closely with families, employers, carers, doctors, nurses and therapists in other professions. Therefore, I work in a variety of settings including clinics, hospital wards, clients' homes and nursing homes.

I most enjoy the challenges that the job offers. Because we work with such a wide range of conditions, I conduct very different types of therapy and assessment in the course of a single day – from advising someone who has had a stroke to help ease their swallowing difficulties, to working with a teacher who has lost or damaged their voice, to exploring different means of communication for someone who is gradually losing their speech through a progressive disease. I also enjoy the creativity of the job. I often have to adapt activities or create my own resources for therapy so that they are specific to the person I am working with.

If you are interested in a career in speech therapy, do your research first! It may not be possible to observe a speech therapist at work before applying for a course, but volunteering at local charities and groups, such as the Stroke Association, can give you an insight into working with people who have communication difficulties.

www.ucas.com

at the heart of connecting people to higher education

Applicant
journey

SIX EASY STEPS TO UNIVERSITY AND COLLEGE

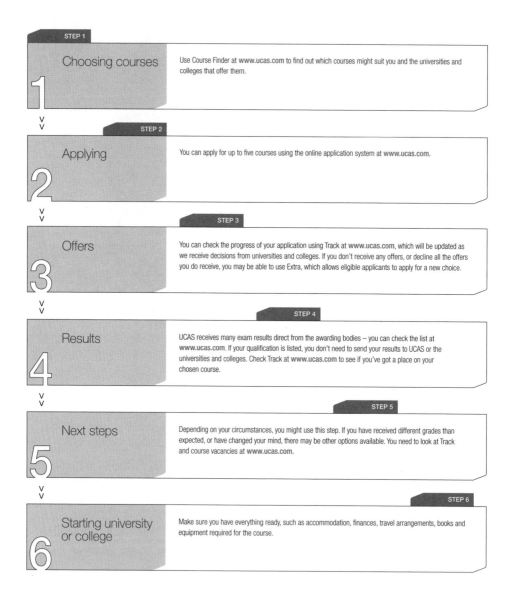

STEP 1

Choosing courses

Use Course Finder at www.ucas.com to find out which courses might suit you and the universities and colleges that offer them.

STEP 2

Applying

You can apply for up to five courses using the online application system at www.ucas.com.

STEP 3

Offers

You can check the progress of your application using Track at www.ucas.com, which will be updated as we receive decisions from universities and colleges. If you don't receive any offers, or decline all the offers you do receive, you may be able to use Extra, which allows eligible applicants to apply for a new choice.

STEP 4

Results

UCAS receives many exam results direct from the awarding bodies – you can check the list at www.ucas.com. If your qualification is listed, you don't need to send your results to UCAS or the universities and colleges. Check Track at www.ucas.com to see if you've got a place on your chosen course.

STEP 5

Next steps

Depending on your circumstances, you might use this step. If you have received different grades than expected, or have changed your mind, there may be other options available. You need to look at Track and course vacancies at www.ucas.com.

STEP 6

Starting university or college

Make sure you have everything ready, such as accommodation, finances, travel arrangements, books and equipment required for the course.

Choosing courses

1

Step 1 – Planning your application

This section covers routes into nursing, health and social care professions from qualifications such as A levels and Scottish Highers, but it is also possible to follow a vocational route – for example, joining the NHS as a healthcare assistant or clinical support worker in the area you are interested in and using this as a springboard into the profession or into higher education.

HEALTH AND SOCIAL CARE APPLICATIONS AT A GLANCE

- Number of applicants*: 119,285
- Number accepted on courses: 48,023
- Average UCAS Tariff (accepted applicants excluding those with no Tariff points): 317

(Figures used are for applications in subjects allied to medicine for entry in 2011)
* Note, an applicant has been defined as making at least one choice to the group - subjects allied to medicine.

HEALTH

Some healthcare professions, such as healthcare science or some of the allied health professions that require the use of technical equipment, will require specific A level subjects for entry onto a course. It is true that having one or two science A levels will stand you in good stead, but course requirements do vary according to each higher education institution. As a general guide, for entry onto a nursing diploma course you will usually be asked for five GCSEs or equivalent at grade C or above, while entry onto a degree programme will require five GCSEs plus two A levels or equivalent. However, diploma courses are being phased out, so by September 2013 all nursing courses will be at degree level and will require appropriate entry qualifications.

SOCIAL CARE

Entry requirements will again vary from institution to institution but course providers usually ask for GCSE grade C or equivalent in maths and English and at least two A levels or equivalent. Candidates applying to social work courses are usually expected to have gained some knowledge of what the work will involve either by completing some work experience, shadowing a social worker or volunteering to work at a youth group, for example. Students will often have an occupational health assessment and will need to disclose details of any criminal records before they can go on their first placement.

Applicants to all courses must be able to demonstrate evidence of literacy, numeracy and good character.

HOW DO I FIND THE BEST COURSE FOR ME?

For courses on offer, see Course Finder at **www.ucas.com**.

Applicants are advised to use various resources of information in order to make their choices for higher education, including Course Finder at **www.ucas.com**. League tables might be a component of this research but applicants should bear in mind that these tables attempt to rank institutions in an overall order, which reflects the interests, preoccupations and decisions of those who have produced and edited the tables. The ways in which they are compiled vary greatly and you will need to look closely at the criteria that have been used. See page 78 for more information about league tables.

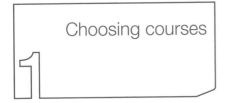

Choosing courses

Choosing courses

USE COURSE FINDER AT WWW.UCAS.COM TO FIND OUT WHICH COURSES MIGHT SUIT YOU, AND THE UNIVERSITIES AND COLLEGES THAT OFFER THEM.

Use the UCAS website – www.ucas.com has lots of advice on how to find a course. Go to the students' section of the website for the best advice or go straight to Course Finder to see all the courses available through UCAS. Our map of the UK at **www.ucas.com/students/choosingcourses/choosinguni/map/** shows you where all the universities and colleges are located.

Watch UCAStv – at **www.ucas.tv** there are videos on *How to choose your course*, *Attending events* and *Open days* as well as case studies from students talking about their experiences of finding a course at university or college.

Attend UCAS conventions – UCAS conventions are held throughout the country. Universities and colleges have exhibition stands where their staff offer information about their courses and institutions. Details of when the conventions are happening and a convention planner to help you prepare at **www.ucas.com/conventions**.

Look at university and college websites and prospectuses – universities and colleges have prospectuses and course-specific leaflets on their undergraduate courses. Your school or college library may have copies or go to the university's website to download a copy or ask them to send one to you.

Go to university and college open days – most institutions offer open days to anyone who wants to attend. See the list of universities and colleges on **www.ucas.com** and the UCAS *Open Days* publication (see the Essential reading chapter) for information on when they are taking place. Aim to visit all of the universities and colleges you are interested in before you apply. It will help with your expectations of university life and make sure the course is the right one for you.

League tables – these can be helpful but bear in mind that they attempt to rank institutions in an overall order reflecting the views of those that produce them. They may not reflect your views and needs.
Examples can be found at **www.thecompleteuniversityguide.co.uk**,
www.guardian.co.uk/education/universityguide, **www.thetimes.co.uk** (subscription service) and
www.thesundaytimes.co.uk (subscription service). See page 78 for more information about league tables.

Do your research – speak and refer to as many trusted sources as you can find. Talk to someone already doing the job you have in mind. The section 'Which area?' on pages 17 to 21 will help you identify the different areas of health and social care you might want to enter.

DECIDING ON YOUR COURSE CHOICES

Through UCAS you can initially apply for up to five courses. How do you find out more information to make an informed decision?

Remember you don't have to make five course choices. Only apply for a course if you're completely happy with both the course and the university or college and you would definitely be prepared to accept a place.

How do you narrow down your course choices? First of all, look up course details in this book or on Course Finder at **www.ucas.com**. This will give you an idea of the full range of courses and topics on offer. You may want to study psychology as a single subject, but there are also many courses which also include additional options, such as a modern language (check out the degree subjects studied by our case studies). You'll quickly be able to eliminate institutions that don't offer the right course, or you can choose a 'hit list' of institutions first, and then see what they have to offer.

Once you've made a short(er) list, look at university or college websites, and generally find out as much as you can about the course, department and institution. Don't be afraid to contact them to ask for more information, request their prospectus or arrange an open day visit.

UCAS CARD

At its simplest, the UCAS Card scheme is the start of your UCAS journey. It can save you a packet on the high street with exclusive offers to UCAS Card holders, as well as providing you with hints and tips about finding the best course at the right university or college. If that's not enough you'll also receive these benefits:

- frequent expert help from UCAS, with all the essential information you need on the application process

- free monthly newsletters providing advice, hints, tips and exclusive discounts

- tailored information on the universities and courses you're interested in

- and much more

If you're in Year 12, S5 or equivalent and thinking about higher education for autumn 2013, sign up for your FREE UCAS Card today to receive all these benefits at **www.ucas.com/ucascard**.

1 Choosing courses

Choosing your institution

Different people look for different things from their university or college course, but the checklist on the next page sets out the kinds of factors all prospective students should consider when choosing their university. Keep this list in mind on open days, when talking to friends about their experiences at various universities and colleges, or while reading prospectuses and websites.

WHAT TO CONSIDER WHEN CHOOSING YOUR HEALTH OR SOCIAL CARE COURSE

Location	Do you want to stay close to home? Would you prefer to study at a city or campus university or college?
Grades required	Use Course Finder at www.ucas.com, to view entry requirements for courses you are interested in. Also, check out the university website or call up the admissions office. Some universities specify grades required, eg AAB, while others specify points required, eg 340. If they ask for points, it means they're using the UCAS Tariff system, which basically awards points to different types and levels of qualification. For example, an A grade at A level = 120 points; a B grade at A level = 100 points. The full Tariff tables are available on pages 109 to 115 and at www.ucas.com.
Employer links	Ask the course tutor and university or college careers office about links with employers, especially for placements or work experience.
Graduate prospects	Ask the university careers office for their list of graduate destinations to find out what former students are now doing.
Cost	Ask the admissions office about variable tuition fees and financial assistance.
Teaching style	How is the course taught? Ask about the number of lectures per week, the number of tutorials and amount of one-to-one work, how you will be involved in project work, etc.
Course assessment	What proportion of the assessment is based on your project work and how much is based on written assignments or exams?
Facilities for students	Check out the campus library and computing facilities and find out if there is a careers adviser dedicated to health and social care students.
'Fit'	Even if all the above criteria stack up, this one relies on gut feel – go and visit the institution if you can and see if it's 'you'.

Choosing courses

1

League tables

The information that follows has been provided by Dr Bernard Kingston of *The Complete University Guide.*

League tables are worth consulting early in your research and perhaps for confirmation later on. But never rely on them in isolation – always use them alongside other information sources available to you. Universities typically report that over a third of prospective students view league tables as important or very important in making their university choices. They give an insight into quality and are mainly based on data from the universities themselves. Somewhat confusingly, tables published in, say, 2012 are referred to as the 2013 tables because they are aimed at applicants going to university in that following year. The well known ones - *The Complete University Guide, The Guardian, The Times*, and *The Sunday Times* - rank the institutions and the subjects they teach using input measures (eg entry standards), throughput measures (eg student : staff ratios) and output measures (eg graduate prospects). Some tables are free to access whilst others are behind pay walls. All are interactive and enable users to create their own tables based on the measures important to them.

The universities are provided with their raw data for checking and are regularly consulted on methodology. But ultimately it is the compilers who decide what measures to use and what weights to put on them. They are competitors and rarely consult amongst themselves. So, for example, *The Times* tables differ significantly from *The Sunday Times* ones even though both newspapers belong to the same media proprietor.

Whilst the main university rankings tend to get the headlines, we would stress that the individual subject tables are as least as important, if not more so, when deciding where to study. All universities, regardless of their overall ranking, have some academic departments that rank highly in their subjects. Beware also giving much weight to an institution being a few places higher or lower in the tables – this is likely to be of little significance. This is particularly true in the lower half of the main table where overall scores show considerable bunching.

Most of the measures used to define quality come from hard factual data provided by the Higher Education Statistics Agency (HESA) but some, like student satisfaction and peer assessment, are derived from surveys of subjective impressions where you might wish to query sample size. We give a brief overview of the common measures here but please go to the individual websites for full details.

- **Student satisfaction** is derived from the annual National Student Survey (NSS) and is heavily used by *The Guardian* and *The Sunday Times.*
- **Research assessment** comes from a 2008 exercise (RAE) aimed at defining the quality of a university's research (excluded by *The Guardian*).
- **Entry standards** are based on the full UCAS Tariff scores obtained by new students.
- **Student : staff ratio** gives the number of students per member of academic staff.
- **Expenditure figures** show the costs of academic and student services.
- **Good honours** lists the proportion of graduates gaining a first or upper second honours degree.
- **Completion** indicates the proportion of students who successfully complete their studies.

- **Graduate prospects** usually reports the proportion of graduates who obtain a graduate job – not any job – or continue studying within six months of leaving.
- **Peer assessment** is used only by *The Sunday Times* which asks academics to rate other universities in their subjects.
- **Value added** is used only by *The Guardian* and compares entry standards with good honours.

All four main publishers of UK league tables (see Table 1) also publish university subject tables. *The Complete University Guide* and *The Times* are based on four measures: student satisfaction, research quality, entry standards and graduate destinations. *The Sunday Times* uses student satisfaction, entry standards, graduate destinations, graduate unemployment, good degrees and drop-out rate, while *The Guardian* uses student satisfaction (as three separate measures), entry standards, graduate destinations, student-staff ratio, spend per student and value added. This use of different measures is one reason why the different tables can yield different results (sometimes very different, especially in the case of *The Guardian* which has least in common with the other tables).

League tables compiled by *The Complete University Guide* (**www.thecompleteuniversityguide.co.uk**) and *The Guardian* (**www.guardian.co.uk**) are available in spring, those by *The Times* (**www.thetimes.co.uk**) and *The Sunday Times* (**www.thesundaytimes.co.uk**) in the summer.

Table 1 – measures used by the main publishers of UK league tables

	Universities	Measures	Subjects	Measures
The Complete University Guide	116	9	62	4
The Guardian	119	8	46	8
The Sunday Times	122	8	39	6
The Times	116	8	62	4

THINGS TO WATCH OUT FOR WHEN READING SUBJECT LEAGUE TABLES

- Nursing data in 2012 or 2013 tables will be from before the change in nursing training to all degree courses from 2012 entry. Prior to that, the data for entry standards and destinations may represent only degree courses and not all of the provision on offer.
- Other healthcare courses will usually be included within a more general table covering subjects allied to medicine.
- The tables make no distinction between universities which offer social work courses that are accredited by the General Social Care Council and those which do not.

WHO PUBLISHES NURSING, HEALTHCARE AND SOCIAL WORK LEAGUE TABLES?

The Complete University Guide	Food science Nursing Other subjects allied to medicine Social work
The Guardian	Nursing and paramedical studies Social work
The Sunday Times	Nursing Subjects allied to medicine Social work
The Times	Food science Nursing Other subjects allied to medicine Social work

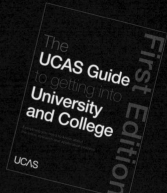

Choosing courses

1

How will they choose you?

Each year university and college departments receive thousands of applications to sift through and consider, so how can you make your application stand out?

SELF-MOTIVATION AND SELF-DISCIPLINE

Studying at university or college is very different from studying at school and in the sixth form. In those settings, you will have followed a set course, normally following a study pattern suggested by teachers. Homework set each night will have ensured that you completed your study regularly and on time.

At university or college, tutors and lecturers do not keep tabs on their students in the same way. Whereas at A level your teachers will have helped motivate you to finish your work on time, university and college tutors will expect you to complete your work on time without constant reminders. This can, understandably, be daunting for some people. Certainly, time management and self-motivation are skills that you will hone during your time at university or college, but it will help your application if your referee can write about any times when you have shown an ability to work well on your own, as this is how you will be studying throughout your undergraduate degree course.

READING

A good way to prove to admissions tutors that you have an interest in the field is to do some reading about the subject, have a good understanding of the area that you want to enter, and be up to date with any new developments in the field – signing up to specialist websites, for example, can be a good way of finding out what's happening in the field at the moment.

Additionally, you could contact the relevant department and ask for their first-year reading list, if this is not available online. You do not need to read everything on it, but if you choose two or three books that most appeal to you and read them in some depth it does show a commitment to the course. Be warned though: don't think that merely mentioning a few key books will automatically get you through. Admissions tutors will know if you have read them or not, so unless you can make a few valid points about why you enjoyed a book or what you found interesting, don't bother – it could do more harm than good.

WORK EXPERIENCE

While relevant work experience is not essential to gain a university or college place, many health and social care course providers will ask for some evidence that you have talked to people working in the profession or have arranged a period of work shadowing to find out what the job involves. Work experience is a really great way of demonstrating to course providers that you are committed to a career in health and social care so try to arrange some if you can. Include details of any experience that you have had in your personal statement. See page 98 for more information about **work experience**.

YOUR PERSONAL STATEMENT

Your personal statement can really enhance your application. It is here that you can show evidence of all the above issues – self-discipline, work experience, additional reading – as well as demonstrate your academic ability and desire for your chosen course. Most universities and colleges place much importance on the personal statement, as this is where your personal voice comes through, so use it to your advantage. Be honest, but don't undersell yourself, and give well-reasoned statements. Above all, make sure that it is free from mistakes and easy to read. There is nothing more offputting for an admissions tutor with hundreds of applications to read than a personal statement that contains glaring errors.

Take your time over your application and ask your family, friends and teacher to check it, not only for mistakes, but also to see if you have left anything out that you should have put in – or if there is anything you have included that should come out. See page 96 for more information about the **personal statement**.

Choosing courses

1

The cost of higher education

The information in this section was up-to-date when this book was published. You should visit the websites mentioned in this section for the very latest information.

THE COST OF STUDYING IN THE UK

As a student, you will usually have to pay for two things: tuition fees for your course, which for most students do not need to be paid for up front, and living costs such as rent, food, books, transport and entertainment. Fees charged vary between courses, between universities and colleges and also according to your normal country of residence, so it's important to check these before you apply. Course fee information is supplied to UCAS by the universities and is displayed in Course Finder at **www.ucas.com**.

STUDENT LOANS

The purpose of student loans from the Government is to help cover the costs of your tuition fees and basic living costs (rent, bills, food and so on). Two types are available: a tuition fee loan to cover the tuition charges and a maintenance loan to help with accommodation and other living costs. Both types of student loan are available to all students who meet the basic eligibility requirements. Interest will be charged at inflation plus a fixed percentage while you are studying. In addition, many other commercial loans are available to students studying at university or college but the interest rate can vary considerably. Loans to help with living costs will be available for all eligible students, irrespective of family income.

Find out more information from the relevant sites below:

England: Student Finance England –
www.direct.gov.uk/studentfinance
Northern Ireland: Student Finance Northern Ireland –
www.studentfinanceni.co.uk
Scotland: Student Awards Agency for Scotland –
www.saas.gov.uk
Wales: Student Finance Wales –
www.studentfinancewales.co.uk or
www.cyllidmyfyrwyrcymru.co.uk

BURSARIES AND SCHOLARSHIPS

- The National Scholarships Programme gives financial help to students studying in England. The scheme is designed to help students whose families have lower incomes.
- Students from families with lower incomes will be entitled to a non-repayable maintenance grant to help with living costs.
- Many universities and colleges also offer non-repayable scholarships and bursaries to help students cover tuition and living costs whilst studying.
- All eligible part-time undergraduates who study for at least 25% of their time will be able to apply for a loan to cover the costs of their tuition, which means they no longer have to pay up front.

There will be extra support for disabled students and students with child or adult dependants. For more information, visit the country-specific websites listed above.

wondering how much higher education costs?

need information about student finance?

Visit www.ucas.com/students/studentfinance
and find sources for all the information on student
money matters you need.

With access to up-to-date information on
bursaries, scholarships and variable fees, plus
our online budget calculator. Visit us today and
get the full picture.

www.ucas.com/students/studentfinance

1 Choosing courses

International students

APPLYING TO STUDY IN THE UK

Deciding to go to university or college in the UK is very exciting. You need to think about what course to do, where to study, and how much it will cost. The decisions you make can have a huge effect on your future but UCAS is here to help.

HOW TO APPLY

Whatever your age or qualifications, if you want to apply for any of the 35,000 courses listed at 300 universities and colleges on the UCAS website, you must apply through UCAS at www.ucas.com. If you are unsure, your school, college, adviser, or local British Council office will be able to help. Further advice and a video guide for international students can be found on the non-UK students' section of the UCAS website at www.ucas.com/international

Students may apply on their own or through their school, college, adviser, or local British Council if they are registered with UCAS to use Apply. If you choose to use an education agent's services, check with the British Council to see if they hold a list of certificated or registered agents in your country. Check also on any charges you may need to pay. UCAS charges only the application fee (see page 88) but agents may charge for additional services.

HOW MUCH WILL MY APPLICATION COST?

If you choose to apply to more than one course, university or college you need to pay UCAS £23 GBP when you apply. If you only apply to one course at one university or college, you pay UCAS £12 GBP.

WHAT LEVEL OF ENGLISH?

UCAS provides a list of English language qualifications and grades that are acceptable to most UK universities and colleges, however you are advised to contact the institutions directly as each have their own entry requirement in English. For more information go to **www.ucas.com/students/wheretostart/ nonukstudents/englangprof.**

INTERNATIONAL STUDENT FEES

If you study in the UK, your fee status (whether you pay full-cost fees or a subsidised fee rate) will be decided by the UK university or college you plan to attend. Before you decide which university or college to attend, you need to be absolutely certain that you can pay the full cost of:

- your tuition fees (the amount is set by universities and colleges, so contact them for more information – visit their websites where many list their fees). Fee details will also be included on Course Finder at **www.ucas.com**
- the everyday living expenses for you and your family for the whole time that you are in the UK, including accommodation, food, gas and electricity bills, clothes, travel and leisure activities
- books and equipment for your course
- travel to and from your country.

You must include everything when you work out how much it will cost. You can get information to help you do this accurately from the international offices at universities and colleges, UKCISA (UK Council for International Student Affairs) and the British Council. There is a useful website tool to help you manage your money at university – **www.studentcalculator.org.uk**.

Scholarships and bursaries are offered at some universities and colleges and you should contact them for more information. In addition, you should check with your local British Council for additional scholarships available to students from your country who want to study in the UK.

LEGAL DOCUMENTS YOU WILL NEED

As you prepare to study in the UK, it is very important to think about the legal documents you will need to enter the country.

Everyone who comes to study in the UK needs a valid passport, details of which will be collected either in you UCAS application or later through Track. If you do not yet have a passport, you should apply for one as soon as possible. People from certain countries also need visas before they come into the UK. They are known as 'visa nationals'. You can check if you require a visa to travel to the UK by visiting the UK Border Agency website and selecting 'Studying in the UK', so please check the UK Border Agency website at **www.ukba.homeoffice.gov.uk** for the most up-to-date guidance and information about the United Kingdom's visa requirements.

When you apply for your visa you need to make sure you have the following documents:

- a confirmation of acceptance for studies (CAS) number from the university of college where you are going to study. The institution must be on the UKBA Register of Sponsors in order to accept international students

- a valid passport
- evidence that you have enough money to pay for your course and living costs
- certificates for all qualifications you have that are relevant to the course you have been accepted for and for any English language qualifications.

You will also have to give your biometric data.

Do check for further information from your local British Embassy or High Commission. Guidance information for international students is also available from UKCISA and from UKBA.

ADDITIONAL RESOURCES

There are a number of organisations that can provide further guidance and information to you as you prepare to study in the UK:

- British Council
  www.britishcouncil.org
- Education UK (British Council website dealing with educational matters)
  www.educationuk.org
- English UK (British Council accredited website listing English language courses in the UK)
  www.englishuk.com
- UK Border Agency (provides information on visa requirements and applications)
  www.ukba.homeoffice.gov.uk
- UKCISA (UK Council for International Student Affairs)
  www.ukcisa.org.uk
- Directgov (the official UK Government website)
  www.direct.gov.uk
- Prepare for Success
  www.prepareforsuccess.org.uk

Step 2 – Applying

You apply through UCAS using the online application system, called Apply, at **www.ucas.com**. You can apply for a maximum of five choices, but you don't have to use them all if you don't want to. If you apply for fewer than five choices, you can add more at a later date if you want to. But be aware of the course application deadlines.

IMPORTANT DATES FOR 2012 ENTRY	
Early June 2012	UCAS Apply opens for 2013 entry registration.
Mid-September 2012	Applications can be sent to UCAS.
15 October 2012	Application deadline for the receipt at UCAS of applications for all medicine, dentistry, veterinary medicine and veterinary science courses and for all courses at the universities of Oxford and Cambridge.
15 January 2013	Application deadline for the receipt at UCAS of applications for all courses except those listed above with a 15 October deadline, and some art and design courses with a 24 March deadline.
25 February 2013	Extra starts (see page 104 for more information about Extra).
24 March 2013	Application deadline for the receipt at UCAS of applications for art and design courses except those listed on Course Finder at www.ucas.com with a 15 January deadline.
31 March 2013	If you apply by 15 January, the universities and colleges should aim to have sent their decisions by this date (but they can take longer).
9 May 2013	If you apply by 15 January, universities and colleges need to send their decisions by this date. If they don't, UCAS will make any outstanding choices unsuccessful on their behalf.
30 June 2013	If you send your application to UCAS by this date, we will send it to your chosen universities and colleges. Applications received after this date are entered into Clearing (see page 118 for more information about Clearing).
3 July 2013	Last date to apply through Extra.
August 2013 (date to be confirmed)	Scottish Qualifications Authority (SQA) results are published.
15 August 2013	GCE and Advanced Diploma results are published (often known as 'A level results day'). Adjustment opens for registration (see page 119 for more information about Adjustment).

DON'T FORGET...

Universities and colleges guarantee to consider your application only if we receive it by the appropriate deadline. Check application deadlines for your courses on Course Finder at www.ucas.com.

If you send it to UCAS after the deadline but before 30 June 2013, universities and colleges will consider your application only if they still have places available.

> Applying
2

How to apply

You apply online at www.ucas.com through Apply – a secure, web-based application service that is designed for all our applicants, whether they are applying through a UCAS-registered centre or as an individual, anywhere in the world. Apply is:

- easy to access – all you need is an internet connection
- easy to use – you don't have to complete your application all in one go: you can save the sections as you complete them and come back to it later
- easy to monitor – once you've applied, you can use Track to check the progress of your application, including any decisions from universities or colleges. You can also reply to your offers using Track.

Watch the UCAStv guide to applying through UCAS at www.ucas.tv.

APPLICATION FEE

For 2013 entry the fee for applying through UCAS is £23 for two or more choices and £12 for one choice.

> 92

DEFERRED ENTRY

If you want to apply for deferred entry in 2014, perhaps because you want to take a year out between school or college and higher education, you should check that the university or college will accept a deferred entry application. Occasionally, tutors are not happy to accept students who take a gap year, because it interrupts the flow of their learning. If you apply for deferred entry, you must meet the conditions of any offers by 31 August 2013 unless otherwise agreed by the university or college. If you accept a deferred place for 2014 entry and then change your mind, you cannot reapply through us in the 2014 entry cycle unless you withdraw your original application.

INVISIBILITY OF CHOICES

Universities and colleges cannot see details of the other choices on your application until you reply to any offers or you are unsuccessful at all your choices. **You can submit only one UCAS application in each year's application cycle.**

APPLYING THROUGH YOUR SCHOOL OR COLLEGE

1 GET SCHOOL OR COLLEGE 'BUZZWORD'

Ask your UCAS application coordinator (may be your sixth form tutor) for your school or college UCAS 'buzzword'. This is a password for the school or college.

2 REGISTER

Go to www.ucas.com/students/apply and click on **Register/Log in to use Apply** and then **register**. After you have entered your registration details, the online system will automatically generate a username for you, but you'll have to come up with a password and answers to security questions.

3 COMPLETE SEVEN SECTIONS

Complete all the sections of the application. To access any section, click on the section name at the left of the screen and follow the instructions. The sections are:

Personal details – contact details, residential status, disability status

Additional information – only UK applicants need to complete this section

Student finance – UK students can share some of their application details with their student finance company. Finance information is provided for other EU and international applicants

Choices – which courses you'd like to apply for

Education – your education and qualifications

Employment – eg work experience, holiday jobs

Statement – see page 96 for personal statement advice.

Before you can send your application you need to go to the **View all details** screen and tick the **section completed** box.

4 PASS TO REFEREE

Once you've completed all the sections, send your application electronically to your referee (normally your form tutor). They'll check it, approve it and add their reference to it, and will then send it to UCAS on your behalf.

USEFUL INFORMATION ABOUT APPLY

- Important details like date of birth and course codes will be checked by Apply. It will alert you if they are not valid.
- We strongly recommend that the personal statement and reference are written in a word processing package and pasted into Apply.
- If you want, you can enter European characters into certain areas of Apply.
- You can change your application at any time before it is completed and sent to UCAS.
- You can print and preview your application at any time. Before you send it you need to go to the **View all details** screen and tick the **section completed** box.
- Your school, college or centre can choose different payment methods. For example, they may want us to bill them, or you may be able to pay online by debit or credit card.

NOT APPLYING THROUGH A SCHOOL OR COLLEGE

If you're not currently studying, you'll probably be applying as an independent applicant rather than through a school, college or other UCAS-registered centre. In this case you won't be able to provide a 'buzzword', but we'll ask you a few extra questions to check you are eligible to apply.

If you're not applying through a UCAS-registered centre, the procedure you use for obtaining a reference will depend on whether or not you want your reference to be provided through a registered centre. For information on the procedures for providing references, visit www.ucas.com/students/applying/howtoapply/reference.

Save with UCAS Card

If you're in Year 12, S5 or equivalent and thinking about higher education, sign up for the **FREE** UCAS Card to receive all these benefits:

- information about courses and unis
- expert advice from UCAS
- exclusive discounts for card holders

UCAS

Register today at
www.ucas.com/ucascard

find us on
Facebook

APPLICATION CHECKLIST

We want this to run smoothly for you and we also want
to process your application as quickly as possible. You
can help us to do this by remembering to do the
following:

✓ check the closing dates for applications – see
  page 91
✓ check the student information at
  www.ucas.com/students/studentfinance/
  and course fees information in Course Finder at
  www.ucas.com
✓ start early and allow plenty of time for completing
  your application – including enough time for your
  referee to complete the reference section
✓ read the online instructions carefully before you start
✓ consider what each question is actually asking for -
  use the 'help'
✓ ask a teacher, parent, friend or careers adviser to
  review your draft application – particularly the
  personal statement
✓ pay special attention to your personal statement
  (see page 96) and start drafting it early
✓ if you get stuck, watch our videos on YouTube where
  we answer your frequently asked questions on
  completing a UCAS application at
  www.youtube.com/ucasonline
✓ if you have extra information that will not fit on your
  application, send it direct to your chosen universities
  or colleges after we have sent you your Welcome
  letter with your Personal ID – don't send it to us
✓ print a copy of the final version of your application, in
  case you are asked questions on it at an interview.

Applying

2

The personal statement

Next to choosing your courses, this section of your application will be the most time-consuming. It is of immense importance as many universities and colleges rely solely on the information in the UCAS application, rather than interviews and admissions tests. The personal statement can be the deciding factor in whether or not they offer you a place. If it is an institution that interviews, it could be the deciding factor in whether you get invited for interview.

Keep a copy of your personal statement – if you are called for interview, you will almost certainly be asked questions based on it.

Tutors will look carefully at your exam results, actual and predicted, your reference and your personal statement. Remember, they are looking for reasons to offer you a place – try to give them every opportunity to do so!

A SALES DOCUMENT

The personal statement is your opportunity to sell yourself, so do so. The university or college admissions tutor wants to get a rounded picture of you to decide whether you will make an interesting member of the university or college both academically and socially. They want to know more about you than the subjects you are studying at school.

HOW TO START

At **www.ucas.com** you'll find several tools to help you write a good personal statement.

- Personal statement timeline, to help you do all your research and plan your statement over several drafts and checks.
- Personal statement mind map, which gives you reminders and hints on preparation, content and presentation, with extra hints for mature and international applicants.
- Personal statement worksheet, which gets you to start writing by asking relevant questions so that you include everything you need. You can also check your work against a list of dos and don'ts.

Include things like hobbies and work experience (see pages 83 and 98), and try to link the skills you have gained to the type of course you are applying for. Describe your career plans and goals. Have you belonged to sports teams or orchestras or held positions of responsibility in the community? Try to give evidence of your ability to undertake higher level study successfully by showing your commitment and maturity. If you left full-time education a while ago, talk about the work you have done and the skills you have gathered or how you have juggled bringing up a family with other activities – that is solid evidence of time management skills. Whoever you are, make sure you explain what appeals to you about the course you are applying for.

WHAT ADMISSIONS TUTORS LOOK FOR
- Your reasons for wanting to take this subject in general and this particular course.
- Your communication skills – not only what you say but how you say it. Your grammar and spelling must be perfect.
- Relevant experience – practical things you've done that are related to your choice of course.
- Evidence of your teamworking ability, leadership capability, independence.
- Evidence of your skills, for example: IT skills, empathy and people skills, debating and public speaking, research and analysis.
- Other activities that show your dedication and ability to apply yourself and maintain your motivation.

WHAT TO TELL THEM
- Why you want to do this subject - how you know it's the subject for you.
- What experience you already have in this field – for example work experience, school projects, hobbies, voluntary work.
- The skills and qualities you have as a person that would make you a good student, for example anything that shows your dedication, communication ability, academic achievement, initiative.
- Examples that show you can knuckle down and apply yourself, for example running a marathon or your Extended Project.
- If you're taking a gap year, why and (if possible) what you're going to do during it.
- About your other interests and activities away from studying – to show you're a 'rounded' person. (But remember that it is mainly your suitability for the particular course that they're looking to judge.)

WORK EXPERIENCE

Universities and colleges look for people who have some knowledge of healthcare or social care: what it is and how it works. Work experience can be a wonderful way to gain this knowledge – with the added bonus of getting a 'taster' and finding out whether you like a particular work environment, area of service or type of job.

Admissions tutors will be looking for applicants with basic skills that are relevant to the health and social care professions: listening, assessing, communicating and working well with others. They will also be interested in people who have a non-judgmental attitude, an appreciation of diversity and self-awareness, a flexible attitude and an openess to new ideas. Working as a volunteer or as an unqualified worker in social care or healthcare settings can be a satisfying and valuable way of finding out more about different kinds of work. It can help you to start thinking about what you want from your future career and gain useful experience – and relevant references!

These are some of the different types of work experience that you could do:

Work shadowing involves closely observing a professional in their daily working life to see if their job interests you. Work shadowing can be for as little as one day or as much as a whole week.

Work tasters are very short placements offered by some organisations, sometimes in conjunction with your school or careers advice service, to give you an insight into a job role or organisation.

Part-time or casual work can be a way to earn money while at the same time gaining important skills.

Whether it's working as a healthcare assistant in the NHS or answering phones at a local council, you can use your experience to illustrate anything from difficult situations you have overcome, to customer service skills and teamwork. There are often opportunities to work as a care assistant or care worker and you won't necessarily need formal training to apply for a job. These jobs are usually advertised in local papers and job centres.

Voluntary work can be anything from helping out at a local charity to setting up a society at school or visiting residents at a nearby hospice. Voluntary work is essentially volunteering your services for free. You may be able to help out in a role that's close to your chosen career route – and even if your work isn't exactly what you want to do, you can use the experience to get a sense of what it's like to work in a healthcare or social care context. Find out about opportunities for volunteering from your local volunteer bureau, NHS Trust, Citizens Advice Bureau or public library. Newspapers such as the *Guardian* on a Wednesday or magazines such as *Community Care* sometimes advertise voluntary work vacancies.

A **gap year**, also known as a year out, can be a great opportunity to gain experience. If you're looking for relevant experience in health and social care, one option is to volunteer full-time on a structured placement with CSV (Community Service Volunteers). These last between four and 12 months and develop skills that are recognised by employers and university and college staff. All placements are based in health and social care settings and could include working with adults with mental health problems, university or college students with physical disabilities, residents in homeless hostels or one-on-one with children in schools. Placements are full-time and you will be given accommodation, meals and a weekly allowance. For more information visit **www.csv.org.uk**.

HOW TO MAKE THE MOST OF YOUR
EXPERIENCE

Wherever you find yourself, here are a few tips to help
you make the most of your work experience, paid or
unpaid.

- Work hard and do what's asked of you willingly
- Ask for feedback on how you're doing – it shows
  your enthusiasm and helps you develop your skills.
- Write down everything you have done and what you
  learned. This will help you write your personal
  statement and give you valuable real examples to
  use at interview
- Make yourself useful – offer to help out.

UCAS

Confused about courses?

Indecisive about institutions?

Stressed about student life?

Unsure about UCAS?

Frowning over finance?

Help is available at
www.ucasbooks.com

Offers

3

Step 3 – Offers

Once we have sent your application to your chosen universities and colleges, they will each consider it independently and tell us whether or not they can offer you a place. Some universities and colleges will take longer to make decisions than others. You may be asked to attend an interview, sit an additional test or provide a piece of work such as an essay before a decision can be made.

Many universities (particularly the more popular ones, running competitive courses) use interviews as part of their selection process. Universities will want to find out why you want to study your chosen course at their institution, and they can make sure the course is suitable for you and your future career plans. Interviews also give you an opportunity to ask the university any questions you may have about the course or their institution.

If you are called for interview, the key areas they are likely to cover will be:

- evidence of your academic ability
- your capacity to study hard
- your awareness of current issues in the news that may have an impact on your chosen field of study
- your logic and reasoning ability
- your manual dexterity, if applying for nursing
- your interpersonal skills.

A lot of the interview will be based on information supplied on your application – especially your **personal statement** – see pages 96-98 for tips about the personal statement.

Whenever a university or college makes a decision about your application we record it and let you know. You can check the progress of your application using Track at **www.ucas.com**. This is our secure online service which gives you access to your application using the same username and password you used when you applied. You can use it to find out if you have been invited for interview or need to provide an additional piece of work, and you can check to see if you have received any offers.

Find out more about how to use Track in the UCAStv video guide at **www.ucas.tv**.

TYPES OF OFFER

Universities can make two types of offer: conditional or unconditional.

Conditional offer

A conditional offer means the university or college will offer you a place if you meet certain conditions – usually based on exam results. The conditions may be based on Tariff points (for example, 300 points from three A levels), or specify certain grades in named subjects (for example, A in English, B in health and social care, C in history).

Unconditional offer

If you've met all the academic requirements for the course and the university or college wants to accept you, they will make you an unconditional offer. If you accept this you'll have a definite place. However, there might be other requirements, like medical or financial

conditions, that you need to meet before you can start your course.

However, for either type of offer there may be some non-academic requirements.

- For courses that involve contact with children and vulnerable adults you may need to have criminal record checks before you can start the course.
- For health courses you will need to have a health check.
- For students who are not resident in either the UK or the EU, there may be some financial conditions to meet.

REPLYING TO OFFERS

When you have received decisions for all your choices, you must decide which offers you want to accept. You will be given a deadline in Track by which you have to make your replies. Before replying, get advice from family, friends or advisers, but remember that you're the one taking the course so it's your decision.

Firm acceptance

- Your firm acceptance is your first choice - this is your preferred choice out of all the offers you have received. You can only have one firm acceptance.
- If you accept an unconditional offer, you are entering a contract that you will attend the course, so you must decline any other offers.
- If you accept a conditional offer, you are entering a contract that you will attend the course at that university or college if you meet the conditions of the offer. You can accept another offer as an insurance choice.

Insurance acceptance

- If your firm acceptance is a conditional offer, you can accept another offer as an insurance choice. Your insurance choice can be conditional or unconditional and acts as a back-up, so if you don't meet the conditions for your firm choice but meet the conditions for your insurance, you will be committed to the insurance choice. You can only have one insurance choice.

- The conditions for your insurance choice would usually be lower than your firm choice.
- You don't have to accept an insurance choice if you don't want one. You need to be certain that it's an offer you would be happy to accept.

For more information watch our video guides *How to use Track, Making sense of your offers*, and *How to reply to your offers* at www.ucas.tv.

WHAT IF YOU HAVE NO OFFERS?

If you have used all five choices on your application and either received no offers, or decided to turn down any offers you have received, you may be eligible to apply for another choice through Extra. Find out more about Extra on page 104.

If you are not eligible for Extra, in the summer you can contact universities and colleges with vacancies in Clearing. See page 118 for more information.

```
┌─────────────────────────────────┐
│        Offers                   │
│  ┌─                             │
│  3                             │
│  └─                             │
└─────────────────────────────────┘
```

Extra

Extra allows you to make additional choices, one at a time, without having to wait for Clearing in July. It is completely optional and free, and is designed to encourage you to continue researching and choosing courses if you need to. You can search for courses available through Extra on Course Finder, at **www.ucas.com**. The Extra service is available to eligible applicants from 25 February to early July 2013 through Track at **www.ucas.com**

WHO IS ELIGIBLE?

You will be eligible for Extra if you have already made five choices and:

- you have had unsuccessful or withdrawal decisions from all five of your choices, or

- you have cancelled your outstanding choices and hold no offers, or
- you have received decisions from all five choices and have declined all offers made to you.

HOW DOES IT WORK?

We contact you and explain what to do if you are eligible for Extra. If you are eligible a special Extra button will be available on your Track screen. If you want to use Extra you should:

- check on Course Finder for courses that are available through Extra. You need to tick the 'Available in extra' box in the Study options section when looking for courses on Course Finder
- choose a course that you would like to apply for and enter the details on your Track screen.

When you have chosen a course the university or college will be able to see your application and consider you for a place.

WHAT HAPPENS NEXT?

We give universities and colleges a maximum of 21 days to consider your Extra application. During this time, you cannot be considered by another university or college. If you have not heard after 21 days you can refer yourself to a different university or college if you wish, but it is a good idea to ring the one currently considering you before doing so. If you are made an offer, you can choose whether or not to accept it.

If you accept any offer, conditional or unconditional, you will not be able to take any further part in Extra.

If you are currently studying for examinations, any offer that you receive is likely to be an offer conditional on exam grades. If you already have your examination results, it is possible that a university or college may make an unconditional offer. If you accept an unconditional offer, you will be placed. If you decide to decline the offer, or the university or college decides they cannot make you an offer, you will be given another opportunity to use Extra, time permitting. Your Extra button on Track will be reactivated.

Once you have accepted an offer in Extra, you are committed to it in the same way as you would be with an offer through the main UCAS system. Conditional offers made through Extra will be treated in the same way as other conditional offers, when your examination results become available.

If your results do not meet the conditions and the university or college decides that they cannot confirm your Extra offer, you will automatically become eligible for Clearing if it is too late for you to be considered by another university or college in Extra.

If you are unsuccessful, decline an offer, or do not receive an offer, or 21 days has elapsed since choosing a course through Extra, you can use Extra to apply for another course, time permitting.

ADVICE

Do some careful research and seek guidance on your Extra choice of university or college and course. If you applied to high-demand courses and institutions in your original application and were unsuccessful, you could consider related or alternative subjects or perhaps apply for the subject you want in combination with another. Your teachers or careers advisers, or the universities and colleges themselves can provide useful guidance. Course Finder at **www.ucas.com** is another important source of information. Be flexible, that is the key to success. But you are the only one who knows how flexible you are prepared to be. Remember that even if you decide to take a degree course other than health and social care, you can take the postgraduate route into the profession.

Visit **www.ucas.tv** to watch the video guide on how to use Extra.

Offers

3

The Tariff

Finding out what qualifications are needed for different higher education courses can be very confusing.

The UCAS Tariff is the system for allocating points to qualifications used for entry to higher education. Universities and colleges can use the UCAS Tariff to make comparisons between applicants with different qualifications. Tariff points are often used in entry requirements, although other factors are often taken into account. Information on Course Finder at www.ucas.com provides a fuller picture of what admissions tutors are seeking.

The tables on the following pages show the qualifications covered by the UCAS Tariff. There may have been changes to these tables since this book was printed. You should visit www.ucas.com to view the most up-to-date tables.

FURTHER INFORMATION?

Although Tariff points can be accumulated in a variety of ways, not all of these will necessarily be acceptable for entry to a particular higher education course. The achievement of a points score therefore does not give an automatic entitlement to entry, and many other factors are taken into account in the admissions process.

The Course Finder facility at www.ucas.com is the best source of reference to find out what qualifications are acceptable for entry to specific courses. Updates to the Tariff, including details on how new qualifications are added, can be found at www.ucas.com/students/ucas_tariff/.

HOW DOES THE TARIFF WORK?

- Students can collect Tariff points from a range of different qualifications, eg GCE A level with BTEC Nationals.
- There is no ceiling to the number of points that can be accumulated.
- There is no double counting. Certain qualifications within the Tariff build on qualifications in the same subject. In these cases only the qualification with the higher Tariff score will be counted. This principle applies to:
  - GCE Advanced Subsidiary level and GCE Advanced level
  - Scottish Highers and Advanced Highers
  - Speech, drama and music awards at grades 6, 7 and 8.
- Tariff points for the Advanced Diploma come from the Progression Diploma score plus the relevant Additional and Specialist Learning (ASL) Tariff points. Please see the appropriate qualification in the Tariff tables to calculate the ASL score.
- The Extended Project Tariff points are included within the Tariff points for Progression and Advanced Diplomas. Extended Project points represented in the Tariff only count when the qualification is taken outside of these Diplomas.
- Where the Tariff tables refer to specific awarding organisations, only qualifications from these awarding organisations attract Tariff points. Qualifications with a similar title, but from a different qualification awarding organisation do not attract Tariff points.

HOW DO UNIVERSITIES AND COLLEGES USE THE TARIFF?

The Tariff provides a facility to help universities and colleges when expressing entrance requirements and when making conditional offers. Entry requirements and conditional offers expressed as Tariff points will often require a minimum level of achievement in a specified subject (for example, '300 points to include grade A at A level chemistry', or '260 points including SQA Higher grade B in mathematics').

Use of the Tariff may also vary from department to department at any one institution, and may in some cases be dependent on the programme being offered.

In July 2010, UCAS announced plans to review the qualifications information provided to universities and colleges. You can read more about the review at **www.ucas.com/qireview**.

The following qualifications are included in the UCAS Tariff. See the number on the qualification title to find the relevant section of the Tariff table.

1   AAT NVQ Level 3 in Accounting
2   AAT Level 3 Diploma in Accounting (QCF)
3   Advanced Diploma
4   Advanced Extension Awards
5   Advanced Placement Programme (US and Canada)
6   Arts Award (Gold)
7   ASDAN Community Volunteering qualification
8   Asset Languages Advanced Stage
9   British Horse Society (Stage 3 Horse Knowledge & Care, Stage 3 Riding and Preliminary Teacher's Certificate)
10 BTEC Awards (NQF)
11 BTEC Certificates and Extended Certificates (NQF)
12 BTEC Diplomas (NQF)
13 BTEC National in Early Years (NQF)
14 BTEC Nationals (NQF)
15 BTEC QCF Qualifications (Suite known as Nationals)
16 BTEC Specialist Qualifications (QCF)
17 CACHE Award, Certificate and Diploma in Child Care and Education
18 CACHE Level 3 Extended Diploma for the Children and Young People's Workforce (QCF)
19 Cambridge ESOL Examinations
20 Cambridge Pre-U
21 Certificate of Personal Effectiveness (COPE)
22 CISI Introduction to Securities and Investment
23 City & Guilds Land Based Services Level 3 Qualifications
24 Graded Dance and Vocational Graded Dance
25 Diploma in Fashion Retail
26 Diploma in Foundation Studies (Art & Design; Art, Design & Media)
27 EDI Level 3 Certificate in Accounting, Certificate in Accounting (IAS)
28 Essential Skills (Northern Ireland)
29 Essential Skills Wales
30 Extended Project (stand alone)
31 Free-standing Mathematics
32 Functional skills
33 GCE (AS, AS Double Award, A level, A level Double Award and A level (with additional AS))
34 Hong Kong Diploma of Secondary Education (from 2012 entry onwards)
35 ifs School of Finance (Certificate and Diploma in Financial Studies)
36 iMedia (OCR level Certificate/Diploma for iMedia Professionals)
37 International Baccalaureate (IB) Diploma
38 International Baccalaureate (IB) Certificate
39 Irish Leaving Certificate (Higher and Ordinary levels)
40 IT Professionals (iPRO) (Certificate and Diploma)
41 Key Skills (Levels 2, 3 and 4)
42 Music examinations (grades 6, 7 and 8)
43 OCR Level 3 Certificate in Mathematics for Engineering
44 OCR Level 3 Certificate for Young Enterprise
45 OCR Nationals (National Certificate, National Diploma and National Extended Diploma)
46 Principal Learning Wales
47 Progression Diploma
48 Rockschool Music Practitioners Qualifications
49 Scottish Qualifications
50 Speech and Drama examinations (grades 6, 7 and 8 and Performance Studies)
51 Sports Leaders UK
52 Welsh Baccalaureate Advanced Diploma (Core)

Updates on the Tariff, including details on the incorporation of any new qualifications, are posted on **www.ucas.com**.

UCAS TARIFF TABLES

1

AAT NVQ LEVEL 3 IN ACCOUNTING	
GRADE	TARIFF POINTS
PASS	160

2

AAT LEVEL 3 DIPLOMA IN ACCOUNTING	
GRADE	TARIFF POINTS
PASS	160

3

ADVANCED DIPLOMA

Advanced Diploma = Progression Diploma plus Additional & Specialist Learning (ASL). Please see the appropriate qualification to calculate the ASL score. Please see the Progression Diploma (Table 47) for Tariff scores

4

ADVANCED EXTENSION AWARDS	
GRADE	TARIFF POINTS
DISTINCTION	40
MERIT	20

Points for Advanced Extension Awards are over and above those gained from the A level grade

5

ADVANCED PLACEMENT PROGRAMME (US & CANADA)	
GRADE	TARIFF POINTS
Group A	
5	120
4	90
3	60
Group B	
5	50
4	35
3	20

Details of the subjects covered by each group can be found at www.ucas.com/students/ucas_tariff/tarifftables

6

ARTS AWARD (GOLD)	
GRADE	TARIFF POINTS
PASS	35

7

ASDAN COMMUNITY VOLUNTEERING QUALIFICATION	
GRADE	TARIFF POINTS
CERTIFICATE	50
AWARD	30

8

ASSET LANGUAGES ADVANCED STAGE			
GRADE	TARIFF POINTS	GRADE	TARIFF POINTS
Speaking		Listening	
GRADE 12	28	GRADE 12	25
GRADE 11	20	GRADE 11	18
GRADE 10	12	GRADE 10	11
Reading		Writing	
GRADE 12	25	GRADE 12	25
GRADE 11	18	GRADE 11	18
GRADE 10	11	GRADE 10	11

9

BRITISH HORSE SOCIETY	
GRADE	TARIFF POINTS
Stage 3 Horse Knowledge & Care	
PASS	35
Stage 3 Riding	
PASS	35
Preliminary Teacher's Certificate	
PASS	35

Awarded by Equestrian Qualifications (GB) Ltd (EQL)

10

BTEC AWARDS (NQF) (EXCLUDING BTEC NATIONAL QUALIFICATIONS)			
GRADE	TARIFF POINTS		
	Group A	Group B	Group C
DISTINCTION	20	30	40
MERIT	13	20	26
PASS	7	10	13

Details of the subjects covered by each group can be found at www.ucas.com/students/ucas_tariff/tarifftables

11

BTEC CERTIFICATES AND EXTENDED CERTIFICATES (NQF) (EXCLUDING BTEC NATIONAL QUALIFICATIONS)					
GRADE	TARIFF POINTS				
	Group A	Group B	Group C	Group D	Extended Certificates
DISTINCTION	40	60	80	100	60
MERIT	26	40	52	65	40
PASS	13	20	26	35	20

Details of the subjects covered by each group can be found at www.ucas.com/students/ucas_tariff/tarifftables

12

BTEC DIPLOMAS (NQF) (EXCLUDING BTEC NATIONAL QUALIFICATIONS)			
GRADE	TARIFF POINTS		
	Group A	Group B	Group C
DISTINCTION	80	100	120
MERIT	52	65	80
PASS	26	35	40

Details of the subjects covered by each group can be found at www.ucas.com/students/ucas_tariff/tarifftables

13

GRADE	TARIFF POINTS	GRADE	TARIFF POINTS	GRADE	TARIFF POINTS
BTEC NATIONAL IN EARLY YEARS (NQF)					
Theory				Practical	
Diploma				D	120
DDD	320	Certificate		M	80
		DD	200	P	40
DDM	280	DM	160		
DMM	240	MM	120		
MMM	220	MP	80		
MMP	160	PP	40		
MPP	120				
PPP	80				

Points apply to the following qualifications only: BTEC National Diploma in Early Years (100/1279/5); BTEC National Certificate in Early Years (100/1280/1)

14

GRADE	TARIFF POINTS	GRADE	TARIFF POINTS	GRADE	TARIFF POINTS
BTEC NATIONALS (NQF)					
Diploma		Certificate		Award	
DDD	360	DD	240	D	120
DDM	320	DM	200	M	80
DMM	280	MM	160	P	40
MMM	240	MP	120		
MMP	200	PP	80		
MPP	160				
PPP	120				

15

EXTENDED DIPLOMA	DIPLOMA	90 CREDIT DIPLOMA	SUBSIDIARY DIPLOMA	CERTIFICATE	TARIFF POINTS
BTEC QUALIFICATIONS (QCF) (SUITE OF QUALIFICATIONS KNOWN AS NATIONALS)					
D*D*D*					420
D*D*D					400
D*DD					380
DDD					360
DDM					320
DMM	D*D*				280
	D*D				260
MMM	DD				240
		D*D*			210
MMP	DM	D*D			200
		DD			180
MPP	MM	DM			160
			D*		140
PPP	MP	MM	D		120
		MP			100
	PP		M		80
				D*	70
		PP		D	60
			P	M	40
				P	20

16

GRADE	TARIFF POINTS		
BTEC SPECIALIST (QCF)			
	Diploma	Certificate	Award
DISTINCTION	120	60	20
MERIT	80	40	13
PASS	40	20	7

UCAS TARIFF TABLES

17

CACHE LEVEL 3 AWARD, CERTIFICATE AND DIPLOMA IN CHILD CARE & EDUCATION					
AWARD		CERTIFICATE		DIPLOMA	
GRADE	TARIFF POINTS	GRADE	TARIFF POINTS	GRADE	TARIFF POINTS
A	30	A	110	A	360
B	25	B	90	B	300
C	20	C	70	C	240
D	15	D	55	D	180
E	10	E	35	E	120

18

CACHE LEVEL 3 EXTENDED DIPLOMA FOR THE CHILDREN AND YOUNG PEOPLE'S WORKFORCE (QCF)	
GRADE	TARIFF POINTS
A*	420
A	340
B	290
C	240
D	140
E	80

19

CAMBRIDGE ESOL EXAMINATIONS	
GRADE	TARIFF POINTS
Certificate of Proficiency in English	
A	140
B	110
C	70
Certificate in Advanced English	
A	70

20

CAMBRIDGE PRE-U							
GRADE	TARIFF POINTS	GRADE	TARIFF POINTS	GRADE	TARIFF POINTS	GRADE	TARIFF POINTS
Principal Subject		Global Perspectives and Research		Short Course			
D1	TBC	D1	TBC	D1	TBC		
D2	145	D2	140	D2	TBC		
D3	130	D3	126	D3	60		
M1	115	M1	112	M1	53		
M2	101	M2	98	M2	46		
M3	87	M3	84	M3	39		
P1	73	P1	70	P1	32		
P2	59	P2	56	P2	26		
P3	46	P3	42	P3	20		

21

CERTIFICATE OF PERSONAL EFFECTIVENESS (COPE)	
GRADE	TARIFF POINTS
PASS	70

Points are awarded for the Certificate of Personal Effectiveness (CoPE) awarded by ASDAN and CCEA

22

CISI INTRODUCTION TO SECURITIES AND INVESTMENT	
GRADE	TARIFF POINTS
PASS WITH DISTINCTION	60
PASS WITH MERIT	40
PASS	20

23

CITY AND GUILDS LAND BASED SERVICES LEVEL 3 QUALIFICATIONS				
GRADE	TARIFF POINTS			
	EXTENDED DIPLOMA	DIPLOMA	SUBSIDIARY DIPLOMA	CERTIFICATE
DISTINCTION*	420	280	140	70
DISTINCTION	360	240	120	60
MERIT	240	160	80	40
PASS	120	80	40	20

24

GRADED DANCE AND VOCATIONAL GRADED DANCE					
GRADE	TARIFF POINTS	GRADE	TARIFF POINTS	GRADE	TARIFF POINTS
Graded Dance					
Grade 8		Grade 7		Grade 6	
DISTINCTION	65	DISTINCTION	55	DISTINCTION	40
MERIT	55	MERIT	45	MERIT	35
PASS	45	PASS	35	PASS	30
Vocational Graded Dance					
Advanced Foundation		Intermediate			
DISTINCTION	70	DISTINCTION	65		
MERIT	55	MERIT	50		
PASS	45	PASS	40		

25

DIPLOMA IN FASHION RETAIL	
GRADE	TARIFF POINTS
DISTINCTION	160
MERIT	120
PASS	80

Applies to the NQF and QCF versions of the qualifications awarded by ABC Awards

UCAS TARIFF TABLES

26

DIPLOMA IN FOUNDATION STUDIES (ART & DESIGN AND ART, DESIGN & MEDIA)	
GRADE	TARIFF POINTS
DISTINCTION	285
MERIT	225
PASS	165

Awarded by ABC, Edexcel, UAL and WJEC

27

EDI LEVEL 3 CERTIFICATE IN ACCOUNTING, CERTIFICATE IN ACCOUNTING (IAS)	
GRADE	TARIFF POINTS
DISTINCTION	120
MERIT	90
PASS	70

28

ESSENTIAL SKILLS (NORTHERN IRELAND)	
GRADE	TARIFF POINTS
LEVEL 2	10

Only allocated at level 2 if studied as part of a wider composite qualification such as 14-19 Diploma or Welsh Baccalaureate

29

ESSENTIAL SKILLS WALES	
GRADE	TARIFF POINTS
LEVEL 4	30
LEVEL 3	20
LEVEL 2	10

Only allocated at level 2 if studied as part of a wider composite qualification such as 14-19 Diploma or Welsh Baccalaureate

30

EXTENDED PROJECT (STAND ALONE)	
GRADE	TARIFF POINTS
A*	70
A	60
B	50
C	40
D	30
E	20

Points for the Extended Project cannot be counted if taken as part of Progression/Advanced Diploma

31

FREE-STANDING MATHEMATICS	
GRADE	TARIFF POINTS
A	20
B	17
C	13
D	10
E	7

Covers free-standing Mathematics - Additional Maths, Using and Applying Statistics, Working with Algebraic and Graphical Techniques, Modelling with Calculus

32

FUNCTIONAL SKILLS	
GRADE	TARIFF POINTS
LEVEL 2	10

Only allocated if studied as part of a wider composite qualification such as 14-19 Diploma or Welsh Baccalaureate

33

GCE AND VCE									
GRADE	TARIFF POINTS	GRADE	TARIFF POINTS	GRADE	TARIFF POINTS	GRADE	TARIFF POINTS	GRADE	TARIFF POINTS
GCE & AVCE Double Award		GCE A level with additional AS (9 units)		GCE A level & AVCE		GCE AS Double Award		GCE AS & AS VCE	
A*A*	280	A*A	200	A*	140	AA	120	A	60
A*A	260	AA	180	A	120	AB	110	B	50
AA	240	AB	170	B	100	BB	100	C	40
AB	220	BB	150	C	80	BC	90	D	30
BB	200	BC	140	D	60	CC	80	E	20
BC	180	CC	120	E	40	CD	70		
CC	160	CD	110			DD	60		
CD	140	DD	90			DE	50		
DD	120	DE	80			EE	40		
DE	100	EE	60						
EE	80								

34

HONG KONG DIPLOMA OF SECONDARY EDUCATION					
GRADE	TARIFF POINTS	GRADE	TARIFF POINTS	GRADE	TARIFF POINTS
All subjects except mathematics		Mathematics compulsory component		Mathematics optional components	
5**	No value	5**	No value	5**	No value
5*	130	5*	60	5*	70
5	120	5	45	5	60
4	80	4	35	4	50
3	40	3	25	3	40

No value for 5** pending receipt of candidate evidence (post 2012)

35

IFS SCHOOL OF FINANCE (NQF & QCF)			
GRADE	TARIFF POINTS	GRADE	TARIFF POINTS
Certificate in Financial Studies (CeFS)		Diploma in Financial Studies (DipFS)	
A	60	A	120
B	50	B	100
C	40	C	80
D	30	D	60
E	20	E	40

Applicants with the ifs Diploma cannot also count points allocated to the ifs Certificate. Completion of both qualifications will result in a maximum of 120 UCAS Tariff points

36

LEVEL 3 CERTIFICATE / DIPLOMA FOR iMEDIA USERS (iMEDIA)	
GRADE	TARIFF POINTS
DIPLOMA	66
CERTIFICATE	40

Awarded by OCR

37

INTERNATIONAL BACCALAUREATE (IB) DIPLOMA			
GRADE	TARIFF POINTS	GRADE	TARIFF POINTS
45	720	34	479
44	698	33	457
43	676	32	435
42	654	31	413
41	632	30	392
40	611	29	370
39	589	28	348
38	567	27	326
37	545	26	304
36	523	25	282
35	501	24	260

38

INTERNATIONAL BACCALAUREATE (IB) CERTIFICATE					
GRADE	TARIFF POINTS	GRADE	TARIFF POINTS	GRADE	TARIFF POINTS
Higher Level		Standard Level		Core	
7	130	7	70	3	120
6	110	6	59	2	80
5	80	5	43	1	40
4	50	4	27	0	10
3	20	3	11		

39

IRISH LEAVING CERTIFICATE			
GRADE	TARIFF POINTS	GRADE	TARIFF POINTS
Higher		Ordinary	
A1	90	A1	39
A2	77	A2	26
B1	71	B1	20
B2	64	B2	14
B3	58	B3	7
C1	52		
C2	45		
C3	39		
D1	33		
D2	26		
D3	20		

40

IT PROFESSIONALS (iPRO)	
GRADE	TARIFF POINTS
DIPLOMA	100
CERTIFICATE	80

Awarded by OCR

41

KEY SKILLS	
GRADE	TARIFF POINTS
LEVEL 4	30
LEVEL 3	20
LEVEL 2	10

Only allocated at level 2 if studied as part of a wider composite qualification such as 14-19 Diploma or Welsh Baccalaureate

42

MUSIC EXAMINATIONS					
GRADE	TARIFF POINTS	GRADE	TARIFF POINTS	GRADE	TARIFF POINTS
Practical					
Grade 8		Grade 7		Grade 6	
DISTINCTION	75	DISTINCTION	60	DISTINCTION	45
MERIT	70	MERIT	55	MERIT	40
PASS	55	PASS	40	PASS	25
Theory					
Grade 8		Grade 7		Grade 6	
DISTINCTION	30	DISTINCTION	20	DISTINCTION	15
MERIT	25	MERIT	15	MERIT	10
PASS	20	PASS	10	PASS	5

Points shown are for the ABRSM, LCMM/University of West London, Rockschool and Trinity Guildhall/Trinity College London Advanced Level music examinations

43

OCR LEVEL 3 CERTIFICATE IN MATHEMATICS FOR ENGINEERING	
GRADE	TARIFF POINTS
A*	TBC
A	90
B	75
C	60
D	45
E	30

44

OCR LEVEL 3 CERTIFICATE FOR YOUNG ENTERPRISE	
GRADE	TARIFF POINTS
DISTINCTION	40
MERIT	30
PASS	20

45

OCR NATIONALS					
GRADE	TARIFF POINTS	GRADE	TARIFF POINTS	GRADE	TARIFF POINTS
National Extended Diploma		National Diploma		National Certificate	
D1	360	D	240	D	120
D2/M1	320	M1	200	M	80
M2	280	M2/P1	160	P	40
M3	240	P2	120		
P1	200	P3	80		
P2	160				
P3	120				

46

PRINCIPAL LEARNING WALES	
GRADE	TARIFF POINTS
A*	210
A	180
B	150
C	120
D	90
E	60

47

PROGRESSION DIPLOMA	
GRADE	TARIFF POINTS
A*	350
A	300
B	250
C	200
D	150
E	100

Advanced Diploma = Progression Diploma plus Additional & Specialist Learning (ASL). Please see the appropriate qualification to calculate the ASL score

UCAS TARIFF TABLES

48

ROCKSCHOOL MUSIC PRACTITIONERS QUALIFICATIONS					
GRADE	TARIFF POINTS				
	Extended Diploma	Diploma	Subsidiary Diploma	Extended Certificate	Certificate
DISTINCTION	240	180	120	60	30
MERIT	160	120	80	40	20
PASS	80	60	40	20	10

49

SCOTTISH QUALIFICATIONS							
GRADE	TARIFF POINTS	GRADE	TARIFF POINTS	GRADE	TARIFF POINTS	GROUP	TARIFF POINTS
Advanced Higher		Higher		Scottish Interdisciplinary Project		Scottish National Certificates	
A	130	A	80	A	65	C	125
B	110	B	65	B	55	B	100
C	90	C	50	C	45	A	75
D	72	D	36				
Ungraded Higher		NPA PC Passport					
PASS	45	PASS	45				
		Core Skills					
		HIGHER	20				

Details of the subjects covered by each Scottish National Certificate can be found at www.ucas.com/students/ucas_tariff/tarifftables

50

SPEECH AND DRAMA EXAMINATIONS							
GRADE	TARIFF POINTS	GRADE	TARIFF POINTS	GRADE	TARIFF POINTS	GRADE	TARIFF POINTS
PCertLAM		Grade 8		Grade 7		Grade 6	
DISTINCTION	90	DISTINCTION	65	DISTINCTION	55	DISTINCTION	40
MERIT	80	MERIT	60	MERIT	50	MERIT	35
PASS	60	PASS	45	PASS	35	PASS	20

Details of the Speech and Drama Qualifications covered by the Tariff can be found at www.ucas.com/students/ucas_tariff/tarifftables

51

SPORTS LEADERS UK	
GRADE	TARIFF POINTS
PASS	30

These points are awarded to Higher Sports Leader Award and Level 3 Certificate in Higher Sports Leadership (QCF)

52

WELSH BACCALAUREATE ADVANCED DIPLOMA (CORE)	
GRADE	TARIFF POINTS
PASS	120

These points are awarded only when a candidate achieves the Welsh Baccalaureate Advanced Diploma

Results

4

Step 4 – Results

You should arrange your holidays so that you are at home when your exam results are published because, if there are any issues to discuss, admissions tutors will want to speak to you in person.

We receive many UK exam results direct from the exam boards – check the list at **www.ucas.com**. If your qualification is listed, we send your results to the universities and colleges that you have accepted as your firm and insurance choices. If your qualification is not listed, you must send your exam results to the universities and colleges where you are holding offers.

After you have received your exam results check Track to find out if you have a place on your chosen course.

If you have met all the conditions for your firm choice, the university or college will confirm that you have a place. Occasionally, they may still confirm you have a place even if you have not quite met all the offer conditions; or they may offer you a place on a similar course.

If you have not met the conditions of your firm choice and the university or college has not confirmed your place, but you have met all the conditions of your insurance offer, your insurance university or college will confirm that you have a place.

When a university or college tells us that you have a place, we send you confirmation by letter.

RE-MARKED EXAMS

If you ask for any of your exams to be re-marked, you must tell the universities or colleges where you're holding offers. If a university or college cannot confirm your place based on the initial results, you should ask them if they would be able to reconsider their decision after the re-mark. They are under no obligation to reconsider their position even if your re-mark results in higher grades. Don't forget that re-marks may also result in lower grades.

The exam boards tell us about any re-marks that result in grade changes. We then send the revised grades to the universities or colleges where you're holding offers. As soon as you know about any grade changes, you should also tell these universities and colleges.

'CASHING IN' A LEVEL RESULTS

If you have taken A levels, your school or college must certificate or 'cash in' all your unit scores before the exam board can award final grades. If when you collect your A level results you have to add up your unit scores to find out your final grades, this means your school or college has not 'cashed in' your results.

We only receive cashed in results from the exam boards, so if your school or college has not cashed in your results, you must ask them to send a 'cash in' request to the exam board. You also need to tell the universities or colleges where you're holding offers that there'll be a delay in receiving your results and call our Customer Service Unit to find out when your results have been received.

When we receive your 'cashed in' results from the exam board we send them straight away to the universities or colleges where you're holding offers.

WHAT IF YOU DON'T HAVE A PLACE?

If you have not met the conditions of either your firm or insurance choice, and your chosen universities or colleges have not confirmed your place, you are eligible for Clearing. In Clearing you can apply for any courses that still have vacancies. Clearing operates from mid-July to late September 2013 (page 118).

BETTER RESULTS THAN EXPECTED?

If you obtain exam results that meet and exceed the conditions of the offer for your firm choice, you can for a short period use a process called Adjustment to look for an alternative place, whilst still keeping your original firm choice. See page 119 for information about Adjustment.

Next steps

5

Step 5 – Next steps

You might find yourself with different exam results than you were expecting, or you may change your mind about what you want to do. If so, there may be other options open to you.

CLEARING

Clearing is a service that helps people without a place find suitable course vacancies. It runs from mid-July until the end of September, but most people use it after the exam results are published in August.

You could consider related or alternative subjects or perhaps combining your original choice of subject with another. Your teachers or careers adviser, or the universities and colleges themselves, can provide useful guidance.

Course vacancies are listed at **www.ucas.com** and in the national media following the publication of exam results in August. **Once you have your exam results**, if you're in Clearing you need to look at the vacancy listings and then contact any university or college you are interested in.

Talk to the institutions; don't be afraid to call them. Make sure you have your Personal ID and Clearing Number ready and prepare notes on what you will say to them about:

- why you want to study the course
- why you want to study at their university or college
- any relevant employment or activities you have done that relate to the course
- your grades.

Accepting an offer - you can contact as many universities and colleges as you like through Clearing, and you may informally be offered more than one place. If this happens, you will need to decide which offer you want to accept. If you're offered a place you want to be formally considered for, you enter the course details in Track, and the university or college will then let you know if they're accepting you.

ADJUSTMENT

If you receive better results than expected, and meet and exceed the conditions of your conditional firm choice, you have the opportunity to reconsider what and where you want to study. This process is called Adjustment.

Adjustment runs from A level results day on 15 August 2013 until the end of August. Your individual Adjustment period starts on A level results day or when your conditional firm choice changes to unconditional firm, whichever is the later. You then have a maximum of five calendar days to register and secure an alternative course, if you decide you want to do this. If you want to try to find an alternative course you must register in Track to use Adjustment, so universities and colleges can view your application.

There are no vacancy listings for Adjustment, so you'll need to talk to the institutions. When you contact a university or college make it clear that you are applying through Adjustment, not Clearing. If they want to consider you they will ask for your Personal ID, so they can view your application.

If you don't find an alternative place then you remain accepted at your original firm choice.

Adjustment is entirely optional; remember that nothing really beats the careful research you carried out to find the right courses before you made your UCAS application. Talk to a careers adviser at your school, college or local careers office, as they can help you decide if registering to use Adjustment is right for you.

More information about Adjustment and Clearing is available at www.ucas.com. You can also view UCAStv video guides on how to use Adjustment and Clearing at www.ucas.tv.

IF YOU ARE STILL WITHOUT A PLACE TO STUDY

If you haven't found a suitable place, or changed your mind about what you want to do, there are lots of other options. Ask for advice from your school, college or careers office. Here are some suggestions you might want to consider:

- studying a part-time course (there's a part-time course search at www.ucas.com from July until September)
- studying a foundation degree
- re-sit your exams
- getting some work experience
- studying in another country
- reapplying next year to university or college through UCAS
- taking a gap year
- doing an apprenticeship (you'll find a vacancy search on the National Apprenticeship Service (NAS) website at www.apprenticeships.org.uk)
- finding a job
- starting a business.

More advice and links to other organisations can be found on the UCAS website at www.ucas.com/students/nextsteps/advice.

Step 6 – Starting university or college

Congratulations! Now that you have confirmed your place at university or college you will need to finalise your plans on how to get there, where to live and how to finance it. Make lists of things to do with deadlines and start contacting people whose help you can call on. Will you have to travel independently or can your parents or relatives help with transport? If you are keeping a car at uni, have you checked out parking facilities and told your insurance company?

Make sure you have everything organised, including travel arrangements, essential documents and paperwork, books and equipment required for the course. The university will send you joining information – contact the Admissions Office or the Students' Union if you have questions about anything to do with starting your course.

Freshers' week will help you settle in and make friends, but don't forget you are there to study. You may find the teaching methods rather alien at first, but remember there are plenty of sources of help, including your tutors, other students or student mentors and the students' union.

Where to live - unless you are planning to live at home, your university or college will usually provide you with guidance on how to find somewhere to live. The earlier you contact them the better your chance of finding a suitable range of options, from hall to private landlords. Find out what facilities are available at the different types of accommodation and check whether it fits within your budget. Check also what you need to bring with you and what is supplied. Don't leave it all to the last minute – especially things like arranging a bank account, checking what proof of identity you might need, gathering together a few essentials like a mug and supplies of coffee, insurance cover, TV licence etc.

Student finance - you will need to budget for living costs, accommodation, travel and books (and tuition fees if you are paying them up front). Learn about budgeting by visiting **www.ucas.com** where you will find further links to useful resources to help you manage your money. Remember that if you do get into financial difficulties the Welfare Office at the university will help you change tack and manage better in future, but it is always better to live within your means from the outset. If you need help, find it before the situation gets too stressful.

Useful contacts

CONNECTING WITH UCAS

You can follow UCAS on Twitter at **www.twitter.com/ucas_online**, and ask a question or see what others are asking on Facebook at **www.facebook.com/ucasonline**. You can also watch videos of UCAS advisers answering frequently asked questions on YouTube at **www.youtube.com/ucasonline**.

There are many UCAStv video guides to help with your journey into higher education, such as *How to choose your courses*, *Attending events*, *Open days* and *How to apply*. These can all be viewed at **www.ucas.tv** or in the relevant section of **www.ucas.com**.

If you need to speak to UCAS, please contact us on 0871 468 0 468 or 0044 871 468 0 468 from outside the UK. Calls from BT landlines within the UK will cost no more than 9p per minute. The cost of calls from mobiles and other networks may vary.

If you have hearing difficulties, you can call the Text Relay service on 18001 0871 468 0 468 (outside the UK 0044 151 494 1260). Calls are charged at normal rates.

CAREERS ADVICE

The Directgov Careers Helpline for Young People is for you if you live in England, are aged 13 to 19 and want advice on getting to where you want to be in life.

Careers advisers can give you information, advice and practical help with all sorts of things, like choosing subjects at school or mapping out your future career options. They can help you with anything that might be affecting you at school, college, work or in your personal or family life.

Contact a careers adviser at **www.direct.gov.uk/en/youngpeople/index.htm**.

Skills Development Scotland provides a starting point for anyone looking for careers information, advice or guidance.
www.myworldofwork.co.uk.

Careers Wales – Wales' national all-age careers guidance service.
www.careerswales.com or **www.gyrfacymru.com**.

Northern Ireland Careers Service website for the new, all-age careers guidance service in Northern Ireland.
www.nidirect.gov.uk/careers.

If you're not sure what job you want or you need help to decide which course to do, give learndirect a call on 0800 101 901 or visit
www.learndirect.co.uk.

GENERAL HIGHER EDUCATION ADVICE

National Union of Students (NUS) is the national voice of students, helping them to campaign, get cheap student discounts and provide advice on living student life to the full - **www.nus.org.uk**.

STUDENTS WITH DISABILITIES

If you have a disability or specific learning difficulty, you are strongly encouraged to make early direct contact with individual institutions before submitting your application. Most universities and colleges have disability coordinators or advisers. You can find their contact details and further advice on the Disability Rights UK website - **www.disabilityalliance.org**.

There is financial help for students with disabilities, known as Disabled Students' Allowances (DSAs). More information is available on the Directgov website at **www.direct.gov.uk/disabledstudents**.

YEAR OUT

For useful information on taking a year out, see **www.gap-year.com**.

The Year Out Group website is packed with information and guidance for young people and their parents and advisers. **www.yearoutgroup.org**.

Essential reading

UCAS has brought together the best books and resources you need to make the important decisions regarding entry to higher education. With guidance on choosing courses, finding the right institution, information about student finance, admissions tests, gap years and lots more, you can find the most trusted guides at www.ucasbooks.com.

The publications listed on the following pages and many others are available through www.ucasbooks.com or from UCAS Publication Services unless otherwise stated.

UCAS PUBLICATION SERVICES
UCAS Publication Services
PO Box 130, Cheltenham, Gloucestershire GL52 3ZF

f: 01242 544 806
e: publicationservices@ucas.ac.uk
// www.ucasbooks.com

ENTIRE RESEARCH AND APPLICATION PROCESS EXPLAINED

The UCAS Guide to getting into University and College
This guide contains advice and up-to-date information about the entire research and application process, and brings together the expertise of UCAS staff, along with insights and tips from well known universities including Oxford and Cambridge, and students who are involved with or have experienced the process first-hand.

The book clearly sets out the information you need in an easy-to-read format, with myth busters, tips from students, checklists and much more; this book will be a companion for applicants throughout their entire journey into higher education.
Published by UCAS
Price £11.99
Publication date January 2011

NEED HELP COMPLETING YOUR APPLICATION?

How to Complete your UCAS Application 2013

A must for anyone applying through UCAS. Contains advice on the preparation needed, a step-by-step guide to filling out the UCAS application, information on the UCAS process and useful tips for completing the personal statement.

Published by Trotman

Price £12.99

Publication date May 2012

Insider's Guide to Applying to University

Full of honest insights, this is a thorough guide to the application process. It reveals advice from careers advisers and current students, guidance on making sense of university information and choosing courses. Also includes tips for the personal statement, interviews, admissions tests, UCAS Extra and Clearing.

Published by Trotman

Price £12.99

Publication date June 2011

How to Write a Winning UCAS Personal Statement

The personal statement is your chance to stand out from the crowd. Based on information from admissions tutors, this book will help you sell yourself. It includes specific guidance for over 30 popular subjects, common mistakes to avoid, information on what admissions tutors look for, and much more.

Published by Trotman

Price £12.99

Publication date March 2010

CHOOSING COURSES

Progression Series 2013 entry

The 'UCAS Guide to getting into…' titles are designed to help you access good quality, useful information on some of the most competitive subject areas. The books cover advice on applying through UCAS, routes to qualifications, course details, job prospects, case studies and career advice.

New for 2013: information on the pros and cons of league tables and how to read them.

The UCAS Guide to getting into…

Art and Design

Economics, Finance and Accountancy

Engineering and Mathematics

Journalism, Broadcasting, Media Production and
   Performing Arts

Law

Medicine, Dentistry and Optometry

Nursing, Healthcare and Social Work

Psychology

Sports Science and Physiotherapy

Teaching and Education

Published by UCAS

Price £15.99 each

Publication date June 2012

UCAS Parent Guide

Free of charge.

Order online at www.ucas.com/parents.

Publication date February 2012

Open Days 2012

Attending open days, taster courses and higher education conventions is an important part of the application process. This publication makes planning attendance at these events quick and easy.
Published annually by UCAS.
Price £3.50
Publication date January 2012

Heap 2013: University Degree Course Offers

An independent, reliable guide to selecting university degree courses in the UK.

The guide lists degree courses available at universities and colleges throughout the UK and the grades, UCAS points or equivalent that you need to achieve to get on to each course listed.
Published by Trotman
Price £32.99
Publication date May 2012

ESSENTIAL READING

Choosing Your Degree Course & University

With so many universities and courses to choose from, it is not an easy decision for students embarking on their journey to higher education. This guide will offer expert guidance on the questions students need to ask when considering the opportunities available.
Published by Trotman
Price £24.99
Publication date April 2012

Degree Course Descriptions

Providing details of the nature of degree courses, the descriptions in this book are written by heads of departments and senior lecturers at major universities. Each description contains an overview of the course area, details of course structures, career opportunities and more.
Published by COA
Price £12.99
Publication date September 2011

CHOOSING WHERE TO STUDY

The Virgin Guide to British Universities

An insider's guide to choosing a university or college. Written by students and using independent statistics, this guide evaluates what you get from a higher education institution.
Published by Virgin
Price £15.99
Publication date May 2011

Times Good University Guide 2013

How do you find the best university for the subject you wish to study? You need a guide that evaluates the quality of what is available, giving facts, figures and comparative assessments of universities. The rankings provide hard data, analysed, interpreted and presented by a team of experts.
Published by Harper Collins
Price £16.99
Publication date June 2012

A Parent's Guide to Graduate Jobs

A must-have guide for any parent who is worried about their child's job prospects when they graduate.
In this guide, the graduate careers guru, Paul Redmond, advises parents how to help their son or daughter:

- increase their employability
- boost their earning potential
- acquire essential work skills
- use their own contacts to get them ahead
- gain the right work experience.

Published by Trotman
Price £12.99
Publication date January 2012

Which Uni?

One person's perfect uni might be hell for someone else. Picking the right one will give you the best chance of future happiness, academic success and brighter job prospects. This guide is packed with tables from a variety of sources, rating universities on everything from the quality of teaching to the make-up of the student population and much more.
Published by Trotman
Price £14.99
Publication date September 2011

Getting into the UK's Best Universities and Courses

This book is for those who set their goals high and dream of studying on a highly regarded course at a good university. It provides information on selecting the best courses for a subject, the application and personal statement, interviews, results day, timescales for applications and much more.
Published by Trotman
Price £12.99
Publication date June 2011

FINANCIAL INFORMATION

Student Finance - e-book

All students need to know about tuition fees, loans, grants, bursaries and much more. Covering all forms of income and expenditure, this comprehensive guide is produced in association with UCAS and offers great value for money.
Published by Constable Robinson
Price £4.99
Publication date May 2012

CAREERS PLANNING

A-Z of Careers and Jobs

It is vital to be well informed about career decisions and this guide will help you make the right choice. It provides full details of the wide range of opportunities on the market, the personal qualities and skills needed for each job, entry qualifications and training, realistic salary expectations and useful contact details.
Published by Kogan Page
Price £16.99
Publication date March 2012

The Careers Directory

An indispensable resource for anyone seeking careers information, covering over 350 careers. It presents up-to-date information in an innovative double-page format. Ideal for students in years 10 to 13 who are considering their futures and for other careers professionals.
Published by COA
Price £14.99
Publication date September 2011

Careers with a Science Degree

Over 100 jobs and areas of work for graduates of biological, chemical and physical sciences are described in this guide.

Whether you have yet to choose your degree subject and want to know where the various choices could lead, or are struggling for ideas about what to do with your science degree, this book will guide and inspire you. The title includes: nature of the work and potential employers, qualifications required for entry, including personal qualities and skills; training routes and opportunities for career development and postgraduate study options.

Published by Lifetime Publishing
Price £12.99
Publication date September 2010

Careers with an Arts and Humanities Degree

Covers careers and graduate opportunities related to these degrees.

The book describes over 100 jobs and areas of work suitable for graduates from a range of disciplines including: English and modern languages, history and geography, music and the fine arts. The guide highlights: graduate opportunities, training routes, postgraduate study options and entry requirements.

Published by Lifetime Publishing
Price £12.99
Publication date September 2010

'Getting into...' guides

Clear and concise guides to help applicants secure places. They include qualifications required, advice on applying, tests, interviews and case studies. The guides give an honest view and discuss current issues and careers.

Getting into Oxford and Cambridge
Publication date April 2011
Getting into Veterinary School
Publication date February 2011
Published by Trotman
Price £12.99 each

DEFERRING ENTRY

Gap Years: The Essential Guide

The essential book for all young people planning a gap year before continuing with their education. This up-to-date guide provides essential information on specialist gap year programmes, as well as the vast range of jobs and voluntary opportunities available to young people around the world.

Published by Crimson Publishing
Price £9.99
Publication date April 2012

Gap Year Guidebook 2012

This thorough and easy-to-use guide contains everything you need to know before taking a gap year. It includes real-life traveller tips, hundreds of contact details, realistic advice on everything from preparing, learning and working abroad, coping with coming home and much more.

Published by John Catt Education
Price £14.99
Publication date November 2011

Summer Jobs Worldwide 2012

This unique and specialist guide contains over
40,000 jobs for all ages. No other book includes
such a variety and wealth of summer work
opportunities in Britain and aboard. Anything from
horse trainer in Iceland, to a guide for nature walks
in Peru, to a yoga centre helper in Greece, to an
animal keeper for London Zoo, can be found.
Published by Crimson Publishing
Price £14.99
Publication date November 2011

Please note all publications incur a postage and packing
charge. All information was correct at the time of
printing.

For a full list of publications, please visit
www.ucasbooks.com.

UCAS HIGHER EDUCATION CONVENTIONS

Meet face-to-face with over 100 UK university representatives, attend seminars on How to Apply through UCAS and Financing yourself through university.

For further details visit
www.ucas.com/conventions

Courses

Courses

Keen to get started on your nursing, healthcare or social work career? This section contains details of the various degree courses available at UK institutions.

EXPLAINING THE LIST OF COURSES

The list of courses has been divided into subject categories (see over for list of subjects). We list the universities and colleges by their UCAS institution codes. Within each institution, courses are listed first by award type (such as BA, BSc, FdA, HND, MA and many others), then alphabetically by course title.

You might find some courses showing an award type '(Mod)', which indicates a combined degree that might be modular in design. A small number of courses have award type '(FYr)'. This indicates a 12-month foundation course, after which students can choose to apply for a degree course. In either case, you should contact the university or college for further details.

Generally speaking, when a course comprises two or more subjects, the word used to connect the subjects indicates the make-up of the award: 'Subject A and Subject B' is a joint award, where both subjects carry equal weight; 'Subject A with Subject B' is a major/minor award, where Subject A accounts for at least 60% of your study. If the title shows 'Subject A/Subject B', it may indicate that students can decide on the weighting of the subjects at the end of the first year. You should check with the university or college for full details.

Each entry shows the UCAS course code and the duration of the course. Where known, the entry contains details of the minimum qualification requirements for the course, as supplied to UCAS by the universities and colleges. Bear in mind that possessing the minimum qualifications does not guarantee acceptance to the course: there may be far more applicants than places. You may be asked to attend an interview,

Courses with entry requirements that require applicants to disclose information about spent and unspent convictions and may require a Criminal Records Bureau (CRB) check, are marked 'CRB Check: Required'.

Before applying for any course, you are advised to contact the university or college to check any changes in entry requirements and to see if any new courses have come on stream since the lists were approved for publication. To make this easy, each institution's entry starts with their address, email, phone and fax details, as well as their website address. You will also find it useful to check Course Finder at **www.ucas.com**.

LIST OF SUBJECT CATEGORIES

The list of courses in this section has been divided into the following subject categories:

AURAL AND ORAL SCIENCES

A80 ASTON UNIVERSITY, BIRMINGHAM
ASTON TRIANGLE
BIRMINGHAM B4 7ET
t: 0121 204 4444 f: 0121 204 3696
e: admissions@aston.ac.uk (automatic response)
// www.aston.ac.uk/prospective-students/ug

B611 BSc Health Care Science (Audiology)
Duration: 3FT Hon   CRB Check: Required
Entry Requirements: *GCE:* ABB-BBB. *IB:* 34.

B25 BIRMINGHAM CITY UNIVERSITY
PERRY BARR
BIRMINGHAM B42 2SU
t: 0121 331 5595 f: 0121 331 7994
// www.bcu.ac.uk

B620 BSc Speech and Language Therapy
Duration: 3FT Hon   CRB Check: Required
Entry Requirements: *GCE:* 280. *IB:* 36. Interview required.

B32 THE UNIVERSITY OF BIRMINGHAM
EDGBASTON
BIRMINGHAM B15 2TT
t: 0121 415 8900 f: 0121 414 7159
e: admissions@bham.ac.uk
// www.birmingham.ac.uk

B750 BSc Dental Hygiene and Therapy
Duration: 3FT Hon   CRB Check: Required
Entry Requirements: *GCE:* ABB. *SQAH:* AABBB-ABBBB. *SQAAH:* AB. *IB:* 34. Interview required.

C15 CARDIFF UNIVERSITY
PO BOX 927
30-36 NEWPORT ROAD
CARDIFF CF24 0DE
t: 029 2087 9999 f: 029 2087 6138
e: admissions@cardiff.ac.uk
// www.cardiff.ac.uk

B752 BSc Dental Therapy and Dental Hygiene
Duration: 3FT Hon   CRB Check: Required
Entry Requirements: *GCE:* BBB. *SQAH:* BBBBB. *IB:* 32. Interview required.

B750 DipHE Dental Hygiene
Duration: 2FT Dip   CRB Check: Required
Entry Requirements: *GCE:* BB. *SQAH:* BBBCC. *IB:* 30. Interview required.

C20 CARDIFF METROPOLITAN UNIVERSITY (UWIC)
ADMISSIONS UNIT
LLANDAFF CAMPUS
WESTERN AVENUE
CARDIFF CF5 2YB
t: 029 2041 6070 f: 029 2041 6286
e: admissions@cardiffmet.ac.uk
// www.cardiffmet.ac.uk

B840 BSc Dental Technology (3 years)
Duration: 3FT Hon
Entry Requirements: *GCE:* 200. *IB:* 24. *BTEC Dip:* DM. *BTEC ExtDip:* MMP. *OCR ND:* M1 *OCR NED:* P1 Interview required.

B620 BSc Speech & Language Therapy
Duration: 4FT Hon   CRB Check: Required
Entry Requirements: *GCE:* BBB. *SQAAH:* ABB-BBB. *IB:* 26. *BTEC ExtDip:* DDD. *OCR NED:* D2

C30 UNIVERSITY OF CENTRAL LANCASHIRE
PRESTON
LANCS PR1 2HE
t: 01772 201201 f: 01772 894954
e: uadmissions@uclan.ac.uk
// www.uclan.ac.uk

BX63 BA Deaf Studies and Education
Duration: 3FT Hon
Entry Requirements: *GCE:* 260-300. *SQAH:* ABBCC-BBBB. *SQAAH:* BBB-CCC. *IB:* 30. *BTEC Dip:* D*D*. *BTEC ExtDip:* DMM. Interview required.

C60 CITY UNIVERSITY
NORTHAMPTON SQUARE
LONDON EC1V 0HB
t: 020 7040 5060 f: 020 7040 8995
e: ugadmissions@city.ac.uk
// www.city.ac.uk

B621 BSc Human Communication
Duration: 3FT Hon
Entry Requirements: *GCE:* 380. *SQAH:* AABBB. *IB:* 32.

B620 BSc Speech and Language Therapy (4 years)
Duration: 4FT Hon
Entry Requirements: *GCE:* A*AA. *SQAH:* AABBB. *IB:* 32.

D26 DE MONTFORT UNIVERSITY
THE GATEWAY
LEICESTER LE1 9BH
t: 0116 255 1551 f: 0116 250 6204
e: enquiries@dmu.ac.uk
// www.dmu.ac.uk

B61A BSc Healthcare Science (Audiology Pathway)
Duration: 3FT Hon   CRB Check: Required
Entry Requirements: *GCE:* 280. *IB:* 28. *BTEC Dip:* D*D*. *BTEC ExtDip:* DMM. *OCR NED:* M2

B620 BSc Human Communication (Speech and Language Therapy)
Duration: 3.5FT Deg   CRB Check: Required
Entry Requirements: *GCE:* BBB. *SQAH:* BBBBC. *IB:* 30. *BTEC ExtDip:* DDM. *OCR NED:* M1

D65 UNIVERSITY OF DUNDEE
NETHERGATE
DUNDEE DD1 4HN
t: 01382 383838 f: 01382 388150
e: contactus@dundee.ac.uk
// www.dundee.ac.uk/admissions/undergraduate/

B750 BSc Oral Health Sciences
Duration: 3FT Ord   CRB Check: Required
Entry Requirements: *GCE:* BCC. *SQAH:* BBBB. *IB:* 30. Interview required.

E14 UNIVERSITY OF EAST ANGLIA
NORWICH NR4 7TJ
t: 01603 591515 f: 01603 591523
e: admissions@uea.ac.uk
// www.uea.ac.uk

B620 BSc Speech and Language Therapy
Duration: 3FT Hon   CRB Check: Required
Entry Requirements: *GCE:* ABB. *SQAH:* AABBB. *SQAAH:* ABB. *IB:* 32. Interview required.

E70 THE UNIVERSITY OF ESSEX
WIVENHOE PARK
COLCHESTER
ESSEX CO4 3SQ
t: 01206 873666 f: 01206 874477
e: admit@essex.ac.uk
// www.essex.ac.uk

QB36 BA English Language, Language Acquisition and Language Disorders (Inc Yr Abroad)
Duration: 4FT Hon
Entry Requirements: *GCE:* BBB. *SQAH:* AABB. *IB:* 32.

B750 FdSc Oral Health Sciences
Duration: 2FT Fdg   CRB Check: Required
Entry Requirements: *GCE:* CC. *SQAH:* BBBB. *SQAAH:* CC. *IB:* 26. *BTEC ExtDip:* MPP. Interview required.

H49 UNIVERSITY OF THE HIGHLANDS AND ISLANDS
UHI EXECUTIVE OFFICE
NESS WALK
INVERNESS
SCOTLAND IV3 5SQ
t: 01463 279000 f: 01463 279001
e: info@uhi.ac.uk
// www.uhi.ac.uk

B750 BSc Oral Health Science
Duration: 3FT Ord
Entry Requirements: *GCE:* BB. *SQAH:* CCC.

H72 THE UNIVERSITY OF HULL
THE UNIVERSITY OF HULL
COTTINGHAM ROAD
HULL HU6 7RX
t: 01482 466100 f: 01482 442290
e: admissions@hull.ac.uk
// www.hull.ac.uk

B750 FdSc Post Qualifying Dental Nursing Practice
Duration: 2FT Fdg   CRB Check: Required
Entry Requirements: Contact the institution for details.

L23 UNIVERSITY OF LEEDS
THE UNIVERSITY OF LEEDS
WOODHOUSE LANE
LEEDS LS2 9JT
t: 0113 343 3999
e: admissions@leeds.ac.uk
// www.leeds.ac.uk

B61A BSc Healthcare Science (Audiology)
Duration: 3FT Hon   CRB Check: Required
Entry Requirements: *GCE:* ABB. *SQAAH:* ABB. *BTEC ExtDip:* DDD.

L27 LEEDS METROPOLITAN UNIVERSITY
COURSE ENQUIRIES OFFICE
CITY CAMPUS
LEEDS LS1 3HE
t: 0113 81 23113 f: 0113 81 23129
// www.leedsmet.ac.uk

B630 BSc Clinical Language Sciences (Speech and Language Therapy)
Duration: 3FT Hon   CRB Check: Required
Entry Requirements: *GCE:* BBB. *SQAAH:* BBB.

M20 THE UNIVERSITY OF MANCHESTER
RUTHERFORD BUILDING
OXFORD ROAD
MANCHESTER M13 9PL
t: 0161 275 2077 f: 0161 275 2106
e: ug-admissions@manchester.ac.uk
// www.manchester.ac.uk

B840 BSc Oral Health Science
Duration: 3FT Hon CRB Check: Required
Entry Requirements: GCE: BBB. SQAH: ABCCC. IB: 33. Interview required.

B620 BSc Speech and Language Therapy
Duration: 4FT Hon CRB Check: Required
Entry Requirements: GCE: AAB. SQAH: AABBB. SQAAH: ABB. IB: 35. Interview required.

B611 BSc (Hons) Healthcare Science (Audiology)
Duration: 3FT Hon
Entry Requirements: GCE: BBB. SQAH: BBB. SQAAH: AABBB. IB: 31. Interview required.

M40 THE MANCHESTER METROPOLITAN UNIVERSITY
ADMISSIONS OFFICE
ALL SAINTS (GMS)
ALL SAINTS
MANCHESTER M15 6BH
t: 0161 247 2000
// www.mmu.ac.uk

B840 BSc Dental Technology
Duration: 3FT/4SW Hon
Entry Requirements: GCE: 240-280. IB: 26.

B841 BSc Dental Technology (Foundation)
Duration: 4FT/5SW Hon
Entry Requirements: GCE: 160. IB: 24. BTEC Dip: MM. BTEC ExtDip: MPP.

BC68 BSc Psychology and Speech Pathology
Duration: 4FT Hon CRB Check: Required
Entry Requirements: GCE: BBB. SQAH: AAAAA-BBBBB. SQAAH: AAA-BBB. IB: 30. BTEC Dip: D*D*. BTEC ExtDip: DDM. OCR ND: D OCR NED: D2 Interview required. Portfolio required.

B630 BSc Speech Pathology and Therapy
Duration: 3.5FT Hon CRB Check: Required
Entry Requirements: GCE: BBB. SQAH: AAAAA-BBBBB. SQAAH: AAA-BBB. IB: 30. BTEC Dip: D*D*. BTEC ExtDip: DDM. OCR ND: D OCR NED: D2 Interview required. Portfolio required.

M80 MIDDLESEX UNIVERSITY
MIDDLESEX UNIVERSITY
THE BURROUGHS
LONDON NW4 4BT
t: 020 8411 5555 f: 020 8411 5649
e: enquiries@mdx.ac.uk
// www.mdx.ac.uk

B610 BSc Healthcare Science (Audiology)
Duration: 3FT Hon
Entry Requirements: Contact the institution for details.

N21 NEWCASTLE UNIVERSITY
KING'S GATE
NEWCASTLE UPON TYNE NE1 7RU
t: 01912083333
// www.ncl.ac.uk

B620 BSc Speech and Language Sciences
Duration: 4FT Hon CRB Check: Required
Entry Requirements: GCE: AAB. SQAH: AAABB. IB: 35.

N38 UNIVERSITY OF NORTHAMPTON
PARK CAMPUS
BOUGHTON GREEN ROAD
NORTHAMPTON NN2 7AL
t: 0800 358 2232 f: 01604 722083
e: admissions@northampton.ac.uk
// www.northampton.ac.uk

B750 FdSc Dental Nursing
Duration: 2FT Fdg CRB Check: Required
Entry Requirements: GCE: 140-160. SQAH: BC-CCC. IB: 24. BTEC Dip: MP. BTEC ExtDip: MPP. OCR ND: P1 OCR NED: P2 Interview required.

O66 OXFORD BROOKES UNIVERSITY
ADMISSIONS OFFICE
HEADINGTON CAMPUS
GIPSY LANE
OXFORD OX3 0BP
t: 01865 483040 f: 01865 483983
e: admissions@brookes.ac.uk
// www.brookes.ac.uk

B610 FdA Hearing Aid Audiology(Mary Hare)
Duration: 2FT Fdg
Entry Requirements: Contact the institution for details.

P63 UCP MARJON - UNIVERSITY COLLEGE PLYMOUTH ST MARK & ST JOHN
DERRIFORD ROAD
PLYMOUTH PL6 8BH
t: 01752 636890 f: 01752 636819
e: admissions@marjon.ac.uk
// www.ucpmarjon.ac.uk

B621 BSc Speech Sciences
Duration: 3FT Hon
Entry Requirements: Contact the institution for details.

B620 BSc Speech and Language Therapy
Duration: 3.5FT Deg   CRB Check: Required
Entry Requirements: *GCE:* BBB. Interview required.

P80 UNIVERSITY OF PORTSMOUTH
ACADEMIC REGISTRY
UNIVERSITY HOUSE
WINSTON CHURCHILL AVENUE
PORTSMOUTH PO1 2UP
t: 023 9284 8484 f: 023 9284 3082
e: admissions@port.ac.uk
// www.port.ac.uk

B750 BSc Dental Hygiene and Dental Therapy
Duration: 3FT Hon   CRB Check: Required
Entry Requirements: *GCE:* 300. *IB:* 27. *BTEC ExtDip:* DMM.
Interview required.

B751 CertHE Dental Nursing
Duration: 1.5FT Cer   CRB Check: Required
Entry Requirements: *GCE:* 80. *IB:* 26. *BTEC SubDip:* M. *BTEC Dip:* PP. *BTEC ExtDip:* PPP. Interview required.

BC68 FdSc Speech, Language and Communication Science
Duration: 2FT Fdg   CRB Check: Required
Entry Requirements: *GCE:* 160. *IB:* 25. *BTEC Dip:* MM. *BTEC ExtDip:* MPP. Interview required.

Q25 QUEEN MARGARET UNIVERSITY, EDINBURGH
QUEEN MARGARET UNIVERSITY DRIVE
EDINBURGH EH21 6UU
t: 0131474 0000 f: 0131 474 0001
e: admissions@qmu.ac.uk
// www.qmu.ac.uk

B630 BSc Speech and Language Therapy
Duration: 4FT Hon   CRB Check: Required
Entry Requirements: *GCE:* 340. *IB:* 32.

R12 THE UNIVERSITY OF READING
THE UNIVERSITY OF READING
PO BOX 217
READING RG6 6AH
t: 0118 378 8619 f: 0118 378 8924
e: student.recruitment@reading.ac.uk
// www.reading.ac.uk

B690 BSc Speech and Language Therapy
Duration: 4FT Hon   CRB Check: Required
Entry Requirements: *GCE:* ABB. *SQAH:* ABBBB. *SQAAH:* ABB.
BTEC ExtDip: DDM. Interview required.

S03 THE UNIVERSITY OF SALFORD
SALFORD M5 4WT
t: 0161 295 4545 f: 0161 295 4646
e: ug-admissions@salford.ac.uk
// www.salford.ac.uk

B984 BSc Prosthetics and Orthotics
Duration: 3FT Hon   CRB Check: Required
Entry Requirements: *GCE:* 280. *SQAH:* BBBCC. *SQAAH:* BBC. *IB:* 24. *OCR NED:* M2

S18 THE UNIVERSITY OF SHEFFIELD
THE UNIVERSITY OF SHEFFIELD
LEVEL 2, ARTS TOWER
WESTERN BANK
SHEFFIELD S10 2TN
t: 0114 222 8030 f: 0114 222 8032
// www.sheffield.ac.uk

B620 BMS Speech Science
Duration: 4FT Hon   CRB Check: Required
Entry Requirements: *GCE:* AAB. *SQAH:* AAABB. *SQAAH:* A. *IB:* 35.
Interview required.

S27 UNIVERSITY OF SOUTHAMPTON
HIGHFIELD
SOUTHAMPTON SO17 1BJ
t: 023 8059 4732 f: 023 8059 3037
e: admissions@soton.ac.uk
// www.southampton.ac.uk

B610 BSc Audiology
Duration: 3FT Hon   CRB Check: Required
Entry Requirements: *GCE:* ABB. *IB:* 36. Interview required.

S78 THE UNIVERSITY OF STRATHCLYDE
GLASGOW G1 1XQ
t: 0141 552 4400 f: 0141 552 0775
// www.strath.ac.uk

B984 BSc Prosthetics and Orthotics
Duration: 4FT Hon   CRB Check: Required
Entry Requirements: *GCE:* ABB. *SQAH:* AAABB-AAAB. *IB:* 34.
Interview required.

B630 BSc Speech and Language Pathology
Duration: 4FT Hon   CRB Check: Required
Entry Requirements: *GCE:* ABB. *SQAH:* AABBB-AABB. *IB:* 32.

S93 SWANSEA UNIVERSITY
SINGLETON PARK
SWANSEA SA2 8PP
t: 01792 295111 f: 01792 295110
e: admissions@swansea.ac.uk
// www.swansea.ac.uk

B610 BSc Audiology
Duration: 4FT Deg   CRB Check: Required
Entry Requirements: *GCE:* BBB. Interview required.

T20 TEESSIDE UNIVERSITY
MIDDLESBROUGH TS1 3BA
t: 01642 218121 f: 01642 384201
e: registry@tees.ac.uk
// www.tees.ac.uk

B750 BSc Dental Hygiene and Dental Therapy
Duration: 3FT Hon   CRB Check: Required
Entry Requirements: *GCE:* 260. *IB:* 24. *BTEC Dip:* D*D. *BTEC ExtDip:* DMM. *OCR NED:* M2 Interview required.

B751 CertHE Dental Nurse Practice
Duration: 1FT Cer   CRB Check: Required
Entry Requirements: *GCE:* 80. *IB:* 24. *BTEC SubDip:* M. *BTEC Dip:* PP. *BTEC ExtDip:* PPP. *OCR ND:* P3 *OCR NED:* P3 Interview required.

U20 UNIVERSITY OF ULSTER
COLERAINE
CO. LONDONDERRY
NORTHERN IRELAND BT52 1SA
t: 028 7012 4221 f: 028 7012 4908
e: online@ulster.ac.uk
// www.ulster.ac.uk

B632 BSc Speech and Language Therapy
Duration: 3FT Hon   CRB Check: Required
Entry Requirements: *GCE:* BBB. *SQAH:* AABCC. *SQAAH:* BBB. *IB:* 25. Admissions Test required.

U80 UNIVERSITY COLLEGE LONDON (UNIVERSITY OF LONDON)
GOWER STREET
LONDON WC1E 6BT
t: 020 7679 3000 f: 020 7679 3001
// www.ucl.ac.uk

CB86 BSc Psychology and Language Sciences
Duration: 3FT Hon
Entry Requirements: *GCE:* A*AAe-AAAe. *SQAAH:* AAA. Interview required.

W75 UNIVERSITY OF WOLVERHAMPTON
ADMISSIONS UNIT
MX207, CAMP STREET
WOLVERHAMPTON
WEST MIDLANDS WV1 1AD
t: 01902 321000 f: 01902 321896
e: admissions@wlv.ac.uk
// www.wlv.ac.uk

BQ53 BA Deaf Studies and English
Duration: 3FT Hon   CRB Check: Required
Entry Requirements: *GCE:* 160-220. *IB:* 24.

BQ61 BA Interpreting (British Sign Language/English)
Duration: 3FT Hon   CRB Check: Required
Entry Requirements: *GCE:* 160-220. *IB:* 24.

BQM1 BA Interpreting (British Sign Language/English) plus Foundation Year
Duration: 4FT Hon   CRB Check: Required
Entry Requirements: *GCE:* 160-220. *IB:* 24.

BL65 BA Social Care and Deaf Studies
Duration: 3FT Hon   CRB Check: Required
Entry Requirements: *GCE:* 160-220. *IB:* 24.

COMPLEMENTARY MEDICINE

A65 ANGLO EUROPEAN COLLEGE OF CHIROPRACTIC
AECC
13-15 PARKWOOD ROAD
BOURNEMOUTH
DORSET BH5 2DF
t: 0044 (0)1202 436200 f: 0044 (0)1202 436252
e: admissions@aecc.ac.uk
// www.aecc.ac.uk

B321 BSc Human Sciences (Chiropractic)
Duration: 3FT Hon   CRB Check: Required
Entry Requirements: *GCE:* 280. *IB:* 25. *BTEC ExtDip:* DMM. Interview required.

B22 UNIVERSITY OF BEDFORDSHIRE
PARK SQUARE
LUTON
BEDS LU1 3JU
t: 0844 8482234 f: 01582 489323
e: admissions@beds.ac.uk
// www.beds.ac.uk

BN32 FdA Beauty Therapy and Spa Management
Duration: 2FT Fdg
Entry Requirements: *GCE:* 80-120.

B35 UNIVERSITY COLLEGE BIRMINGHAM
SUMMER ROW
BIRMINGHAM B3 1JB
t: 0121 604 1040 f: 0121 604 1166
e: admissions@ucb.ac.uk
// www.ucb.ac.uk

NB23 FdA Salon Business Management (Beauty Therapy)
Duration: 2FT Fdg
Entry Requirements: *GCE:* 120.

B40 BLACKBURN COLLEGE
FEILDEN STREET
BLACKBURN BB2 1LH
t: 01254 292594 f: 01254 679647
e: he-admissions@blackburn.ac.uk
// www.blackburn.ac.uk

B301 BSc Complementary Medicine (Top-Up)
Duration: 1FT Hon
Entry Requirements: Contact the institution for details.

B300 FdSc Complementary Medicine
Duration: 2FT Fdg
Entry Requirements: *GCE:* 80.

B44 UNIVERSITY OF BOLTON
DEANE ROAD
BOLTON BL3 5AB
t: 01204 903903 f: 01204 399074
e: enquiries@bolton.ac.uk
// www.bolton.ac.uk

B301 BSc (Hons) Professional Studies (Complementary Health)
Duration: 1FT Hon
Entry Requirements: Interview required.

B300 FdA Complementary Therapies
Duration: 2FT Fdg
Entry Requirements: *GCE:* 100. Interview required.

B54 BPP UNIVERSITY COLLEGE OF PROFESSIONAL STUDIES LIMITED
142-144 UXBRIDGE ROAD
LONDON W12 8AW
t: 02031 312 298
e: admissions@bpp.com
// undergraduate.bpp.com/

B320 MChiro Chiropractic (with Integrated Masters)
Duration: 4FT Oth
Entry Requirements: Contact the institution for details.

B60 BRADFORD COLLEGE: AN ASSOCIATE COLLEGE OF LEEDS METROPOLITAN UNIVERSITY
GREAT HORTON ROAD
BRADFORD
WEST YORKSHIRE BD7 1AY
t: 01274 433008 f: 01274 431652
e: heregistry@bradfordcollege.ac.uk
// www.bradfordcollege.ac.uk/university-centre

B391 BA Beauty Therapy Management (Top-up)
Duration: 1FT Hon
Entry Requirements: HND required.

B72 UNIVERSITY OF BRIGHTON
MITHRAS HOUSE 211
LEWES ROAD
BRIGHTON BN2 4AT
t: 01273 644644 f: 01273 642607
e: admissions@brighton.ac.uk
// www.brighton.ac.uk

B340 FdSc Complementary Healthcare
Duration: 2FT Fdg
Entry Requirements: *GCE:* 100. *IB:* 24. Interview required.

B81 BRITISH COLLEGE OF OSTEOPATHIC MEDICINE
LIEF HOUSE
120-122 FINCHLEY ROAD
LONDON NW3 5HR
t: 020 7435 6464 f: 020 7431 3630
e: kt@bcom.ac.uk
// www.bcom.ac.uk

B312 MOst Masters in Osteopathy
Duration: 4FT Hon **CRB Check:** Required
Entry Requirements: Interview required.

B87 BRITISH SCHOOL OF OSTEOPATHY
275 BOROUGH HIGH STREET
LONDON SE1 1JE
t: 020 7089 5316 f: 020 7089 5300
e: admissions@bso.ac.uk
// www.bso.ac.uk

B110 MOst Osteopathy
Duration: 4FT Deg **CRB Check:** Required
Entry Requirements: *GCE:* BBC. *SQAH:* AAAAA-BBCCC. *SQAAH:* AAA-BCC. *IB:* 28. Interview required. Admissions Test required.

B94 BUCKINGHAMSHIRE NEW UNIVERSITY
QUEEN ALEXANDRA ROAD
HIGH WYCOMBE
BUCKINGHAMSHIRE HP11 2JZ
t: 0800 0565 660 f: 01494 605 023
e: admissions@bucks.ac.uk
// bucks.ac.uk

B390 FdSc Advanced Beauty Therapy Practices
Duration: 2FT Fdg
Entry Requirements: *GCE:* 100-140. *IB:* 24. *OCR ND:* P2 *OCR NED:* P3 Interview required.

C10 CANTERBURY CHRIST CHURCH UNIVERSITY
NORTH HOLMES ROAD
CANTERBURY
KENT CT1 1QU
t: 01227 782900 f: 01227 782888
e: admissions@canterbury.ac.uk
// www.canterbury.ac.uk

053B HNC Hair and Beauty Management
Duration: 1FT HNC
Entry Requirements: Contact the institution for details.

C20 CARDIFF METROPOLITAN UNIVERSITY (UWIC)
ADMISSIONS UNIT
LLANDAFF CAMPUS
WESTERN AVENUE
CARDIFF CF5 2YB
t: 029 2041 6070 f: 029 2041 6286
e: admissions@cardiffmet.ac.uk
// www.cardiffmet.ac.uk

B390 BSc Complementary Therapies (3 years)
Duration: 3FT Hon   CRB Check: Required
Entry Requirements: *GCE:* 200. *IB:* 24. *BTEC Dip:* DM. *BTEC ExtDip:* MMP. *OCR ND:* M1 *OCR NED:* P1 Interview required.

B300 BSc Complementary Therapies (4 years including Foundation)
Duration: 4FT Hon
Entry Requirements: *Foundation:* Pass. *GCE:* 80. *IB:* 24. *BTEC Dip:* PP. *BTEC ExtDip:* PPP. *OCR ND:* P3 *OCR NED:* P3

B301 CertHE Complementary Therapies
Duration: 1FT Cer   CRB Check: Required
Entry Requirements: *GCE:* 200. *IB:* 24. *BTEC Dip:* DM. *BTEC ExtDip:* MMP. *OCR ND:* M1 *OCR NED:* P1 Interview required.

B302 DipHE Complementary Therapies
Duration: 2FT Dip   CRB Check: Required
Entry Requirements: *GCE:* 200. *IB:* 24. *BTEC Dip:* DM. *BTEC ExtDip:* MMP. *OCR ND:* M1 *OCR NED:* P1 Interview required.

C30 UNIVERSITY OF CENTRAL LANCASHIRE
PRESTON
LANCS PR1 2HE
t: 01772 201201 f: 01772 894954
e: uadmissions@uclan.ac.uk
// www.uclan.ac.uk

CB63 BSc Sports Therapy
Duration: 3FT Hon   CRB Check: Required
Entry Requirements: *GCE:* 280. *IB:* 30. *OCR ND:* D *OCR NED:* M2 Interview required.

C57 CHICHESTER COLLEGE
WESTGATE FIELDS
CHICHESTER
WEST SUSSEX PO19 1SB
t: 01243 786321 x2127 f: 01243 539481
e: sally.billingham@chichester.ac.uk
// www.chichester.ac.uk

093B HND Beauty Therapy Sciences
Duration: 2FT HND
Entry Requirements: *Foundation:* Merit. *SQAH:* AAAAA-CCCDD. *SQAAH:* AAA-CCC. *BTEC SubDip:* M. *BTEC Dip:* MM. *BTEC ExtDip:* MPP. *OCR ND:* M2 *OCR NED:* M3 Interview required.

C78 CORNWALL COLLEGE
POOL
REDRUTH
CORNWALL TR15 3RD
t: 01209 616161 f: 01209 611612
e: he.admissions@cornwall.ac.uk
// www.cornwall.ac.uk

B301 FdSc Complementary Health Therapies
Duration: 2FT Fdg
Entry Requirements: *GCE:* 120. *IB:* 24. Interview required. Portfolio required.

003B HNC Complementary Health Therapies
Duration: 1FT HNC   CRB Check: Required
Entry Requirements: *GCE:* 80-120. Interview required.

C99 UNIVERSITY OF CUMBRIA
FUSEHILL STREET
CARLISLE
CUMBRIA CA1 2HH
t: 01228 616234 f: 01228 616235
// www.cumbria.ac.uk

CB63 FdSc Sports Massage Therapy
Duration: 2FT Fdg
Entry Requirements: Contact the institution for details.

D39 UNIVERSITY OF DERBY
KEDLESTON ROAD
DERBY DE22 1GB
t: 01332 591167 f: 01332 597724
e: askadmissions@derby.ac.uk
// www.derby.ac.uk

B392 FdA Spa
Duration: 2FT Fdg
Entry Requirements: *Foundation:* Pass. *GCE:* 160. *IB:* 26. *BTEC Dip:* D*D*. *BTEC ExtDip:* DMM. *OCR ND:* M2 *OCR NED:* P2

D55 DUCHY COLLEGE
STOKE CLIMSLAND
CALLINGTON
CORNWALL PL17 8PB
t: 01579 372327 f: 01579 372200
e: uni@duchy.ac.uk
// www.duchy.ac.uk

DB43 FdSc Horticultural Therapy
Duration: 2FT Fdg
Entry Requirements: *GCE:* 100-120.

E42 EDGE HILL UNIVERSITY
ORMSKIRK
LANCASHIRE L39 4QP
t: 01695 657000 f: 01695 584355
e: study@edgehill.ac.uk
// www.edgehill.ac.uk

CB63 BSc Sports Therapy
Duration: 3FT Hon   CRB Check: Required
Entry Requirements: *GCE:* 300. *IB:* 26. *OCR ND:* D *OCR NED:* M1

E56 THE UNIVERSITY OF EDINBURGH
STUDENT RECRUITMENT & ADMISSIONS
57 GEORGE SQUARE
EDINBURGH EH8 9JU
t: 0131 650 4360 f: 0131 651 1236
e: sra.enquiries@ed.ac.uk
// www.ed.ac.uk/studying/undergraduate/

BR31 MA Chinese and French
Duration: 4FT Hon
Entry Requirements: *GCE:* AAA-BBB. *SQAH:* AAAA-BBBB. *IB:* 34.

BR32 MA Chinese and German
Duration: 4FT Hon
Entry Requirements: *GCE:* AAA-BBB. *SQAH:* AAAA-BBBB. *IB:* 34.

BR37 MA Chinese and Russian Studies
Duration: 4FT Hon
Entry Requirements: *GCE:* AAA-BBB. *SQAH:* AAAA-BBBB. *IB:* 34.

BR34 MA Chinese and Spanish
Duration: 4FT Hon
Entry Requirements: *GCE:* AAA-BBB. *SQAH:* AAAA-BBBB. *IB:* 34.

E80 EUROPEAN SCHOOL OF OSTEOPATHY
EUROPEAN SCHOOL OF OSTEOPATHY
BOXLEY HOUSE
BOXLEY
MAIDSTONE ME14 3DZ
t: +44 (0)1622 671558 f: +44(0)1622 662165
e: bernadetteranger@eso.ac.uk
// www.eso.ac.uk

B310 MOst Osteopathy
Duration: 4FT Deg
Entry Requirements: *GCE:* BCC. *IB:* 29. Interview required.

E81 EXETER COLLEGE
HELE ROAD
EXETER
DEVON EX4 4JS
t: 0845 111 6000
e: info@exe-coll.ac.uk
// www.exe-coll.ac.uk/he

BC36 FdSc Sports Therapy
Duration: 2FT Fdg
Entry Requirements: *GCE:* 160.

F66 FARNBOROUGH COLLEGE OF TECHNOLOGY
BOUNDARY ROAD
FARNBOROUGH
HAMPSHIRE GU14 6SB
t: 01252 407028 f: 01252 407041
e: admissions@farn-ct.ac.uk
// www.farn-ct.ac.uk

B390 BSc Complementary Therapies (Top-Up)
Duration: 1FT Hon
Entry Requirements: Contact the institution for details.

B300 FdSc Complementary Therapies
Duration: 2FT Fdg
Entry Requirements: *GCE:* 160.

G14 UNIVERSITY OF GLAMORGAN, CARDIFF AND PONTYPRIDD
ENQUIRIES AND ADMISSIONS UNIT
PONTYPRIDD CF37 1DL
t: 08456 434030 f: 01443 654050
e: enquiries@glam.ac.uk
// www.glam.ac.uk

B326 FYr Chiropractic Foundation Year
Duration: 1FT FYr   CRB Check: Required
Entry Requirements: *IB:* 32. *BTEC Dip:* D*D. *BTEC ExtDip:* DMM. Interview required.

B320 MChiro Master of Chiropractic
Duration: 4FT Hon   CRB Check: Required
Entry Requirements: *GCE:* ABB. *IB:* 32. *BTEC ExtDip:* DDM. Interview required.

G53 GLYNDWR UNIVERSITY
PLAS COCH
MOLD ROAD
WREXHAM LL11 2AW
t: 01978 293439 f: 01978 290008
e: sid@glyndwr.ac.uk
// www.glyndwr.ac.uk

B341 BSc Acupuncture
Duration: 3FT Hon   CRB Check: Required
Entry Requirements: GCE: 240.

B343 BSc Complementary Therapies for Healthcare
Duration: 3FT Hon   CRB Check: Required
Entry Requirements: GCE: 240.

G59 GOWER COLLEGE SWANSEA
TY COCH ROAD
SWANSEA SA2 9EB
t: 01792 284000 f: 01792 284074
e: fiona.john@gowercollegeswansea.ac.uk
// www.gowercollegeswansea.ac.uk

003B HND Advanced Therapies and Spa Management
Duration: 2FT HND
Entry Requirements: Contact the institution for details.

G80 GRIMSBY INSTITUTE OF FURTHER AND HIGHER EDUCATION
NUNS CORNER
GRIMSBY
NE LINCOLNSHIRE DN34 5BQ
t: 0800 328 3631
e: headmissions@grimsby.ac.uk
// www.grimsby.ac.uk

B390 FdA Management for Beauty Industries
Duration: 2FT Fdg
Entry Requirements: GCE: 120. Interview required.

H12 HARPER ADAMS UNIVERSITY COLLEGE
NEWPORT
SHROPSHIRE TF10 8NB
t: 01952 820280 f: 01952 813210
e: admissions@harper-adams.ac.uk
// www.harper-adams.ac.uk

BD34 FdSc Equine Science, Complementary Therapy and Natural Horsemanship
Duration: 2FT Fdg
Entry Requirements: Contact the institution for details.

H36 UNIVERSITY OF HERTFORDSHIRE
UNIVERSITY ADMISSIONS SERVICE
COLLEGE LANE
HATFIELD
HERTS AL10 9AB
t: 01707 284800
// www.herts.ac.uk

CB63 BSc Sports Therapy
Duration: 3FT/4SW Hon   CRB Check: Required
Entry Requirements: GCE: 300. Interview required.

H49 UNIVERSITY OF THE HIGHLANDS AND ISLANDS
UHI EXECUTIVE OFFICE
NESS WALK
INVERNESS
SCOTLAND IV3 5SQ
t: 01463 279000 f: 01463 279001
e: info@uhi.ac.uk
// www.uhi.ac.uk

113B HNC Beauty Therapy
Duration: 1FT HNC
Entry Requirements: GCE: D. SQAH: C.

103B HNC Complementary Therapies
Duration: 1FT HNC
Entry Requirements: GCE: D. SQAH: C.

013B HND Beauty Therapy
Duration: 2FT HND
Entry Requirements: GCE: C. SQAH: CC.

003B HND Complementary Therapies
Duration: 2FT HND
Entry Requirements: GCE: C. SQAH: CC.

L27 LEEDS METROPOLITAN UNIVERSITY
COURSE ENQUIRIES OFFICE
CITY CAMPUS
LEEDS LS1 3HE
t: 0113 81 23113 f: 0113 81 23129
// www.leedsmet.ac.uk

B311 MOst Osteopathy
Duration: 4FT Oth   CRB Check: Required
Entry Requirements: Contact the institution for details.

L39 UNIVERSITY OF LINCOLN
ADMISSIONS
BRAYFORD POOL
LINCOLN LN6 7TS
t: 01522 886097 f: 01522 886146
e: admissions@lincoln.ac.uk
// www.lincoln.ac.uk

B343 BSc Acupuncture
Duration: 3FT Hon
Entry Requirements: GCE: 240. Interview required.

B342 BSc Herbal Medicine
Duration: 3FT Hon
Entry Requirements: *GCE:* 240. Interview required.

L42 LINCOLN COLLEGE
MONKS ROAD
LINCOLN LN2 5HQ
t: 01522 876000 f: 01522 876200
e: enquiries@lincolncollege.ac.uk
// www.lincolncollege.ac.uk

B350 HND Hair and Beauty Management
Duration: 2FT HND
Entry Requirements: Contact the institution for details.

L68 LONDON METROPOLITAN UNIVERSITY
166-220 HOLLOWAY ROAD
LONDON N7 8DB
t: 020 7133 4200
e: admissions@londonmet.ac.uk
// www.londonmet.ac.uk

B342 BSc Herbal Medicinal Science (Top-Up)
Duration: 1FT Hon
Entry Requirements: Contact the institution for details.

CB63 BSc Sports Therapy
Duration: 3FT Hon
Entry Requirements: *GCE:* 280. *IB:* 28.

L75 LONDON SOUTH BANK UNIVERSITY
ADMISSIONS AND RECRUITMENT CENTRE
90 LONDON ROAD
LONDON SE1 6LN
t: 0800 923 8888 f: 020 7815 8273
e: course.enquiry@lsbu.ac.uk
// www.lsbu.ac.uk

B343 MCM Acupuncture
Duration: 4FT Deg   CRB Check: Required
Entry Requirements: *GCE:* 200. *IB:* 24. Interview required.
Portfolio required.

M10 THE MANCHESTER COLLEGE
OPENSHAW CAMPUS
ASHTON OLD ROAD
OPENSHAW
MANCHESTER M11 2WH
t: 0800 068 8585 f: 0161 920 4103
e: enquiries@themanchestercollege.ac.uk
// www.themanchestercollege.ac.uk

B353 BA Make-up Artistry Fashion and Media
Duration: 1FT Hon
Entry Requirements: Contact the institution for details.

B3W4 BA Make-up Artistry and Special Effects
Duration: 3FT Hon
Entry Requirements: Contact the institution for details.

B354 FdA Make-up Artistry Fashion and Media
Duration: 2FT Fdg
Entry Requirements: Contact the institution for details.

M40 THE MANCHESTER METROPOLITAN UNIVERSITY
ADMISSIONS OFFICE
ALL SAINTS (GMS)
ALL SAINTS
MANCHESTER M15 6BH
t: 0161 247 2000
// www.mmu.ac.uk

B343 BSc Acupuncture
Duration: 3FT Hon   CRB Check: Required
Entry Requirements: *GCE:* 280. *SQAH:* AABBB. *SQAAH:* B. *IB:* 30.
Interview required.

M80 MIDDLESEX UNIVERSITY
MIDDLESEX UNIVERSITY
THE BURROUGHS
LONDON NW4 4BT
t: 020 8411 5555 f: 020 8411 5649
e: enquiries@mdx.ac.uk
// www.mdx.ac.uk

B348 BSc Acupuncture
Duration: 3FT Hon
Entry Requirements: *GCE:* 200-300. *IB:* 28.

B347 BSc Herbal Medicine
Duration: 3FT Hon
Entry Requirements: *GCE:* 200-300. *IB:* 28.

BT31 BSc Traditional Chinese Medicine
Duration: 4FT Hon
Entry Requirements: *GCE:* 200-300. *IB:* 28.

N23 NEWCASTLE COLLEGE
STUDENT SERVICES
RYE HILL CAMPUS
SCOTSWOOD ROAD
NEWCASTLE UPON TYNE NE4 7SA
t: 0191 200 4110 f: 0191 200 4349
e: enquiries@ncl-coll.ac.uk
// www.newcastlecollege.co.uk

BN32 FdA Beauty Therapy and Spa Management
Duration: 2FT Fdg
Entry Requirements: *GCE:* 120-160. *OCR ND:* P2 *OCR NED:* P3
Interview required.

N28 NEW COLLEGE DURHAM
FRAMWELLGATE MOOR CAMPUS
DURHAM DH1 5ES
t: 0191 375 4210/4211 f: 0191 375 4222
e: admissions@newdur.ac.uk
// www.newcollegedurham.ac.uk

B301 FdA Complementary Health
Duration: 3FT Hon
Entry Requirements: Contact the institution for details.

B300 FdSc Complementary Health Care
Duration: 2FT Fdg
Entry Requirements: *GCE:* 40.

N31 NEWHAM COLLEGE OF FURTHER EDUCATION
EAST HAM CAMPUS
HIGH STREET SOUTH
LONDON E6 6ER
t: 020 8257 4000 f: 020 8257 4325
e: admissions@newham.ac.uk
// www.newham.ac.uk

053B HND Hair and Beauty Management
Duration: 2FT HND
Entry Requirements: Contact the institution for details.

N49 NESCOT, SURREY
REIGATE ROAD
EWELL
EPSOM
SURREY KT17 3DS
t: 020 8394 3038 f: 020 8394 3030
e: info@nescot.ac.uk
// www.nescot.ac.uk

B310 MOst Osteopathic Medicine BSc/MOst
Duration: 4.5FT Hon   CRB Check: Required
Entry Requirements: *GCE:* 280.

O66 OXFORD BROOKES UNIVERSITY
ADMISSIONS OFFICE
HEADINGTON CAMPUS
GIPSY LANE
OXFORD OX3 0BP
t: 01865 483040 f: 01865 483983
e: admissions@brookes.ac.uk
// www.brookes.ac.uk

B310 BOst Osteopathy
Duration: 4FT Hon   CRB Check: Required
Entry Requirements: *GCE:* BBB.

S27 UNIVERSITY OF SOUTHAMPTON
HIGHFIELD
SOUTHAMPTON SO17 1BJ
t: 023 8059 4732 f: 023 8059 3037
e: admissions@soton.ac.uk
// www.southampton.ac.uk

B985 BSc Podiatry
Duration: 3FT Hon   CRB Check: Required
Entry Requirements: *GCE:* BBB. *IB:* 28.

S41 SOUTH CHESHIRE COLLEGE
DANE BANK AVENUE
CREWE CW2 8AB
t: 01270 654654 f: 01270 651515
e: admissions@s-cheshire.ac.uk
// www.s-cheshire.ac.uk

B300 FdA Complementary Therapeutic Practices for Health and Wellbeing
Duration: 2FT Fdg   CRB Check: Required
Entry Requirements: Interview required.

S51 ST HELENS COLLEGE
WATER STREET
ST HELENS
MERSEYSIDE WA10 1PP
t: 01744 733766 f: 01744 623400
e: enquiries@sthelens.ac.uk
// www.sthelens.ac.uk

B390 FdSc Complementary Therapy
Duration: 2FT Fdg
Entry Requirements: *GCE:* 40-80.

S93 SWANSEA UNIVERSITY
SINGLETON PARK
SWANSEA SA2 8PP
t: 01792 295111 f: 01792 295110
e: admissions@swansea.ac.uk
// www.swansea.ac.uk

B310 MOst Osteopathy
Duration: 4FT Hon   CRB Check: Required
Entry Requirements: *GCE:* BBB. Interview required.

T85 TRURO AND PENWITH COLLEGE
TRURO COLLEGE
COLLEGE ROAD
TRURO
CORNWALL TR1 3XX
t: 01872 267122 f: 01872 267526
e: heinfo@trurocollege.ac.uk
// www.truro-penwith.ac.uk

B300 FdSc Complementary Body Therapies
Duration: 2FT Fdg
Entry Requirements: *GCE:* 60. *IB:* 24. *BTEC Dip:* MP. *BTEC ExtDip:* PPP. Interview required.

W25 WARWICKSHIRE COLLEGE
WARWICK NEW ROAD
LEAMINGTON SPA
WARWICKSHIRE CV32 5JE
t: 01926 884223 f: 01926 318 111
e: kgooch@warkscol.ac.uk
// www.warwickshire.ac.uk

NB23 FdA Beauty Therapies Management
Duration: 2FT Fdg
Entry Requirements: Contact the institution for details.

B390 FdA Holistic Therapies Management
Duration: 2FT Fdg
Entry Requirements: Contact the institution for details.

W50 UNIVERSITY OF WESTMINSTER
2ND FLOOR, CAVENDISH HOUSE
101 NEW CAVENDISH STREET,
LONDON W1W 6XH
t: 020 7915 5511
e: course-enquiries@westminster.ac.uk
// www.westminster.ac.uk

B343 BSc Chinese Medicine: Acupuncture
Duration: 3FT Hon
Entry Requirements: *GCE:* CCD. *SQAH:* CCCC. *IB:* 26. Interview required.

B342 BSc Herbal Medicine
Duration: 3FT Hon
Entry Requirements: *GCE:* CCD. *SQAH:* CCCC. *IB:* 26. Interview required.

B341 BSc/MSci Chinese Medicine: Acupuncture with Foundation
Duration: 4FT/5FT Hon
Entry Requirements: *GCE:* CCD. *SQAH:* CCCC. *IB:* 26. Interview required.

B340 BSc/MSci Herbal Medicine with Foundation Year
Duration: 4FT/5FT Hon
Entry Requirements: *GCE:* CCD. *SQAH:* CCCC. *IB:* 26. Interview required.

B303 MSci Chinese Medicine Acupuncture (with Foundation Year)
Duration: 5FT Hon
Entry Requirements: Contact the institution for details.

B347 MSci Chinese Medicine: Acupuncture
Duration: 4FT Hon
Entry Requirements: Contact the institution for details.

B348 MSci Herbal Medicine
Duration: 4FT Hon
Entry Requirements: Contact the institution for details.

B34F MSci Herbal Medicine with Foundation Year
Duration: 5FT Hon
Entry Requirements: Contact the institution for details.

W73 WIRRAL METROPOLITAN COLLEGE
CONWAY PARK CAMPUS
EUROPA BOULEVARD
BIRKENHEAD, WIRRAL
MERSEYSIDE CH41 4NT
t: 0151 551 7777 f: 0151 551 7001
// www.wmc.ac.uk

B300 FdSc Complementary Therapies
Duration: 2FT Fdg   CRB Check: Required
Entry Requirements: Contact the institution for details.

W81 WORCESTER COLLEGE OF TECHNOLOGY
DEANSWAY
WORCESTER WR1 2JF
t: 01905 725555 f: 01905 28906
// www.wortech.ac.uk

B350 FdA Management, Innovation and Practice for Hair Beauty and Spa
Duration: 2FT Fdg
Entry Requirements: Contact the institution for details.

BN32 FdA Salon Management
Duration: 2FT Fdg
Entry Requirements: Interview required.

Y70 YORK COLLEGE
SIM BALK LANE
YORK YO23 2BB
t: 01904 770448 f: 01904 770499
e: admissions.team@yorkcollege.ac.uk
// www.yorkcollege.ac.uk

BN32 FdA Holistic and Spa Treatments
Duration: 2FT Fdg
Entry Requirements: *GCE:* CC.

B06 BANGOR UNIVERSITY
BANGOR UNIVERSITY
BANGOR
GWYNEDD LL57 2DG
t: 01248 388484 f: 01248 370451
e: admissions@bangor.ac.uk
// www.bangor.ac.uk

B820 BSc Diagnostic Radiography and Imaging
Duration: 3FT Hon   CRB Check: Required
Entry Requirements: *GCE:* 220-240. *IB:* 28. Interview required.

B25 BIRMINGHAM CITY UNIVERSITY
PERRY BARR
BIRMINGHAM B42 2SU
t: 0121 331 5595 f: 0121 331 7994
// www.bcu.ac.uk

B821 BSc Diagnostic Radiography
Duration: 3FT Hon   CRB Check: Required
Entry Requirements: *GCE:* 280. *IB:* 25. Interview required.

B822 BSc Radiotherapy
Duration: 3FT Hon   CRB Check: Required
Entry Requirements: *GCE:* 280. *IB:* 25. Interview required.

B32 THE UNIVERSITY OF BIRMINGHAM
EDGBASTON
BIRMINGHAM B15 2TT
t: 0121 415 8900 f: 0121 414 7159
e: admissions@bham.ac.uk
// www.birmingham.ac.uk

BJ95 BMedSc Biomedical Materials Science
Duration: 3FT Hon   CRB Check: Required
Entry Requirements: *GCE:* ABB. *SQAH:* AABBB-ABBBB. *SQAAH:* AB. *IB:* 34.

B56 THE UNIVERSITY OF BRADFORD
RICHMOND ROAD
BRADFORD
WEST YORKSHIRE BD7 1DP
t: 0800 073 1225 f: 01274 235585
e: course-enquiries@bradford.ac.uk
// www.bradford.ac.uk

B821 BSc Diagnostic Radiography
Duration: 3FT Hon   CRB Check: Required
Entry Requirements: *GCE:* 300. *IB:* 26. Interview required.

B80 UNIVERSITY OF THE WEST OF ENGLAND, BRISTOL
FRENCHAY CAMPUS
COLDHARBOUR LANE
BRISTOL BS16 1QY
t: +44 (0)117 32 83333 f: +44 (0)117 32 82810
e: admissions@uwe.ac.uk
// www.uwe.ac.uk

B821 BSc Diagnostic Imaging
Duration: 3FT Hon   CRB Check: Required
Entry Requirements: *GCE:* 300. Interview required.

B822 BSc Radiotherapy and Oncology
Duration: 3FT Hon   CRB Check: Required
Entry Requirements: *GCE:* 280. Interview required.

C10 CANTERBURY CHRIST CHURCH UNIVERSITY
NORTH HOLMES ROAD
CANTERBURY
KENT CT1 1QU
t: 01227 782900 f: 01227 782888
e: admissions@canterbury.ac.uk
// www.canterbury.ac.uk

B821 BSc Diagnostic Radiography
Duration: 3FT Hon   CRB Check: Required
Entry Requirements: *GCE:* 240. *IB:* 24. Interview required.

C15 CARDIFF UNIVERSITY
PO BOX 927
30-36 NEWPORT ROAD
CARDIFF CF24 0DE
t: 029 2087 9999 f: 029 2087 6138
e: admissions@cardiff.ac.uk
// www.cardiff.ac.uk

H1B8 BEng Medical Engineering
Duration: 3FT Hon
Entry Requirements: *GCE:* AAB. *IB:* 32.

B821 BSc Diagnostic Radiography and Imaging
Duration: 3FT Hon   CRB Check: Required
Entry Requirements: *GCE:* BBB. *SQAAH:* BBB. *IB:* 26. *OCR NED:* M2 Interview required.

B822 BSc Radiotherapy and Oncology
Duration: 3FT Hon   CRB Check: Required
Entry Requirements: *GCE:* BBC. *IB:* 25. *OCR NED:* M2 Interview required.

H1BV MEng Medical Engineering
Duration: 4FT Hon
Entry Requirements: *GCE:* AAB. *SQAAH:* AAB.

C60 CITY UNIVERSITY
NORTHAMPTON SQUARE
LONDON EC1V 0HB
t: 020 7040 5060 f: 020 7040 8995
e: ugadmissions@city.ac.uk
// www.city.ac.uk

BH81 BEng Biomedical Engineering
Duration: 3FT Hon
Entry Requirements: *GCE:* 340. *IB:* 30.

BHV1 BEng Biomedical Engineering
Duration: 4SW Hon
Entry Requirements: *GCE:* 340. *IB:* 30.

B821 BSc Radiography (Diagnostic Imaging)
Duration: 3FT Hon
Entry Requirements: *SQAH:* BBCCC. *IB:* 28.

B822 BSc Radiography (Radiotherapy and Oncology)
Duration: 3FT Hon
Entry Requirements: *SQAH:* BBCCC. *IB:* 28.

C99 UNIVERSITY OF CUMBRIA
FUSEHILL STREET
CARLISLE
CUMBRIA CA1 2HH
t: 01228 616234 f: 01228 616235
// www.cumbria.ac.uk

B821 BSc Diagnostic Radiography
Duration: 3FT Hon   CRB Check: Required
Entry Requirements: *GCE:* 280. *IB:* 28. *OCR NED:* M3 Interview required.

D39 UNIVERSITY OF DERBY
KEDLESTON ROAD
DERBY DE22 1GB
t: 01332 591167 f: 01332 597724
e: askadmissions@derby.ac.uk
// www.derby.ac.uk

B821 BSc Diagnostic Radiography
Duration: 3FT Hon   CRB Check: Required
Entry Requirements: *GCE:* 300. *IB:* 28. *BTEC Dip:* D*D*. *BTEC ExtDip:* DMM. *OCR NED:* D2 Interview required.

E84 UNIVERSITY OF EXETER
LAVER BUILDING
NORTH PARK ROAD
EXETER
DEVON EX4 4QE
t: 01392 723044 f: 01392 722479
e: admissions@exeter.ac.uk
// www.exeter.ac.uk

B821 BSc Medical Imaging (Diagnostic Radiography)
Duration: 3FT Hon   CRB Check: Required
Entry Requirements: *GCE:* ABB-BBC. *SQAH:* ABBBB-BBBBB. *SQAAH:* BBC-BCC. Interview required.

G42 GLASGOW CALEDONIAN UNIVERSITY
STUDENT RECRUITMENT & ADMISSIONS SERVICE
CITY CAMPUS
COWCADDENS ROAD
GLASGOW G4 0BA
t: 0141 331 3000 f: 0141 331 8676
e: undergraduate@gcu.ac.uk
// www.gcu.ac.uk

B821 BSc Diagnostic Imaging
Duration: 4FT Hon   CRB Check: Required
Entry Requirements: *GCE:* BCC. *SQAH:* BBBC. *IB:* 26.

B82C BSc Diagnostic Imaging Studies (International only)
Duration: 1FT Hon   CRB Check: Required
Entry Requirements: Contact the institution for details.

B823 BSc Radiotherapy & Oncology Studies (International)
Duration: 1FT Hon   CRB Check: Required
Entry Requirements: Contact the institution for details.

B822 BSc Radiotherapy and Oncology
Duration: 4FT Hon   CRB Check: Required
Entry Requirements: *GCE:* BCC. *SQAH:* BBBC. *IB:* 26.

H36 UNIVERSITY OF HERTFORDSHIRE
UNIVERSITY ADMISSIONS SERVICE
COLLEGE LANE
HATFIELD
HERTS AL10 9AB
t: 01707 284800
// www.herts.ac.uk

B821 BSc Diagnostic Radiography and Imaging
Duration: 3FT Hon   CRB Check: Required
Entry Requirements: *GCE:* 280. *IB:* 24. Interview required. Admissions Test required.

B822 BSc Radiotherapy and Oncology
Duration: 3FT Hon   CRB Check: Required
Entry Requirements: *GCE:* 280. Interview required.

H72 THE UNIVERSITY OF HULL
THE UNIVERSITY OF HULL
COTTINGHAM ROAD
HULL HU6 7RX
t: 01482 466100 f: 01482 442290
e: admissions@hull.ac.uk
// www.hull.ac.uk

HB38 BEng Mechanical and Medical Engineering
Duration: 3FT Hon
Entry Requirements: **GCE:** 280. **IB:** 27. **BTEC ExtDip:** DMM.

HBH8 MEng Mechanical and Medical Engineering
Duration: 4FT Hon
Entry Requirements: **GCE:** 320. **IB:** 30. **BTEC ExtDip:** DDD.

I50 IMPERIAL COLLEGE LONDON
REGISTRY
SOUTH KENSINGTON CAMPUS
IMPERIAL COLLEGE LONDON
LONDON SW7 2AZ
t: 020 7589 5111 f: 020 7594 8004
// www.imperial.ac.uk

BH81 BEng Biomedical Engineering
Duration: 3FT Hon
Entry Requirements: **GCE:** AAA. **SQAAH:** AAA. **IB:** 38.

BJ95 MEng Biomaterials and Tissue Engineering
Duration: 4FT Hon
Entry Requirements: **GCE:** AAA. **SQAAH:** AAB. **IB:** 36.

L23 UNIVERSITY OF LEEDS
THE UNIVERSITY OF LEEDS
WOODHOUSE LANE
LEEDS LS2 9JT
t: 0113 343 3999
e: admissions@leeds.ac.uk
// www.leeds.ac.uk

B810 BSc Healthcare Science (Cardiology)
Duration: 3FT Hon   CRB Check: Required
Entry Requirements: **GCE:** ABB. **SQAAH:** ABB. **BTEC ExtDip:** DDD.

B821 BSc Radiography
Duration: 3FT Hon   CRB Check: Required
Entry Requirements: **GCE:** ABB. **SQAAH:** ABB. **BTEC ExtDip:** DDD.

L41 THE UNIVERSITY OF LIVERPOOL
THE FOUNDATION BUILDING
BROWNLOW HILL
LIVERPOOL L69 7ZX
t: 0151 794 2000 f: 0151 708 6502
e: ugrecruitment@liv.ac.uk
// www.liv.ac.uk

B821 BSc Diagnostic Radiography
Duration: 3FT Hon   CRB Check: Required
Entry Requirements: **GCE:** BBB. **SQAH:** BBBCC. **SQAAH:** BCC. **IB:** 28.

B822 BSc Radiotherapy
Duration: 3FT Hon   CRB Check: Required
Entry Requirements: **GCE:** BBB. **SQAH:** BBBBB. **SQAAH:** BBB. **IB:** 28.

L75 LONDON SOUTH BANK UNIVERSITY
ADMISSIONS AND RECRUITMENT CENTRE
90 LONDON ROAD
LONDON SE1 6LN
t: 0800 923 8888 f: 020 7815 8273
e: course.enquiry@lsbu.ac.uk
// www.lsbu.ac.uk

B821 BSc Diagnostic Radiography
Duration: 3FT Hon   CRB Check: Required
Entry Requirements: **GCE:** 280-300. **IB:** 24. **BTEC ExtDip:** DMM.
OCR NED: M2 Interview required. Admissions Test required.

B822 BSc Therapeutic Radiography
Duration: 3FT Hon   CRB Check: Required
Entry Requirements: **GCE:** 280-300. **IB:** 24. **BTEC ExtDip:** DMM.
OCR NED: M2 Interview required. Admissions Test required.

M20 THE UNIVERSITY OF MANCHESTER
RUTHERFORD BUILDING
OXFORD ROAD
MANCHESTER M13 9PL
t: 0161 275 2077 f: 0161 275 2106
e: ug-admissions@manchester.ac.uk
// www.manchester.ac.uk

J2BV BSc Biomaterials Science and Tissue Engineering
Duration: 3FT Hon
Entry Requirements: **GCE:** AAB. **SQAAH:** AAB. **IB:** 35.

J2B8 MEng Biomaterials Science and Tissue Engineering with Industrial Experience
Duration: 4FT Hon
Entry Requirements: **GCE:** AAA. **SQAAH:** AAA. **IB:** 37. **OCR NED:** D1

N84 THE UNIVERSITY OF NOTTINGHAM
THE ADMISSIONS OFFICE
THE UNIVERSITY OF NOTTINGHAM
UNIVERSITY PARK
NOTTINGHAM NG7 2RD
t: 0115 951 5151 f: 0115 951 4668
// www.nottingham.ac.uk

BJ85 BSc Biomedical Materials Science
Duration: 3FT Hon
Entry Requirements: *GCE:* ABB. *SQAAH:* ABB. *IB:* 32.

P80 UNIVERSITY OF PORTSMOUTH
ACADEMIC REGISTRY
UNIVERSITY HOUSE
WINSTON CHURCHILL AVENUE
PORTSMOUTH PO1 2UP
t: 023 9284 8484 f: 023 9284 3082
e: admissions@port.ac.uk
// www.port.ac.uk

B821 BSc Radiography (Diagnostic)
Duration: 3FT Hon   CRB Check: Required
Entry Requirements: *GCE:* 300. *IB:* 26.   *BTEC ExtDip:* DMM.
Interview required.

B822 BSc Radiography (Therapeutic)
Duration: 3FT Hon   CRB Check: Required
Entry Requirements: *GCE:* 300. *IB:* 26.   *BTEC ExtDip:* DMM.
Interview required.

Q25 QUEEN MARGARET UNIVERSITY, EDINBURGH
QUEEN MARGARET UNIVERSITY DRIVE
EDINBURGH EH21 6UU
t: 0131474 0000 f: 0131 474 0001
e: admissions@qmu.ac.uk
// www.qmu.ac.uk

B821 BSc Diagnostic Radiography
Duration: 4FT Hon   CRB Check: Required
Entry Requirements: *GCE:* 200. *IB:* 26.

B822 BSc Therapeutic Radiography
Duration: 4FT Hon   CRB Check: Required
Entry Requirements: *GCE:* 200. *IB:* 26.

Q50 QUEEN MARY, UNIVERSITY OF LONDON
QUEEN MARY, UNIVERSITY OF LONDON
MILE END ROAD
LONDON E1 4NS
t: 020 7882 5555 f: 020 7882 5500
e: admissions@qmul.ac.uk
// www.qmul.ac.uk

HBC8 BEng Medical Engineering
Duration: 3FT Hon
Entry Requirements: *GCE:* 300. *IB:* 32.

HBD8 BEng Medical Engineering with Industrial Experience
Duration: 4FT Hon
Entry Requirements: *GCE:* 300. *IB:* 32.

B890 BEng Medical Materials
Duration: 3FT Hon
Entry Requirements: *GCE:* 300. *IB:* 32.

B893 BEng Medical Materials with Industrial Experience
Duration: 4FT Hon
Entry Requirements: *GCE:* 300. *IB:* 32.

B892 BSc Medical Materials
Duration: 3FT Hon
Entry Requirements: *GCE:* 320. *IB:* 32.

HB18 MEng Medical Engineering
Duration: 4FT Hon
Entry Requirements: *GCE:* 360. *IB:* 36.

HB1V MEng Medical Engineering with Industrial Experience
Duration: 5FT Hon
Entry Requirements: *GCE:* 360. *IB:* 36.

B891 MEng Medical Materials
Duration: 4FT Hon
Entry Requirements: *GCE:* 360. *IB:* 36.

BV90 MEng Medical Materials with Industrial Experience
Duration: 5FT Hon
Entry Requirements: *GCE:* 360. *IB:* 36.

R36 ROBERT GORDON UNIVERSITY
ROBERT GORDON UNIVERSITY
SCHOOLHILL
ABERDEEN
SCOTLAND AB10 1FR
t: 01224 26 27 28 f: 01224 26 21 47
e: UGOffice@rgu.ac.uk
// www.rgu.ac.uk

B821 BSc Diagnostic Radiography
Duration: 4FT Hon   CRB Check: Required
Entry Requirements: *GCE:* 240. *SQAH:* BBCC. *IB:* 26. Interview required.

S03 THE UNIVERSITY OF SALFORD
SALFORD M5 4WT
t: 0161 295 4545 f: 0161 295 4646
e: ug-admissions@salford.ac.uk
// www.salford.ac.uk

B821 BSc Diagnostic Radiography
Duration: 3FT Hon   CRB Check: Required
Entry Requirements: *GCE:* 300. *IB:* 26. *OCR NED:* M2 Interview required.

S21 SHEFFIELD HALLAM UNIVERSITY
CITY CAMPUS
HOWARD STREET
SHEFFIELD S1 1WB
t: 0114 225 5555 f: 0114 225 2167
e: admissions@shu.ac.uk
// www.shu.ac.uk

B821 BSc Diagnostic Radiography
Duration: 3FT Hon
Entry Requirements: *GCE:* 320. Interview required.

B822 BSc Radiotherapy and Oncology
Duration: 3FT Hon
Entry Requirements: *GCE:* 280.

S49 ST GEORGE'S, UNIVERSITY OF LONDON
CRANMER TERRACE
LONDON SW17 0RE
t: +44 (0)20 8725 2333 f: +44 (0)20 8725 0841
e: enquiries@sgul.ac.uk
// www.sgul.ac.uk

B821 BSc Diagnostic Radiography
Duration: 3FT Hon   CRB Check: Required
Entry Requirements: *GCE:* 260-300. *IB:* 26. Interview required.

B822 BSc Therapeutic Radiography
Duration: 3FT Hon   CRB Check: Required
Entry Requirements: *GCE:* 260-300. Interview required.

S82 UNIVERSITY CAMPUS SUFFOLK (UCS)
WATERFRONT BUILDING
NEPTUNE QUAY
IPSWICH
SUFFOLK IP4 1QJ
t: 01473 338833 f: 01473 339900
e: info@ucs.ac.uk
// www.ucs.ac.uk

B821 BSc Diagnostic Radiography
Duration: 3FT Hon   CRB Check: Required
Entry Requirements: *GCE:* 280. *IB:* 28. *BTEC ExtDip:* DMM.
Interview required. Admissions Test required.

B822 BSc Radiotherapy and Oncology
Duration: 3FT Hon   CRB Check: Required
Entry Requirements: *GCE:* 280. *IB:* 28. *BTEC ExtDip:* DMM.
Interview required. Admissions Test required.

B82C CertHE Health Sciences (Mammography)
Duration: 1FT Cer
Entry Requirements: *BTEC ExtDip:* DMM. Interview required.

S85 UNIVERSITY OF SURREY
STAG HILL
GUILDFORD
SURREY GU2 7XH
t: +44(0)1483 689305 f: +44(0)1483 689388
e: ugteam@surrey.ac.uk
// www.surrey.ac.uk

HBJ8 BEng Medical Engineering (4 years)
Duration: 4SW Hon
Entry Requirements: *GCE:* ABB. *SQAH:* BBBB. Interview required.

HB38 MEng Medical Engineering (3 years)
Duration: 3FT Hon
Entry Requirements: *GCE:* ABB. *SQAH:* BBBB. Interview required.

HB3V MEng Medical Engineering (4 years)
Duration: 4FT Hon
Entry Requirements: *GCE:* AAA. Interview required.

HBH8 MEng Medical Engineering (5 years)
Duration: 5SW Hon
Entry Requirements: *GCE:* AAA. Interview required.

S93 SWANSEA UNIVERSITY
SINGLETON PARK
SWANSEA SA2 8PP
t: 01792 295111 f: 01792 295110
e: admissions@swansea.ac.uk
// www.swansea.ac.uk

HB18 BEng Medical Engineering
Duration: 3FT Hon
Entry Requirements: *GCE:* BBB. *IB:* 32.

B1B8 BSc Clinical Physiology with Cardiology
Duration: 4FT Hon   CRB Check: Required
Entry Requirements: *GCE:* BBB. Interview required.

HB1V MEng Medical Engineering
Duration: 4FT Hon
Entry Requirements: *GCE:* AAB. *IB:* 32.

T20 TEESSIDE UNIVERSITY
MIDDLESBROUGH TS1 3BA
t: 01642 218121 f: 01642 384201
e: registry@tees.ac.uk
// www.tees.ac.uk

B821 BSc Diagnostic Radiography
Duration: 3FT Hon   CRB Check: Required
Entry Requirements: *GCE:* 260. *IB:* 24. *BTEC Dip:* D*D. *BTEC ExtDip:* DMM. *OCR NED:* M2 Interview required.

U20 UNIVERSITY OF ULSTER
COLERAINE
CO. LONDONDERRY
NORTHERN IRELAND BT52 1SA
t: 028 7012 4221 f: 028 7012 4908
e: online@ulster.ac.uk
// www.ulster.ac.uk

BH81 BSc Biomedical Engineering
Duration: 4SW Hon
Entry Requirements: *GCE:* 280. *IB:* 24. Interview required. Admissions Test required.

B821 BSc Radiography (Diagnostic)
Duration: 3FT Hon   CRB Check: Required
Entry Requirements: *GCE:* BBB. *SQAH:* AABCC. *SQAAH:* BBB. *IB:* 25. Admissions Test required.

B822 BSc Radiography (Therapeutic)
Duration: 3FT Hon   CRB Check: Required
Entry Requirements: *GCE:* BBB. *SQAH:* AABCC. *SQAAH:* BBB. *IB:* 25. Admissions Test required.

NURSING AND MIDWIFERY

A30 UNIVERSITY OF ABERTAY DUNDEE
BELL STREET
DUNDEE DD1 1HG
t: 01382 308080 f: 01382 308081
e: sro@abertay.ac.uk
// www.abertay.ac.uk

B760 BSc Mental Health Nursing
Duration: 4FT Hon   CRB Check: Required
Entry Requirements: *GCE:* CC. *SQAH:* BBB. *IB:* 26. Interview required.

B700 BSc Nursing
Duration: 4FT Hon   CRB Check: Required
Entry Requirements: *GCE:* CC. *SQAH:* BBB. *IB:* 26. Interview required.

A60 ANGLIA RUSKIN UNIVERSITY
BISHOP HALL LANE
CHELMSFORD
ESSEX CM1 1SQ
t: 0845 271 3333 f: 01245 251789
e: answers@anglia.ac.uk
// www.anglia.ac.uk

B700 BSc International Nursing Studies
Duration: 1FT Hon
Entry Requirements: Contact the institution for details.

B720 BSc Midwifery
Duration: 3FT Hon   CRB Check: Required
Entry Requirements: *GCE:* 240. *SQAH:* BBCC. *SQAAH:* BC. *IB:* 26. Interview required.

B740 BSc Nursing (Adult)
Duration: 3FT Hon   CRB Check: Required
Entry Requirements: *GCE:* 180. *SQAH:* BBCC. *SQAAH:* CC. *IB:* 24. Interview required.

B730 BSc Nursing (Child)
Duration: 3FT Hon   CRB Check: Required
Entry Requirements: *GCE:* 160. *SQAH:* BBCC. *SQAAH:* CC. *IB:* 24. Interview required.

B760 BSc Nursing (Mental Health)
Duration: 3FT Hon   CRB Check: Required
Entry Requirements: *GCE:* 160. *SQAH:* BBCC. *SQAAH:* CC. *IB:* 24. Interview required.

B990 DipHE Operating Department Practice
Duration: 2FT Dip   CRB Check: Required
Entry Requirements: *GCE:* 160. *SQAH:* CCCC. *SQAAH:* CC. *IB:* 24. Interview required. Portfolio required.

A65 ANGLO EUROPEAN COLLEGE OF CHIROPRACTIC
AECC
13-15 PARKWOOD ROAD
BOURNEMOUTH
DORSET BH5 2DF
t: 0044 (0)1202 436200 f: 0044 (0)1202 436252
e: admissions@aecc.ac.uk
// www.aecc.ac.uk

L510 BSc Community Health and Rehabilitation
Duration: 3FT Hon   CRB Check: Required
Entry Requirements: Contact the institution for details.

B06 BANGOR UNIVERSITY
BANGOR UNIVERSITY
BANGOR
GWYNEDD LL57 2DG
t: 01248 388484 f: 01248 370451
e: admissions@bangor.ac.uk
// www.bangor.ac.uk

B720 BM Midwifery
Duration: 3FT Hon   CRB Check: Required
Entry Requirements: *GCE:* 240. *IB:* 28. Interview required.

B740 BN Bachelor of Nursing (Adult)
Duration: 3FT Hon   CRB Check: Required
Entry Requirements: *GCE:* 240. *IB:* 28. Interview required.

B761 BN Bachelor of Nursing (Learning Disability)
Duration: 3FT Hon   CRB Check: Required
Entry Requirements: *GCE:* 240. *IB:* 28. Interview required.

B760 BN Bachelor of Nursing (Mental Health)
Duration: 3FT Hon   CRB Check: Required
Entry Requirements: *GCE:* 240. *IB:* 28. Interview required.

B22 UNIVERSITY OF BEDFORDSHIRE
PARK SQUARE
LUTON
BEDS LU1 3JU
t: 0844 8482234 f: 01582 489323
e: admissions@beds.ac.uk
// www.beds.ac.uk

B740 BSc Adult Nursing
Duration: 3FT Hon   CRB Check: Required
Entry Requirements: *GCE:* 200. *SQAH:* CCCC. Interview required.

B730 BSc Children's Nursing
Duration: 3FT Hon   CRB Check: Required
Entry Requirements: *GCE:* 200. *SQAH:* CCCC. Interview required.

B760 BSc Mental Health Nursing
Duration: 3FT Hon   CRB Check: Required
Entry Requirements: *GCE:* 200. *SQAH:* CCCC. Interview required.

B711 BSc Midwifery
Duration: 3FT Hon   CRB Check: Required
Entry Requirements: *Foundation:* Pass. *GCE:* 240. *SQAH:* BBBB-BBBC. *SQAAH:* BCC. *IB:* 24. *OCR ND:* D *OCR NED:* M3 Interview required. Admissions Test required.

B990 DipHE Operating Department Practice
Duration: 2FT Dip   CRB Check: Required
Entry Requirements: Interview required.

B25 BIRMINGHAM CITY UNIVERSITY
PERRY BARR
BIRMINGHAM B42 2SU
t: 0121 331 5595 f: 0121 331 7994
// www.bcu.ac.uk

B740 BSc Adult Nursing (Registered Nurse) (Apr)
Duration: 3FT Hon   CRB Check: Required
Entry Requirements: *GCE:* 260. *IB:* 34. *OCR ND:* D *OCR NED:* M2 Interview required.

B741 BSc Adult Nursing (Registered Nurse) (Oct)
Duration: 3FT Hon   CRB Check: Required
Entry Requirements: *GCE:* 260. *IB:* 34. *OCR ND:* D *OCR NED:* M2 Interview required.

B730 BSc Children's Nursing (Registered Nurse) (Apr)
Duration: 3FT Hon   CRB Check: Required
Entry Requirements: *GCE:* 260. *IB:* 34. *OCR ND:* D *OCR NED:* M2 Interview required.

B731 BSc Children's Nursing (Registered Nurse) (Oct)
Duration: 3FT Hon   CRB Check: Required
Entry Requirements: *GCE:* 260. *IB:* 34. *OCR ND:* D *OCR NED:* M2 Interview required.

B761 BSc Learning Disability Nursing (RN) (Oct)
Duration: 3FT Hon   CRB Check: Required
Entry Requirements: *GCE:* 260. *IB:* 34. *OCR ND:* D *OCR NED:* M2 Interview required.

B763 BSc Learning Disability Nursing (Registered Nurse) (Apr)
Duration: 3FT Hon   CRB Check: Required
Entry Requirements: *GCE:* 260. *IB:* 34. *OCR ND:* D *OCR NED:* M2 Interview required.

B760 BSc Mental Health Nursing (RN) (APR)
Duration: 3FT Hon   CRB Check: Required
Entry Requirements: *GCE:* 260. *IB:* 34. *OCR ND:* D *OCR NED:* M2 Interview required.

B762 BSc Mental Health Nursing (RN) (OCT)
Duration: 3FT Hon   CRB Check: Required
Entry Requirements: *GCE:* 260. *IB:* 34. *OCR ND:* D *OCR NED:* M2 Interview required.

B720 BSc Midwifery
Duration: 3FT Hon   CRB Check: Required
Entry Requirements: *GCE:* 280. *SQAH:* CCCCC. *IB:* 36. Interview required.

B32 THE UNIVERSITY OF BIRMINGHAM
EDGBASTON
BIRMINGHAM B15 2TT
t: 0121 415 8900 f: 0121 414 7159
e: admissions@bham.ac.uk
// www.birmingham.ac.uk

B700 BNurs Nursing
Duration: 3FT Hon   CRB Check: Required
Entry Requirements: *GCE:* ABB. *SQAH:* AAABB-AABBB. *SQAAH:* AB. *IB:* 34. Interview required.

B50 BOURNEMOUTH UNIVERSITY
TALBOT CAMPUS
FERN BARROW
POOLE
DORSET BH12 5BB
t: 01202 524111
// www.bournemouth.ac.uk

B700 BSc Adult Nursing
Duration: 3FT Hon   CRB Check: Required
Entry Requirements: *GCE:* 300. *IB:* 31. *BTEC Dip:* DM. *BTEC ExtDip:* DDM. Interview required.

B702 BSc Child Health Nursing
Duration: 3FT Hon   CRB Check: Required
Entry Requirements: *GCE:* 300. *IB:* 31. *BTEC Dip:* DM. *BTEC ExtDip:* DDM. Interview required.

B701 BSc Mental Health Nursing
Duration: 3FT Hon   CRB Check: Required
Entry Requirements: *GCE:* 300. *IB:* 31. *BTEC Dip:* DM. *BTEC ExtDip:* DDM. Interview required.

B720 BSc Midwifery
Duration: 3FT Hon   CRB Check: Required
Entry Requirements: *GCE:* 340. *IB:* 33. *BTEC Dip:* DD. *BTEC ExtDip:* DDD. Interview required.

3060 DipNurse Advanced Diploma Adult Nursing
Duration: 3FT ADN   CRB Check: Required
Entry Requirements: Interview required.

B56 THE UNIVERSITY OF BRADFORD
RICHMOND ROAD
BRADFORD
WEST YORKSHIRE BD7 1DP
t: 0800 073 1225 f: 01274 235585
e: course-enquiries@bradford.ac.uk
// www.bradford.ac.uk

B720 BSc Midwifery Studies/Registered Midwife
Duration: 3FT Hon   CRB Check: Required
Entry Requirements: *GCE:* 280. *IB:* 25. Interview required.

B740 BSc Nursing/Registered Nurse (Adult)
Duration: 3FT Hon   CRB Check: Required
Entry Requirements: *GCE:* 280. Interview required.

B730 BSc Nursing/Registered Nurse (Child)
Duration: 3FT Hon   CRB Check: Required
Entry Requirements: *GCE:* 280. Interview required.

B760 BSc Nursing/Registered Nurse (Mental Health)
Duration: 3FT Hon   CRB Check: Required
Entry Requirements: *GCE:* 280. Interview required.

B72 UNIVERSITY OF BRIGHTON
MITHRAS HOUSE 211
LEWES ROAD
BRIGHTON BN2 4AT
t: 01273 644644 f: 01273 642607
e: admissions@brighton.ac.uk
// www.brighton.ac.uk

B720 BSc Midwifery
Duration: 3FT Hon   CRB Check: Required
Entry Requirements: *GCE:* BBC. *IB:* 28. Interview required.

B721 BSc Midwifery (18 Months)
Duration: 1.5FT Hon
Entry Requirements: Contact the institution for details.

B7L0 BSc Nursing (Adult)
Duration: 3FT Hon   CRB Check: Required
Entry Requirements: *GCE:* BBB. *IB:* 30. Interview required.

B730 BSc Nursing (Child)
Duration: 3FT Hon   CRB Check: Required
Entry Requirements: *GCE:* BBB. *IB:* 30. Interview required.

B760 BSc Nursing (Mental Health)
Duration: 3FT Hon   CRB Check: Required
Entry Requirements: *GCE:* BBB.

B80 UNIVERSITY OF THE WEST OF ENGLAND, BRISTOL
FRENCHAY CAMPUS
COLDHARBOUR LANE
BRISTOL BS16 1QY
t: +44 (0)117 32 83333 f: +44 (0)117 32 82810
e: admissions@uwe.ac.uk
// www.uwe.ac.uk

B760 BA Mental Health (Top-up)
Duration: 1FT Hon
Entry Requirements: Contact the institution for details.

B701 BSc Adult Nursing
Duration: 3FT Hon   CRB Check: Required
Entry Requirements: *GCE:* 300. Interview required.

B731 BSc Children's Health (Top-up)
Duration: 1FT Hon
Entry Requirements: Contact the institution for details.

B702 BSc Children's Nursing
Duration: 3FT Hon   CRB Check: Required
Entry Requirements: *GCE:* 300. Interview required.

B790 BSc Emergency Care (Top-up)
Duration: 1FT Hon
Entry Requirements: Contact the institution for details.

B703 BSc Learning Disabilities Nursing
Duration: 3FT Hon **CRB Check:** Required
Entry Requirements: *GCE:* 260. Interview required.

B704 BSc Mental Health Nursing
Duration: 3FT Hon **CRB Check:** Required
Entry Requirements: *GCE:* 280. Interview required.

B711 BSc Midwifery
Duration: 3FT Hon **CRB Check:** Required
Entry Requirements: *GCE:* 320. Interview required.

B94 BUCKINGHAMSHIRE NEW UNIVERSITY
QUEEN ALEXANDRA ROAD
HIGH WYCOMBE
BUCKINGHAMSHIRE HP11 2JZ
t: 0800 0565 660 f: 01494 605 023
e: admissions@bucks.ac.uk
// bucks.ac.uk

B740 BSc Health Care Practice (Adult Nursing)
Duration: 1FT Hon
Entry Requirements: Interview required.

B730 BSc Health Care Practice (Child Health Nursing)
Duration: 1FT Hon
Entry Requirements: Interview required.

B760 BSc Health Care Practice (Mental Health Nursing)
Duration: 1FT Hon
Entry Requirements: Interview required.

B703 BSc Health Care Practice (Top-Up)
Duration: 1FT Hon
Entry Requirements: Interview required.

B701 BSc Nursing (Adult)
Duration: 3FT Hon **CRB Check:** Required
Entry Requirements: *GCE:* 200-240. *IB:* 24. *OCR ND:* M1 *OCR NED:* M3 Interview required.

B731 BSc Nursing (Child)
Duration: 3FT Hon **CRB Check:** Required
Entry Requirements: *GCE:* 200-240. *IB:* 24. *OCR ND:* M1 *OCR NED:* M3 Interview required.

B761 BSc Nursing (Mental Health)
Duration: 3FT Hon **CRB Check:** Required
Entry Requirements: *GCE:* 200-240. *IB:* 24. *OCR ND:* M1 *OCR NED:* M3 Interview required.

BR40 PG DIP Nursing (Adult)
Duration: 2FT GDN **CRB Check:** Required
Entry Requirements: Contact the institution for details.

B732 PGDip Nursing (Child)
Duration: 2FT GDN **CRB Check:** Required
Entry Requirements: Interview required.

BR60 PGDip Nursing (Mental Health)
Duration: 2FT GDN **CRB Check:** Required
Entry Requirements: Contact the institution for details.

C10 CANTERBURY CHRIST CHURCH UNIVERSITY
NORTH HOLMES ROAD
CANTERBURY
KENT CT1 1QU
t: 01227 782900 f: 01227 782888
e: admissions@canterbury.ac.uk
// www.canterbury.ac.uk

B720 BSc Midwifery
Duration: 3FT Hon **CRB Check:** Required
Entry Requirements: *GCE:* 260. *IB:* 24. Interview required.

B740 BSc Nursing (Adult)
Duration: 3FT Hon **CRB Check:** Required
Entry Requirements: *GCE:* 260. *IB:* 24. Interview required.

B730 BSc Nursing (Child)
Duration: 3FT Hon **CRB Check:** Required
Entry Requirements: *GCE:* 260. *IB:* 24. Interview required.

B760 BSc Nursing (Mental Health)
Duration: 3FT Hon **CRB Check:** Required
Entry Requirements: *GCE:* 240. *IB:* 24. Interview required.

C15 CARDIFF UNIVERSITY
PO BOX 927
30-36 NEWPORT ROAD
CARDIFF CF24 0DE
t: 029 2087 9999 f: 029 2087 6138
e: admissions@cardiff.ac.uk
// www.cardiff.ac.uk

B720 BMid Midwifery
Duration: 3FT Hon **CRB Check:** Required
Entry Requirements: *GCE:* BBB. *SQAH:* AAAB. *SQAAH:* BBB. *IB:* 28. *OCR ND:* M1 *OCR NED:* M1 Interview required. Admissions Test required.

B740 BN Nursing (Adult)
Duration: 3FT Hon **CRB Check:** Required
Entry Requirements: *GCE:* BBB. *SQAH:* AAAB. *SQAAH:* BBB. *IB:* 28. *OCR ND:* M1 *OCR NED:* M1 Interview required. Admissions Test required.

B741 BN Nursing (Adult) March start
Duration: 3FT Hon **CRB Check:** Required
Entry Requirements: *GCE:* BBB. *SQAH:* AAAB. *SQAAH:* BBB. *IB:* 28. *OCR ND:* M1 *OCR NED:* M1 Interview required. Admissions Test required.

B730 BN Nursing (Child Health)
Duration: 3FT Hon   CRB Check: Required
Entry Requirements: *GCE:* BBB. *SQAH:* AAAB. *SQAAH:* BBB. *IB:* 28. *OCR ND:* M1 *OCR NED:* M1 Interview required. Admissions Test required.

B731 BN Nursing (Child) March Start
Duration: 3FT Hon   CRB Check: Required
Entry Requirements: *GCE:* BBB. *SQAH:* AAAB. *SQAAH:* BBB. *IB:* 28. *OCR ND:* M1 *OCR NED:* M1 Interview required. Admissions Test required.

B760 BN Nursing (Mental Health)
Duration: 3FT Hon   CRB Check: Required
Entry Requirements: *GCE:* BBB. *SQAH:* AAAB. *SQAAH:* BBB. *IB:* 28. *OCR ND:* M1 *OCR NED:* M1 Interview required. Admissions Test required.

B761 BN Nursing (Mental Health) March start
Duration: 3FT Hon   CRB Check: Required
Entry Requirements: *GCE:* BBB. *SQAH:* AAAB. *SQAAH:* BBB. *IB:* 28. *OCR ND:* M1 *OCR NED:* M1 Interview required. Admissions Test required.

C30 UNIVERSITY OF CENTRAL LANCASHIRE
PRESTON
LANCS PR1 2HE
t: 01772 201201 f: 01772 894954
e: uadmissions@uclan.ac.uk
// www.uclan.ac.uk

B720 BSc Midwifery
Duration: 3FT Hon   CRB Check: Required
Entry Requirements: *GCE:* 280. *IB:* 28. *OCR ND:* D *OCR NED:* M2 Interview required.

B711 BSc Midwifery (18 month Shortened course)
Duration: 1.5FT Hon   CRB Check: Required
Entry Requirements: Interview required.

B740 BSc Nursing Pre-Registration Adult
Duration: 3FT Hon   CRB Check: Required
Entry Requirements: *GCE:* 240. *IB:* 28. *OCR ND:* M1 *OCR NED:* M3 Interview required.

B730 BSc Nursing Pre-Registration Child
Duration: 3FT Hon   CRB Check: Required
Entry Requirements: *GCE:* 240. *IB:* 28. *OCR ND:* M1 *OCR NED:* M3 Interview required.

B760 BSc Nursing Pre-Registration Mental Health
Duration: 3FT Hon   CRB Check: Required
Entry Requirements: *GCE:* 240. *IB:* 28. *OCR ND:* M1 *OCR NED:* M3 Interview required.

C55 UNIVERSITY OF CHESTER
PARKGATE ROAD
CHESTER CH1 4BJ
t: 01244 511000 f: 01244 511300
e: enquiries@chester.ac.uk
// www.chester.ac.uk

B740 BSc Adult Nursing
Duration: 3FT Hon   CRB Check: Required
Entry Requirements: *GCE:* 240-280. *SQAH:* BBBB. *IB:* 24. Interview required.

B730 BSc Child Nursing
Duration: 3FT Hon   CRB Check: Required
Entry Requirements: *GCE:* 240-280. *SQAH:* BBBB. *IB:* 24. *OCR ND:* M1 *OCR NED:* P1 Interview required.

B761 BSc Learning Disability Nursing
Duration: 3FT Hon   CRB Check: Required
Entry Requirements: *GCE:* 240-280. *SQAH:* BBBB. *IB:* 24. *OCR ND:* M1 *OCR NED:* P1 Interview required.

B760 BSc Mental Health Nursing
Duration: 3FT Hon   CRB Check: Required
Entry Requirements: *GCE:* 240-280. *SQAH:* BBBB. *IB:* 24. *OCR ND:* M1 *OCR NED:* P1 Interview required.

B720 BSc Midwifery
Duration: 3FT Hon   CRB Check: Required
Entry Requirements: *GCE:* 240-280. *SQAH:* BBBB. *IB:* 24. Interview required.

C60 CITY UNIVERSITY
NORTHAMPTON SQUARE
LONDON EC1V 0HB
t: 020 7040 5060 f: 020 7040 8995
e: ugadmissions@city.ac.uk
// www.city.ac.uk

B701 BSc Adult Nursing
Duration: 3FT Hon
Entry Requirements: *GCE:* 280. Interview required. Admissions Test required.

B703 BSc Child Nursing
Duration: 3FT Hon
Entry Requirements: *GCE:* 280. Admissions Test required.

B702 BSc Mental Health Nursing
Duration: 3FT Hon
Entry Requirements: *GCE:* 280. Admissions Test required.

B715 BSc Midwifery
Duration: 3FT Hon
Entry Requirements: *GCE:* 300. Admissions Test required.

C85 COVENTRY UNIVERSITY
THE STUDENT CENTRE
COVENTRY UNIVERSITY
1 GULSON RD
COVENTRY CV1 2JH
t: 024 7615 2222 f: 024 7615 2223
e: studentenquiries@coventry.ac.uk
// www.coventry.ac.uk

B740 BSc Adult Nursing
Duration: 3FT Hon   CRB Check: Required
Entry Requirements: *GCE:* CCC. *SQAH:* CCCCC. *IB:* 30. *BTEC ExtDip:* MMM. *OCR NED:* M3 Interview required.

B730 BSc Children and Young People's Nursing
Duration: 3FT Hon   CRB Check: Required
Entry Requirements: *GCE:* BCC. *SQAH:* BCCCC. *BTEC ExtDip:* DDM. *OCR NED:* M1 Interview required.

B761 BSc Learning Disabilities Nursing
Duration: 3FT Hon   CRB Check: Required
Entry Requirements: *GCE:* CCC. *SQAH:* CCCCC. *IB:* 30. *BTEC ExtDip:* MMM. *OCR NED:* M3 Interview required.

B760 BSc Mental Health Nursing
Duration: 3FT Hon   CRB Check: Required
Entry Requirements: *GCE:* CCC. *SQAH:* CCCCC. *BTEC ExtDip:* MMM. *OCR NED:* M3 Interview required.

B720 BSc Midwifery
Duration: 3FT Hon   CRB Check: Required
Entry Requirements: *GCE:* BCC. *SQAH:* BCCCC. *IB:* 28. *BTEC ExtDip:* DMM. *OCR NED:* M2 Interview required.

C99 UNIVERSITY OF CUMBRIA
FUSEHILL STREET
CARLISLE
CUMBRIA CA1 2HH
t: 01228 616234 f: 01228 616235
// www.cumbria.ac.uk

B720 BSc Midwifery
Duration: 3FT Hon   CRB Check: Required
Entry Requirements: *GCE:* 300. Interview required. Admissions Test required.

B730 BSc Nursing (Child)
Duration: 3FT Hon   CRB Check: Required
Entry Requirements: *GCE:* 240. *IB:* 24. *OCR NED:* M3 Interview required.

B763 BSc Nursing (Learning Disabilities)
Duration: 3FT Hon   CRB Check: Required
Entry Requirements: *GCE:* 220. *IB:* 24. *OCR NED:* M3 Interview required.

B700 BSc Nursing - Adult
Duration: 3FT Hon   CRB Check: Required
Entry Requirements: *GCE:* 240. *IB:* 24. *OCR NED:* M3 Interview required.

B760 BSc Nursing - Mental Health
Duration: 3FT Hon   CRB Check: Required
Entry Requirements: *GCE:* 220. *IB:* 24. *OCR NED:* M3 Interview required.

D26 DE MONTFORT UNIVERSITY
THE GATEWAY
LEICESTER LE1 9BH
t: 0116 255 1551 f: 0116 250 6204
e: enquiries@dmu.ac.uk
// www.dmu.ac.uk

B720 BSc Midwifery
Duration: 3FT Hon   CRB Check: Required
Entry Requirements: *IB:* 28. *BTEC Dip:* D*D*. *BTEC ExtDip:* DMM. *OCR NED:* M2 Interview required.

B990 BSc Nursing (Adult and Child - Dual Registration)
Duration: 4FT Hon   CRB Check: Required
Entry Requirements: *GCE:* 280. *IB:* 28. *BTEC Dip:* D*D*. *BTEC ExtDip:* DMM. *OCR NED:* M2 Interview required. Admissions Test required.

B700 BSc Nursing (Adult Nursing)
Duration: 3FT Hon   CRB Check: Required
Entry Requirements: *GCE:* 280. *IB:* 28. *BTEC Dip:* D*D*. *BTEC ExtDip:* DMM. *OCR NED:* M2 Interview required. Admissions Test required.

B740 BSc Nursing (Adult Nursing:Decelerated)
Duration: 4FT Hon   CRB Check: Required
Entry Requirements: *GCE:* 280. *IB:* 28. *BTEC Dip:* D*D*. *BTEC ExtDip:* DMM. *OCR NED:* M2 Interview required. Admissions Test required.

B99A BSc Nursing (Adult and Learning Disability - Dual Registration)
Duration: 4FT Hon   CRB Check: Required
Entry Requirements: *GCE:* 280. *IB:* 28. *BTEC Dip:* D*D*. *BTEC ExtDip:* DMM. *OCR NED:* M2 Interview required. Admissions Test required.

B99B BSc Nursing (Adult and Mental Health) Dual Registration
Duration: 4FT Hon   CRB Check: Required
Entry Requirements: *GCE:* 280. *IB:* 28. *BTEC Dip:* D*D*. *BTEC ExtDip:* DMM. *OCR NED:* M2 Interview required. Admissions Test required.

B99C BSc Nursing (Child and Learning Disability - Dual registration)
Duration: 4FT Hon   CRB Check: Required
Entry Requirements: *GCE:* 280. *IB:* 28. *BTEC Dip:* D*D*. *BTEC ExtDip:* DMM. *OCR NED:* M2 Interview required. Admissions Test required.

B702 BSc Nursing (Children's Nursing)
Duration: 3FT Hon   CRB Check: Required
Entry Requirements: *GCE:* 280. *IB:* 28. *BTEC Dip:* D*D*. *BTEC ExtDip:* DMM. *OCR NED:* M2 Interview required. Admissions Test required.

B76A BSc Nursing (Learning Disability: Decelerated)
Duration: 4FT Hon   CRB Check: Required
Entry Requirements: *GCE:* 280. *IB:* 28. *BTEC Dip:* D*D*. *BTEC ExtDip:* DMM. *OCR NED:* M2 Interview required. Admissions Test required.

B701 BSc Nursing (Mental Health Nursing)
Duration: 3FT Hon   CRB Check: Required
Entry Requirements: *GCE:* 280. *IB:* 28. *BTEC Dip:* D*D*. *BTEC ExtDip:* DMM. *OCR NED:* M2 Interview required. Admissions Test required.

B99F BSc Nursing (Mental Health and Child)
Duration: 4FT Hon   CRB Check: Required
Entry Requirements: *GCE:* 280. *IB:* 28. *BTEC Dip:* D*D*. *BTEC ExtDip:* DMM. *OCR NED:* M2 Interview required. Admissions Test required.

B992 BSc Nursing (Mental Health and Learning Disability - Dual Registration)
Duration: 4FT Hon   CRB Check: Required
Entry Requirements: Interview required. Admissions Test required.

B76B BSc Nursing (Mental Health: Decelerated)
Duration: 4FT Hon   CRB Check: Required
Entry Requirements: Admissions Test required.

B761 BSc Nursing with Registration (Learning Disability)
Duration: 3FT Hon   CRB Check: Required
Entry Requirements: *GCE:* 280. *IB:* 28. *BTEC Dip:* D*D*. *BTEC ExtDip:* DMM. *OCR NED:* M2 Interview required. Admissions Test required.

B73A BSc Nursing: (Children's Nursing: Decelerated)
Duration: 4FT Hon   CRB Check: Required
Entry Requirements: *GCE:* 280. *IB:* 28. *BTEC Dip:* D*D*. *BTEC ExtDip:* DMM. *OCR NED:* M2 Interview required. Admissions Test required.

D39 UNIVERSITY OF DERBY
KEDLESTON ROAD
DERBY DE22 1GB
t: 01332 591167 f: 01332 597724
e: askadmissions@derby.ac.uk
// www.derby.ac.uk

B770 BSc Nursing (Adult)
Duration: 3FT Hon   CRB Check: Required
Entry Requirements: *Foundation:* Distinction. *GCE:* 240. *IB:* 28. *BTEC Dip:* D*D*. *BTEC ExtDip:* DMM. *OCR ND:* D *OCR NED:* M3 Interview required.

B780 BSc Nursing (Mental Health)
Duration: 3FT Hon   CRB Check: Required
Entry Requirements: *Foundation:* Distinction. *GCE:* 240. *IB:* 28. *BTEC Dip:* D*D*. *BTEC ExtDip:* DMM. *OCR ND:* D *OCR NED:* M3 Interview required.

D65 UNIVERSITY OF DUNDEE
NETHERGATE
DUNDEE DD1 4HN
t: 01382 383838 f: 01382 388150
e: contactus@dundee.ac.uk
// www.dundee.ac.uk/admissions/undergraduate/

B740 BSc Adult Nursing
Duration: 3FT Ord   CRB Check: Required
Entry Requirements: *GCE:* DD. *SQAH:* CC. *IB:* 24. Interview required.

B743 BSc Adult Nursing (Conversion Course)
Duration: 2FT Deg
Entry Requirements: Interview required.

B730 BSc Child Nursing
Duration: 3FT Ord   CRB Check: Required
Entry Requirements: *GCE:* DD. *SQAH:* CC. *IB:* 24. Interview required.

B731 BSc Child Nursing (Conversion Course)
Duration: 2FT Deg
Entry Requirements: Interview required.

B760 BSc Mental Health Nursing
Duration: 3FT Ord   CRB Check: Required
Entry Requirements: *GCE:* DD. *SQAH:* CC. *IB:* 24. Interview required.

B763 BSc Mental Health Nursing (Conversion Course)
Duration: 2FT Deg
Entry Requirements: Interview required.

E14 UNIVERSITY OF EAST ANGLIA
NORWICH NR4 7TJ
t: 01603 591515 f: 01603 591523
e: admissions@uea.ac.uk
// www.uea.ac.uk

B720 BSc Midwifery
Duration: 3FT Hon   CRB Check: Required
Entry Requirements: *GCE:* ABB. *SQAH:* AABBB. *SQAAH:* ABB. *IB:* 32. *BTEC ExtDip:* DDD. Interview required. Admissions Test required.

B701 BSc Nursing (Adult)
Duration: 3FT Hon   CRB Check: Required
Entry Requirements: *GCE:* BBC. *SQAH:* BBBBC. *SQAAH:* BBC. *IB:* 30. *BTEC ExtDip:* DMM. Interview required. Admissions Test required.

B730 BSc Nursing (Children)
Duration: 3FT Hon   CRB Check: Required
Entry Requirements: *GCE:* BBB. *SQAH:* BBBBB. *SQAAH:* BBB. *IB:* 31. *BTEC ExtDip:* DDM. Interview required. Admissions Test required.

B761 BSc Nursing (Learning Disability)
Duration: 3FT Hon   CRB Check: Required
Entry Requirements: *GCE:* BBC. *SQAH:* BBBBC. *SQAAH:* BBC. *IB:* 30. *BTEC ExtDip:* DMM. Interview required. Admissions Test required.

B760 BSc Nursing (Mental Health)
Duration: 3FT Hon   CRB Check: Required
Entry Requirements: *GCE:* BBC. *SQAH:* BBBBC. *SQAAH:* BBC. *IB:* 30. *BTEC ExtDip:* DMM. Interview required. Admissions Test required.

E42 EDGE HILL UNIVERSITY
ORMSKIRK
LANCASHIRE L39 4QP
t: 01695 657000 f: 01695 584355
e: study@edgehill.ac.uk
// www.edgehill.ac.uk

B740 BSc Adult Nursing
Duration: 3FT Hon   CRB Check: Required
Entry Requirements: *GCE:* 280. *IB:* 26. *OCR ND:* D *OCR NED:* M2 Interview required.

B730 BSc Children's Nursing
Duration: 3FT Hon   CRB Check: Required
Entry Requirements: *GCE:* 280. *IB:* 26. *OCR ND:* D *OCR NED:* M2 Interview required.

B731 BSc Children's Nursing and Social Work
Duration: 3FT Hon   CRB Check: Required
Entry Requirements: *GCE:* 280. *IB:* 26. *OCR ND:* D *OCR NED:* M2 Interview required.

B761 BSc Learning Disabilities Nursing
Duration: 3FT Hon   CRB Check: Required
Entry Requirements: *GCE:* 280. *IB:* 26. *OCR ND:* D *OCR NED:* M2 Interview required.

B762 BSc Learning Disabilities Nursing and Social Work
Duration: 3FT Hon   CRB Check: Required
Entry Requirements: *GCE:* 280. *IB:* 26. *OCR ND:* D *OCR NED:* M2 Interview required.

B760 BSc Mental Health Nursing
Duration: 3FT Hon   CRB Check: Required
Entry Requirements: *GCE:* 280. *IB:* 26. *OCR ND:* D *OCR NED:* M2 Interview required.

B720 BSc Midwifery
Duration: 3FT Hon   CRB Check: Required
Entry Requirements: *GCE:* 300. *IB:* 26. *OCR ND:* D *OCR NED:* M1 Interview required.

E56 THE UNIVERSITY OF EDINBURGH
STUDENT RECRUITMENT & ADMISSIONS
57 GEORGE SQUARE
EDINBURGH EH8 9JU
t: 0131 650 4360 f: 0131 651 1236
e: sra.enquiries@ed.ac.uk
// www.ed.ac.uk/studying/undergraduate/

B700 BNurs Nursing
Duration: 4FT Hon   CRB Check: Required
Entry Requirements: *GCE:* AAA-BBB. *SQAH:* AAAA-BBBB. *IB:* 34. Interview required.

E59 EDINBURGH NAPIER UNIVERSITY
CRAIGLOCKHART CAMPUS
EDINBURGH EH14 1DJ
t: +44 (0)8452 60 60 40 f: 0131 455 6464
e: info@napier.ac.uk
// www.napier.ac.uk

B720 BM Midwifery
Duration: 3FT Ord   CRB Check: Required
Entry Requirements: Interview required.

3010 BN Nursing (Adult - Shortened Pathway for Graduates)
Duration: 2.5FT Ord   CRB Check: Required
Entry Requirements: Interview required.

B740 BN Nursing (Adult)
Duration: 3FT Ord   CRB Check: Required
Entry Requirements: Interview required.

B731 BN Nursing (Child Health)
Duration: 3FT Ord   CRB Check: Required
Entry Requirements: Interview required.

3020 BN Nursing (Conversion to Adult)
Duration: 1.5FT Ord   CRB Check: Required
Entry Requirements: Interview required.

3320 BN Nursing (Conversion to Child Health)
Duration: 1.5FT Ord   CRB Check: Required
Entry Requirements: Interview required.

3220 BN Nursing (Conversion to Learning Disability)
Duration: 1.5FT Ord   CRB Check: Required
Entry Requirements: Interview required.

3120 BN Nursing (Conversion to Mental Health)
Duration: 1.5FT Ord   CRB Check: Required
Entry Requirements: Interview required.

B761 BN Nursing (Learning Disability)
Duration: 3FT Ord   CRB Check: Required
Entry Requirements: Interview required.

3110 BN Nursing (Mental Health - Shortened Pathway for Graduates)
Duration: 2FT Ord   CRB Check: Required
Entry Requirements: Interview required.

B760 BN Nursing (Mental Health)
Duration: 3FT Ord   CRB Check: Required
Entry Requirements: Interview required.

E70 THE UNIVERSITY OF ESSEX
WIVENHOE PARK
COLCHESTER
ESSEX CO4 3SQ
t: 01206 873666 f: 01206 874477
e: admit@essex.ac.uk
// www.essex.ac.uk

B740 BSc Nursing (Adult)
Duration: 3FT Hon   CRB Check: Required
Entry Requirements: *GCE:* CC. *IB:* 26. *BTEC ExtDip:* MPP.
Interview required.

B760 BSc Nursing (Mental Health)
Duration: 3FT Hon   CRB Check: Required
Entry Requirements: *GCE:* CC. *IB:* 26. *BTEC ExtDip:* MPP.
Interview required.

G14 UNIVERSITY OF GLAMORGAN, CARDIFF AND PONTYPRIDD
ENQUIRIES AND ADMISSIONS UNIT
PONTYPRIDD CF37 1DL
t: 08456 434030 f: 01443 654050
e: enquiries@glam.ac.uk
// www.glam.ac.uk

B720 BMid Midwifery
Duration: 3FT Hon   CRB Check: Required
Entry Requirements: *GCE:* BBB. *BTEC ExtDip:* DDM. Interview required.

B740 BN Nursing (Adult) March Entry
Duration: 3FT Hon   CRB Check: Required
Entry Requirements: *GCE:* BBB. *BTEC ExtDip:* DDM. Interview required.

B701 BN Nursing (Adult) September Entry
Duration: 3FT Hon   CRB Check: Required
Entry Requirements: *GCE:* BBB. *BTEC ExtDip:* DDM. Interview required.

B702 BN Nursing (Child)
Duration: 3FT Hon   CRB Check: Required
Entry Requirements: *GCE:* BBB. *BTEC ExtDip:* DDM. Interview required.

B703 BN Nursing (Learning Disabilities) September Entry
Duration: 3FT Hon   CRB Check: Required
Entry Requirements: *GCE:* BBB. *BTEC ExtDip:* DDM. Interview required.

B760 BN Nursing (Mental Health) March Entry
Duration: 3FT Hon   CRB Check: Required
Entry Requirements: *GCE:* BBB. *BTEC ExtDip:* DDM. Interview required.

B704 BN Nursing (Mental Health) September Entry
Duration: 3FT Hon   CRB Check: Required
Entry Requirements: *GCE:* BBB. *BTEC ExtDip:* DDM. Interview required.

G28 UNIVERSITY OF GLASGOW
71 SOUTHPARK AVENUE
UNIVERSITY OF GLASGOW
GLASGOW G12 8QQ
t: 0141 330 6062 f: 0141 330 2961
e: student.recruitment@glasgow.ac.uk
// www.glasgow.ac.uk

B700 BN Nursing
Duration: 4FT Hon
Entry Requirements: *GCE:* BBB. *SQAH:* BBBB. *IB:* 28. Interview required.

G42 GLASGOW CALEDONIAN UNIVERSITY
STUDENT RECRUITMENT & ADMISSIONS SERVICE
CITY CAMPUS
COWCADDENS ROAD
GLASGOW G4 0BA
t: 0141 331 3000 f: 0141 331 8676
e: undergraduate@gcu.ac.uk
// www.gcu.ac.uk

B700 BA Nursing Studies
Duration: 4FT Hon   CRB Check: Required
Entry Requirements: *GCE:* BCC. *SQAH:* BBBB-BBBCC. *IB:* 24.
Interview required.

B730 BN Child Nursing
Duration: 3FT Ord   **CRB Check:** Required
Entry Requirements: *GCE:* CCC. *SQAH:* BBC. *IB:* 24. Interview required.

B761 BN Nursing (Learning Disability)
Duration: 3FT Ord   **CRB Check:** Required
Entry Requirements: *GCE:* CCC. *SQAH:* BBC. *IB:* 24. Interview required.

B760 BN Nursing (Mental Health)
Duration: 3FT Ord   **CRB Check:** Required
Entry Requirements: *GCE:* CCC. *SQAH:* BBC. *IB:* 24. Interview required.

B740 BNurse Adult Nursing
Duration: 3FT Ord   **CRB Check:** Required
Entry Requirements: *GCE:* CCC. *SQAH:* BBC. *IB:* 24. Interview required.

3020 DipN Adult Nursing (Conversion)
Duration: 1.5FT DNM   **CRB Check:** Required
Entry Requirements: Contact the institution for details.

3320 DipN Child Nursing (Conversion)
Duration: 1.5FT DNM   **CRB Check:** Required
Entry Requirements: Contact the institution for details.

3120 DipN Mental Health Nursing (Conversion Course)
Duration: 1.5FT DNM   **CRB Check:** Required
Entry Requirements: Contact the institution for details.

3220 DipN Nursing Learning Disability (Conversion)
Duration: 1.5FT DNM   **CRB Check:** Required
Entry Requirements: Contact the institution for details.

G53 GLYNDWR UNIVERSITY
PLAS COCH
MOLD ROAD
WREXHAM LL11 2AW
t: 01978 293439 f: 01978 290008
e: sid@glyndwr.ac.uk
// www.glyndwr.ac.uk

B703 BN Nursing (Adult - March entry)
Duration: 3FT Hon   **CRB Check:** Required
Entry Requirements: Contact the institution for details.

B700 BN Nursing (Adult - September entry)
Duration: 3FT Hon   **CRB Check:** Required
Entry Requirements: *GCE:* 300. Interview required.

B701 BN Nursing (Mental)
Duration: 3FT Hon   **CRB Check:** Required
Entry Requirements: Contact the institution for details.

G70 UNIVERSITY OF GREENWICH
GREENWICH CAMPUS
OLD ROYAL NAVAL COLLEGE
PARK ROW
LONDON SE10 9LS
t: 020 8331 9000 f: 020 8331 8145
e: courseinfo@gre.ac.uk
// www.gre.ac.uk

B710 BSc Midwifery
Duration: 3FT Hon
Entry Requirements: *GCE:* 240. *IB:* 24. Interview required.

B730 BSc Nursing (Adult Branch Registration)
Duration: 3FT Hon
Entry Requirements: *GCE:* 240. *IB:* 24. Interview required.

B720 BSc Nursing (Children's Nursing)
Duration: 3FT Hon
Entry Requirements: *GCE:* 240. *IB:* 24. Interview required.

B761 BSc Nursing (Learning Disabilities Nursing)
Duration: 3FT Hon   **CRB Check:** Required
Entry Requirements: *GCE:* 240. *IB:* 24. Interview required.

B760 BSc Nursing (Mental Health Registration)
Duration: 3FT Hon   **CRB Check:** Required
Entry Requirements: *GCE:* 240. *IB:* 24. Interview required.

B741 PgDip Nursing (Adult Nursing)
Duration: 2FT GDN
Entry Requirements: Interview required.

B731 PgDip Nursing (Children's Nursing)
Duration: 2FT GDN
Entry Requirements: Interview required.

B763 PgDip Nursing (Mental Health Nursing)
Duration: 2FT GDN
Entry Requirements: Interview required.

G80 GRIMSBY INSTITUTE OF FURTHER AND HIGHER EDUCATION
NUNS CORNER
GRIMSBY
NE LINCOLNSHIRE DN34 5BQ
t: 0800 328 3631
e: headmissions@grimsby.ac.uk
// www.grimsby.ac.uk

BL75 FdSc Hospital and Health Care
Duration: 3FT Fdg
Entry Requirements: *GCE:* CC. Interview required.

H36 UNIVERSITY OF HERTFORDSHIRE
UNIVERSITY ADMISSIONS SERVICE
COLLEGE LANE
HATFIELD
HERTS AL10 9AB
t: 01707 284800
// www.herts.ac.uk

B720 BSc Midwifery
Duration: 3FT Hon   CRB Check: Required
Entry Requirements: *GCE:* 300. Interview required.

B700 BSc Nursing with Registration (Adult)
Duration: 3FT Hon   CRB Check: Required
Entry Requirements: *GCE:* 240. Interview required.

B702 BSc Nursing with Registration (Child)
Duration: 3FT Hon   CRB Check: Required
Entry Requirements: *GCE:* 240. Interview required. Admissions Test required.

B761 BSc Nursing with Registration (Learning Disabilities)
Duration: 3FT Hon   CRB Check: Required
Entry Requirements: *GCE:* 240. Interview required. Admissions Test required. HND required.

B701 BSc Nursing with Registration (Mental Health)
Duration: 3FT Hon   CRB Check: Required
Entry Requirements: *GCE:* 160-240. Interview required.

H60 THE UNIVERSITY OF HUDDERSFIELD
QUEENSGATE
HUDDERSFIELD HD1 3DH
t: 01484 473969 f: 01484 472765
e: admissionsandrecords@hud.ac.uk
// www.hud.ac.uk

B720 BSc Midwifery Studies
Duration: 3FT Hon   CRB Check: Required
Entry Requirements: *GCE:* 300. *SQAH:* BBBB. *IB:* 28. Interview required.

B700 BSc Nursing (Adult)
Duration: 3FT Hon   CRB Check: Required
Entry Requirements: *GCE:* 320. Interview required.

B7H0 BSc Nursing (Child)
Duration: 3FT Hon   CRB Check: Required
Entry Requirements: *GCE:* 320. Interview required.

B762 BSc Nursing (Learning Disability)
Duration: 3FT Hon   CRB Check: Required
Entry Requirements: *GCE:* 320. Interview required.

B7P0 BSc Nursing (Mental Health)
Duration: 3FT Hon   CRB Check: Required
Entry Requirements: *GCE:* 320. Interview required.

H72 THE UNIVERSITY OF HULL
THE UNIVERSITY OF HULL
COTTINGHAM ROAD
HULL HU6 7RX
t: 01482 466100 f: 01482 442290
e: admissions@hull.ac.uk
// www.hull.ac.uk

B740 BSc Nursing (Adult Nursing)
Duration: 3FT Hon   CRB Check: Required
Entry Requirements: *GCE:* 240. *IB:* 28. *BTEC ExtDip:* MMM. Interview required.

B730 BSc Nursing (Children's Nursing)
Duration: 3FT Hon   CRB Check: Required
Entry Requirements: *GCE:* 280. *IB:* 28. *BTEC ExtDip:* DMM. Interview required.

B761 BSc Nursing (Learning Disability Nursing)
Duration: 3FT Hon   CRB Check: Required
Entry Requirements: *GCE:* 240. *IB:* 28. *BTEC ExtDip:* MMM. Interview required.

B760 BSc Nursing (Mental Health Nursing)
Duration: 3FT Hon   CRB Check: Required
Entry Requirements: *GCE:* 240. *IB:* 28. *BTEC ExtDip:* MMM. Interview required.

3010 GradDip Adult Nursing (Graduate Entry Programme)
Duration: 2FT GDN   CRB Check: Required
Entry Requirements: Interview required.

3310 GradDip Children's Nursing (Graduate Entry Programme)
Duration: 2FT GDN   CRB Check: Required
Entry Requirements: Interview required.

3210 GradDip Learning Disability Nursing (Graduate Entry Programme)
Duration: 2FT GDN   CRB Check: Required
Entry Requirements: Interview required.

3110 GradDip Mental Health Nursing (Graduate Entry Programme)
Duration: 2FT GDN   CRB Check: Required
Entry Requirements: Interview required.

K12 KEELE UNIVERSITY
KEELE UNIVERSITY
STAFFORDSHIRE ST5 5BG
t: 01782 734005 f: 01782 632343
e: undergraduate@keele.ac.uk
// www.keele.ac.uk

B721 BMid Midwifery with Health Foundation Year
Duration: 4FT Hon   CRB Check: Required
Entry Requirements: *GCE:* CC.

B742 BN Adult Nursing with Health Foundation Year
Duration: 4FT Hon   CRB Check: Required
Entry Requirements: *GCE:* CD. Interview required.

B731 BN Children's Nursing with Health Foundation Year
Duration: 4FT Hon   CRB Check: Required
Entry Requirements: *GCE:* CD. Interview required.

B762 BN Learning Disability Nursing with Health Foundation Year
Duration: 4FT Hon   CRB Check: Required
Entry Requirements: *GCE:* CD. Interview required.

B763 BN Mental Health Nursing with Health Foundation Year
Duration: 4FT Hon   CRB Check: Required
Entry Requirements: *GCE:* CD. Interview required.

B740 BSc Adult Nursing
Duration: 3FT Hon   CRB Check: Required
Entry Requirements: *GCE:* 180-240. *SQAH:* AAAB-BBCC. *BTEC ExtDip:* MMP. *OCR ND:* M1 *OCR NED:* P1 Interview required.

B730 BSc Children's Nursing
Duration: 3FT Hon   CRB Check: Required
Entry Requirements: *GCE:* 180-240. *SQAH:* AAAB-BBCC. *BTEC ExtDip:* MMP. *OCR ND:* M1 *OCR NED:* P1 Interview required.

B761 BSc Learning Disability Nursing
Duration: 3FT Hon   CRB Check: Required
Entry Requirements: *GCE:* 180-240. *SQAH:* AAAB-BBCC. *BTEC ExtDip:* MMP. *OCR ND:* M1 *OCR NED:* P1 Interview required.

B760 BSc Mental Health Nursing
Duration: 3FT Hon   CRB Check: Required
Entry Requirements: *GCE:* 180-240. *SQAH:* AAAB-BBCC. *BTEC ExtDip:* MMP. *OCR ND:* M1 *OCR NED:* P1 Interview required.

B720 BSc (Hons) Midwifery
Duration: 3FT Hon   CRB Check: Required
Entry Requirements: *GCE:* 240-260. *SQAH:* AAAB-BBCC. *BTEC ExtDip:* DMM. *OCR ND:* P1 *OCR NED:* M3 Interview required.

K60 KING'S COLLEGE LONDON (UNIVERSITY OF LONDON)
STRAND
LONDON WC2R 2LS
t: 020 7836 5454 f: 020 7848 7171
e: prospective@kcl.ac.uk
// www.kcl.ac.uk/prospectus

B720 BSc Midwifery Studies with Registration as a Midwife
Duration: 3FT Hon   CRB Check: Required
Entry Requirements: *GCE:* BBBc. *SQAH:* ABBBB. *IB:* 32. Admissions Test required.

B740 BSc Nursing Studies with registration as a nurse (Adult Nursing)
Duration: 3FT Hon   CRB Check: Required
Entry Requirements: *GCE:* BBBc. *SQAH:* BBBBB. *IB:* 32. Admissions Test required.

B730 BSc Nursing Studies with registration as a nurse (Children's Nursing)
Duration: 3FT Hon   CRB Check: Required
Entry Requirements: *GCE:* BBBc. *SQAH:* ABBBB. *IB:* 32. Admissions Test required.

B760 BSc Nursing Studies with registration as a nurse (Mental Health Nursing)
Duration: 3FT Hon   CRB Check: Required
Entry Requirements: *GCE:* BBBc. *SQAH:* ABBBB. *IB:* 32. Admissions Test required.

B721 PgDip Midwifery Practice and Registration as a Midwife
Duration: 1.5FT GDN   CRB Check: Required
Entry Requirements: Admissions Test required.

B741 PgDip Nursing Studies with Registration (Adult)
Duration: 2FT GDN   CRB Check: Required
Entry Requirements: Admissions Test required.

B731 PgDip Nursing Studies with Registration (Child)
Duration: 2FT GDN   CRB Check: Required
Entry Requirements: Admissions Test required.

B761 PgDip Nursing Studies with Registration (Mental Health)
Duration: 2FT GDN   CRB Check: Required
Entry Requirements: Admissions Test required.

K84 KINGSTON UNIVERSITY
STUDENT INFORMATION & ADVICE CENTRE
COOPER HOUSE
40-46 SURBITON ROAD
KINGSTON UPON THAMES KT1 2HX
t: 0844 8552177 f: 020 8547 7080
e: aps@kingston.ac.uk
// www.kingston.ac.uk

B740 BSc Adult Nursing
Duration: 3FT Hon   CRB Check: Required
Entry Requirements: *GCE:* 240. Interview required. Admissions Test required.

B732 BSc Children's Nursing
Duration: 3FT Hon   CRB Check: Required
Entry Requirements: *GCE:* 240. Interview required. Admissions Test required.

B763 BSc Learning Disability Nursing
Duration: 3FT Hon   CRB Check: Required
Entry Requirements: *GCE:* 240. Interview required. Admissions Test required.

B765 BSc Mental Health Nursing
Duration: 3FT Hon   CRB Check: Required
Entry Requirements: *GCE:* 240. Interview required. Admissions Test required.

B720 BSc Midwifery (Registered Midwife)
Duration: 3FT Hon   CRB Check: Required
Entry Requirements: *GCE:* 300. Interview required. Admissions Test required.

B741 PgDip Adult Nursing
Duration: 2FT PMD   CRB Check: Required
Entry Requirements: Interview required. Admissions Test required.

B731 PgDip Children's Nursing
Duration: 2FT GDN   CRB Check: Required
Entry Requirements: Interview required. Admissions Test required.

B764 PgDip Learning Disability Nursing
Duration: 2FT GDN   CRB Check: Required
Entry Requirements: Interview required. Admissions Test required.

B766 PgDip Mental Health Nursing
Duration: 2FT PMD   CRB Check: Required
Entry Requirements: Interview required. Admissions Test required.

L23 UNIVERSITY OF LEEDS
THE UNIVERSITY OF LEEDS
WOODHOUSE LANE
LEEDS LS2 9JT
t: 0113 343 3999
e: admissions@leeds.ac.uk
// www.leeds.ac.uk

B720 BHSc Midwifery
Duration: 3FT Hon   CRB Check: Required
Entry Requirements: *GCE:* BBB. *SQAAH:* BBB. *BTEC ExtDip:* DDD.

B700 BHSc Nursing (Adult)
Duration: 3FT Hon   CRB Check: Required
Entry Requirements: *GCE:* BBB. *SQAAH:* BBB. *BTEC ExtDip:* DDD.

B730 BSc Nursing (Child)
Duration: 3FT Hon   CRB Check: Required
Entry Requirements: *GCE:* BBB. *SQAAH:* BBB. *BTEC ExtDip:* DDD.

B760 BSc Nursing (Mental Health) with registration
Duration: 3FT Hon   CRB Check: Required
Entry Requirements: *GCE:* BBB. *SQAAH:* BBB. *BTEC ExtDip:* DDD.

L27 LEEDS METROPOLITAN UNIVERSITY
COURSE ENQUIRIES OFFICE
CITY CAMPUS
LEEDS LS1 3HE
t: 0113 81 23113 f: 0113 81 23129
// www.leedsmet.ac.uk

B741 BSc Adult Nursing
Duration: 3FT Hon   CRB Check: Required
Entry Requirements: *GCE:* 240.

B761 BSc Mental Health Nursing
Duration: 3FT Hon   CRB Check: Required
Entry Requirements: *GCE:* 240. *IB:* 24.

L39 UNIVERSITY OF LINCOLN
ADMISSIONS
BRAYFORD POOL
LINCOLN LN6 7TS
t: 01522 886097 f: 01522 886146
e: admissions@lincoln.ac.uk
// www.lincoln.ac.uk

B710 BSc Nursing (Adult)
Duration: 3FT Hon   CRB Check: Required
Entry Requirements: *GCE:* 260.

B760 BSc Nursing (Mental Health)
Duration: 3FT Hon   CRB Check: Required
Entry Requirements: *GCE:* 260.

L41 THE UNIVERSITY OF LIVERPOOL
THE FOUNDATION BUILDING
BROWNLOW HILL
LIVERPOOL L69 7ZX
t: 0151 794 2000 f: 0151 708 6502
e: ugrecruitment@liv.ac.uk
// www.liv.ac.uk

B700 BN Nursing
Duration: 3FT Hon   CRB Check: Required
Entry Requirements: *GCE:* BBB. *SQAH:* BBBBC. *IB:* 30. Interview required.

L51 LIVERPOOL JOHN MOORES UNIVERSITY
KINGSWAY HOUSE
HATTON GARDEN
LIVERPOOL L3 2AJ
t: 0151 231 5090 f: 0151 904 6368
e: courses@ljmu.ac.uk
// www.ljmu.ac.uk

B720 BA Midwifery
Duration: 3FT Hon   CRB Check: Required
Entry Requirements: *GCE:* 300. *IB:* 24. Interview required.

B740 BSc Nursing with Registered Nurse Status (Adult)
Duration: 3FT Hon   **CRB Check:** Required
Entry Requirements: *GCE:* 260. *IB:* 24. Interview required.

B760 BSc Nursing with Registered Nurse Status (Mental Health)
Duration: 3FT Hon   **CRB Check:** Required
Entry Requirements: *GCE:* 260. *IB:* 24. Interview required.

L75 LONDON SOUTH BANK UNIVERSITY
ADMISSIONS AND RECRUITMENT CENTRE
90 LONDON ROAD
LONDON SE1 6LN
t: 0800 923 8888 f: 020 7815 8273
e: course.enquiry@lsbu.ac.uk
// www.lsbu.ac.uk

B740 BSc Adult Nursing
Duration: 3FT Hon   **CRB Check:** Required
Entry Requirements: *GCE:* 200. *IB:* 24. *BTEC Dip:* DM. *BTEC ExtDip:* MMP. *OCR ND:* M1 *OCR NED:* P1 Interview required.
Admissions Test required.

B730 BSc Children's Nursing
Duration: 3FT Hon   **CRB Check:** Required
Entry Requirements: *GCE:* 200. *IB:* 24. *BTEC Dip:* DM. *BTEC ExtDip:* MMP. *OCR ND:* M1 *OCR NED:* P1 Interview required.
Admissions Test required.

B761 BSc Learning Disability Nursing
Duration: 3FT Hon   **CRB Check:** Required
Entry Requirements: *GCE:* 200. *IB:* 24. *BTEC Dip:* DM. *BTEC ExtDip:* MMP. *OCR ND:* M1 *OCR NED:* P1 Interview required.
Admissions Test required.

B760 BSc Mental Health Nursing
Duration: 3FT Hon   **CRB Check:** Required
Entry Requirements: *GCE:* 200. *IB:* 24. *BTEC Dip:* DM. *BTEC ExtDip:* MMP. *OCR ND:* M1 *OCR NED:* P1 Interview required.
Admissions Test required.

B720 BSc Midwifery Practice
Duration: 3FT Hon   **CRB Check:** Required
Entry Requirements: *GCE:* 240. *IB:* 24. *BTEC Dip:* DD. *BTEC ExtDip:* MMM. *OCR ND:* D *OCR NED:* M3 Interview required.
Admissions Test required.

B772 BSc Operating Department Practice
Duration: 3FT Hon   **CRB Check:** Required
Entry Requirements: Contact the institution for details.

B741 PgDip Adult Nursing
Duration: 2FT GDN   **CRB Check:** Required
Entry Requirements: Contact the institution for details.

B731 PgDip Children's Nursing
Duration: 2FT GDN   **CRB Check:** Required
Entry Requirements: Interview required. Admissions Test required.
Portfolio required.

B762 PgDip Mental Health Nursing
Duration: 2FT GDN   **CRB Check:** Required
Entry Requirements: Interview required. Admissions Test required.
Portfolio required.

M20 THE UNIVERSITY OF MANCHESTER
RUTHERFORD BUILDING
OXFORD ROAD
MANCHESTER M13 9PL
t: 0161 275 2077 f: 0161 275 2106
e: ug-admissions@manchester.ac.uk
// www.manchester.ac.uk

B760 BA Learning Disability Studies
Duration: 3FT Hon   **CRB Check:** Required
Entry Requirements: *GCE:* ABB-BBB. *SQAH:* ABBBB-BBBBB. *SQAAH:* ABB-BBB. Interview required.

B720 BMidwif Midwifery
Duration: 3FT Hon   **CRB Check:** Required
Entry Requirements: *GCE:* ABB. *SQAH:* BBBBB. *SQAAH:* BBB.
Interview required.

B740 BNurs Adult Nursing
Duration: 3FT Hon   **CRB Check:** Required
Entry Requirements: *GCE:* BBC. *SQAH:* BBCCC. *SQAAH:* BBC. *IB:* 28. Interview required.

B730 BNurs Children's Nursing
Duration: 3FT Hon   **CRB Check:** Required
Entry Requirements: *GCE:* BBB. *SQAH:* BBCCC. *SQAAH:* BBB. *IB:* 30. Interview required.

B762 BNurs Mental Health Nursing
Duration: 3FT Hon   **CRB Check:** Required
Entry Requirements: *GCE:* BCC. *SQAH:* BBCCC. *SQAAH:* BCC. *IB:* 29. Interview required.

M40 THE MANCHESTER METROPOLITAN UNIVERSITY
ADMISSIONS OFFICE
ALL SAINTS (GMS)
ALL SAINTS
MANCHESTER M15 6BH
t: 0161 247 2000
// www.mmu.ac.uk

B700 BSc Adult Nursing
Duration: 3FT Hon   **CRB Check:** Required
Entry Requirements: *GCE:* 300. *IB:* 29. *BTEC SubDip:* D*. *BTEC Dip:* D*D*. *BTEC ExtDip:* DDM. *OCR ND:* D *OCR NED:* D2 Interview required.

M80 MIDDLESEX UNIVERSITY
MIDDLESEX UNIVERSITY
THE BURROUGHS
LONDON NW4 4BT
t: 020 8411 5555 f: 020 8411 5649
e: enquiries@mdx.ac.uk
// www.mdx.ac.uk

B74A BSc European Nursing (Adult)
Duration: 3FT Hon   CRB Check: Required
Entry Requirements: Contact the institution for details.

B73A BSc European Nursing (Child)
Duration: 3FT Hon   CRB Check: Required
Entry Requirements: Contact the institution for details.

B76A BSc European Nursing (Mental Health)
Duration: 3FT Hon   CRB Check: Required
Entry Requirements: Contact the institution for details.

B702 BSc Healthcare Science (Cardiac and Vascular Sciences)
Duration: 3FT Hon
Entry Requirements: Contact the institution for details.

B762 BSc Mental Health (Top-Up)
Duration: 1FT Hon
Entry Requirements: Contact the institution for details.

B728 BSc Midwifery (Long)
Duration: 3FT Hon   CRB Check: Required
Entry Requirements: GCE: 200-300. IB: 28. Interview required.

B724 BSc Midwifery (Short)
Duration: 1.5FT Hon
Entry Requirements: Contact the institution for details.

B740 BSc Nursing (Adult)
Duration: 3FT Hon   CRB Check: Required
Entry Requirements: GCE: 200-300. IB: 28. Interview required.

B730 BSc Nursing (Child)
Duration: 3FT Hon   CRB Check: Required
Entry Requirements: GCE: 200-300. IB: 28. Interview required.

B760 BSc Nursing (Mental Health)
Duration: 3FT Hon   CRB Check: Required
Entry Requirements: GCE: 200-300. IB: 28. Interview required.

BR40 PGDip Nursing (Adult)
Duration: 2FT DNM   CRB Check: Required
Entry Requirements: Interview required.

BR60 PGDip Nursing (Mental Health)
Duration: 2FT PMD   CRB Check: Required
Entry Requirements: Interview required.

N38 UNIVERSITY OF NORTHAMPTON
PARK CAMPUS
BOUGHTON GREEN ROAD
NORTHAMPTON NN2 7AL
t: 0800 358 2232 f: 01604 722083
e: admissions@northampton.ac.uk
// www.northampton.ac.uk

B720 BSc Midwifery
Duration: 3FT Hon   CRB Check: Required
Entry Requirements: GCE: 240-280. SQAH: AAA-BBBB. IB: 24. BTEC Dip: DD. BTEC ExtDip: DMM. OCR ND: D OCR NED: M2 Interview required.

B700 BSc Nursing (Adult)
Duration: 3FT Hon   CRB Check: Required
Entry Requirements: GCE: 240-280. SQAH: AAB-BBBC. IB: 24. BTEC Dip: DD. BTEC ExtDip: DMM. OCR ND: D OCR NED: M2 Interview required.

B702 BSc Nursing (Child)
Duration: 3FT Hon   CRB Check: Required
Entry Requirements: GCE: 240-280. SQAH: AAB-BBBC. IB: 24. BTEC Dip: DD. BTEC ExtDip: DMM. OCR ND: D OCR NED: M2 Interview required.

B703 BSc Nursing (Learning Disabilities)
Duration: 3FT Hon   CRB Check: Required
Entry Requirements: GCE: 240-280. SQAH: AAB-BBBC. IB: 24. BTEC Dip: DD. BTEC ExtDip: DMM. OCR ND: D OCR NED: M2 Interview required.

B710 BSc Nursing (Mental Health)
Duration: 3FT Hon   CRB Check: Required
Entry Requirements: GCE: 240-280. SQAH: AAB-BBBC. IB: 24. BTEC Dip: DD. BTEC ExtDip: DMM. OCR ND: D OCR NED: M2 Interview required.

N77 NORTHUMBRIA UNIVERSITY
TRINITY BUILDING
NORTHUMBERLAND ROAD
NEWCASTLE UPON TYNE NE1 8ST
t: 0191 243 7420 f: 0191 227 4561
e: er.admissions@northumbria.ac.uk
// www.northumbria.ac.uk

BL75 BA Childhood Studies and Early Years
Duration: 3FT Hon   CRB Check: Required
Entry Requirements: SQAH: BBCCC. SQAAH: BCC. IB: 25.

BB79 BA Guidance & Counselling and Early Years
Duration: 3FT Hon   CRB Check: Required
Entry Requirements: SQAH: BBCCC. SQAAH: BCC. IB: 25.

B720 BSc Midwifery Studies, Registered Midwife
Duration: 3FT Hon   CRB Check: Required
Entry Requirements: SQAH: BBBBC. SQAAH: BBC. IB: 26. BTEC Dip: D*D*. BTEC ExtDip: DDM. OCR NED: M1 Interview required.

B700 BSc Nursing Studies, Registered Nurse (Adult)
Duration: 3FT Hon   CRB Check: Required
Entry Requirements: *SQAH:* BBCCC. *SQAAH:* BCC. *IB:* 25. *BTEC Dip:* D*D*. *BTEC ExtDip:* DMM. *OCR NED:* M2 Interview required.

B701 BSc Nursing Studies, Registered Nurse (Child)
Duration: 3FT Hon   CRB Check: Required
Entry Requirements: *SQAH:* BBCCC. *SQAAH:* BCC. *IB:* 25. *BTEC Dip:* D*D*. *BTEC ExtDip:* DMM. *OCR NED:* M2 Interview required.

B741 BSc Nursing Studies, Registered Nurse (Learning Disability)
Duration: 3FT Hon   CRB Check: Required
Entry Requirements: *SQAH:* BBCCC. *SQAAH:* BCC. *IB:* 25. *BTEC Dip:* D*D*. *BTEC ExtDip:* DMM. *OCR NED:* M2 Interview required.

B740 BSc Nursing Studies, Registered Nurse (Mental Health)
Duration: 3FT Hon   CRB Check: Required
Entry Requirements: *SQAH:* BBCCC. *SQAAH:* BCC. *IB:* 25. *BTEC Dip:* D*D*. *BTEC ExtDip:* DMM. *OCR NED:* M2 Interview required.

N84 THE UNIVERSITY OF NOTTINGHAM
THE ADMISSIONS OFFICE
THE UNIVERSITY OF NOTTINGHAM
UNIVERSITY PARK
NOTTINGHAM NG7 2RD
t: 0115 951 5151 f: 0115 951 4668
// www.nottingham.ac.uk

B721 BMid Midwifery
Duration: 3FT Hon   CRB Check: Required
Entry Requirements: *GCE:* BBB. *SQAAH:* BBB. *IB:* 30. Interview required.

B722 BMid Midwifery (Extended)
Duration: 3.5FT Hon   CRB Check: Required
Entry Requirements: *GCE:* BCC. *SQAAH:* BCC. *IB:* 28. Interview required.

B740 BSc Nursing (Adult)
Duration: 3FT Hon   CRB Check: Required
Entry Requirements: *GCE:* BBC-BCC. *SQAAH:* BBC-BCC. *IB:* 28. Interview required.

B730 BSc Nursing (Children)
Duration: 3FT Hon   CRB Check: Required
Entry Requirements: *GCE:* BCC. *SQAAH:* BCC. *IB:* 28.

B768 BSc Nursing (Learning Disability)
Duration: 3FT Hon   CRB Check: Required
Entry Requirements: *GCE:* BCC. *SQAAH:* BCC. *IB:* 26. Interview required.

B767 BSc Nursing (Mental Health and Social Care)
Duration: 3FT Hon   CRB Check: Required
Entry Requirements: *GCE:* BBC-BCC. *SQAAH:* BBC-BCC. *IB:* 28. Interview required.

3010 GradDip Nursing (Graduate Entry) - Adult
Duration: 2FT GDN   CRB Check: Required
Entry Requirements: Interview required.

3310 GradDip Nursing (Graduate Entry) - Child
Duration: 2FT GDN
Entry Requirements: Interview required.

3110 GradDip Nursing (Graduate Entry) - Mental Health
Duration: 2FT GDN   CRB Check: Required
Entry Requirements: Interview required.

B700 MN Nursing Science
Duration: 4FT Hon   CRB Check: Required
Entry Requirements: *GCE:* ABB. *SQAAH:* ABB. *IB:* 32.

O66 OXFORD BROOKES UNIVERSITY
ADMISSIONS OFFICE
HEADINGTON CAMPUS
GIPSY LANE
OXFORD OX3 0BP
t: 01865 483040 f: 01865 483983
e: admissions@brookes.ac.uk
// www.brookes.ac.uk

B702 BA Nursing (Mental Health)
Duration: 3FT Hon   CRB Check: Required
Entry Requirements: *GCE:* BCC. *BTEC ExtDip:* DMM.

B792 BSc Adult and Mental Health Nursing
Duration: 4FT Hon   CRB Check: Required
Entry Requirements: Contact the institution for details.

B791 BSc Children's and Mental Health Nursing
Duration: 4FT Hon   CRB Check: Required
Entry Requirements: Contact the institution for details.

B720 BSc Midwifery
Duration: 3FT Hon   CRB Check: Required
Entry Requirements: *GCE:* BBB. *IB:* 32. *BTEC ExtDip:* DDD.

B701 BSc Nursing (Adult)
Duration: 3FT Hon   CRB Check: Required
Entry Requirements: *GCE:* BCC. *BTEC ExtDip:* DDM.

B704 BSc Nursing (Children's)
Duration: 3FT Hon   CRB Check: Required
Entry Requirements: *GCE:* BBC. *BTEC ExtDip:* DDM.

B700 BSc Nursing Adult (Swindon)
Duration: 3FT Hon   CRB Check: Required
Entry Requirements: *GCE:* BCC.

B793 GradDip Person Centred Health Care
Duration: 1FT GDN   CRB Check: Required
Entry Requirements: Contact the institution for details.

B794 GradDip Pregnancy and Childbirth
Duration: 1FT GDN   CRB Check: Required
Entry Requirements: Contact the institution for details.

P60 PLYMOUTH UNIVERSITY
DRAKE CIRCUS
PLYMOUTH PL4 8AA
t: 01752 585858 f: 01752 588055
e: admissions@plymouth.ac.uk
// www.plymouth.ac.uk

B720 BSc Midwifery (Pre-Registration)
Duration: 3FT Hon CRB Check: Required
Entry Requirements: *GCE:* 300. *IB:* 29. *BTEC ExtDip:* DMM. *OCR ND:* D *OCR NED:* M2

B740 BSc Nursing (Adult)
Duration: 3FT Hon CRB Check: Required
Entry Requirements: *GCE:* 240. *IB:* 27. *BTEC ExtDip:* MMM. *OCR ND:* D *OCR NED:* M3

B730 BSc Nursing (Child Health)
Duration: 3FT Hon CRB Check: Required
Entry Requirements: *GCE:* 280. *IB:* 27. *OCR ND:* D *OCR NED:* M2

B760 BSc Nursing (Mental Health)
Duration: 3FT Hon CRB Check: Required
Entry Requirements: *GCE:* 240. *OCR ND:* D *OCR NED:* M3

B712 BSc Specialist Community Public Health Nursing (Health Visiting)
Duration: 1FT Hon
Entry Requirements: Contact the institution for details.

B711 BSc Specialist Community Public Health Nursing (Occupational Health Nursing)
Duration: 1FT Hon
Entry Requirements: Contact the institution for details.

B713 BSc Specialist Community Public Health Nursing (School Nursing)
Duration: 1FT Hon
Entry Requirements: Contact the institution for details.

Q25 QUEEN MARGARET UNIVERSITY, EDINBURGH
QUEEN MARGARET UNIVERSITY DRIVE
EDINBURGH EH21 6UU
t: 0131474 0000 f: 0131 474 0001
e: admissions@qmu.ac.uk
// www.qmu.ac.uk

B740 BSc Nursing
Duration: 4FT Hon CRB Check: Required
Entry Requirements: *GCE:* 220. *IB:* 28. Interview required.

R36 ROBERT GORDON UNIVERSITY
ROBERT GORDON UNIVERSITY
SCHOOLHILL
ABERDEEN
SCOTLAND AB10 1FR
t: 01224 26 27 28 f: 01224 26 21 47
e: UGOffice@rgu.ac.uk
// www.rgu.ac.uk

B720 BM Midwifery
Duration: 3FT Ord CRB Check: Required
Entry Requirements: *GCE:* CD. *SQAH:* CC. *IB:* 24. Interview required.

B741 BN Nursing - Adult
Duration: 3FT Ord CRB Check: Required
Entry Requirements: *GCE:* C. *SQAH:* C. *IB:* 24. Interview required.

B731 BN Nursing - Children and Young People's Nursing
Duration: 3FT Ord CRB Check: Required
Entry Requirements: Contact the institution for details.

B760 BN Nursing - Mental Health
Duration: 3FT Ord CRB Check: Required
Entry Requirements: *GCE:* C. *SQAH:* C. *IB:* 24. Interview required.

B740 BNur Nursing - Adult
Duration: 4FT Hon CRB Check: Required
Entry Requirements: *GCE:* 220-240. *SQAH:* BBCC. *IB:* 26. Interview required.

S03 THE UNIVERSITY OF SALFORD
SALFORD M5 4WT
t: 0161 295 4545 f: 0161 295 4646
e: ug-admissions@salford.ac.uk
// www.salford.ac.uk

B720 BSc Midwifery
Duration: 3FT Hon CRB Check: Required
Entry Requirements: *GCE:* BBB. *IB:* 24. *OCR NED:* M2 Interview required.

B701 BSc Nursing - Registered Nurse (Adult)
Duration: 3FT Hon CRB Check: Required
Entry Requirements: *GCE:* 280. *IB:* 25. *OCR ND:* D *OCR NED:* M2 Interview required.

B702 BSc Nursing - Registered Nurse (Child)
Duration: 3FT Hon CRB Check: Required
Entry Requirements: *GCE:* 280. *IB:* 25. *OCR ND:* D *OCR NED:* M2 Interview required.

B760 BSc Nursing - Registered Nurse (Mental Health)
Duration: 3FT Hon CRB Check: Required
Entry Requirements: *GCE:* 280. *IB:* 25. *OCR ND:* D *OCR NED:* M2 Interview required.

BL75 BSc Professional Studies in Nursing and Social Work
Duration: 3FT Hon   CRB Check: Required
Entry Requirements: *GCE:* 280. *IB:* 24. *OCR NED:* M2 Interview required.

S18 THE UNIVERSITY OF SHEFFIELD
THE UNIVERSITY OF SHEFFIELD
LEVEL 2, ARTS TOWER
WESTERN BANK
SHEFFIELD S10 2TN
t: 0114 222 8030 f: 0114 222 8032
// www.sheffield.ac.uk

3010 PGDip Nursing Studies leading to professional registration as an Adult Nurse
Duration: 2FT PMD   CRB Check: Required
Entry Requirements: Contact the institution for details.

S21 SHEFFIELD HALLAM UNIVERSITY
CITY CAMPUS
HOWARD STREET
SHEFFIELD S1 1WB
t: 0114 225 5555 f: 0114 225 2167
e: admissions@shu.ac.uk
// www.shu.ac.uk

3060 ADV Dip N Adult Nursing
Duration: 3FT ADN
Entry Requirements: *GCE:* 120.

3360 ADV Dip N Children's Nursing
Duration: 3FT ADN
Entry Requirements: *GCE:* 120.

3160 ADV Dip N Mental Health Nursing
Duration: 3FT ADN
Entry Requirements: *GCE:* 120.

B761 BA Applied Nursing and Social Work (Learning Disability)
Duration: 3FT Hon
Entry Requirements: *GCE:* 240.

B701 BA Nursing Studies (Adult Care)
Duration: 3FT Hon
Entry Requirements: *GCE:* 240.

B702 BA Nursing Studies (Child Care)
Duration: 3FT Hon
Entry Requirements: *GCE:* 240.

B703 BA Nursing Studies (Mental Health Care)
Duration: 3FT Hon
Entry Requirements: *GCE:* 240.

B720 BSc Midwifery
Duration: 3FT Hon
Entry Requirements: *GCE:* 300.

B791 BSc Nursing
Duration: 1FT Hon
Entry Requirements: Interview required.

3010 GradDip Adult Nursing
Duration: 2FT GDN
Entry Requirements: HND required.

3110 GradDip Mental Health Nursing
Duration: 2FT GDN
Entry Requirements: HND required.

S27 UNIVERSITY OF SOUTHAMPTON
HIGHFIELD
SOUTHAMPTON SO17 1BJ
t: 023 8059 4732 f: 023 8059 3037
e: admissions@soton.ac.uk
// www.southampton.ac.uk

B720 BMid Midwifery
Duration: 3FT Hon   CRB Check: Required
Entry Requirements: *GCE:* ABB. Interview required.

B747 BN Adult and Mental Health Nursing
Duration: 4FT Hon   CRB Check: Required
Entry Requirements: Contact the institution for details.

B746 BN Children's and Adult Nursing
Duration: 4FT Hon   CRB Check: Required
Entry Requirements: Contact the institution for details.

B748 BN Children's and Mental Health Nursing
Duration: 4FT Hon   CRB Check: Required
Entry Requirements: Contact the institution for details.

B745 BN Nursing (Degree) Adult Branch
Duration: 3FT Hon   CRB Check: Required
Entry Requirements: Interview required.

B735 BN Nursing (Degree) Child Branch
Duration: 3FT Hon   CRB Check: Required
Entry Requirements: *GCE:* BBB. Interview required.

B760 BN Nursing (Degree) Mental Health Branch
Duration: 3FT Hon   CRB Check: Required
Entry Requirements: *GCE:* BBC. Interview required.

S32 SOUTH DEVON COLLEGE
LONG ROAD
PAIGNTON
DEVON TQ4 7EJ
t: 08000 213181 f: 01803 540541
e: university@southdevon.ac.uk
// www.southdevon.ac.uk/
welcome-to-university-level

BX71 FdSc Early Years Care and Education
Duration: 2FT Fdg   CRB Check: Required
Entry Requirements: *GCE:* 60-160. *SQAH:* C. *SQAAH:* C. Interview required.

S72 STAFFORDSHIRE UNIVERSITY
COLLEGE ROAD
STOKE ON TRENT ST4 2DE
t: 01782 292753 f: 01782 292740
e: admissions@staffs.ac.uk
// www.staffs.ac.uk

B720 BSc Midwifery Practice
Duration: 3FT Hon   CRB Check: Required
Entry Requirements: *GCE:* 280. *IB:* 24. *OCR ND:* D Interview required.

B740 BSc Nursing Practice (Adult)
Duration: 3FT Hon   CRB Check: Required
Entry Requirements: *GCE:* 240. *IB:* 24. Interview required.

B730 BSc Nursing Practice (Child)
Duration: 3FT Hon   CRB Check: Required
Entry Requirements: *GCE:* 240. *IB:* 24. Interview required.

B760 BSc Nursing Practice (Mental Health)
Duration: 3FT Hon   CRB Check: Required
Entry Requirements: *GCE:* 240. *IB:* 24. Interview required.

S75 THE UNIVERSITY OF STIRLING
STUDENT RECRUITMENT & ADMISSIONS SERVICE
UNIVERSITY OF STIRLING
STIRLING
SCOTLAND FK9 4LA
t: 01786 467044 f: 01786 466800
e: admissions@stir.ac.uk
// www.stir.ac.uk

B740 BSc Nursing (Adult)
Duration: 3FT Ord   CRB Check: Required
Entry Requirements: *GCE:* CD. *SQAH:* BB. *IB:* 25. *BTEC ExtDip:* MMP. Interview required.

B742 BSc Nursing (Adult) (conversion course for registered nurses)
Duration: 2FT Ord   CRB Check: Required
Entry Requirements: *IB:* 32. *BTEC ExtDip:* DMM. Interview required.

B760 BSc Nursing (Mental Health)
Duration: 3FT Ord   CRB Check: Required
Entry Requirements: *GCE:* CD. *SQAH:* BB. *IB:* 25. *BTEC ExtDip:* MMP. Interview required.

B762 BSc Nursing (Mental Health) (conversion course for registered nurses)
Duration: 2FT Ord   CRB Check: Required
Entry Requirements: Interview required.

B700 BSc Professional Practice
Duration: 3FT Ord   CRB Check: Required
Entry Requirements: Contact the institution for details.

S82 UNIVERSITY CAMPUS SUFFOLK (UCS)
WATERFRONT BUILDING
NEPTUNE QUAY
IPSWICH
SUFFOLK IP4 1QJ
t: 01473 338833 f: 01473 339900
e: info@ucs.ac.uk
// www.ucs.ac.uk

B700 BSc Adult Nursing
Duration: 3FT Hon   CRB Check: Required
Entry Requirements: *GCE:* 280. *IB:* 28. *BTEC ExtDip:* DMM. Interview required. Admissions Test required.

B730 BSc Child Health Nursing
Duration: 3FT Hon   CRB Check: Required
Entry Requirements: *GCE:* 280. *IB:* 28. *BTEC ExtDip:* DMM. Interview required. Admissions Test required.

B760 BSc Mental Health Nursing
Duration: 3FT Hon   CRB Check: Required
Entry Requirements: *GCE:* 280. *IB:* 28. *BTEC ExtDip:* DMM. Interview required. Admissions Test required.

B701 FdA Health Care Practice (Management of Acute Conditions)
Duration: 2FT Fdg
Entry Requirements: *GCE:* 200. *IB:* 28. *BTEC ExtDip:* DMM. Interview required.

B702 FdA Health Care Practice (Management of Long-Term Conditions)
Duration: 2FT Fdg
Entry Requirements: *GCE:* 200. *IB:* 28. *BTEC ExtDip:* DMM. Interview required.

BB9R FdA Health Care Practice (Mental Health)
Duration: 2FT Fdg
Entry Requirements: *GCE:* 200. *IB:* 28. *BTEC ExtDip:* DMM. Interview required.

S84 UNIVERSITY OF SUNDERLAND
STUDENT HELPLINE
THE STUDENT GATEWAY
CHESTER ROAD
SUNDERLAND SR1 3SD
t: 0191 515 3000 f: 0191 515 3805
e: student.helpline@sunderland.ac.uk
// www.sunderland.ac.uk

B700 BSc Nursing (Top-up)
Duration: 1FT Hon
Entry Requirements: Contact the institution for details.

S85 UNIVERSITY OF SURREY
STAG HILL
GUILDFORD
SURREY GU2 7XH
t: +44(0)1483 689305 f: +44(0)1483 689388
e: ugteam@surrey.ac.uk
// www.surrey.ac.uk

B760 BSc Mental Health Nursing
Duration: 3FT Hon   CRB Check: Required
Entry Requirements: *GCE:* ABB-BBB. Interview required.

B720 BSc Midwifery (for Registered Nurses only)
Duration: 1.5FT Hon   CRB Check: Required
Entry Requirements: Interview required.

B711 BSc Midwifery - Registered Midwife (3 years)
Duration: 3FT Hon   CRB Check: Required
Entry Requirements: *GCE:* AAB-ABB. Interview required.

B744 BSc Nursing Studies - Registered Nurse: Adult Nursing (3 years)
Duration: 3FT Hon   CRB Check: Required
Entry Requirements: *GCE:* ABB-BBB. Interview required.

B745 BSc Nursing Studies - Registered Nurse: Child Nursing (3 years)
Duration: 3FT Hon   CRB Check: Required
Entry Requirements: *GCE:* ABB-BBB. Interview required.

3060 Dip Nurse Adult Nursing
Duration: 3FT Dip   CRB Check: Required
Entry Requirements: Contact the institution for details.

S93 SWANSEA UNIVERSITY
SINGLETON PARK
SWANSEA SA2 8PP
t: 01792 295111 f: 01792 295110
e: admissions@swansea.ac.uk
// www.swansea.ac.uk

B720 BMid Midwifery
Duration: 3FT Hon   CRB Check: Required
Entry Requirements: *GCE:* BBB. Interview required.

B702 BN Nursing (Adult)
Duration: 3FT Hon   CRB Check: Required
Entry Requirements: *GCE:* BBC. Interview required.

B740 BN Nursing (Adult) - Carmarthen campus
Duration: 3FT Hon   CRB Check: Required
Entry Requirements: *GCE:* BBC. Interview required.

B703 BN Nursing (Child)
Duration: 3FT Hon   CRB Check: Required
Entry Requirements: *GCE:* BBB. Interview required.

B704 BN Nursing (Mental Health)
Duration: 3FT Hon   CRB Check: Required
Entry Requirements: *GCE:* BBC. Interview required.

B760 BN Nursing (Mental Health) - Carmarthen campus
Duration: 3FT Hon   CRB Check: Required
Entry Requirements: *GCE:* BBC. Interview required.

T20 TEESSIDE UNIVERSITY
MIDDLESBROUGH TS1 3BA
t: 01642 218121 f: 01642 384201
e: registry@tees.ac.uk
// www.tees.ac.uk

B720 BSc Midwifery (Pre-Registration)
Duration: 3FT Hon   CRB Check: Required
Entry Requirements: *GCE:* 260. *IB:* 32. *BTEC SubDip:* D. *BTEC Dip:* DD. *BTEC ExtDip:* DDM. *OCR ND:* D *OCR NED:* D2 Interview required.

B700 BSc Nursing Studies (Adult) (Pre-Registration)
Duration: 3FT Hon   CRB Check: Required
Entry Requirements: *GCE:* 240. *IB:* 24. *BTEC Dip:* DD. *BTEC ExtDip:* MMM. Interview required.

B701 BSc Nursing Studies (Child) (Pre-Registration)
Duration: 3FT Hon   CRB Check: Required
Entry Requirements: *GCE:* 240. *IB:* 24. *BTEC Dip:* DD. *BTEC ExtDip:* MMM. Interview required.

B761 BSc Nursing Studies (Learning Disabilities) (Pre-Registration)
Duration: 3FT Hon   CRB Check: Required
Entry Requirements: *GCE:* 240. *IB:* 24. *BTEC Dip:* DD. *BTEC ExtDip:* MMM. Interview required.

B702 BSc Nursing Studies (Mental Health) (Pre-Registration)
Duration: 3FT Hon   CRB Check: Required
Entry Requirements: *GCE:* 240. *IB:* 24. *BTEC Dip:* DD. *BTEC ExtDip:* MMM. Interview required.

U20 UNIVERSITY OF ULSTER
COLERAINE
CO. LONDONDERRY
NORTHERN IRELAND BT52 1SA
t: 028 7012 4221 f: 028 7012 4908
e: online@ulster.ac.uk
// www.ulster.ac.uk

B740 BSc Nursing (Adult)
Duration: 3FT Hon   CRB Check: Required
Entry Requirements: *GCE:* 280. *IB:* 24. Interview required.

B760 BSc Nursing (Mental Health)
Duration: 3FT Hon   CRB Check: Required
Entry Requirements: *GCE:* 280. *IB:* 24. Interview required.

U40 UNIVERSITY OF THE WEST OF SCOTLAND
PAISLEY
RENFREWSHIRE
SCOTLAND PA1 2BE
t: 0141 848 3727 f: 0141 848 3623
e: admissions@uws.ac.uk
// www.uws.ac.uk

B740 BSc Adult Nursing
Duration: 3FT Ord   CRB Check: Required
Entry Requirements: *GCE:* CD. *SQAH:* CCC. Admissions Test required.

B760 BSc Mental Health Nursing
Duration: 3FT Ord   CRB Check: Required
Entry Requirements: *GCE:* CD. *SQAH:* CCC. Admissions Test required.

B720 BSc Midwifery
Duration: 3FT Ord   CRB Check: Required
Entry Requirements: *GCE:* CD. *SQAH:* BBCC. Interview required.

BR40 MSc Adult Nursing with Registration
Duration: 2FT PMD   CRB Check: Required
Entry Requirements: Admissions Test required.

BR60 MSc Mental Health Nursing with Registration
Duration: 2FT PMD   CRB Check: Required
Entry Requirements: Admissions Test required.

W05 THE UNIVERSITY OF WEST LONDON
ST MARY'S ROAD
EALING
LONDON W5 5RF
t: 0800 036 8888 f: 020 8566 1353
e: learning.advice@uwl.ac.uk
// www.uwl.ac.uk

B740 BSc Adult Nursing
Duration: 3FT Hon   CRB Check: Required
Entry Requirements: *GCE:* 240-260. *IB:* 28. Interview required.

B761 BSc Learning Disabilities Nursing
Duration: 3FT Hon   CRB Check: Required
Entry Requirements: *GCE:* 240-260. *IB:* 28. Interview required.

B760 BSc Mental Health Nursing
Duration: 3FT Hon   CRB Check: Required
Entry Requirements: *GCE:* 240-260. *IB:* 28. Interview required.

B720 BSc Midwifery
Duration: 3FT Hon   CRB Check: Required
Entry Requirements: *GCE:* 300. *IB:* 28. Interview required.

B730 BSc Nursing (Children's Nursing)
Duration: 3FT Hon   CRB Check: Required
Entry Requirements: *GCE:* 240-260. *IB:* 28. Interview required.

BL75 BSc Nursing and Healthcare (top-up)
Duration: 1FT Hon
Entry Requirements: Contact the institution for details.

B721 BSc (Hons) Midwifery (for registered nurses)
Duration: 1.5FT Hon   CRB Check: Required
Entry Requirements: Contact the institution for details.

B742 PGDip Nursing (Adult)
Duration: 2FT GDN   CRB Check: Required
Entry Requirements: Interview required.

BR60 PGDip Nursing (Mental Health)
Duration: 2FT GDN   CRB Check: Required
Entry Requirements: Interview required.

W75 UNIVERSITY OF WOLVERHAMPTON
ADMISSIONS UNIT
MX207, CAMP STREET
WOLVERHAMPTON
WEST MIDLANDS WV1 1AD
t: 01902 321000 f: 01902 321896
e: admissions@wlv.ac.uk
// www.wlv.ac.uk

B740 BNur Adult Nursing
Duration: 3FT Hon   CRB Check: Required
Entry Requirements: Interview required.

B730 BNur Children's Nursing
Duration: 3FT Hon   CRB Check: Required
Entry Requirements: Interview required.

B761 BNur Learning Disability Nursing
Duration: 3FT Hon   CRB Check: Required
Entry Requirements: Interview required.

B760 BNur Mental Health Nursing
Duration: 3FT Hon   CRB Check: Required
Entry Requirements: Interview required.

B721 BSc Midwifery (Shortened Route)
Duration: 1.5FT Hon   CRB Check: Required
Entry Requirements: Contact the institution for details.

B720 BSc Midwifery (leading to Registered Midwife)
Duration: 3FT Hon   CRB Check: Required
Entry Requirements: *GCE:* 200-260. *IB:* 26.   Interview required.

W80 UNIVERSITY OF WORCESTER
HENWICK GROVE
WORCESTER WR2 6AJ
t: 01905 855111 f: 01905 855377
e: admissions@worc.ac.uk
// www.worcester.ac.uk

B720 BSc Midwifery with NMC Registration
Duration: 3FT Hon   CRB Check: Required
Entry Requirements: *GCE:* CC. *IB:* 24. Interview required.

B740 BSc Nursing Studies (Adult) with NMC Registration
Duration: 3FT/3FT Hon/Ord   CRB Check: Required
Entry Requirements: *GCE:* 200. *IB:* 24. Interview required.

B730 BSc Nursing Studies (Child) with NMC Registration
Duration: 3FT/3FT Hon/Ord   CRB Check: Required
Entry Requirements: *GCE:* 240. *IB:* 24. Interview required.

B760 BSc Nursing Studies (Mental Health) with NMC Registration
Duration: 3FT/3FT Hon/Ord   CRB Check: Required
Entry Requirements: *GCE:* 200. *IB:* 24. Interview required.

B790 FdSc Pre-hospital Unscheduled and Emergency Care
Duration: 2FT Fdg   CRB Check: Required
Entry Requirements: *GCE:* 120. *IB:* 24. Interview required.

Y50 THE UNIVERSITY OF YORK
STUDENT RECRUITMENT AND ADMISSIONS
UNIVERSITY OF YORK
HESLINGTON
YORK YO10 5DD
t: 01904 324000 f: 01904 323538
e: ug-admissions@york.ac.uk
// www.york.ac.uk

B720 BA Midwifery
Duration: 3FT Hon   CRB Check: Required
Entry Requirements: *GCE:* BBB. *SQAH:* AABBB. *IB:* 31.

B705 BSc Nursing
Duration: 3FT Hon   CRB Check: Required
Entry Requirements: *GCE:* BBC. *SQAH:* BBBBB. *IB:* 30.

B700 BSc Nursing (Extended Degree)
Duration: 4FT Hon   CRB Check: Required
Entry Requirements: Contact the institution for details.

NUTRITION

A30 UNIVERSITY OF ABERTAY DUNDEE
BELL STREET
DUNDEE DD1 1HG
t: 01382 308080 f: 01382 308081
e: sro@abertay.ac.uk
// www.abertay.ac.uk

BD46 BSc Food, Nutrition and Health
Duration: 4FT Hon
Entry Requirements: *GCE:* CDD. *SQAH:* BBC. *IB:* 26.

CB64 BSc Sport & Exercise Nutrition
Duration: 4FT Hon   CRB Check: Required
Entry Requirements: *GCE:* DDD. *SQAH:* ABB. *IB:* 26. Interview required.

A45 THE COLLEGE OF AGRICULTURE, FOOD AND RURAL ENTERPRISE
GREENMOUNT CAMPUS
45 TIRGRACY ROAD
MUCKAMORE
ANTRIM BT41 4PS
t: 0800 0284291 f: 028 94 426606
e: enquiries@cafre.ac.uk
// www.cafre.ac.uk

DB64 BSc Food Design and Nutrition
Duration: 4FT Hon
Entry Requirements: *GCE:* 200. *SQAH:* AAA-CCC. *SQAAH:* AA-CC.

BD46 FdSc Food, Nutrition and Health
Duration: 2FT Fdg
Entry Requirements: *GCE:* 100. *SQAH:* AA-CC. *SQAAH:* A-C.

B20 BATH SPA UNIVERSITY
NEWTON PARK
NEWTON ST LOE
BATH BA2 9BN
t: 01225 875875 f: 01225 875444
e: enquiries@bathspa.ac.uk
// www.bathspa.ac.uk/clearing

D6B4 BSc Food with Nutrition
Duration: 3FT Hon
Entry Requirements: *GCE:* 220-280. *IB:* 24.

B400 BSc Human Nutrition
Duration: 3FT Hon
Entry Requirements: *GCE:* 220-280. *IB:* 24.

B901 DipHE Diet & Health
Duration: 2FT Dip
Entry Requirements: *GCE:* 220-280. *IB:* 24.

D6BK DipHE Food with Nutrition
Duration: 2FT Dip
Entry Requirements: *GCE:* 220-280. *IB:* 24.

B401 DipHE Human Nutrition
Duration: 2FT Dip
Entry Requirements: *GCE:* 220-280. *IB:* 24.

B25 BIRMINGHAM CITY UNIVERSITY
PERRY BARR
BIRMINGHAM B42 2SU
t: 0121 331 5595 f: 0121 331 7994
// www.bcu.ac.uk

BB94 BSc Health and Well-being (Nutrition Science)
Duration: 3FT Hon   **CRB Check:** Required
Entry Requirements: *GCE:* 240. *IB:* 32. *OCR ND:* D

B50 BOURNEMOUTH UNIVERSITY
TALBOT CAMPUS
FERN BARROW
POOLE
DORSET BH12 5BB
t: 01202 524111
// www.bournemouth.ac.uk

B400 BSc Nutrition
Duration: 3FT Hon
Entry Requirements: *GCE:* 300. *IB:* 31. *BTEC Dip:* DM. *BTEC ExtDip:* DDM. Interview required.

B60 BRADFORD COLLEGE: AN ASSOCIATE COLLEGE OF LEEDS METROPOLITAN UNIVERSITY
GREAT HORTON ROAD
BRADFORD
WEST YORKSHIRE BD7 1AY
t: 01274 433008 f: 01274 431652
e: heregistry@bradfordcollege.ac.uk
// www.bradfordcollege.ac.uk/
university-centre

BB49 BSc Diet, Nutrition & Health
Duration: 3FT Hon   **CRB Check:** Required
Entry Requirements: Interview required.

C20 CARDIFF METROPOLITAN UNIVERSITY (UWIC)
ADMISSIONS UNIT
LLANDAFF CAMPUS
WESTERN AVENUE
CARDIFF CF5 2YB
t: 029 2041 6070 f: 029 2041 6286
e: admissions@cardiffmet.ac.uk
// www.cardiffmet.ac.uk

B402 BSc Human Nutrition and Dietetics
Duration: 4SW Hon   **CRB Check:** Required
Entry Requirements: *GCE:* 300. *IB:* 26. *BTEC ExtDip:* DDD. *OCR NED:* M1 Interview required.

B490 BSc Public Health Nutrition
Duration: 3FT Hon
Entry Requirements: *GCE:* 240. *IB:* 24. *BTEC Dip:* DD. *BTEC ExtDip:* MMM. *OCR ND:* D *OCR NED:* M3

BB49 BSc Public Health Nutrition (4 years inc Foundation)
Duration: 4FT Hon
Entry Requirements: *Foundation:* Pass. *GCE:* 80. *IB:* 24. *BTEC Dip:* PP. *BTEC ExtDip:* PPP. *OCR ND:* P3 *OCR NED:* P3

CB6K BSc Sport Biomedicine & Nutrition (4 yrs inc Foundation)
Duration: 4FT Hon
Entry Requirements: *Foundation:* Pass. *GCE:* 80. *IB:* 24. *BTEC Dip:* PP. *BTEC ExtDip:* PPP. *OCR ND:* P3 *OCR NED:* P3

CB64 BSc Sport Biomedicine and Nutrition (3 years)
Duration: 3FT Hon
Entry Requirements: *GCE:* 240. *IB:* 24. *BTEC Dip:* DD. *BTEC ExtDip:* MMM. *OCR ND:* D *OCR NED:* M3

C30 UNIVERSITY OF CENTRAL LANCASHIRE
PRESTON
LANCS PR1 2HE
t: 01772 201201 f: 01772 894954
e: uadmissions@uclan.ac.uk
// www.uclan.ac.uk

B4C6 BSc Nutrition & Exercise Sciences (Human Nutrition)
Duration: 3FT Hon
Entry Requirements: Contact the institution for details.

B4C1 BSc Nutrition & Exercise Sciences (Personal Fitness Training)
Duration: 3FT Hon
Entry Requirements: Contact the institution for details.

B4C0 BSc Nutrition and Exercise Sciences
Duration: 3FT Hon
Entry Requirements: Contact the institution for details.

C55 UNIVERSITY OF CHESTER
PARKGATE ROAD
CHESTER CH1 4BJ
t: 01244 511000 f: 01244 511300
e: enquiries@chester.ac.uk
// www.chester.ac.uk

B400 BSc Human Nutrition
Duration: 3FT Hon
Entry Requirements: *GCE:* 240-280. *SQAH:* BBBB. *IB:* 26.

B401 BSc Nutrition and Dietetics
Duration: 4FT Hon   **CRB Check:** Required
Entry Requirements: *GCE:* 280-300. *SQAH:* BBBB. *IB:* 28. Interview required.

C85 COVENTRY UNIVERSITY
THE STUDENT CENTRE
COVENTRY UNIVERSITY
1 GULSON RD
COVENTRY CV1 2JH
t: 024 7615 2222 f: 024 7615 2223
e: studentenquiries@coventry.ac.uk
// www.coventry.ac.uk

B410 BSc Dietetics
Duration: 4FT Hon   CRB Check: Required
Entry Requirements: *GCE:* BCC. *SQAH:* BCCCC. *IB:* 28. *BTEC*
ExtDip: DMM. *OCR NED:* M2 Interview required.

BB94 BSc Exercise, Nutrition and Health
Duration: 3FT/4SW Hon
Entry Requirements: *GCE:* CCC. *SQAH:* CCCCC. *IB:* 27. *BTEC*
ExtDip: MMM. *OCR NED:* M3

DB64 BSc Food and Nutrition
Duration: 3FT/4SW Hon
Entry Requirements: *GCE:* CCC. *SQAH:* CCCCC. *IB:* 27. *BTEC*
ExtDip: MMM. *OCR NED:* M3

E42 EDGE HILL UNIVERSITY
ORMSKIRK
LANCASHIRE L39 4QP
t: 01695 657000 f: 01695 584355
e: study@edgehill.ac.uk
// www.edgehill.ac.uk

B400 BSc Nutrition and Health
Duration: 3FT Hon
Entry Requirements: *GCE:* 280. *IB:* 26. *OCR ND:* D *OCR NED:* M2

G14 UNIVERSITY OF GLAMORGAN, CARDIFF AND PONTYPRIDD
ENQUIRIES AND ADMISSIONS UNIT
PONTYPRIDD CF37 1DL
t: 08456 434030 f: 01443 654050
e: enquiries@glam.ac.uk
// www.glam.ac.uk

BL45 BSc Nutrition, Physical Activity and Community Health
Duration: 3FT Hon
Entry Requirements: *GCE:* 220-260. *IB:* 28. *BTEC Dip:* D*D.
BTEC ExtDip: DMM.

G28 UNIVERSITY OF GLASGOW
71 SOUTHPARK AVENUE
UNIVERSITY OF GLASGOW
GLASGOW G12 8QQ
t: 0141 330 6062 f: 0141 330 2961
e: student.recruitment@glasgow.ac.uk
// www.glasgow.ac.uk

BC46 BSc Physiology, Sports Science and Nutrition
Duration: 4FT Hon
Entry Requirements: *GCE:* ABB. *SQAH:* AAAB-BBBB. *IB:* 32.

G42 GLASGOW CALEDONIAN UNIVERSITY
STUDENT RECRUITMENT & ADMISSIONS SERVICE
CITY CAMPUS
COWCADDENS ROAD
GLASGOW G4 0BA
t: 0141 331 3000 f: 0141 331 8676
e: undergraduate@gcu.ac.uk
// www.gcu.ac.uk

B400 BSc Human Nutrition and Dietetics
Duration: 4SW Hon   CRB Check: Required
Entry Requirements: *GCE:* BB-BCC. *SQAH:* BBBB. *IB:* 24. *OCR*
NED: M2 Interview required.

G70 UNIVERSITY OF GREENWICH
GREENWICH CAMPUS
OLD ROYAL NAVAL COLLEGE
PARK ROW
LONDON SE10 9LS
t: 020 8331 9000 f: 020 8331 8145
e: courseinfo@gre.ac.uk
// www.gre.ac.uk

B401 BSc Human Nutrition
Duration: 3FT Hon
Entry Requirements: *GCE:* 300. *IB:* 24.

CB94 BSc Sport Exercise and Nutrition
Duration: 3FT Hon
Entry Requirements: Contact the institution for details.

H12 HARPER ADAMS UNIVERSITY COLLEGE
NEWPORT
SHROPSHIRE TF10 8NB
t: 01952 820280 f: 01952 813210
e: admissions@harper-adams.ac.uk
// www.harper-adams.ac.uk

DB64 BSc Food, Nutrition and Well-Being
Duration: 4SW/4SW Hon/Ord
Entry Requirements: *GCE:* 220-260. *SQAH:* BBBC. Interview
required.

H36 UNIVERSITY OF HERTFORDSHIRE
UNIVERSITY ADMISSIONS SERVICE
COLLEGE LANE
HATFIELD
HERTS AL10 9AB
t: 01707 284800
// www.herts.ac.uk

B410 BSc Dietetics
Duration: 3FT Hon   CRB Check: Required
Entry Requirements: Interview required.

B400 BSc Nutrition
Duration: 3FT Hon
Entry Requirements: Contact the institution for details.

H60 THE UNIVERSITY OF HUDDERSFIELD
QUEENSGATE
HUDDERSFIELD HD1 3DH
t: 01484 473969 f: 01484 472765
e: admissionsandrecords@hud.ac.uk
// www.hud.ac.uk

B4D6 BSc Food, Nutrition and Health
Duration: 4SW Hon
Entry Requirements: GCE: 240.

BB4X BSc Nutrition and Public Health
Duration: 4SW Hon
Entry Requirements: GCE: 240.

K60 KING'S COLLEGE LONDON (UNIVERSITY OF LONDON)
STRAND
LONDON WC2R 2LS
t: 020 7836 5454 f: 020 7848 7171
e: prospective@kcl.ac.uk
// www.kcl.ac.uk/prospectus

B400 BSc Nutrition
Duration: 3FT Hon
Entry Requirements: GCE: ABBb. IB: 34. Interview required.

B401 BSc Nutrition and Dietetics (4 years)
Duration: 4FT Hon   CRB Check: Required
Entry Requirements: GCE: AABb. SQAH: AAABB. IB: 36. Interview required.

K84 KINGSTON UNIVERSITY
STUDENT INFORMATION & ADVICE CENTRE
COOPER HOUSE
40-46 SURBITON ROAD
KINGSTON UPON THAMES KT1 2HX
t: 0844 8552177 f: 020 8547 7080
e: aps@kingston.ac.uk
// www.kingston.ac.uk

BB4X BSc Exercise Nutrition & Health
Duration: 4SW Hon
Entry Requirements: GCE: 220-280.

BB49 BSc Exercise, Nutrition & Health
Duration: 3FT Hon
Entry Requirements: GCE: 220-280.

B400 BSc Nutrition
Duration: 3FT Hon
Entry Requirements: GCE: 200-280.

B402 BSc Nutrition
Duration: 4SW Hon
Entry Requirements: GCE: 200-280.

B401 BSc Nutrition (Foundation)
Duration: 4FT Hon
Entry Requirements: GCE: 60.

L23 UNIVERSITY OF LEEDS
THE UNIVERSITY OF LEEDS
WOODHOUSE LANE
LEEDS LS2 9JT
t: 0113 343 3999
e: admissions@leeds.ac.uk
// www.leeds.ac.uk

DB64 BSc Food Studies and Nutrition
Duration: 3FT/4FT Hon
Entry Requirements: GCE: ABB. SQAAH: ABB. IB: 34.

B400 BSc Nutrition
Duration: 3FT Hon
Entry Requirements: GCE: ABB. SQAAH: ABB. IB: 34.

L24 LEEDS TRINITY UNIVERSITY COLLEGE
BROWNBERRIE LANE
HORSFORTH
LEEDS LS18 5HD
t: 0113 283 7150 f: 0113 283 7222
e: enquiries@leedstrinity.ac.uk
// www.leedstrinity.ac.uk

BD46 BSc Nutrition and Food
Duration: 3FT Hon
Entry Requirements: GCE: 280. IB: 25. OCR ND: D OCR NED: M2

CB64 BSc Sport, Health, Exercise and Nutrition
Duration: 3FT Hon
Entry Requirements: GCE: 280. IB: 25. OCR ND: D OCR NED: M2

L27 LEEDS METROPOLITAN UNIVERSITY
COURSE ENQUIRIES OFFICE
CITY CAMPUS
LEEDS LS1 3HE
t: 0113 81 23113 f: 0113 81 23129
// www.leedsmet.ac.uk

B410 BSc Dietetics
Duration: 4FT Hon   CRB Check: Required
Entry Requirements: *GCE:* BCC. *SQAAH:* BCC. *IB:* 24.

LB44 BSc Public Health Nutrition
Duration: 3FT/4SW Hon   CRB Check: Required
Entry Requirements: *GCE:* 200. *IB:* 26.

L46 LIVERPOOL HOPE UNIVERSITY
HOPE PARK
LIVERPOOL L16 9JD
t: 0151 291 3331 f: 0151 291 3434
e: administration@hope.ac.uk
// www.hope.ac.uk

XB34 BA Education and Nutrition
Duration: 3FT Hon   CRB Check: Required
Entry Requirements: *GCE:* 300-320. *IB:* 25.

LB74 BSc Geography and Nutrition
Duration: 3FT Hon
Entry Requirements: *GCE:* 300-320. *IB:* 25.

BB9L BSc Health and Nutrition
Duration: 3FT Hon
Entry Requirements: *GCE:* 300-320. *IB:* 25.

CB84 BSc Nutrition and Psychology
Duration: 3FT Hon
Entry Requirements: *GCE:* 300-320. *IB:* 25.

B4B9 BSc Nutrition with Health Promotion
Duration: 3FT Hon
Entry Requirements: *GCE:* 300-320. *IB:* 25.

L51 LIVERPOOL JOHN MOORES UNIVERSITY
KINGSWAY HOUSE
HATTON GARDEN
LIVERPOOL L3 2AJ
t: 0151 231 5090 f: 0151 904 6368
e: courses@ljmu.ac.uk
// www.ljmu.ac.uk

DB64 BSc Food and Nutrition
Duration: 3FT Hon
Entry Requirements: *GCE:* 260. Interview required.

L68 LONDON METROPOLITAN UNIVERSITY
166-220 HOLLOWAY ROAD
LONDON N7 8DB
t: 020 7133 4200
e: admissions@londonmet.ac.uk
// www.londonmet.ac.uk

B401 BSc Dietetics and Nutrition (4 years)
Duration: 4FT Hon   CRB Check: Required
Entry Requirements: *GCE:* 300. *IB:* 28. Interview required.

B400 BSc Human Nutrition
Duration: 3FT Hon
Entry Requirements: *GCE:* 240. *IB:* 28.

L75 LONDON SOUTH BANK UNIVERSITY
ADMISSIONS AND RECRUITMENT CENTRE
90 LONDON ROAD
LONDON SE1 6LN
t: 0800 923 8888 f: 020 7815 8273
e: course.enquiry@lsbu.ac.uk
// www.lsbu.ac.uk

BD46 BSc Food and Nutrition
Duration: 3FT Hon
Entry Requirements: *GCE:* 200. *IB:* 24.

B401 BSc Human Nutrition
Duration: 3FT Hon
Entry Requirements: Contact the institution for details.

M40 THE MANCHESTER METROPOLITAN UNIVERSITY
ADMISSIONS OFFICE
ALL SAINTS (GMS)
ALL SAINTS
MANCHESTER M15 6BH
t: 0161 247 2000
// www.mmu.ac.uk

BD46 BSc Food and Nutrition
Duration: 3FT Hon
Entry Requirements: *GCE:* 280. *IB:* 28. *OCR ND:* D *OCR NED:* M3

DB64 BSc Food and Nutrition
Duration: 4SW Hon
Entry Requirements: *GCE:* 280. *IB:* 28. *OCR ND:* D *OCR NED:* M3

B400 BSc Human Nutrition
Duration: 3FT Hon
Entry Requirements: *GCE:* 280. *IB:* 28. *OCR ND:* D *OCR NED:* M3

B402 BSc Human Nutrition
Duration: 4SW Hon
Entry Requirements: *GCE:* 280. *IB:* 28. *OCR ND:* D *OCR NED:* M3

N21 NEWCASTLE UNIVERSITY
KING'S GATE
NEWCASTLE UPON TYNE NE1 7RU
t: 01912083333
// www.ncl.ac.uk

DB64 BSc Food Marketing and Nutrition
Duration: 3FT/4SW Hon
Entry Requirements: *GCE:* AAB. *SQAH:* AAABB. *SQAAH:* ABB.
BTEC ExtDip: DDD.

B4D6 BSc Food and Human Nutrition
Duration: 4SW Hon
Entry Requirements: *GCE:* AAB. *SQAH:* AAABB. *BTEC ExtDip:*
DDD.

BC48 BSc Nutrition and Psychology
Duration: 3FT/4SW Hon
Entry Requirements: *GCE:* AAB. *SQAH:* AAAAB. *IB:* 35. *BTEC
ExtDip:* DDD.

N37 UNIVERSITY OF WALES, NEWPORT
ADMISSIONS
LODGE ROAD
CAERLEON
NEWPORT NP18 3QT
t: 01633 432030 f: 01633 432850
e: admissions@newport.ac.uk
// www.newport.ac.uk

B400 BSc Nutrition
Duration: 3FT Hon   CRB Check: Required
Entry Requirements: Contact the institution for details.

N77 NORTHUMBRIA UNIVERSITY
TRINITY BUILDING
NORTHUMBERLAND ROAD
NEWCASTLE UPON TYNE NE1 8ST
t: 0191 243 7420 f: 0191 227 4561
e: er.admissions@northumbria.ac.uk
// www.northumbria.ac.uk

BD46 BSc Food Science and Nutrition
Duration: 3FT/4SW Hon
Entry Requirements: *GCE:* 280. *SQAH:* BBCCC. *SQAAH:* BCC. *IB:*
25. *OCR ND:* M1 *OCR NED:* P1

B400 BSc Human Nutrition
Duration: 3FT/4SW Hon
Entry Requirements: *GCE:* 280. *SQAH:* BBCCC. *SQAAH:* BCC. *IB:*
25. *OCR ND:* M1 *OCR NED:* P1

CB64 BSc Sport, Exercise and Nutrition
Duration: 3FT Hon
Entry Requirements: *GCE:* 300. *SQAH:* BBBBC. *SQAAH:* BBC. *IB:*
26. *BTEC Dip:* DM. *BTEC ExtDip:* DDM. *OCR ND:* M1 *OCR NED:*
M1

N84 THE UNIVERSITY OF NOTTINGHAM
THE ADMISSIONS OFFICE
THE UNIVERSITY OF NOTTINGHAM
UNIVERSITY PARK
NOTTINGHAM NG7 2RD
t: 0115 951 5151 f: 0115 951 4668
// www.nottingham.ac.uk

B400 BSc Nutrition
Duration: 3FT Hon
Entry Requirements: *GCE:* BBB-BBC. *SQAAH:* BBC-BCC.

B4R9 BSc Nutrition also with a Certificate in European Studies (Biosciences)
Duration: 4FT Hon
Entry Requirements: *GCE:* BBB-BBC. *SQAAH:* BBC-BCC.

B4D6 BSc Nutrition and Food Science
Duration: 3FT Hon
Entry Requirements: *GCE:* BBB-BCC. *SQAAH:* BBC-BCC.

B4RX BSc Nutrition and Food Science also with a Cert in European Studies (Biosciences)
Duration: 4FT Hon
Entry Requirements: *GCE:* BBB-BCC. *SQAAH:* BBB-BCC.

B401 MNutr Nutrition (with state registration in dietetics)
Duration: 4FT Hon   CRB Check: Required
Entry Requirements: *GCE:* ABB-BBB. *SQAAH:* BBB-BBC. Interview
required.

N91 NOTTINGHAM TRENT UNIVERSITY
DRYDEN BUILDING
BURTON STREET
NOTTINGHAM NG1 4BU
t: +44 (0) 115 848 4200 f: +44 (0) 115 848 8869
e: applications@ntu.ac.uk
// www.ntu.ac.uk

CB64 BSc Exercise, Nutrition and Health
Duration: 3FT Hon
Entry Requirements: *GCE:* 260. *BTEC ExtDip:* DMM. *OCR NED:*
M2

O66 OXFORD BROOKES UNIVERSITY
ADMISSIONS OFFICE
HEADINGTON CAMPUS
GIPSY LANE
OXFORD OX3 0BP
t: 01865 483040 f: 01865 483983
e: admissions@brookes.ac.uk
// www.brookes.ac.uk

B401 BSc Nutrition
Duration: 3FT Hon
Entry Requirements: *GCE:* BBC.

P60 PLYMOUTH UNIVERSITY
DRAKE CIRCUS
PLYMOUTH PL4 8AA
t: 01752 585858 f: 01752 588055
e: admissions@plymouth.ac.uk
// www.plymouth.ac.uk

B410 BSc Dietetics
Duration: 3FT Hon   CRB Check: Required
Entry Requirements: *GCE:* 300. *IB:* 31. *OCR ND:* D

CB64 BSc Exercise, Nutrition and Health
Duration: 3FT Hon
Entry Requirements: *GCE:* 280-320. *IB:* 26.

BC46 BSc Nutrition Exercise and Health
Duration: 3FT/4SW Hon
Entry Requirements: *GCE:* 280. *IB:* 26.

Q25 QUEEN MARGARET UNIVERSITY, EDINBURGH
QUEEN MARGARET UNIVERSITY DRIVE
EDINBURGH EH21 6UU
t: 0131474 0000 f: 0131 474 0001
e: admissions@qmu.ac.uk
// www.qmu.ac.uk

B400 BSc Dietetics
Duration: 4FT Hon   CRB Check: Required
Entry Requirements: *GCE:* 200. *IB:* 26.

B403 BSc Nutrition
Duration: 4FT Hon
Entry Requirements: *GCE:* 160. *IB:* 26.

Q75 QUEEN'S UNIVERSITY BELFAST
UNIVERSITY ROAD
BELFAST BT7 1NN
t: 028 9097 3838 f: 028 9097 5151
e: admissions@qub.ac.uk
// www.qub.ac.uk

DB6K BSc Food Quality, Safety and Nutrition
Duration: 3FT Hon
Entry Requirements: *GCE:* BBB-BBCb. *IB:* 32.

BDK6 BSc Food Quality, Safety and Nutrition with Professional Studies
Duration: 4SW Hon
Entry Requirements: *GCE:* BBB-BBCb. *IB:* 32.

R12 THE UNIVERSITY OF READING
THE UNIVERSITY OF READING
PO BOX 217
READING RG6 6AH
t: 0118 378 8619 f: 0118 378 8924
e: student.recruitment@reading.ac.uk
// www.reading.ac.uk

BD46 BSc Nutrition and Food Science
Duration: 3FT Hon
Entry Requirements: *GCE:* 300. Interview required.

BDK6 BSc Nutrition and Food Science with Professional Training
Duration: 4SW Hon
Entry Requirements: *GCE:* 300. Interview required.

B4D6 BSc Nutrition with Food Consumer Sciences
Duration: 3FT Hon
Entry Requirements: *GCE:* 320. Interview required.

B4DP BSc Nutrition with Food Consumer Sciences with Professional Training
Duration: 4FT Hon
Entry Requirements: *GCE:* 320. Interview required.

R36 ROBERT GORDON UNIVERSITY
ROBERT GORDON UNIVERSITY
SCHOOLHILL
ABERDEEN
SCOTLAND AB10 1FR
t: 01224 26 27 28 f: 01224 26 21 47
e: UGOffice@rgu.ac.uk
// www.rgu.ac.uk

B400 BSc Nutrition
Duration: 4FT Hon
Entry Requirements: *GCE:* CC. *SQAH:* BBC. *IB:* 24.

B401 BSc Nutrition and Dietetics
Duration: 4FT Hon   CRB Check: Required
Entry Requirements: *GCE:* CCC. *SQAH:* ABBC. *IB:* 24.

R48 ROEHAMPTON UNIVERSITY
ROEHAMPTON LANE
LONDON SW15 5PU
t: 020 8392 3232 f: 020 8392 3470
e: enquiries@roehampton.ac.uk
// www.roehampton.ac.uk

B400 BSc Nutrition and Health
Duration: 3FT Hon
Entry Requirements: *Foundation:* Distinction. *GCE:* 280. *IB:* 25. *BTEC Dip:* D*D*. *BTEC ExtDip:* DMM. *OCR NED:* M2 Interview required.

S21 SHEFFIELD HALLAM UNIVERSITY
CITY CAMPUS
HOWARD STREET
SHEFFIELD S1 1WB
t: 0114 225 5555 f: 0114 225 2167
e: admissions@shu.ac.uk
// www.shu.ac.uk

DB44 BSc Food and Nutrition
Duration: 3FT/4SW Hon
Entry Requirements: *GCE:* 280.

DB64 BSc Food and Nutrition (Top Up)
Duration: 1FT Hon
Entry Requirements: HND required.

BB49 BSc Nutrition, Health and Lifestyles (Top Up)
Duration: 1FT Hon
Entry Requirements: HND required.

B400 BSc Public Health Nutrition
Duration: 3FT Hon
Entry Requirements: *GCE:* 280.

S64 ST MARY'S UNIVERSITY COLLEGE, TWICKENHAM
WALDEGRAVE ROAD
STRAWBERRY HILL
MIDDLESEX TW1 4SX
t: 020 8240 4029 f: 020 8240 2361
e: admit@smuc.ac.uk
// www.smuc.ac.uk

BBY4 BSc Health, Exercise & Physical Activity and Nutrition
Duration: 3FT Hon
Entry Requirements: *GCE:* 220. *IB:* 28. *OCR ND:* M1 *OCR NED:* P1 Interview required.

B400 BSc Nutrition
Duration: 3FT Hon
Entry Requirements: *GCE:* 220. *IB:* 28. *OCR ND:* M1 *OCR NED:* P1 Interview required.

BC4V BSc Nutrition and Psychology
Duration: 3FT Hon
Entry Requirements: *GCE:* 240. *SQAH:* BBBC. *IB:* 28. *OCR ND:* D *OCR NED:* M3 Interview required.

BC4P BSc Nutrition and Sport Science
Duration: 3FT Hon
Entry Requirements: *GCE:* 240. *SQAH:* BBBC. *IB:* 28. *OCR ND:* D *OCR NED:* M3 Interview required.

S82 UNIVERSITY CAMPUS SUFFOLK (UCS)
WATERFRONT BUILDING
NEPTUNE QUAY
IPSWICH
SUFFOLK IP4 1QJ
t: 01473 338833 f: 01473 339900
e: info@ucs.ac.uk
// www.ucs.ac.uk

BB49 BSc Nutrition & Human Health
Duration: 3FT Hon
Entry Requirements: *GCE:* 280. *IB:* 28. *BTEC ExtDip:* DMM.

B401 BSc Nutrition and Human Health (with Science Foundation Year)
Duration: 4FT Hon
Entry Requirements: *GCE:* 280. *IB:* 28. *BTEC ExtDip:* DMM.

S85 UNIVERSITY OF SURREY
STAG HILL
GUILDFORD
SURREY GU2 7XH
t: +44(0)1483 689305 f: +44(0)1483 689388
e: ugteam@surrey.ac.uk
// www.surrey.ac.uk

BD46 BSc Nutrition & Food Science (3 or 4 years)
Duration: 3FT Hon
Entry Requirements: *GCE:* 300. *SQAH:* AABBB. *SQAAH:* AAB. *IB:* 28. Interview required.

B400 BSc Nutrition (3 or 4 years)
Duration: 3FT Hon
Entry Requirements: *GCE:* BBB-BBC. *SQAH:* AABBB. *SQAAH:* AAB. *IB:* 32. Interview required.

B401 BSc Nutrition/Dietetics (4 years)
Duration: 4SW Hon   CRB Check: Required
Entry Requirements: *GCE:* ABB-BBB. *SQAH:* AABBB. *SQAAH:* AAB. *IB:* 34. Interview required.

T20 TEESSIDE UNIVERSITY
MIDDLESBROUGH TS1 3BA
t: 01642 218121 f: 01642 384201
e: registry@tees.ac.uk
// www.tees.ac.uk

BB49 BSc Food, Nutrition and Health Science
Duration: 3FT/4SW Hon
Entry Requirements: *GCE:* 260-280. *IB:* 30. *BTEC SubDip:* M. *BTEC Dip:* D*D*. *BTEC ExtDip:* DDM. Interview required.

T80 UNIVERSITY OF WALES TRINITY SAINT DAVID
COLLEGE ROAD
CARMARTHEN SA31 3EP
t: 01267 676767 f: 01267 676766
e: registry@trinitysaintdavid.ac.uk
// www.tsd.ac.uk

BC46 BA Health & Exercise and Sports Studies
Duration: 3FT Hon
Entry Requirements: *GCE:* 180-360. *IB:* 26. Interview required.

LB54 BSc Health, Nutrition and Lifestyle
Duration: 3FT Hon
Entry Requirements: *GCE:* 180-360. *IB:* 26. Interview required.

T85 TRURO AND PENWITH COLLEGE
TRURO COLLEGE
COLLEGE ROAD
TRURO
CORNWALL TR1 3XX
t: 01872 267122 f: 01872 267526
e: heinfo@trurocollege.ac.uk
// www.truro-penwith.ac.uk

BB94 FdSc Health and Nutrition
Duration: 2FT Fdg
Entry Requirements: *GCE:* 60. *IB:* 24. *BTEC Dip:* MP. *BTEC ExtDip:* PPP. Interview required.

U20 UNIVERSITY OF ULSTER
COLERAINE
CO. LONDONDERRY
NORTHERN IRELAND BT52 1SA
t: 028 7012 4221 f: 028 7012 4908
e: online@ulster.ac.uk
// www.ulster.ac.uk

B460 BSc Dietetics
Duration: 4SW Hon   CRB Check: Required
Entry Requirements: *GCE:* BBB. *IB:* 25. Admissions Test required.

B450 BSc Food and Nutrition with DPP/DIAS
Duration: 4SW Hon
Entry Requirements: *GCE:* 240. *IB:* 24.

B400 BSc Human Nutrition
Duration: 4SW Hon
Entry Requirements: *GCE:* 260. *IB:* 24.

W50 UNIVERSITY OF WESTMINSTER
2ND FLOOR, CAVENDISH HOUSE
101 NEW CAVENDISH STREET,
LONDON W1W 6XH
t: 020 7915 5511
e: course-enquiries@westminster.ac.uk
// www.westminster.ac.uk

B401 BSc Human Nutrition
Duration: 3FT Hon
Entry Requirements: *GCE:* CCD. *SQAH:* CCCC. *IB:* 26. Interview required.

BC46 BSc Human Nutrition (Nutrition & Exercise Science)
Duration: 3FT Hon
Entry Requirements: *GCE:* CCD. *SQAH:* CCCC. *IB:* 26. Interview required.

BCK6 BSc Human Nutrition (Nutrition and Exercise Science) with Foundation
Duration: 4FT Hon
Entry Requirements: *GCE:* CCD. *SQAH:* CCCC. *IB:* 26. Interview required.

B408 BSc Human Nutrition with Foundation
Duration: 4FT Hon
Entry Requirements: *GCE:* CCD. *SQAH:* CCCC. *IB:* 26. Interview required.

W80 UNIVERSITY OF WORCESTER
HENWICK GROVE
WORCESTER WR2 6AJ
t: 01905 855111 f: 01905 855377
e: admissions@worc.ac.uk
// www.worcester.ac.uk

BL45 BA/BSc Human Nutrition and Social Welfare
Duration: 3FT Hon
Entry Requirements: Contact the institution for details.

BCK6 BA/BSc Human Nutrition and Sports Studies
Duration: 3FT Hon
Entry Requirements: Contact the institution for details.

CBC4 BSc Human Biology and Human Nutrition
Duration: 3FT Hon
Entry Requirements: *Foundation:* Merit. *GCE:* 240-280. *IB:* 24. *OCR ND:* D *OCR NED:* M3

LB74 BSc Human Geography and Human Nutrition
Duration: 3FT Hon
Entry Requirements: Contact the institution for details.

B400 BSc Human Nutrition
Duration: 3FT Hon
Entry Requirements: *GCE:* 240-280. *IB:* 24. *OCR ND:* D *OCR NED:* M3

BCK8 BSc Human Nutrition and Psychology
Duration: 3FT Hon
Entry Requirements: Contact the institution for details.

OTHER HEALTH AND MEDICAL SUBJECTS

A20 THE UNIVERSITY OF ABERDEEN
UNIVERSITY OFFICE
KING'S COLLEGE
ABERDEEN AB24 3FX
t: +44 (0) 1224 273504 f: +44 (0) 1224 272034
e: sras@abdn.ac.uk
// www.abdn.ac.uk/sras

B90A BSc Medical Sciences (International Foundation)
Duration: 4FT Hon
Entry Requirements: Contact the institution for details.

A30 UNIVERSITY OF ABERTAY DUNDEE
BELL STREET
DUNDEE DD1 1HG
t: 01382 308080 f: 01382 308081
e: sro@abertay.ac.uk
// www.abertay.ac.uk

B901 BSc Biomedical Sciences
Duration: 4FT Hon
Entry Requirements: *GCE:* CCC. *SQAH:* BBBC. *IB:* 28.

A60 ANGLIA RUSKIN UNIVERSITY
BISHOP HALL LANE
CHELMSFORD
ESSEX CM1 1SQ
t: 0845 271 3333 f: 01245 251789
e: answers@anglia.ac.uk
// www.anglia.ac.uk

B902 BSc Healthcare Science
Duration: 3FT Hon
Entry Requirements: *GCE:* 180. Interview required.

B912 BSc Public Health
Duration: 3FT Hon
Entry Requirements: *GCE:* 160. *IB:* 24.

B771 FdSc Secondary Care
Duration: 2FT Fdg **CRB Check:** Required
Entry Requirements: *GCE:* 80. *IB:* 24. Interview required.

B06 BANGOR UNIVERSITY
BANGOR UNIVERSITY
BANGOR
GWYNEDD LL57 2DG
t: 01248 388484 f: 01248 370451
e: admissions@bangor.ac.uk
// www.bangor.ac.uk

CB69 BSc Sport, Health and Exercise Sciences
Duration: 3FT Hon
Entry Requirements: *GCE:* 260-300. *IB:* 28.

B20 BATH SPA UNIVERSITY
NEWTON PARK
NEWTON ST LOE
BATH BA2 9BN
t: 01225 875875 f: 01225 875444
e: enquiries@bathspa.ac.uk
// www.bathspa.ac.uk/clearing

BV95 BA/BSc Health Studies/Philosophy & Ethics
Duration: 3FT Hon
Entry Requirements: *GCE:* 220-280. *IB:* 24.

BV9M DipHE Health Studies/Philosophy & Ethics
Duration: 2FT Dip
Entry Requirements: *GCE:* 220-280. *IB:* 24.

B940 FdSc Counselling
Duration: 2FT Fdg **CRB Check:** Required
Entry Requirements: *GCE:* 220-280. *IB:* 24. Interview required.

B22 UNIVERSITY OF BEDFORDSHIRE
PARK SQUARE
LUTON
BEDS LU1 3JU
t: 0844 8482234 f: 01582 489323
e: admissions@beds.ac.uk
// www.beds.ac.uk

BC99 BSc Biomedical Science
Duration: 3FT Hon
Entry Requirements: *Foundation:* Pass. *GCE:* 240. *SQAH:* BBBB-BBBC. *SQAAH:* BCC. *IB:* 24. *OCR ND:* D *OCR NED:* M3

CB89 BSc Psychology, Counselling and Therapies
Duration: 3FT Hon
Entry Requirements: *GCE:* 200.

B25 BIRMINGHAM CITY UNIVERSITY
PERRY BARR
BIRMINGHAM B42 2SU
t: 0121 331 5595 f: 0121 331 7994
// www.bcu.ac.uk

BL95 BSc Health and Well-being (Individuals and Communities)
Duration: 3FT Hon   CRB Check: Required
Entry Requirements: *GCE:* 240. *IB:* 32. *OCR ND:* D

B990 DipHE Operating Department Practice
Duration: 2FT Dip   CRB Check: Required
Entry Requirements: *GCE:* 180. *SQAAH:* CCCCC. *IB:* 24. Interview required.

B32 THE UNIVERSITY OF BIRMINGHAM
EDGBASTON
BIRMINGHAM B15 2TT
t: 0121 415 8900 f: 0121 414 7159
e: admissions@bham.ac.uk
// www.birmingham.ac.uk

B900 BMedSc Medical Science
Duration: 3FT Hon
Entry Requirements: *GCE:* AAB. *SQAH:* AAABB-AABBB. *SQAAH:* AA.

B40 BLACKBURN COLLEGE
FEILDEN STREET
BLACKBURN BB2 1LH
t: 01254 292594 f: 01254 679647
e: he-admissions@blackburn.ac.uk
// www.blackburn.ac.uk

B990 FdA Counselling with Brief Interventions
Duration: 2FT Fdg   CRB Check: Required
Entry Requirements: Contact the institution for details.

B940 FdA Counselling with Coaching and Mentoring
Duration: 2FT Fdg   CRB Check: Required
Entry Requirements: Contact the institution for details.

BC96 FdA Health and Personal Training
Duration: 2FT Fdg
Entry Requirements: *GCE:* 80.

B44 UNIVERSITY OF BOLTON
DEANE ROAD
BOLTON BL3 5AB
t: 01204 903903 f: 01204 399074
e: enquiries@bolton.ac.uk
// www.bolton.ac.uk

CB89 BSc Counselling & Psychology
Duration: 3FT Hon
Entry Requirements: *GCE:* 300. Interview required.

B50 BOURNEMOUTH UNIVERSITY
TALBOT CAMPUS
FERN BARROW
POOLE
DORSET BH12 5BB
t: 01202 524111
// www.bournemouth.ac.uk

CB69 BSc Exercise Science (Health and Rehabilitation)
Duration: 3FT Hon
Entry Requirements: *GCE:* 300. *IB:* 31. *BTEC Dip:* DM. *BTEC ExtDip:* DDM. Interview required.

B930 BSc Occupational Therapy
Duration: 3FT Hon   CRB Check: Required
Entry Requirements: *GCE:* 320. *IB:* 32. *BTEC Dip:* DM. *BTEC ExtDip:* DDM. Interview required.

B991 DipHE Operating Department Practice
Duration: 2FT Dip   CRB Check: Required
Entry Requirements: *GCE:* 260. *IB:* 28. *BTEC Dip:* D*D. *BTEC ExtDip:* DMM. Interview required.

B780 FdSc Paramedic Science
Duration: 2FT Fdg   CRB Check: Required
Entry Requirements: *GCE:* 280. *IB:* 30. Interview required.

B56 THE UNIVERSITY OF BRADFORD
RICHMOND ROAD
BRADFORD
WEST YORKSHIRE BD7 1DP
t: 0800 073 1225 f: 01274 235585
e: course-enquiries@bradford.ac.uk
// www.bradford.ac.uk

B990 BSc Clinical Sciences
Duration: 3FT Hon   CRB Check: Required
Entry Requirements: *GCE:* 300. *IB:* 26. Interview required.

B991 BSc Clinical Sciences/Medicine Foundation (Year 0)
Duration: 4FT Hon   CRB Check: Required
Entry Requirements: *GCE:* 200. *IB:* 24. Interview required.

FB49 BSc Forensic and Medical Sciences
Duration: 3FT Hon
Entry Requirements: *GCE:* 260. *IB:* 24.

FBK9 BSc Forensic and Medical Sciences (4 years)
Duration: 4SW Hon
Entry Requirements: *GCE:* 260. *IB:* 24.

BL95 BSc Health, Wellbeing and Social Care
Duration: 1FT Deg
Entry Requirements: Contact the institution for details.

BL9M BSc Health, Wellbeing and Social Care
Duration: 3FT Hon
Entry Requirements: *GCE:* 220.

B930 BSc Occupational Therapy
Duration: 3FT Hon   CRB Check: Required
Entry Requirements: *GCE:* 280. *IB:* 25. Interview required.

C8B9 BSc Psychology with Counselling
Duration: 3FT Hon
Entry Requirements: *GCE:* 260. *IB:* 24.

FBL9 MSci Forensic and Medical Sciences (4 years)
Duration: 4FT Hon
Entry Requirements: *GCE:* 260. *IB:* 24.

B72 UNIVERSITY OF BRIGHTON
MITHRAS HOUSE 211
LEWES ROAD
BRIGHTON BN2 4AT
t: 01273 644644 f: 01273 642607
e: admissions@brighton.ac.uk
// www.brighton.ac.uk

B940 BSc Biomedical Science
Duration: 3FT/4SW Hon
Entry Requirements: *GCE:* BBB. *IB:* 28.

B780 BSc Paramedic Practice
Duration: 3FT Hon   CRB Check: Required
Entry Requirements: *GCE:* BBB. *IB:* 28. *OCR NED:* M2 Interview required.

B80 UNIVERSITY OF THE WEST OF ENGLAND, BRISTOL
FRENCHAY CAMPUS
COLDHARBOUR LANE
BRISTOL BS16 1QY
t: +44 (0)117 32 83333 f: +44 (0)117 32 82810
e: admissions@uwe.ac.uk
// www.uwe.ac.uk

B920 BSc Occupational Therapy
Duration: 3FT Hon   CRB Check: Required
Entry Requirements: *GCE:* 340. Interview required.

B999 BSc Professional Studies (Top-up)
Duration: 1FT Hon
Entry Requirements: Contact the institution for details.

B917 BSc Public and Environmental Health
Duration: 1FT Hon
Entry Requirements: *GCE:* 160.

B990 BSc Specialist Practice (Top-up)
Duration: 1FT Hon
Entry Requirements: HND required.

BC96 BSc Sports Therapy and Rehabilitation
Duration: 3FT Hon   CRB Check: Required
Entry Requirements: *GCE:* 340. Interview required.

B900 FYr Health Professionals (Foundation Year)
Duration: 1FT FYr   CRB Check: Required
Entry Requirements: Interview required.

BCF0 FYr Science Foundation (Year 0) option - Environmental Science
Duration: 1FT FYr
Entry Requirements: *GCE:* 80-120.

BCF0 FYr Science Foundation (Year 0) option - Forensic Chemistry
Duration: 1FT FYr
Entry Requirements: *GCE:* 80-120.

BCF0 FYr Science Foundation (Year 0)
Duration: 1FT FYr
Entry Requirements: *GCE:* 120.

BCF0 FYr Science Foundation (Year 0) option - Forensic Biology
Duration: 1FT FYr
Entry Requirements: *GCE:* 80-120.

BCF0 FYr Science Foundation (Year 0) option - Psychology
Duration: 1FT FYr
Entry Requirements: *GCE:* 80-120.

BCF0 FYr Science Foundation (Year 0) option - Forensic Science
Duration: 1FT FYr
Entry Requirements: *GCE:* 80-120.

BCF0 FYr Science Foundation (Year 0) option - Biomedical Sciences
Duration: 1FT FYr
Entry Requirements: *GCE:* 80-120.

BCF0 FYr Science Foundation (Year 0) option - Biological Sciences
Duration: 1FT FYr
Entry Requirements: *GCE:* 80-120.

BCF0 FYr Science Foundation (Year 0) option - Conservation Biology
Duration: 1FT FYr
Entry Requirements: *GCE:* 80-120.

BCF0 FYr Science Foundation (Year 0) option - Human Biology
Duration: 1FT FYr
Entry Requirements: *GCE:* 80-120.

B901 FdSc Health Care Practice
Duration: 2FT Hon
Entry Requirements: *GCE:* 80.

B780 FdSc Paramedic Science
Duration: 2FT Fdg
Entry Requirements: *GCE:* 240.

B916 FdSc Public and Environmental Health
Duration: 2FT Fdg
Entry Requirements: *GCE:* 120.

B84 BRUNEL UNIVERSITY
UXBRIDGE
MIDDLESEX UB8 3PH
t: 01895 265265 f: 01895 269790
e: admissions@brunel.ac.uk
// www.brunel.ac.uk

B990 BSc Biomedical Sciences (Human Health)
Duration: 3FT Hon
Entry Requirements: *GCE:* ABB. *SQAAH:* ABB. *IB:* 33. *BTEC ExtDip:* D*DD.

B991 BSc Biomedical Sciences (Human Health) (4 year Thick SW)
Duration: 4SW Hon
Entry Requirements: *GCE:* ABB. *SQAAH:* ABB. *IB:* 33. *BTEC ExtDip:* D*DD.

B920 BSc Occupational Therapy
Duration: 3FT Hon   CRB Check: Required
Entry Requirements: *GCE:* BBB. *SQAAH:* BBB. *IB:* 32. *BTEC ExtDip:* DDD.

B90 THE UNIVERSITY OF BUCKINGHAM
YEOMANRY HOUSE
HUNTER STREET
BUCKINGHAM MK18 1EG
t: 01280 820313 f: 01280 822245
e: info@buckingham.ac.uk
// www.buckingham.ac.uk

B900 CertHE Medical Science
Duration: 1FT Cer
Entry Requirements: Contact the institution for details.

B94 BUCKINGHAMSHIRE NEW UNIVERSITY
QUEEN ALEXANDRA ROAD
HIGH WYCOMBE
BUCKINGHAMSHIRE HP11 2JZ
t: 0800 0565 660 f: 01494 605 023
e: admissions@bucks.ac.uk
// bucks.ac.uk

B990 DipHE Operating Department Practitioner
Duration: 2FT Dip
Entry Requirements: Interview required.

C10 CANTERBURY CHRIST CHURCH UNIVERSITY
NORTH HOLMES ROAD
CANTERBURY
KENT CT1 1QU
t: 01227 782900 f: 01227 782888
e: admissions@canterbury.ac.uk
// www.canterbury.ac.uk

T7B9 BA American Studies with Health Studies
Duration: 3FT Hon
Entry Requirements: *GCE:* 240. *IB:* 24.

MB99 BA Applied Criminology and Health Studies
Duration: 3FT Hon
Entry Requirements: *GCE:* 240. *IB:* 24.

M9B9 BA Applied Criminology with Health Studies
Duration: 3FT Hon
Entry Requirements: *GCE:* 240. *IB:* 24.

G5B9 BA Computing with Health Studies
Duration: 3FT Hon
Entry Requirements: *GCE:* 240. *IB:* 24.

X3B9 BA Early Childhood Studies with Health Studies
Duration: 3FT Hon   CRB Check: Required
Entry Requirements: *GCE:* 240. *IB:* 24.

QB39 BA English Language & Communication and Health Studies
Duration: 3FT Hon
Entry Requirements: *GCE:* 240. *IB:* 24.

Q3B9 BA English Literature with Health Studies
Duration: 3FT Hon
Entry Requirements: *GCE:* 240. *IB:* 24.

W1B9 BA Fine & Applied Arts with Health Studies
Duration: 3FT Hon
Entry Requirements: *GCE:* 240. *IB:* 24.

BX93 BA Health Studies and Early Childhood Studies
Duration: 3FT Hon   CRB Check: Required
Entry Requirements: *GCE:* 240. *IB:* 24.

BW91 BA Health Studies and Fine & Applied Arts
Duration: 3FT Hon
Entry Requirements: *GCE:* 240. *IB:* 24.

BW93 BA Health Studies and Music
Duration: 3FT Hon
Entry Requirements: *GCE:* 240. *IB:* 24.

BL93 BA Health Studies and Sociology & Social Science
Duration: 3FT Hon
Entry Requirements: *GCE:* 240. *IB:* 24.

V1B9 BA History with Health Studies
Duration: 3FT Hon
Entry Requirements: *GCE:* 240. *IB:* 24.

P3B9 BA Media and Communications with Health Studies
Duration: 3FT Hon
Entry Requirements: *GCE:* 240. *IB:* 24.

W3B9 BA Music with Health Studies
Duration: 3FT Hon
Entry Requirements: *GCE:* 240. *IB:* 24.

V6B9 BA Religious Studies with Health Studies
Duration: 3FT Hon
Entry Requirements: *GCE:* 240. *IB:* 24.

L3B9 BA Sociology & Social Science with Health Studies
Duration: 3FT Hon
Entry Requirements: *GCE:* 240. *IB:* 24.

N8B9 BA Tourism & Leisure Studies with Health Studies
Duration: 3FT Hon
Entry Requirements: *GCE:* 240. *IB:* 24.

TRB9 BA/BSc American Studies with Health Studies (With a Year in USA)
Duration: 4FT Hon
Entry Requirements: Contact the institution for details.

N1B9 BA/BSc Business Studies with Health Studies
Duration: 3FT Hon
Entry Requirements: *GCE:* 240. *IB:* 24.

G4BX BA/BSc Digital Media with Health Studies
Duration: 3FT Hon
Entry Requirements: *GCE:* 240. *IB:* 24.

Q3BX BA/BSc English Language & Communication with Health Studies
Duration: 3FT Hon
Entry Requirements: *GCE:* 240. *IB:* 24.

N1BX BA/BSc Entrepreneurship with Health Studies
Duration: 3FT Hon
Entry Requirements: *GCE:* 240. *IB:* 24.

R1B9 BA/BSc French with Health Studies
Duration: 3FT Hon
Entry Requirements: Contact the institution for details.

L7B9 BA/BSc Geography with Health Studies
Duration: 3FT Hon
Entry Requirements: *GCE:* 240. *IB:* 24.

BT97 BA/BSc Health Studies and American Studies
Duration: 3FT Hon
Entry Requirements: *GCE:* 240. *IB:* 24.

BN91 BA/BSc Health Studies and Business Studies
Duration: 3FT Hon
Entry Requirements: *GCE:* 240. *IB:* 24.

BG95 BA/BSc Health Studies and Computing
Duration: 3FT Hon
Entry Requirements: *GCE:* 240. *IB:* 24.

BQ93 BA/BSc Health Studies and English Literature
Duration: 3FT Hon
Entry Requirements: *GCE:* 240. *IB:* 24.

BR91 BA/BSc Health Studies and French
Duration: 3FT Hon
Entry Requirements: *GCE:* 240. *IB:* 24.

LB79 BA/BSc Health Studies and Geography
Duration: 3FT Hon
Entry Requirements: *GCE:* 240. *IB:* 24.

BV91 BA/BSc Health Studies and History
Duration: 3FT Hon
Entry Requirements: *GCE:* 240. *IB:* 24.

BN95 BA/BSc Health Studies and Marketing
Duration: 3FT Hon
Entry Requirements: *GCE:* 240. *IB:* 24.

BP93 BA/BSc Health Studies and Media and Communications
Duration: 3FT Hon
Entry Requirements: *GCE:* 240. *IB:* 24.

BC98 BA/BSc Health Studies and Psychology
Duration: 3FT Hon
Entry Requirements: *GCE:* 260. *IB:* 24.

BV96 BA/BSc Health Studies and Religious Studies
Duration: 3FT Hon
Entry Requirements: *GCE:* 240. *IB:* 24.

BN98 BA/BSc Health Studies and Tourism & Leisure Studies
Duration: 3FT Hon
Entry Requirements: *GCE:* 240. *IB:* 24.

B9T7 BA/BSc Health Studies with American Studies
Duration: 3FT Hon
Entry Requirements: *GCE:* 240. *IB:* 24.

B9M9 BA/BSc Health Studies with Applied Criminology
Duration: 3FT Hon
Entry Requirements: *GCE:* 240. *IB:* 24.

B9GL BA/BSc Health Studies with Digital Media
Duration: 3FT Hon
Entry Requirements: *GCE:* 240. *IB:* 24.

B9X3 BA/BSc Health Studies with Early Childhood Studies
Duration: 3FT Hon   CRB Check: Required
Entry Requirements: *GCE:* 240. *IB:* 24.

B9QH BA/BSc Health Studies with English Language & Communication
Duration: 3FT Hon
Entry Requirements: *GCE:* 240. *IB:* 24.

B9Q3 BA/BSc Health Studies with English Literature
Duration: 3FT Hon
Entry Requirements: *GCE:* 240. *IB:* 24.

B9NC BA/BSc Health Studies with Entrepreneurship
Duration: 3FT Hon
Entry Requirements: *GCE:* 240. *IB:* 24.

B9W1 BA/BSc Health Studies with Fine & Applied Arts
Duration: 3FT Hon
Entry Requirements: *GCE:* 240. *IB:* 24.

B9R1 BA/BSc Health Studies with French
Duration: 3FT Hon
Entry Requirements: *GCE:* 240. *IB:* 24.

B9V1 BA/BSc Health Studies with History
Duration: 3FT Hon
Entry Requirements: *GCE:* 240. *IB:* 24.

B9M2 BA/BSc Health Studies with Legal Studies
Duration: 3FT Hon
Entry Requirements: *GCE:* 240. *IB:* 24.

B9P3 BA/BSc Health Studies with Media and Communications
Duration: 3FT Hon
Entry Requirements: *GCE:* 240. *IB:* 24.

B9W3 BA/BSc Health Studies with Music
Duration: 3FT Hon
Entry Requirements: *GCE:* 240. *IB:* 24.

B9V6 BA/BSc Health Studies with Religious Studies
Duration: 3FT Hon
Entry Requirements: *GCE:* 240. *IB:* 24.

B9L3 BA/BSc Health Studies with Sociology & Social Science
Duration: 3FT Hon
Entry Requirements: *GCE:* 240. *IB:* 24.

B9VP BA/BSc Health Studies with Theology
Duration: 3FT Hon
Entry Requirements: *GCE:* 240. *IB:* 24.

B9N8 BA/BSc Health Studies with Tourism & Leisure Studies
Duration: 3FT Hon
Entry Requirements: *GCE:* 240. *IB:* 24.

M2B9 BA/BSc Legal Studies with Health Studies
Duration: 3FT Hon
Entry Requirements: *GCE:* 240. *IB:* 24.

VB69 BA/BSc Theology and Health Studies
Duration: 3FT Hon
Entry Requirements: *GCE:* 240. *IB:* 24.

V6BX BA/BSc Theology with Health Studies
Duration: 3FT Hon
Entry Requirements: *GCE:* 240. *IB:* 24.

D3B9 BSc Animal Science with Health Studies
Duration: 3FT Hon
Entry Requirements: *GCE:* 240. *IB:* 24.

G5BX BSc Business Computing with Health Studies
Duration: 3FT Hon
Entry Requirements: *GCE:* 240. *IB:* 24.

BL95 BSc Health Promotion
Duration: 3FT Hon
Entry Requirements: *GCE:* 240. *IB:* 24.

B900 BSc Health Studies
Duration: 3FT Hon
Entry Requirements: *GCE:* 240. *IB:* 24.

B901 BSc Health Studies 'International Only'
Duration: 4FT Hon
Entry Requirements: Interview required.

BD93 BSc Health Studies and Animal Science
Duration: 3FT Hon
Entry Requirements: *GCE:* 240. *IB:* 24.

BG9M BSc Health Studies and Business Computing
Duration: 3FT Hon
Entry Requirements: *GCE:* 240. *IB:* 24.

BG94 BSc Health Studies and Digital Media
Duration: 3FT Hon
Entry Requirements: *GCE:* 240. *IB:* 24.

BQ9H BSc Health Studies and English Language & Communication
Duration: 3FT Hon
Entry Requirements: *GCE:* 240. *IB:* 24.

BN9C BSc Health Studies and Entrepreneurship
Duration: 3FT Hon
Entry Requirements: *GCE:* 240. *IB:* 24.

BG9K BSc Health Studies and Internet Computing
Duration: 3FT Hon
Entry Requirements: *GCE:* 240. *IB:* 24.

BM92 BSc Health Studies and Legal Studies
Duration: 3FT Hon
Entry Requirements: *GCE:* 240. *IB:* 24.

B9D3 BSc Health Studies with Animal Science
Duration: 3FT Hon
Entry Requirements: *GCE:* 240. *IB:* 24.

B9C9 BSc Health Studies with Biosciences
Duration: 3FT Hon
Entry Requirements: *GCE:* 240. *IB:* 24.

B9CX BSc Health Studies with Biosciences (with Foundation Year)
Duration: 4FT Hon
Entry Requirements: Contact the institution for details.

B9G5 BSc Health Studies with Business Computing
Duration: 3FT Hon
Entry Requirements: *GCE:* 240. *IB:* 24.

B9N1 BSc Health Studies with Business Studies
Duration: 3FT Hon
Entry Requirements: *GCE:* 240. *IB:* 24.

B9GK BSc Health Studies with Computing
Duration: 3FT Hon
Entry Requirements: *GCE:* 240. *IB:* 24.

B9F8 BSc Health Studies with Geography
Duration: 3FT Hon
Entry Requirements: *GCE:* 240. *IB:* 24.

B9G4 BSc Health Studies with Internet Computing
Duration: 3FT Hon
Entry Requirements: *GCE:* 240. *IB:* 24.

B9N5 BSc Health Studies with Marketing
Duration: 3FT Hon
Entry Requirements: *GCE:* 240. *IB:* 24.

B9C8 BSc Health Studies with Psychology
Duration: 3FT Hon
Entry Requirements: *GCE:* 260. *IB:* 24.

G4BY BSc Internet Computing with Health Studies
Duration: 3FT Hon
Entry Requirements: *GCE:* 240. *IB:* 24.

N5B9 BSc Marketing with Health Studies
Duration: 3FT Hon
Entry Requirements: *GCE:* 240. *IB:* 24.

B920 BSc Occupational Therapy
Duration: 3FT Hon   CRB Check: Required
Entry Requirements: *GCE:* 240. *IB:* 24. Interview required.

B991 BSc Operating Department Practice
Duration: 3FT Hon   CRB Check: Required
Entry Requirements: *GCE:* 240. *IB:* 24. Interview required.

B780 BSc Paramedic Science
Duration: 3FT Hon   CRB Check: Required
Entry Requirements: *GCE:* 300. *IB:* 26. Interview required.

C8B9 BSc Psychology with Health Studies
Duration: 3FT Hon
Entry Requirements: *GCE:* 260. *IB:* 24.

BL9M BSc Public Health
Duration: 3FT Hon
Entry Requirements: *GCE:* 240. *IB:* 24.

C15 CARDIFF UNIVERSITY
PO BOX 927
30-36 NEWPORT ROAD
CARDIFF CF24 0DE
t: 029 2087 9999 f: 029 2087 6138
e: admissions@cardiff.ac.uk
// www.cardiff.ac.uk

BH99 BEng Medical Engineering (Year in Industry)
Duration: 4SW Hon
Entry Requirements: *GCE:* AAB. *IB:* 32.

BC9R BSc Biomedical Science (Standard Route Including Professional Training Year)
Duration: 4SW Hon
Entry Requirements: *GCE:* AAB-ABB. *SQAH:* AAABB-AABBB.
SQAAH: AAB-ABB. *IB:* 34. *OCR NED:* D1

B901 BSc Biomedical Science (Standard Route w Preliminary Yr & Professional Training Yr)
Duration: 5SW Hon
Entry Requirements: *GCE:* AAB-ABB. *SQAAH:* AAB-ABB. *IB:* 34.

B900 BSc Biomedical Science (Standard Route) (Including Preliminary Year)
Duration: 4FT Hon
Entry Requirements: *GCE:* AAB-ABB. *SQAAH:* AAB-ABB. *IB:* 34.

BC97 BSc Biomedical Sciences (Standard Route)
Duration: 3FT Hon
Entry Requirements: *GCE:* AAB-ABB. *SQAH:* AAABB-AABBB. *SQAAH:* AAB-ABB. *IB:* 34. *OCR NED:* D1

B920 BSc Occupational Therapy
Duration: 3FT Hon   CRB Check: Required
Entry Requirements: *GCE:* ABB. *SQAH:* AABBB. *SQAAH:* ABB. *IB:* 27. Interview required.

B990 DipHE Operating Department Practice
Duration: 2FT Dip   CRB Check: Required
Entry Requirements: *GCE:* CCC. *IB:* 24. Interview required.
Admissions Test required.

HB99 MEng Medical Engineering (Year in Industry)
Duration: 5SW Hon
Entry Requirements: *GCE:* AAB. *SQAAH:* AAB. Interview required.
Admissions Test required.

C20 CARDIFF METROPOLITAN UNIVERSITY (UWIC)
ADMISSIONS UNIT
LLANDAFF CAMPUS
WESTERN AVENUE
CARDIFF CF5 2YB
t: 029 2041 6070 f: 029 2041 6286
e: admissions@cardiffmet.ac.uk
// www.cardiffmet.ac.uk

XB39 BA Educational Studies and Sport & Physical Activity
Duration: 3FT Hon   CRB Check: Required
Entry Requirements: *GCE:* 260. *IB:* 24. *BTEC ExtDip:* DMM. *OCR NED:* M2

B900 BSc Biomedical Science (3 years)
Duration: 3FT/4SW Hon
Entry Requirements: *GCE:* 260-280. *IB:* 24. *BTEC ExtDip:* DMM. *OCR NED:* M2

B902 BSc Biomedical Science (4 years including Foundation)
Duration: 4FT Hon
Entry Requirements: *Foundation:* Pass. *GCE:* 80. *IB:* 24. *BTEC Dip:* PP. *BTEC ExtDip:* PPP. *OCR ND:* P3 *OCR NED:* P3

B910 BSc Environmental Health (3 years)
Duration: 3FT Hon
Entry Requirements: *GCE:* 220-240. *IB:* 24. *BTEC Dip:* DD. *BTEC ExtDip:* MMM. *OCR ND:* D *OCR NED:* M3

B911 BSc Environmental Health (4 yrs including Foundation)
Duration: 4FT Hon
Entry Requirements: *Foundation:* Pass. *GCE:* 80. *IB:* 24. *BTEC Dip:* PP. *BTEC ExtDip:* PPP. *OCR ND:* P3 *OCR NED:* P3

B901 BSc Health Sciences (with Foundation Year)
Duration: 4FT/5SW Hon
Entry Requirements: *Foundation:* Pass. *GCE:* 80. *IB:* 24. *BTEC Dip:* PP. *BTEC ExtDip:* PPP. *OCR ND:* P3 *OCR NED:* P3

C30 UNIVERSITY OF CENTRAL LANCASHIRE
PRESTON
LANCS PR1 2HE
t: 01772 201201 f: 01772 894954
e: uadmissions@uclan.ac.uk
// www.uclan.ac.uk

BC98 BA Counselling and Psychotherapy Studies
Duration: 3FT Hon
Entry Requirements: *GCE:* 240. *IB:* 28. *OCR ND:* D *OCR NED:* M3

BL95 BA Health and Social Change
Duration: 3FT Hon
Entry Requirements: *GCE:* 200. *IB:* 24. *OCR ND:* M1 *OCR NED:* P1

B940 BSc Biomedical Sciences
Duration: 3FT Hon
Entry Requirements: *GCE:* 240-260. *SQAH:* BBBB-BBBC. *SQAAH:* AAA. *IB:* 28. *OCR ND:* D *OCR NED:* M3

B991 BSc Operating Department Practice
Duration: 3FT Hon   CRB Check: Required
Entry Requirements: Contact the institution for details.

C8B9 BSc Psychology and Counselling & Psychotherapy
Duration: 3FT Hon
Entry Requirements: *Foundation:* Distinction. *GCE:* 260-300. *IB:* 25. *BTEC Dip:* D*D*. *BTEC ExtDip:* DMM. *OCR NED:* M2

B901 BSc Sexual Health Studies
Duration: 3FT Hon
Entry Requirements: *GCE:* 240. *IB:* 28. *OCR ND:* D *OCR NED:* M3

CB69 BSc Strength and Conditioning
Duration: 3FT Hon
Entry Requirements: *GCE:* 260. *OCR ND:* D *OCR NED:* M2

B781 DipHE Paramedic Practice
Duration: 2FT Dip   CRB Check: Required
Entry Requirements: *GCE:* 240. *OCR ND:* D *OCR NED:* M3
Interview required.

BC96 FdA Health & Personal Training
Duration: 2FT Fdg
Entry Requirements: *GCE:* 80.

C55 UNIVERSITY OF CHESTER
PARKGATE ROAD
CHESTER CH1 4BJ
t: 01244 511000 f: 01244 511300
e: enquiries@chester.ac.uk
// www.chester.ac.uk

LC58 BA Counselling Skills and Psychology
Duration: 3FT Hon
Entry Requirements: *Foundation:* Pass. *GCE:* 260-300. *SQAH:* BBBB. *IB:* 28.

B940 BSc Biomedical Sciences
Duration: 3FT Hon
Entry Requirements: *GCE:* 240-280. *SQAH:* BBBB. *IB:* 26.

C58 UNIVERSITY OF CHICHESTER
BISHOP OTTER CAMPUS
COLLEGE LANE
CHICHESTER
WEST SUSSEX PO19 6PE
t: 01243 816002 f: 01243 816161
e: admissions@chi.ac.uk
// www.chiuni.ac.uk

CB69 BSc Sports Therapy
Duration: 3FT Hon
Entry Requirements: *GCE:* 300. *SQAAH:* BBB. *IB:* 32. *BTEC Dip:* DD. *BTEC ExtDip:* DDD.

C75 COLCHESTER INSTITUTE
SHEEPEN ROAD
COLCHESTER
ESSEX CO3 3LL
t: 01206 712777 f: 01206 712800
e: info@colchester.ac.uk
// www.colchester.ac.uk

B940 BA Counselling Studies
Duration: 3FT Hon   CRB Check: Required
Entry Requirements: *GCE:* 120. Interview required.

B941 DipHE Person-centred Counselling
Duration: 2FT Dip   CRB Check: Required
Entry Requirements: *GCE:* 80. Interview required.

C78 CORNWALL COLLEGE
POOL
REDRUTH
CORNWALL TR15 3RD
t: 01209 616161 f: 01209 611612
e: he.admissions@cornwall.ac.uk
// www.cornwall.ac.uk

B941 BA Counselling Studies (top up)
Duration: 1FT Hon
Entry Requirements: Interview required.

B942 Cert Certificate in Advanced Counselling Studies
Duration: 1FT Cer   CRB Check: Required
Entry Requirements: *GCE:* 80-120. Interview required.

B900 FdSc Healthcare Practice
Duration: 2FT Fdg   CRB Check: Required
Entry Requirements: *GCE:* 120. Interview required.

CB69 FdSc Sport, Health & Fitness
Duration: 2FT Fdg   CRB Check: Required
Entry Requirements: *GCE:* 120. *IB:* 24. Interview required. Portfolio required.

C85 COVENTRY UNIVERSITY
THE STUDENT CENTRE
COVENTRY UNIVERSITY
1 GULSON RD
COVENTRY CV1 2JH
t: 024 7615 2222 f: 024 7615 2223
e: studentenquiries@coventry.ac.uk
// www.coventry.ac.uk

B940 BSc Biomedical Science
Duration: 3FT/4SW Hon
Entry Requirements: *GCE:* CCC. *SQAH:* CCCCC. *IB:* 27. *BTEC ExtDip:* MMM. *OCR NED:* M3

B910 BSc Environmental Health
Duration: 3FT/4SW Hon
Entry Requirements: *GCE:* CDD. *SQAH:* CCCCC. *IB:* 27. *BTEC ExtDip:* MMM. *OCR NED:* M3

BB92 BSc Medical and Pharmacological Sciences
Duration: 3FT/4SW Hon
Entry Requirements: *GCE:* CCC. *SQAH:* CCCCC. *IB:* 27. *BTEC ExtDip:* MMM. *OCR NED:* M3

B920 BSc Occupational Therapy
Duration: 3FT Hon   CRB Check: Required
Entry Requirements: *GCE:* BCC. *SQAH:* BCCCC. *BTEC ExtDip:* DMM. *OCR NED:* M2 Interview required.

B930 BSc Occupational Therapy (Post Registration)
Duration: 1FT Hon   CRB Check: Required
Entry Requirements: Interview required.

BC96 BSc Sports Therapy
Duration: 3FT Hon
Entry Requirements: *GCE:* BCC. *SQAH:* BCCCC. *IB:* 28. *BTEC ExtDip:* DMM. *OCR NED:* M2

B990 DipHE Operating Department Practice
Duration: 2FT Dip   CRB Check: Required
Entry Requirements: Interview required.

B780 FdSc Paramedic Science
Duration: 2FT Fdg   CRB Check: Required
Entry Requirements: *GCE:* CDD. *SQAH:* CCDDD. *IB:* 24.   *BTEC ExtDip:* MMP.   *OCR NED:* P1 Interview required.

C99 UNIVERSITY OF CUMBRIA
FUSEHILL STREET
CARLISLE
CUMBRIA CA1 2HH
t: 01228 616234 f: 01228 616235
// www.cumbria.ac.uk

B920 BSc Occupational Therapy
Duration: 3FT Hon   CRB Check: Required
Entry Requirements: *GCE:* 260. *IB:* 28. *OCR NED:* M3 Interview required.

CB69 BSc Sport Rehabilitation
Duration: 3FT Hon
Entry Requirements: *GCE:* 240.

D26 DE MONTFORT UNIVERSITY
THE GATEWAY
LEICESTER LE1 9BH
t: 0116 255 1551 f: 0116 250 6204
e: enquiries@dmu.ac.uk
// www.dmu.ac.uk

B991 BA Health Studies
Duration: 3FT Hon
Entry Requirements: *GCE:* 260. *IB:* 28. *BTEC Dip:* D*D. *BTEC ExtDip:* DMM. *OCR NED:* M2

B940 BSc Biomedical Science
Duration: 3FT/4SW Hon
Entry Requirements: *GCE:* 260. *IB:* 28. *BTEC Dip:* D*D. *BTEC ExtDip:* DDM. *OCR NED:* M2

B902 BSc Medical Science
Duration: 3FT/3FT Hon/Ord
Entry Requirements: *GCE:* 260. *IB:* 28. *BTEC Dip:* D*D. *BTEC ExtDip:* DDM. *OCR NED:* M2

C8B9 BSc Psychology with Health Studies
Duration: 3FT Hon
Entry Requirements: *GCE:* 300. *IB:* 30. *BTEC ExtDip:* DDM. *OCR NED:* M1

B901 BSc Public and Community Health
Duration: 3FT Hon
Entry Requirements: Interview required.

D39 UNIVERSITY OF DERBY
KEDLESTON ROAD
DERBY DE22 1GB
t: 01332 591167 f: 01332 597724
e: askadmissions@derby.ac.uk
// www.derby.ac.uk

B920 BSc Occupational Therapy
Duration: 3FT Hon   CRB Check: Required
Entry Requirements: *GCE:* 280. *IB:* 28. *BTEC Dip:* D*D*. *BTEC ExtDip:* DMM. *OCR NED:* M2 Interview required.

D65 UNIVERSITY OF DUNDEE
NETHERGATE
DUNDEE DD1 4HN
t: 01382 383838 f: 01382 388150
e: contactus@dundee.ac.uk
// www.dundee.ac.uk/admissions/undergraduate/

B900 BSc Biomedical Sciences
Duration: 4FT Hon
Entry Requirements: *GCE:* AAB. *SQAH:* ABBB. *IB:* 30.

CB69 BSc Sports Biomedicine
Duration: 4FT Hon
Entry Requirements: *GCE:* AAB. *SQAH:* ABBB. *IB:* 30.

D86 DURHAM UNIVERSITY
DURHAM UNIVERSITY
UNIVERSITY OFFICE
DURHAM DH1 3HP
t: 0191 334 2000 f: 0191 334 6055
e: admissions@durham.ac.uk
// www.durham.ac.uk

B940 BSc Biomedical Sciences
Duration: 3FT Hon
Entry Requirements: *GCE:* AAB. *SQAH:* AAABB. *SQAAH:* AAB. *IB:* 36.

B941 BSc Biomedical Sciences (4 year SW)
Duration: 4FT Hon
Entry Requirements: *GCE:* AAB. *SQAH:* AAABB. *SQAAH:* AAB. *IB:* 36.

B991 BSc Health and Human Sciences
Duration: 3FT Hon
Entry Requirements: *GCE:* BBB. *SQAH:* BBBBB. *SQAAH:* BBB. *IB:* 32.

E14 UNIVERSITY OF EAST ANGLIA
NORWICH NR4 7TJ
t: 01603 591515 f: 01603 591523
e: admissions@uea.ac.uk
// www.uea.ac.uk

B920 BSc Occupational Therapy
Duration: 3FT Hon CRB Check: Required
Entry Requirements: *GCE:* BBB. *SQAH:* BBBBB. *SQAAH:* BBB. *IB:*
31. *BTEC ExtDip:* DDM. Interview required.

B990 DipHE Operating Department Practice
Duration: 2FT Dip CRB Check: Required
Entry Requirements: *GCE:* EE. *SQAH:* DDDD. *SQAAH:* DD.
Interview required. Admissions Test required.

E28 UNIVERSITY OF EAST LONDON
DOCKLANDS CAMPUS
UNIVERSITY WAY
LONDON E16 2RD
t: 020 8223 3333 f: 020 8223 2978
e: study@uel.ac.uk
// www.uel.ac.uk

PB99 BA Communication Studies/Health Promotion
Duration: 3FT Hon
Entry Requirements: *GCE:* 240. *IB:* 24.

BP9X BA Communication Studies/Health Services Management
Duration: 3FT Hon
Entry Requirements: *GCE:* 240. *IB:* 24.

PB9Y BA Communication Studies/Public Health
Duration: 3FT Hon
Entry Requirements: *GCE:* 240. *IB:* 24.

LB69 BA Cultural Studies/Health Promotion
Duration: 3FT Hon
Entry Requirements: *GCE:* 240. *IB:* 24.

LB6X BA Cultural Studies/Health Services Management
Duration: 3FT Hon
Entry Requirements: *GCE:* 240. *IB:* 24.

LBP9 BA Cultural Studies/Public Health
Duration: 3FT Hon
Entry Requirements: *GCE:* 240. *IB:* 24.

XBH9 BA Education Studies with Health Promotion
Duration: 3FT Hon
Entry Requirements: *GCE:* 240. *IB:* 24.

B990 BA Health Promotion
Duration: 3FT Hon
Entry Requirements: *GCE:* 240. *IB:* 24.

B9PY BA Health Promotion with Communication Studies
Duration: 3FT Hon
Entry Requirements: *GCE:* 240. *IB:* 24.

B9LP BA Health Promotion with Cultural Studies
Duration: 3FT Hon
Entry Requirements: *GCE:* 240. *IB:* 24.

CB8X BA Health Services Management/Psychosocial Studies
Duration: 3FT Hon
Entry Requirements: *GCE:* 240. *IB:* 24.

N1B9 BA International Business with Public Health
Duration: 3FT Hon
Entry Requirements: *GCE:* 240. *IB:* 24.

N5B9 BA Marketing with Health Promotion
Duration: 3FT Hon
Entry Requirements: *GCE:* 240. *IB:* 24.

CB89 BA Psychosocial Studies/Health Promotion
Duration: 3FT Hon
Entry Requirements: *GCE:* 240. *IB:* 24.

CB8Y BA Psychosocial Studies/Public Health
Duration: 3FT Hon
Entry Requirements: *GCE:* 240. *IB:* 24.

X1BX BA Special Needs and Inclusive Education with Public Health
Duration: 3FT Hon
Entry Requirements: *GCE:* 240. *IB:* 24.

L9B9 BA Third World Development with Public Health
Duration: 3FT Hon
Entry Requirements: *GCE:* 240. *IB:* 24.

L5B9 BA Youth & Community Work with Public Health
Duration: 3FT Hon
Entry Requirements: *GCE:* 240. *IB:* 24.

BN96 BA/BSc Clinical Science/Human Resource Management
Duration: 3FT Hon
Entry Requirements: *GCE:* 240. *IB:* 24.

B9P9 BA/BSc Fitness & Health/Communication Studies
Duration: 3FT Hon
Entry Requirements: *GCE:* 240. *IB:* 24.

BW98 BA/BSc Fitness & Health/Creative & Professional Writing
Duration: 3FT Hon
Entry Requirements: *GCE:* 240. *IB:* 24.

BV91 BA/BSc Health Promotion/History
Duration: 3FT Hon
Entry Requirements: *GCE:* 240. *IB:* 24.

BN9P BA/BSc Public Health/Human Resource Management
Duration: 3FT Hon
Entry Requirements: *GCE:* 240. *IB:* 24.

H6B9 BEng Electrical & Electronic Engineering with Health Promotion
Duration: 3FT Hon
Entry Requirements: *GCE:* 240. *IB:* 26.

C7B9 BSc Biochemistry with Health Promotion
Duration: 3FT Hon
Entry Requirements: *GCE:* 240. *IB:* 24.

B940 BSc Biomedical Sciences
Duration: 4SW Hon
Entry Requirements: *GCE:* 240. *IB:* 26.

GB5X BSc Business Information Systems/Health Promotion
Duration: 3FT Hon
Entry Requirements: *GCE:* 240. *IB:* 24.

GB59 BSc Business Information Systems/Health Services Management
Duration: 3FT Hon
Entry Requirements: *GCE:* 240. *IB:* 24.

GB5Y BSc Business Information Systems/Public Health
Duration: 3FT Hon
Entry Requirements: *GCE:* 240. *IB:* 24.

B9C7 BSc Clinical Science with Biochemistry
Duration: 3FT Hon
Entry Requirements: *GCE:* 240. *IB:* 24.

B9BC BSc Clinical Science with Medical Physiology
Duration: 3FT Hon
Entry Requirements: *GCE:* 240. *IB:* 24.

B9CV BSc Clinical Science with Psychology
Duration: 3FT Hon
Entry Requirements: *GCE:* 240. *IB:* 24.

B9L4 BSc Clinical Science with Public Health
Duration: 3FT Hon
Entry Requirements: *GCE:* 240. *IB:* 24.

BC95 BSc Clinical Science/Immunology
Duration: 3FT Hon
Entry Requirements: *GCE:* 240. *IB:* 24.

G4BX BSc Computer Networks with Health Promotion
Duration: 3FT Hon
Entry Requirements: *GCE:* 240. *IB:* 24.

G4BY BSc Computer Networks with Public Health
Duration: 3FT Hon
Entry Requirements: *GCE:* 240. *IB:* 24.

IB19 BSc Computing and Health Promotion
Duration: 3FT Hon
Entry Requirements: *GCE:* 240. *IB:* 24.

IBC9 BSc Computing and Health Services Management
Duration: 3FT Hon
Entry Requirements: *GCE:* 240. *IB:* 24.

BX92 BSc Counselling and Mentoring
Duration: 3FT Hon
Entry Requirements: *GCE:* 240. *IB:* 24. Interview required.

BC99 BSc Extended Health and BioScience
Duration: 4FT/5SW Hon
Entry Requirements: *GCE:* 120.

B901 BSc Fitness & Health with Health Promotion
Duration: 3FT Hon
Entry Requirements: *GCE:* 240. *IB:* 24.

B992 BSc Fitness and Health
Duration: 3FT Hon
Entry Requirements: *GCE:* 240. *IB:* 24.

B9NM BSc Health Promotion with Advertising
Duration: 3FT Hon
Entry Requirements: *GCE:* 240. *IB:* 24.

B9XH BSc Health Promotion with Early Childhood Studies
Duration: 3FT Hon
Entry Requirements: *GCE:* 240. *IB:* 24.

B9B1 BSc Health Promotion with Human Biology
Duration: 3FT Hon
Entry Requirements: *GCE:* 240. *IB:* 24.

B9N5 BSc Health Promotion with Marketing
Duration: 3FT Hon
Entry Requirements: *GCE:* 240. *IB:* 24.

B9CW BSc Health Promotion with Psychosocial Studies
Duration: 3FT Hon
Entry Requirements: *GCE:* 240. *IB:* 24.

B9C6 BSc Health Promotion with Sports Development
Duration: 3FT Hon
Entry Requirements: *GCE:* 240. *IB:* 24.

B9WK BSc Health Promotion with Theatre Studies
Duration: 3FT Hon
Entry Requirements: *GCE:* 240. *IB:* 24.

B9NF BSc Health Services Management
Duration: 3FT Hon
Entry Requirements: *GCE:* 240. *IB:* 24.

B9NG BSc Health Services Management with Business Management
Duration: 3FT Hon
Entry Requirements: *GCE:* 240.

B991 BSc Health Services Management with Public Health
Duration: 3FT Hon
Entry Requirements: *GCE:* 240. *IB:* 24.

B1BX BSc Human Biology with Clinical Science
Duration: 3FT Hon
Entry Requirements: *GCE:* 240. *IB:* 24.

B1B9 BSc Human Biology with Public Health
Duration: 3FT Hon
Entry Requirements: *GCE:* 240. *IB:* 24.

C5BX BSc Immunology with Clinical Science
Duration: 3FT Hon
Entry Requirements: *GCE:* 240. *IB:* 24.

CB59 BSc Immunology/Fitness & Health
Duration: 3FT Hon
Entry Requirements: *GCE:* 240. *IB:* 24.

J7B9 BSc Medical Biotechnology with Clinical Science
Duration: 3FT Hon
Entry Requirements: *GCE:* 240.

C5B9 BSc Medical Microbiology with Public Health
Duration: 3FT Hon
Entry Requirements: *GCE:* 240. *IB:* 24.

CB5X BSc Medical Microbiology/Clinical Science
Duration: 3FT Hon
Entry Requirements: *GCE:* 240. *IB:* 24.

B191 BSc Medical Physiology with Clinical Science
Duration: 3FT Hon
Entry Requirements: *GCE:* 240.

B910 BSc Public Health
Duration: 3FT Hon
Entry Requirements: *GCE:* 240. *IB:* 24.

B995 BSc Public Health / Health Promotion
Duration: 3FT Hon
Entry Requirements: *GCE:* 240. *IB:* 24.

B9PX BSc Public Health with Communication Studies
Duration: 3FT Hon
Entry Requirements: *GCE:* 240. *IB:* 24.

B9I1 BSc Public Health with Computing
Duration: 3FT Hon
Entry Requirements: *GCE:* 240. *IB:* 24.

B9LA BSc Public Health with Cultural Studies
Duration: 3FT Hon
Entry Requirements: *GCE:* 240. *IB:* 24.

B904 BSc Public Health with Health Promotion
Duration: 3FT Hon
Entry Requirements: *GCE:* 240. *IB:* 24.

B9CB BSc Public Health with Psychosocial Studies
Duration: 3FT Hon
Entry Requirements: *GCE:* 240. *IB:* 24.

C6B9 BSc Sports Coaching with Clinical Science
Duration: 3FT Hon
Entry Requirements: *GCE:* 240. *IB:* 24.

B993 BSc Sports Development
Duration: 3FT Hon
Entry Requirements: *GCE:* 240. *IB:* 24.

C6BY BSc Sports Development with Public Health
Duration: 3FT Hon
Entry Requirements: *GCE:* 240. *IB:* 24.

B2B9 BSc Toxicology with Clinical Science
Duration: 3FT Hon
Entry Requirements: *GCE:* 240. *IB:* 24.

BB29 BSc Toxicology/Clinical Science
Duration: 3FT Hon
Entry Requirements: *GCE:* 240. *IB:* 24.

B942 FdA Counselling
Duration: 2FT Fdg
Entry Requirements: *GCE:* 120.

E42 EDGE HILL UNIVERSITY
ORMSKIRK
LANCASHIRE L39 4QP
t: 01695 657000 f: 01695 584355
e: study@edgehill.ac.uk
// www.edgehill.ac.uk

WB49 BA Performance and Health
Duration: 3FT Hon   CRB Check: Required
Entry Requirements: *GCE:* 280. *IB:* 26. *OCR ND:* D *OCR NED:* M2
Interview required.

B991 BSc Operating Department Practice
Duration: 3FT Hon   CRB Check: Required
Entry Requirements: *GCE:* 280. *IB:* 26. *OCR ND:* D *OCR NED:* M2
Interview required.

B780 DipHE Paramedic Practice
Duration: 2FT Dip   CRB Check: Required
Entry Requirements: *GCE:* 240. *OCR ND:* M2 *OCR NED:* M2
Interview required. Admissions Test required.

B940 FdA Counselling
Duration: 2FT Fdg   CRB Check: Required
Entry Requirements: *GCE:* 40. *OCR ND:* P3 *OCR NED:* P3 Interview required.

B910 FdSc Public Health
Duration: 2FT Fdg   CRB Check: Required
Entry Requirements: *GCE:* 40. *OCR ND:* P3 *OCR NED:* P3 Interview required.

E59 EDINBURGH NAPIER UNIVERSITY
CRAIGLOCKHART CAMPUS
EDINBURGH EH14 1DJ
t: +44 (0)8452 60 60 40 f: 0131 455 6464
e: info@napier.ac.uk
// www.napier.ac.uk

B940 BSc Biomedical Science
Duration: 3FT/4FT Ord/Hon
Entry Requirements: *GCE:* 230.

CB69 BSc Sport & Exercise Science (Sports Coaching top up)
Duration: 1FT Ord
Entry Requirements: Contact the institution for details.

CB6X BSc Sport and Exercise Science (Sports Injuries)
Duration: 3FT/4FT Ord/Hon
Entry Requirements: *GCE:* 260.

E70 THE UNIVERSITY OF ESSEX
WIVENHOE PARK
COLCHESTER
ESSEX CO4 3SQ
t: 01206 873666 f: 01206 874477
e: admit@essex.ac.uk
// www.essex.ac.uk

B990 BSc Biomedical Science
Duration: 3FT Hon
Entry Requirements: *GCE:* BBC-CCC. *SQAH:* AABB-ABBB.

E84 UNIVERSITY OF EXETER
LAVER BUILDING
NORTH PARK ROAD
EXETER
DEVON EX4 4QE
t: 01392 723044 f: 01392 722479
e: admissions@exeter.ac.uk
// www.exeter.ac.uk

B901 BClinSci Clinical Science
Duration: 3FT Hon   CRB Check: Required
Entry Requirements: *GCE:* AAB-ABB. *SQAH:* AAABB-AABBB. *SQAAH:* ABB-BBB.

B900 BClinSci Clinical Science with Professional Training (4 years)
Duration: 4FT Hon   CRB Check: Required
Entry Requirements: *GCE:* AAB-ABB. *SQAH:* AAABB-AABBB. *SQAAH:* ABB-BBB.

G14 UNIVERSITY OF GLAMORGAN, CARDIFF AND PONTYPRIDD
ENQUIRIES AND ADMISSIONS UNIT
PONTYPRIDD CF37 1DL
t: 08456 434030 f: 01443 654050
e: enquiries@glam.ac.uk
// www.glam.ac.uk

B901 BSc Medical Sciences
Duration: 3FT Hon   CRB Check: Required
Entry Requirements: *GCE:* ABB. *IB:* 32. *BTEC ExtDip:* DDM.
Interview required.

G28 UNIVERSITY OF GLASGOW
71 SOUTHPARK AVENUE
UNIVERSITY OF GLASGOW
GLASGOW G12 8QQ
t: 0141 330 6062 f: 0141 330 2961
e: student.recruitment@glasgow.ac.uk
// www.glasgow.ac.uk

CB69 BSc Sports Medicine
Duration: 4FT Hon
Entry Requirements: *GCE:* ABB. *SQAH:* AAAB-BBBB. *IB:* 32.

G42 GLASGOW CALEDONIAN UNIVERSITY
STUDENT RECRUITMENT & ADMISSIONS SERVICE
CITY CAMPUS
COWCADDENS ROAD
GLASGOW G4 0BA
t: 0141 331 3000 f: 0141 331 8676
e: undergraduate@gcu.ac.uk
// www.gcu.ac.uk

B940 BSc Biomedical Science
Duration: 4FT Hon
Entry Requirements: *GCE:* BCC. *SQAH:* AAA-BBBC. *IB:* 24.

B930 BSc Occupational Therapy
Duration: 4FT Hon **CRB Check:** Required
Entry Requirements: *GCE:* CCC. *SQAH:* BBCC.

B932 BSc Occupational Therapy Studies (International)
Duration: 1FT Hon **CRB Check:** Required
Entry Requirements: Contact the institution for details.

B990 BSc Operating Department Practice
Duration: 3FT Deg **CRB Check:** Required
Entry Requirements: *GCE:* DD. *SQAH:* CC. Interview required.

G45 GLOUCESTERSHIRE COLLEGE
PRINCESS ELIZABETH WAY
CHELTENHAM GL51 7SJ
t: 01242 532008 f: 01242 532023
e: admissions@gloscol.ac.uk
// www.gloscol.ac.uk

B940 FdA Therapeutic Counselling
Duration: 2FT Fdg
Entry Requirements: *Foundation:* Pass. Interview required.

G50 THE UNIVERSITY OF GLOUCESTERSHIRE
PARK CAMPUS
THE PARK
CHELTENHAM GL50 2RH
t: 01242 714501 f: 01242 714869
e: admissions@glos.ac.uk
// www.glos.ac.uk

B940 BA Counselling
Duration: 1FT Hon
Entry Requirements: Contact the institution for details.

G56 GOLDSMITHS, UNIVERSITY OF LONDON
GOLDSMITHS, UNIVERSITY OF LONDON
NEW CROSS
LONDON SE14 6NW
t: 020 7048 5300 f: 020 7919 7509
e: admissions@gold.ac.uk
// www.gold.ac.uk

BL93 BA Psychosocial Studies
Duration: 3FT Hon
Entry Requirements: *GCE:* BBB. *SQAH:* BBBBC. *SQAAH:* BBC.
Interview required.

G70 UNIVERSITY OF GREENWICH
GREENWICH CAMPUS
OLD ROYAL NAVAL COLLEGE
PARK ROW
LONDON SE10 9LS
t: 020 8331 9000 f: 020 8331 8145
e: courseinfo@gre.ac.uk
// www.gre.ac.uk

B943 BA Counselling (Top-up)
Duration: 1FT Hon
Entry Requirements: Contact the institution for details.

B903 BSc Applied Biomedical Science
Duration: 4SW Hon
Entry Requirements: *GCE:* 300. *IB:* 24.

B940 BSc Biomedical Sciences
Duration: 3FT Hon
Entry Requirements: *GCE:* 300. *IB:* 24.

B901 BSc Health & Wellbeing
Duration: 3FT Hon
Entry Requirements: *GCE:* 240.

B781 BSc Paramedic Science
Duration: 3FT Hon
Entry Requirements: *GCE:* 240. *IB:* 24. Interview required.

C8B9 BSc Psychology with Counselling
Duration: 3FT Hon
Entry Requirements: *GCE:* 320. *IB:* 24.

B902 BSc Public Health
Duration: 3FT Hon
Entry Requirements: *GCE:* 240. *IB:* 24. Interview required.

B900 FdSc Biomedical Science
Duration: 2FT Fdg
Entry Requirements: *GCE:* 240. *IB:* 24.

G80 GRIMSBY INSTITUTE OF FURTHER AND HIGHER EDUCATION
NUNS CORNER
GRIMSBY
NE LINCOLNSHIRE DN34 5BQ
t: 0800 328 3631
e: headmissions@grimsby.ac.uk
// www.grimsby.ac.uk

B940 BA Counselling Studies
Duration: 3FT Hon
Entry Requirements: *GCE:* 120-240. Interview required.

BC96 FdSc Health Related Exercise and Fitness
Duration: 2FT Fdg
Entry Requirements: *GCE:* 120. Interview required. HND required.

G90 GUILDFORD COLLEGE
STOKE ROAD
GUILDFORD
SURREY GU1 1EZ
t: 01483 448585 f: 01483 448600
e: info@guildford.ac.uk
// www.guildford.ac.uk

B940 BA Counselling (Top-up)
Duration: 1.5SW/1SW Hon/Ord   CRB Check: Required
Entry Requirements: Interview required.

B941 FdSc Counselling
Duration: 2FT Fdg   CRB Check: Required
Entry Requirements: Interview required.

H14 HAVERING COLLEGE OF FURTHER AND HIGHER EDUCATION
ARDLEIGH GREEN ROAD
HORNCHURCH
ESSEX RM11 2LL
t: 01708 462793 f: 01708 462736
e: HE@havering-college.ac.uk
// www.havering-college.ac.uk

BCX8 BA Integrative Counselling and Psychotherapy
Duration: 3FT Hon
Entry Requirements: Contact the institution for details.

BCY8 BA Integrative Counselling and Psychotherapy
Duration: 1.5FT Hon
Entry Requirements: Interview required.

H24 HERIOT-WATT UNIVERSITY, EDINBURGH
EDINBURGH CAMPUS
EDINBURGH EH14 4AS
t: 0131 449 5111 f: 0131 451 3630
e: ugadmissions@hw.ac.uk
// www.hw.ac.uk

CB99 BSc Biological Sciences (Human Health)
Duration: 4FT Hon
Entry Requirements: *GCE:* BBB. *SQAH:* BBBBC. *SQAAH:* BB. *IB:* 26.

C8B9 BSc Psychology with Human Health
Duration: 4FT Hon
Entry Requirements: *GCE:* BBB. *SQAH:* BBBBC. *SQAAH:* BB. *IB:* 27.

H36 UNIVERSITY OF HERTFORDSHIRE
UNIVERSITY ADMISSIONS SERVICE
COLLEGE LANE
HATFIELD
HERTS AL10 9AB
t: 01707 284800
// www.herts.ac.uk

BCF0 BA/BSc Extended Degree in Science
Duration: 4FT/5SW Hon
Entry Requirements: *GCE:* 80.

BCF0 BA/BSc Extended Degree in Science option - Pharmaceutical Sciences
Duration: 4FT/5SW Hon
Entry Requirements: Contact the institution for details.

BCF0 BA/BSc Extended Degree in Science option - Astronomy
Duration: 4FT/5SW Hon
Entry Requirements: Contact the institution for details.

B990 BSc Biomedical Science
Duration: 3FT/4SW Hon
Entry Requirements: *GCE:* 260.

B991 BSc Biomedical Science with a year in Europe
Duration: 4FT Hon
Entry Requirements: *GCE:* 260.

B992 BSc Biomedical Science with a year in North America
Duration: 4FT Hon
Entry Requirements: *GCE:* 260.

G4B9 BSc Computing/Health Studies
Duration: 3FT/4SW Hon
Entry Requirements: *GCE:* 280.

L1B9 BSc Economics/Health Studies
Duration: 3FT/4SW Hon
Entry Requirements: *GCE:* 280.

Q1B9 BSc English Language & Communication/Health Studies
Duration: 3FT/4SW Hon
Entry Requirements: Contact the institution for details.

F9B9 BSc Environmental Studies/Health Studies
Duration: 3FT/4SW Hon
Entry Requirements: *GCE:* 280.

R8B9 BSc European Studies/Health Studies
Duration: 3FT/4SW Hon
Entry Requirements: Contact the institution for details.

B9G4 BSc Health Studies/Computing
Duration: 3FT/4SW Hon
Entry Requirements: *GCE:* 280.

B9L1 BSc Health Studies/Economics
Duration: 3FT/4SW Hon
Entry Requirements: *GCE:* 280.

B9Q1 BSc Health Studies/English Language & Communication
Duration: 3FT/4SW Hon
Entry Requirements: *GCE:* 300.

B9F9 BSc Health Studies/Environmental Studies
Duration: 3FT/4SW Hon
Entry Requirements: *GCE:* 280.

B9R8 BSc Health Studies/European Studies
Duration: 3FT/4SW Hon
Entry Requirements: *GCE:* 280.

B9R1 BSc Health Studies/French
Duration: 3FT/4SW Hon
Entry Requirements: *GCE:* 280.

B9P5 BSc Health Studies/Journalism & Media Cultures
Duration: 3FT/4SW Hon
Entry Requirements: *GCE:* 300.

B9M1 BSc Health Studies/Law
Duration: 3FT/4SW Hon
Entry Requirements: *GCE:* 320.

B9G1 BSc Health Studies/Mathematics
Duration: 3FT/4SW Hon
Entry Requirements: *GCE:* 280.

B9C8 BSc Health Studies/Psychology
Duration: 3FT/4SW Hon
Entry Requirements: *GCE:* 320.

B9R4 BSc Health Studies/Spanish
Duration: 3FT/4SW Hon
Entry Requirements: *GCE:* 280.

B9C6 BSc Health Studies/Sports Studies
Duration: 3FT/4SW Hon
Entry Requirements: *GCE:* 280.

P5B9 BSc Journalism & Media Cultures/Health Studies
Duration: 3FT/4SW Hon
Entry Requirements: *GCE:* 300.

M1B9 BSc Law/Health Studies
Duration: 3FT/4SW Hon
Entry Requirements: *GCE:* 320.

G1B9 BSc Mathematics/Health Studies
Duration: 3FT/4SW Hon
Entry Requirements: *GCE:* 280.

B780 BSc Paramedic Science
Duration: 4SW Hon   CRB Check: Required
Entry Requirements: *GCE:* 280. Interview required.

C8B9 BSc Psychology/Health Studies
Duration: 3FT/4SW Hon
Entry Requirements: *GCE:* 320.

C6B9 BSc Sports Studies/Health Studies
Duration: 3FT/4SW Hon
Entry Requirements: *GCE:* 280.

B781 FdSc Paramedic Science
Duration: 3FT Fdg   CRB Check: Required
Entry Requirements: *GCE:* 180. Interview required.

H60 THE UNIVERSITY OF HUDDERSFIELD
QUEENSGATE
HUDDERSFIELD HD1 3DH
t: 01484 473969 f: 01484 472765
e: admissionsandrecords@hud.ac.uk
// www.hud.ac.uk

B940 BSc Counselling Studies
Duration: 3FT Hon
Entry Requirements: *GCE:* 280. Interview required.

B900 BSc Exercise, Physical Activity & Health
Duration: 3FT Hon   CRB Check: Required
Entry Requirements: *GCE:* 280.

B930 BSc Occupational Therapy
Duration: 3FT Hon   CRB Check: Required
Entry Requirements: *GCE:* 280. Interview required.

C8B9 BSc Psychology with Counselling
Duration: 3FT Hon
Entry Requirements: *GCE:* 300. *SQAH:* BBBB.

BCF0 BSc Science (Extended)
Duration: 4FT/5SW Hon
Entry Requirements: *GCE:* 140. *SQAH:* CC. Admissions Test required.

B990 DipHE Operating Department Practice
Duration: 2FT Dip   CRB Check: Required
Entry Requirements: *GCE:* 200. Interview required.

B991 FYr Health Professions Foundation Year
Duration: 1FT FYr   CRB Check: Required
Entry Requirements: *GCE:* 200. Interview required.

H72 THE UNIVERSITY OF HULL
THE UNIVERSITY OF HULL
COTTINGHAM ROAD
HULL HU6 7RX
t: 01482 466100 f: 01482 442290
e: admissions@hull.ac.uk
// www.hull.ac.uk

B945 BA Counselling Studies (Top-up)
Duration: 1FT Hon   CRB Check: Required
Entry Requirements: Interview required.

BC99 BSc Biomedical Science
Duration: 3FT Hon
Entry Requirements: *GCE:* 280-320. *IB:* 32. *BTEC ExtDip:* DDM.

BC9Y BSc Biomedical Science (with foundation year)
Duration: 4FT Hon
Entry Requirements: Contact the institution for details.

CB69 BSc Sports Coaching and Performance
Duration: 3FT Hon   CRB Check: Required
Entry Requirements: *GCE:* 280. *IB:* 30. *BTEC ExtDip:* DDD.

B990 DipHE Operating Department Practice
Duration: 2FT Dip   CRB Check: Required
Entry Requirements: *GCE:* 220. *IB:* 28. *BTEC ExtDip:* MMM.
Interview required.

B943 FdA Theory and Practice of Counselling
Duration: 2FT Fdg   CRB Check: Required
Entry Requirements: Interview required.

B944 FdA Theory and Practice of Integrative Counselling
Duration: 2FT Fdg   CRB Check: Required
Entry Requirements: Interview required.

H73 HULL COLLEGE
QUEEN'S GARDENS
HULL HU1 3DG
t: 01482 329943 f: 01482 598733
e: info@hull-college.ac.uk
// www.hull-college.ac.uk/higher-education

B940 BA Counselling Practice
Duration: 1FT Hon
Entry Requirements: Interview required.

I50 IMPERIAL COLLEGE LONDON
REGISTRY
SOUTH KENSINGTON CAMPUS
IMPERIAL COLLEGE LONDON
LONDON SW7 2AZ
t: 020 7589 5111 f: 020 7594 8004
// www.imperial.ac.uk

B900 BSc Biomedical Science
Duration: 3FT Hon
Entry Requirements: *GCE:* AAAb. *SQAAH:* AAA. *IB:* 38.
Admissions Test required.

B9N2 BSc Biomedical Science with Management
Duration: 4FT Hon
Entry Requirements: Contact the institution for details.

BH9C MEng Biomedical Engineering
Duration: 4FT Hon
Entry Requirements: *GCE:* AAA. *SQAAH:* AAA. *IB:* 38.

K12 KEELE UNIVERSITY
KEELE UNIVERSITY
STAFFORDSHIRE ST5 5BG
t: 01782 734005 f: 01782 632343
e: undergraduate@keele.ac.uk
// www.keele.ac.uk

B1B9 BSc Physiotherapy with Health Foundation Year
Duration: 4FT Hon   CRB Check: Required
Entry Requirements: *GCE:* BBB. *SQAAH:* BBB. *IB:* 28. Interview required.

K24 THE UNIVERSITY OF KENT
RECRUITMENT & ADMISSIONS OFFICE
REGISTRY
UNIVERSITY OF KENT
CANTERBURY, KENT CT2 7NZ
t: 01227 827272 f: 01227 827077
e: information@kent.ac.uk
// www.kent.ac.uk

B940 BSc Biomedical Sciences
Duration: 3FT Hon
Entry Requirements: *GCE:* BBB. *SQAH:* AABBB. *SQAAH:* BBB. *IB:* 33. *OCR ND:* D *OCR NED:* D1

B942 BSc Biomedical Sciences (4-year sandwich)
Duration: 4SW Hon
Entry Requirements: *GCE:* BBB. *SQAH:* AABBB. *SQAAH:* BBB. *IB:* 33. *OCR ND:* D *OCR NED:* D1

K60 KING'S COLLEGE LONDON (UNIVERSITY OF LONDON)
STRAND
LONDON WC2R 2LS
t: 020 7836 5454 f: 020 7848 7171
e: prospective@kcl.ac.uk
// www.kcl.ac.uk/prospectus

BC99 BSc Biomedical Science
Duration: 3FT Hon
Entry Requirements: *GCE:* AABc. *SQAH:* AAABB. *IB:* 36.

K84 KINGSTON UNIVERSITY
STUDENT INFORMATION & ADVICE CENTRE
COOPER HOUSE
40-46 SURBITON ROAD
KINGSTON UPON THAMES KT1 2HX
t: 0844 8552177 f: 020 8547 7080
e: aps@kingston.ac.uk
// www.kingston.ac.uk

B930 BSc Biomedical Science
Duration: 3FT Hon
Entry Requirements: *GCE:* 200-280.

B931 BSc Biomedical Science
Duration: 4SW Hon
Entry Requirements: *GCE:* 200-280.

B948 BSc Biomedical Science (Foundation)
Duration: 4FT Hon
Entry Requirements: *GCE:* 60.

L14 LANCASTER UNIVERSITY
THE UNIVERSITY
LANCASTER
LANCASHIRE LA1 4YW
t: 01524 592029 f: 01524 846243
e: ugadmissions@lancaster.ac.uk
// www.lancs.ac.uk

C1B9 BSc Biological Sciences with Biomedicine
Duration: 3FT Hon
Entry Requirements: *GCE:* AAB. *SQAH:* ABBBB. *SQAAH:* AAB. *IB:* 35.

B990 BSc Biomedical Science
Duration: 3FT Hon
Entry Requirements: *GCE:* AAB. *SQAH:* ABBBB. *SQAAH:* AAB. *IB:* 35.

L23 UNIVERSITY OF LEEDS
THE UNIVERSITY OF LEEDS
WOODHOUSE LANE
LEEDS LS2 9JT
t: 0113 343 3999
e: admissions@leeds.ac.uk
// www.leeds.ac.uk

BCF0 MNatSci Natural Sciences
Duration: 4FT Hon
Entry Requirements: *GCE:* AAA. *SQAAH:* AAA. *IB:* 38.

L27 LEEDS METROPOLITAN UNIVERSITY
COURSE ENQUIRIES OFFICE
CITY CAMPUS
LEEDS LS1 3HE
t: 0113 81 23113 f: 0113 81 23129
// www.leedsmet.ac.uk

B900 BSc Biomedical Sciences
Duration: 3FT Hon
Entry Requirements: *GCE:* 180. *IB:* 24.

B940 BSc Counselling and Therapeutic Studies
Duration: 3FT Hon
Entry Requirements: *GCE:* 220. *IB:* 26.

B990 BSc Health Care Sciences
Duration: 3FT Hon
Entry Requirements: *GCE:* 160. *IB:* 26.

B910 BSc Public Health - Environmental Health
Duration: 3FT Hon
Entry Requirements: *GCE:* 160-200. *IB:* 26.

CB6X BSc Sports & Exercise Therapy
Duration: 3FT Hon   CRB Check: Required
Entry Requirements: *GCE:* 260.

L39 UNIVERSITY OF LINCOLN
ADMISSIONS
BRAYFORD POOL
LINCOLN LN6 7TS
t: 01522 886097 f: 01522 886146
e: admissions@lincoln.ac.uk
// www.lincoln.ac.uk

B940 BSc Biomedical Science
Duration: 3FT Hon
Entry Requirements: *GCE:* 280.

L41 THE UNIVERSITY OF LIVERPOOL
THE FOUNDATION BUILDING
BROWNLOW HILL
LIVERPOOL L69 7ZX
t: 0151 794 2000 f: 0151 708 6502
e: ugrecruitment@liv.ac.uk
// www.liv.ac.uk

BCG0 BSc Combined Honours option - Philosophy
Duration: 3FT Hon
Entry Requirements: *GCE:* AAB-BBC. *SQAAH:* AAB-BBC.

BCG0 BSc Combined Honours option - Geography
Duration: 3FT Hon
Entry Requirements: *GCE:* AAB-BBC. *SQAAH:* AAB-BBC.

BCG0 BSc Combined Honours option - Genetics
Duration: 3FT Hon
Entry Requirements: *GCE:* AAB-BBC. *SQAAH:* AAB-BBC.

BCG0 BSc Combined Honours option - Biochemistry
Duration: 3FT Hon
Entry Requirements: *GCE:* AAB-BBC. *SQAAH:* AAB-BBC.

BCG0 BSc Combined Honours option - Psychology
Duration: 3FT Hon
Entry Requirements: *GCE:* AAB-BBC. *SQAAH:* AAB-BBC.

BCG0 BSc Combined Honours option - Mathematics
Duration: 3FT Hon
Entry Requirements: *GCE:* AAB-BBC. *SQAAH:* AAB-BBC.

BCG0 BSc Combined Honours option - Computer Science
Duration: 3FT Hon
Entry Requirements: *GCE:* AAB-BBC. *SQAAH:* AAB-BBC.

BCG0 BSc Combined Honours option - Archaeology
Duration: 3FT Hon
Entry Requirements: *GCE:* AAB-BBC. *SQAAH:* AAB-BBC.

BCG0 BSc Combined Honours option - Chemistry
Duration: 3FT Hon
Entry Requirements: *GCE:* AAB-BBC. *SQAAH:* AAB-BBC.

BCG0 BSc Combined Honours option - Zoology
Duration: 3FT Hon
Entry Requirements: *GCE:* AAB-BBC. *SQAAH:* AAB-BBC.

BCG0 BSc Combined Honours option - Microbiology
Duration: 3FT Hon
Entry Requirements: *GCE:* AAB-BBC. *SQAAH:* AAB-BBC.

BCG0 BSc Combined Honours option - Business Studies
Duration: 3FT Hon
Entry Requirements: *GCE:* AAB-BBC. *SQAAH:* AAB-BBC.

BCG0 BSc Combined Honours option - Geology
Duration: 3FT Hon
Entry Requirements: *GCE:* AAB-BBC. *SQAAH:* AAB-BBC.

BCG0 BSc Combined Honours option - Biology
Duration: 3FT Hon
Entry Requirements: *GCE:* AAB-BBC. *SQAAH:* AAB-BBC.

BCG0 BSc Combined Honours option - Ocean and Earth Sciences
Duration: 3FT Hon
Entry Requirements: *GCE:* AAB-BBC. *SQAAH:* AAB-BBC.

B920 BSc Occupational Therapy
Duration: 3FT Hon   CRB Check: Required
Entry Requirements: *GCE:* BBB. *SQAH:* BBBBB. *SQAAH:* BBB. *IB:* 30.

L42 LINCOLN COLLEGE
MONKS ROAD
LINCOLN LN2 5HQ
t: 01522 876000 f: 01522 876200
e: enquiries@lincolncollege.ac.uk
// www.lincolncollege.ac.uk

B900 FdSc Health and Active Lifestyles
Duration: 2FT Fdg
Entry Requirements: *GCE:* 120. Interview required.

CB69 FdSc Sport Performance and Exercise Development
Duration: 2FT Hon
Entry Requirements: *GCE:* 120. Interview required.

L46 LIVERPOOL HOPE UNIVERSITY
HOPE PARK
LIVERPOOL L16 9JD
t: 0151 291 3331 f: 0151 291 3434
e: administration@hope.ac.uk
// www.hope.ac.uk

BX93 BA Education and Health
Duration: 3FT Hon   CRB Check: Required
Entry Requirements: *GCE:* 300-320. *IB:* 25.

CB19 BSc Biology and Health
Duration: 3FT Hon
Entry Requirements: *GCE:* 300-320. *IB:* 25.

BG95 BSc Health and Information Technology
Duration: 3FT Hon
Entry Requirements: *GCE:* 300-320. *IB:* 25.

BCX8 BSc Health and Psychology
Duration: 3FT Hon
Entry Requirements: *GCE:* 300-320. *IB:* 25.

CBP9 BSc Health and Sport Studies
Duration: 3FT Hon
Entry Requirements: *GCE:* 300-320. *IB:* 25.

B902 BSc Health, Nutrition & Fitness
Duration: 3FT Hon
Entry Requirements: *GCE:* 300-320. *IB:* 25.

L51 LIVERPOOL JOHN MOORES UNIVERSITY
KINGSWAY HOUSE
HATTON GARDEN
LIVERPOOL L3 2AJ
t: 0151 231 5090 f: 0151 904 6368
e: courses@ljmu.ac.uk
// www.ljmu.ac.uk

B940 BSc Biomedical Science
Duration: 3FT/4SW Hon
Entry Requirements: *GCE:* 260-300. *IB:* 25.

B911 BSc Environmental Health
Duration: 3FT Hon
Entry Requirements: *GCE:* 260.

B781 DipHE Paramedic Practice
Duration: 2FT Dip   **CRB Check:** Required
Entry Requirements: *GCE:* 260. Interview required.

L68 LONDON METROPOLITAN UNIVERSITY
166-220 HOLLOWAY ROAD
LONDON N7 8DB
t: 020 7133 4200
e: admissions@londonmet.ac.uk
// www.londonmet.ac.uk

B900 BSc Biomedical Science
Duration: 3FT Hon
Entry Requirements: *GCE:* 300. *IB:* 28.

B901 BSc/MD Biomedical Science (Leading to MD)
Duration: 6FT Hon
Entry Requirements: *GCE:* 320. *IB:* 28. Interview required.

L75 LONDON SOUTH BANK UNIVERSITY
ADMISSIONS AND RECRUITMENT CENTRE
90 LONDON ROAD
LONDON SE1 6LN
t: 0800 923 8888 f: 020 7815 8273
e: course.enquiry@lsbu.ac.uk
// www.lsbu.ac.uk

B930 BSc Occupational Therapy
Duration: 3FT Hon   **CRB Check:** Required
Entry Requirements: *GCE:* 300. *IB:* 24. *BTEC ExtDip:* DDM.
Interview required. Admissions Test required.

M20 THE UNIVERSITY OF MANCHESTER
RUTHERFORD BUILDING
OXFORD ROAD
MANCHESTER M13 9PL
t: 0161 275 2077 f: 0161 275 2106
e: ug-admissions@manchester.ac.uk
// www.manchester.ac.uk

B940 BSc Biomedical Sciences
Duration: 3FT Hon
Entry Requirements: *GCE:* AAA-ABB. *SQAH:* AAAAA-AAABB.
SQAAH: AAA-AAB. Interview required.

B941 BSc Biomedical Sciences with Industrial / Professional Experience (4 years)
Duration: 4SW Hon
Entry Requirements: *GCE:* AAA-ABB. *SQAH:* AAAAA-AAABB.
SQAAH: AAA-AAB. Interview required.

B9R9 BSc Biomedical Sciences with a Modern Language
Duration: 4FT Hon
Entry Requirements: *GCE:* AAA-ABB. *SQAH:* AAAAA-AAABB.
SQAAH: AAA-ABB. Interview required.

M40 THE MANCHESTER METROPOLITAN UNIVERSITY
ADMISSIONS OFFICE
ALL SAINTS (GMS)
ALL SAINTS
MANCHESTER M15 6BH
t: 0161 247 2000
// www.mmu.ac.uk

B990 BSc Healthcare Science
Duration: 3FT Hon
Entry Requirements: *GCE:* 240-280. *IB:* 27. Interview required.

M80 MIDDLESEX UNIVERSITY
MIDDLESEX UNIVERSITY
THE BURROUGHS
LONDON NW4 4BT
t: 020 8411 5555 f: 020 8411 5649
e: enquiries@mdx.ac.uk
// www.mdx.ac.uk

B942 BA Counselling (Top-Up)
Duration: 1FT Hon
Entry Requirements: Interview required.

B910 BSc Environmental Health
Duration: 3FT/4SW Hon
Entry Requirements: *GCE:* 200-300. *IB:* 28.

B912 BSc Environmental and Public Health
Duration: 3FT Hon
Entry Requirements: *GCE:* 200-300. *IB:* 28.

B920 BSc Occupational Health and Safety (Top-Up)
Duration: 1FT Hon
Entry Requirements: Contact the institution for details.

C8B9 BSc Psychology with Counselling Skills
Duration: 3FT Hon
Entry Requirements: *GCE:* 200-300. *IB:* 28.

B914 CertHE Environmental Health
Duration: 1FT Cer
Entry Requirements: Contact the institution for details.

KB49 CertHE Housing Practice in Environmental Health
Duration: 1FT Cer
Entry Requirements: Contact the institution for details.

B941 FdA Counselling
Duration: 2FT Fdg
Entry Requirements: Interview required.

N21 NEWCASTLE UNIVERSITY
KING'S GATE
NEWCASTLE UPON TYNE NE1 7RU
t: 01912083333
// www.ncl.ac.uk

B901 BSc Biomedical Genetics
Duration: 3FT Hon
Entry Requirements: *GCE:* AAB. *SQAH:* AAABB.

B940 BSc Biomedical Sciences
Duration: 3FT Hon
Entry Requirements: *GCE:* AAB. *SQAH:* AAABB.

B9N2 BSc Biomedical Sciences with Business
Duration: 3FT Hon
Entry Requirements: *GCE:* AAB. *SQAH:* AAABB.

BC95 BSc Biomedical Sciences with Medical Microbiology
Duration: 3FT Hon
Entry Requirements: *GCE:* AAB. *SQAH:* AAABB.

B902 BSc Medical Science
Duration: 3FT Hon
Entry Requirements: *GCE:* AAB. *SQAH:* AAABB.

B900 MSci Biomedical Sciences (Integrated Masters)
Duration: 4FT Hon
Entry Requirements: *GCE:* AAB. *SQAH:* AAABB.

N23 NEWCASTLE COLLEGE
STUDENT SERVICES
RYE HILL CAMPUS
SCOTSWOOD ROAD
NEWCASTLE UPON TYNE NE4 7SA
t: 0191 200 4110 f: 0191 200 4349
e: enquiries@ncl-coll.ac.uk
// www.newcastlecollege.co.uk

BC96 BSc Applied Health & Exercise Science (Top-up)
Duration: 1FT Hon   CRB Check: Required
Entry Requirements: Interview required.

CB6X BSc Sports Therapy (Top-up)
Duration: 1FT Hon
Entry Requirements: Contact the institution for details.

CB69 FdSc Sports Training and Rehabilitation
Duration: 2FT Fdg
Entry Requirements: *GCE:* 160-200. *OCR ND:* P1 *OCR NED:* P2 Interview required.

N28 NEW COLLEGE DURHAM
FRAMWELLGATE MOOR CAMPUS
DURHAM DH1 5ES
t: 0191 375 4210/4211 f: 0191 375 4222
e: admissions@newdur.ac.uk
// www.newcollegedurham.ac.uk

B910 FdA Public Health
Duration: 2FT Fdg
Entry Requirements: Contact the institution for details.

N31 NEWHAM COLLEGE OF FURTHER EDUCATION
EAST HAM CAMPUS
HIGH STREET SOUTH
LONDON E6 6ER
t: 020 8257 4000 f: 020 8257 4325
e: admissions@newham.ac.uk
// www.newham.ac.uk

B941 BA Counselling Studies (Integrative Therapy)
Duration: 3FT Hon
Entry Requirements: Contact the institution for details.

B942 BA Counselling Studies (Pastoral Counselling)
Duration: 3FT Hon
Entry Requirements: Contact the institution for details.

BQ9H BA Counselling Studies and English
Duration: 3FT Hon
Entry Requirements: Contact the institution for details.

BL9H BA Counselling Studies and Sociology
Duration: 3FT Hon
Entry Requirements: Contact the institution for details.

BN92 BA (Hons) Counselling Studies and Business Management
Duration: 3FT Hon
Entry Requirements: Contact the institution for details.

XB39 BA (Hons) Education and Counselling Studies
Duration: 3FT Hon
Entry Requirements: Contact the institution for details.

BC9W BA/BSc Counselling Studies and Psychology
Duration: 3FT Hon
Entry Requirements: Contact the institution for details.

BC9V BSc Counselling Studies (Cognitive Behaviour Therapy)
Duration: 3FT Hon
Entry Requirements: Contact the institution for details.

N36 NEWMAN UNIVERSITY COLLEGE, BIRMINGHAM
GENNERS LANE
BARTLEY GREEN
BIRMINGHAM B32 3NT
t: 0121 476 1181 f: 0121 476 1196
e: Admissions@newman.ac.uk
// www.newman.ac.uk

CB89 BA Applied Psychology and Counselling Studies
Duration: 3FT Hon
Entry Requirements: *Foundation:* Distinction. *GCE:* 260. *IB:* 24.
BTEC ExtDip: DMM. *OCR ND:* M2 *OCR NED:* M2

B940 BA Counselling (top up)
Duration: 1FT Hon
Entry Requirements: Interview required. HND required.

BP93 BA Counselling Studies and Media & Communication
Duration: 3FT Hon
Entry Requirements: *Foundation:* Distinction. *GCE:* 260. *IB:* 24.
BTEC ExtDip: DMM. *OCR ND:* M2 *OCR NED:* M2

BV95 BA Counselling Studies and Philosophy, Religion and Ethics
Duration: 3FT Hon
Entry Requirements: *Foundation:* Distinction. *GCE:* 260. *IB:* 24.
BTEC ExtDip: DMM. *OCR ND:* M2 *OCR NED:* M2

BL95 BA Counselling Studies and Working with Children, Young People & Families
Duration: 3FT Hon
Entry Requirements: *Foundation:* Distinction. *GCE:* 260. *IB:* 24.
BTEC ExtDip: DMM. *OCR ND:* M2 *OCR NED:* M2

WB49 BA Drama and Counselling Studies
Duration: 3FT Hon
Entry Requirements: *Foundation:* Distinction. *GCE:* 260. *IB:* 24.
BTEC ExtDip: DMM. *OCR ND:* M2 *OCR NED:* M2

W4B9 BA Drama with Counselling Studies
Duration: 3FT Hon
Entry Requirements: *Foundation:* Distinction. *GCE:* 260. *IB:* 24.
BTEC ExtDip: DMM. *OCR ND:* M2 *OCR NED:* M2

XB39 BA Education Studies and Counselling Studies
Duration: 3FT Hon
Entry Requirements: *Foundation:* Distinction. *GCE:* 260. *IB:* 24.
BTEC ExtDip: DMM. *OCR ND:* M2 *OCR NED:* M2

X3B9 BA Education Studies with Counselling Studies
Duration: 3FT Hon
Entry Requirements: *Foundation:* Distinction. *GCE:* 260. *IB:* 24.
BTEC ExtDip: DMM. *OCR ND:* M2 *OCR NED:* M2

BV91 BA History and Counselling Studies
Duration: 3FT Hon
Entry Requirements: *Foundation:* Distinction. *GCE:* 260. *IB:* 24.
BTEC ExtDip: DMM. *OCR ND:* M2 *OCR NED:* M2

V1B9 BA History with Counselling Studies
Duration: 3FT Hon
Entry Requirements: *Foundation:* Distinction. *GCE:* 260. *IB:* 24.
BTEC ExtDip: DMM. *OCR ND:* M2 *OCR NED:* M2

GB59 BA Information Technology and Counselling Studies
Duration: 3FT Hon
Entry Requirements: *Foundation:* Distinction. *GCE:* 260. *IB:* 24.
BTEC ExtDip: DMM. *OCR ND:* M2 *OCR NED:* M2

G5B9 BA Information Technology with Counselling Studies
Duration: 3FT Hon
Entry Requirements: *Foundation:* Distinction. *GCE:* 260. *IB:* 24.
BTEC ExtDip: DMM. *OCR ND:* M2 *OCR NED:* M2

XB19 BA Primary Education (QTS) Physical Education
Duration: 3FT/4FT Hon   CRB Check: Required
Entry Requirements: *Foundation:* Merit. *GCE:* 280. *IB:* 25. *OCR ND:* M2 *OCR NED:* M2 Interview required. Admissions Test required.

C8B9 BA Psychology with Counselling Studies
Duration: 3FT Hon
Entry Requirements: *Foundation:* Distinction. *GCE:* 280. *IB:* 25.
BTEC ExtDip: DMM. *OCR ND:* M2 *OCR NED:* M2

CB69 BA Sports Studies and Counselling Studies
Duration: 3FT Hon
Entry Requirements: *Foundation:* Distinction. *GCE:* 260. *IB:* 24.
BTEC ExtDip: DMM. *OCR ND:* M2 *OCR NED:* M2

C6B9 BA Sports Studies with Counselling Studies
Duration: 3FT Hon
Entry Requirements: *Foundation:* Distinction. *GCE:* 280. *IB:* 25.
BTEC ExtDip: DMM. *OCR ND:* M2 *OCR NED:* M2

VB69 BA Theology and Counselling Studies
Duration: 3FT Hon
Entry Requirements: *Foundation:* Distinction. *GCE:* 260. *IB:* 24.
BTEC ExtDip: DMM. *OCR ND:* M2 *OCR NED:* M2

V6B9 BA Theology with Counselling Studies
Duration: 3FT Hon
Entry Requirements: *Foundation:* Distinction. *GCE:* 260. *IB:* 24.
BTEC ExtDip: DMM. *OCR ND:* M2 *OCR NED:* M2

L5B9 BA Working with Children, Young People & Families with Counselling Studies
Duration: 3FT Hon
Entry Requirements: *Foundation:* Distinction. *GCE:* 260. *IB:* 24.
BTEC ExtDip: DMM. *OCR ND:* M2 *OCR NED:* M2

N37 UNIVERSITY OF WALES, NEWPORT
ADMISSIONS
LODGE ROAD
CAERLEON
NEWPORT NP18 3QT
t: 01633 432030 f: 01633 432850
e: admissions@newport.ac.uk
// www.newport.ac.uk

BM92 BA Counselling Studies and Youth Justice
Duration: 3FT Hon
Entry Requirements: *GCE:* 240. *IB:* 24. Interview required.

LB39 BA Criminology & Criminal Justice and Counselling Studies
Duration: 3FT Hon
Entry Requirements: *GCE:* 240. *IB:* 24. Interview required.

LB3X BA Social Studies and Counselling Studies
Duration: 3FT Hon
Entry Requirements: *GCE:* 240. *IB:* 24. Interview required.

C8B9 BA/BSc Psychology with Counselling Studies
Duration: 3FT Hon
Entry Requirements: *GCE:* 240. *IB:* 24. Interview required.

N38 UNIVERSITY OF NORTHAMPTON
PARK CAMPUS
BOUGHTON GREEN ROAD
NORTHAMPTON NN2 7AL
t: 0800 358 2232 f: 01604 722083
e: admissions@northampton.ac.uk
// www.northampton.ac.uk

B930 BSc Occupational Therapy
Duration: 3FT Hon   CRB Check: Required
Entry Requirements: *GCE:* 260-280. *SQAH:* AAA-BBBB. *IB:* 24. *BTEC Dip:* DD. *BTEC ExtDip:* DMM. *OCR ND:* D *OCR NED:* M2 Interview required.

BC98 BSc Psychology and Counselling
Duration: 3FT Hon
Entry Requirements: *GCE:* 280-320. *SQAH:* AABB. *IB:* 26. *BTEC Dip:* DD. *BTEC ExtDip:* DMM. *OCR ND:* D *OCR NED:* M2 Interview required.

F8LL BSc Wastes Management/Health Studies
Duration: 3FT Hon
Entry Requirements: *GCE:* 260-280. *SQAH:* AAA-BBBB. *IB:* 24. *BTEC Dip:* DD. *BTEC ExtDip:* DMM. *OCR ND:* D *OCR NED:* M2

B781 FdSc Paramedic Science
Duration: 2FT Fdg   CRB Check: Required
Entry Requirements: *GCE:* 220-260. *SQAH:* BC-CCC. *IB:* 24. *BTEC Dip:* DD. *BTEC ExtDip:* DMM. *OCR ND:* D *OCR NED:* M2 Interview required.

N49 NESCOT, SURREY
REIGATE ROAD
EWELL
EPSOM
SURREY KT17 3DS
t: 020 8394 3038 f: 020 8394 3030
e: info@nescot.ac.uk
// www.nescot.ac.uk

B940 BSc Biomedical Science
Duration: 3FT Hon
Entry Requirements: *GCE:* 240.

B991 BSc Osteopathic Medicine
Duration: 4FT Hon
Entry Requirements: *GCE:* 240.

N77 NORTHUMBRIA UNIVERSITY
TRINITY BUILDING
NORTHUMBERLAND ROAD
NEWCASTLE UPON TYNE NE1 8ST
t: 0191 243 7420 f: 0191 227 4561
e: er.admissions@northumbria.ac.uk
// www.northumbria.ac.uk

BX99 BA Childhood Studies and Guidance & Counselling
Duration: 3FT Hon   CRB Check: Required
Entry Requirements: *SQAH:* BBCCC. *SQAAH:* BCC. *IB:* 25.

BL95 BA Disability Studies and Guidance & Counselling
Duration: 3FT Hon   CRB Check: Required
Entry Requirements: *SQAH:* BBCCC. *SQAAH:* BCC. *IB:* 25.

LB59 BA Health in Contemporary Society and Guidance & Counselling
Duration: 3FT Hon   CRB Check: Required
Entry Requirements: *SQAH:* BBCCC. *SQAAH:* BCC. *IB:* 25.

B940 BSc Biomedical Science
Duration: 3FT/4SW Hon
Entry Requirements: *GCE:* 300. *SQAH:* BBBBC. *SQAAH:* BBC. *IB:* 26. *OCR ND:* M1 *OCR NED:* P1

F1B9 BSc Chemistry with Biomedical Sciences
Duration: 3FT/4SW Hon
Entry Requirements: *GCE:* 280. *SQAH:* BBCCC. *SQAAH:* BCC. *IB:* 25. *OCR ND:* M1 *OCR NED:* P1

B910 BSc Environmental Health
Duration: 3FT Hon
Entry Requirements: *GCE:* 280. *SQAH:* BBCCC. *SQAAH:* BCC. *IB:* 25. *BTEC Dip:* D*D*. *BTEC ExtDip:* DMM. *OCR ND:* M1 *OCR NED:* P1

B920 BSc Occupational Therapy
Duration: 3FT Hon   CRB Check: Required
Entry Requirements: *SQAH:* BBBBC. *SQAAH:* BBC. *IB:* 26. *BTEC Dip:* D*D*. *BTEC ExtDip:* DDM. *OCR NED:* M1 Interview required.

B990 DipHE Operating Department Practice
Duration: 2FT Dip   CRB Check: Required
Entry Requirements: *IB:* 24. Interview required.

N82 NORWICH CITY COLLEGE OF FURTHER AND HIGHER EDUCATION (AN ASSOCIATE COLLEGE OF UEA)
IPSWICH ROAD
NORWICH
NORFOLK NR2 2LJ
t: 01603 773012 f: 01603 773301
e: he_office@ccn.ac.uk
// www.ccn.ac.uk

B900 FdSc Health Studies
Duration: 2FT Fdg
Entry Requirements: Contact the institution for details.

N84 THE UNIVERSITY OF NOTTINGHAM
THE ADMISSIONS OFFICE
THE UNIVERSITY OF NOTTINGHAM
UNIVERSITY PARK
NOTTINGHAM NG7 2RD
t: 0115 951 5151 f: 0115 951 4668
// www.nottingham.ac.uk

B940 BA Humanistic Counselling Practice
Duration: 3FT Hon   CRB Check: Required
Entry Requirements: *GCE:* BCC. *SQAAH:* BCC. *IB:* 28. Interview required.

B902 BSc Health Care Science with Foundation Year
Duration: 4FT Hon   CRB Check: Required
Entry Requirements: Contact the institution for details.

B900 BSc Healthcare Science
Duration: 3FT Hon   CRB Check: Required
Entry Requirements: *GCE:* ABB-BBB. *SQAAH:* ABB-BBB. *IB:* 32.

N91 NOTTINGHAM TRENT UNIVERSITY
DRYDEN BUILDING
BURTON STREET
NOTTINGHAM NG1 4BU
t: +44 (0) 115 848 4200 f: +44 (0) 115 848 8869
e: applications@ntu.ac.uk
// www.ntu.ac.uk

B940 BSc Biomedical Sciences
Duration: 3FT/4SW Hon
Entry Requirements: *GCE:* 300. *BTEC ExtDip:* DDM.

O33 OXFORD UNIVERSITY
UNDERGRADUATE ADMISSIONS OFFICE
UNIVERSITY OF OXFORD
WELLINGTON SQUARE
OXFORD OX1 2JD
t: 01865 288000 f: 01865 270212
e: undergraduate.admissions@admin.ox.ac.uk
// www.admissions.ox.ac.uk

BC98 BA Biomedical Sciences
Duration: 3FT Hon
Entry Requirements: *GCE:* AAA. *SQAH:* AAAAA. *SQAAH:* AAB.
Interview required. Admissions Test required.

O66 OXFORD BROOKES UNIVERSITY
ADMISSIONS OFFICE
HEADINGTON CAMPUS
GIPSY LANE
OXFORD OX3 0BP
t: 01865 483040 f: 01865 483983
e: admissions@brookes.ac.uk
// www.brookes.ac.uk

B900 BSc Biomedical Science
Duration: 3FT/4SW Hon
Entry Requirements: *GCE:* BBC.

B920 BSc Occupational Therapy
Duration: 3FT Hon   CRB Check: Required
Entry Requirements: *GCE:* BBB. *IB:* 32. *BTEC ExtDip:* DDD.

B990 DipHE Operating Department Practice (Swindon)
Duration: 2FT Dip   CRB Check: Required
Entry Requirements: *GCE:* BCC. *BTEC ExtDip:* DMM.

B780 FdSc Paramedic Emergency Care
Duration: 2FT Fdg   CRB Check: Required
Entry Requirements: Contact the institution for details.

P60 PLYMOUTH UNIVERSITY
DRAKE CIRCUS
PLYMOUTH PL4 8AA
t: 01752 585858 f: 01752 588055
e: admissions@plymouth.ac.uk
// www.plymouth.ac.uk

B900 BSc Biomedical Sciences
Duration: 3FT Hon
Entry Requirements: *GCE:* 300. *IB:* 26.

B901 BSc Healthcare Science (Life Sciences)
Duration: 3FT Hon   CRB Check: Required
Entry Requirements: *GCE:* 280-320. *IB:* 26. Interview required.

B902 BSc Healthcare Science (Physiological Sciences)
Duration: 3FT Hon   CRB Check: Required
Entry Requirements: *GCE:* 280-320. *IB:* 26. Interview required.

B920 BSc Occupational Therapy
Duration: 3FT Hon   CRB Check: Required
Entry Requirements: *GCE:* 300. *IB:* 27. *OCR ND:* D

B781 BSc Paramedic Practitioner (Community Emergency Health)
Duration: 3FT Hon   CRB Check: Required
Entry Requirements: *GCE:* 300. *OCR ND:* D

B990 DipHE Operating Department Practice
Duration: 2FT Dip   CRB Check: Required
Entry Requirements: *GCE:* 200. *OCR ND:* M1 *OCR NED:* P1

B783 DipHE Paramedic Studies (Community Emergency Health)
Duration: 1FT Dip
Entry Requirements: Contact the institution for details.

P63 UCP MARJON - UNIVERSITY COLLEGE PLYMOUTH ST MARK & ST JOHN
DERRIFORD ROAD
PLYMOUTH PL6 8BH
t: 01752 636890 f: 01752 636819
e: admissions@marjon.ac.uk
// www.ucpmarjon.ac.uk

CB69 BSC Health Exercise and Physical Activity
Duration: 3FT Hon   CRB Check: Required
Entry Requirements: *GCE:* 240.

P80 UNIVERSITY OF PORTSMOUTH
ACADEMIC REGISTRY
UNIVERSITY HOUSE
WINSTON CHURCHILL AVENUE
PORTSMOUTH PO1 2UP
t: 023 9284 8484 f: 023 9284 3082
e: admissions@port.ac.uk
// www.port.ac.uk

B901 BSc Acute Clinical Healthcare
Duration: 1FT Hon
Entry Requirements: Contact the institution for details.

B940 BSc Biomedical Science
Duration: 3FT Hon
Entry Requirements: *GCE:* BBC. *IB:* 30. *BTEC ExtDip:* DMM.

B902 BSc Healthcare Science
Duration: 3FT Hon   CRB Check: Required
Entry Requirements: *GCE:* BBC. *IB:* 30. *BTEC ExtDip:* DMM.
Interview required.

B990 DipHE Operating Department Practice (RODP)
Duration: 2FT Dip   CRB Check: Required
Entry Requirements: *GCE:* 160. *IB:* 26. *BTEC Dip:* MM. *BTEC ExtDip:* MMP. Interview required.

B780 FdSc Paramedic Science
Duration: 2FT Fdg   CRB Check: Required
Entry Requirements: *GCE:* 220. *IB:* 26. *BTEC Dip:* DM. *BTEC ExtDip:* MMM. Interview required.

Q25 QUEEN MARGARET UNIVERSITY, EDINBURGH
QUEEN MARGARET UNIVERSITY DRIVE
EDINBURGH EH21 6UU
t: 0131474 0000 f: 0131 474 0001
e: admissions@qmu.ac.uk
// www.qmu.ac.uk

B920 BSc Occupational Therapy
Duration: 4FT Hon   CRB Check: Required
Entry Requirements: *GCE:* 260. *IB:* 28. Interview required.

Q50 QUEEN MARY, UNIVERSITY OF LONDON
QUEEN MARY, UNIVERSITY OF LONDON
MILE END ROAD
LONDON E1 4NS
t: 020 7882 5555 f: 020 7882 5500
e: admissions@qmul.ac.uk
// www.qmul.ac.uk

B990 BSc Biomedical Sciences
Duration: 3FT Hon
Entry Requirements: *GCE:* AAB. *SQAAH:* AAB. *IB:* 34.

Q75 QUEEN'S UNIVERSITY BELFAST
UNIVERSITY ROAD
BELFAST BT7 1NN
t: 028 9097 3838 f: 028 9097 5151
e: admissions@qub.ac.uk
// www.qub.ac.uk

B940 BSc Biomedical Science
Duration: 3FT Hon
Entry Requirements: *GCE:* ABB. *IB:* 33.

F3B9 BSc Physics with Medical Applications
Duration: 3FT/4FT Hon
Entry Requirements: *GCE:* BBC-BBDb. *IB:* 30.

F3BX MSci Physics with Medical Applications
Duration: 4FT Hon
Entry Requirements: *GCE:* AAB-ABBa. *IB:* 34.

R36 ROBERT GORDON UNIVERSITY
ROBERT GORDON UNIVERSITY
SCHOOLHILL
ABERDEEN
SCOTLAND AB10 1FR
t: 01224 26 27 28 f: 01224 26 21 47
e: UGOffice@rgu.ac.uk
// www.rgu.ac.uk

C9B9 BSc Biosciences with Biomedical Science
Duration: 3FT Hon
Entry Requirements: Contact the institution for details.

B920 BSc Occupational Therapy
Duration: 4FT Hon   CRB Check: Required
Entry Requirements: *GCE:* 240-260. *SQAH:* BBCC. *IB:* 26.
Interview required.

B902 BSc (Hons) Biomedical Science
Duration: 4FT Hon   CRB Check: Required
Entry Requirements: *GCE:* CCC. *SQAH:* BBCC. *IB:* 26.

R48 ROEHAMPTON UNIVERSITY
ROEHAMPTON LANE
LONDON SW15 5PU
t: 020 8392 3232 f: 020 8392 3470
e: enquiries@roehampton.ac.uk
// www.roehampton.ac.uk

B940 BSc Biomedical Sciences
Duration: 3FT Hon
Entry Requirements: *Foundation:* Distinction. *GCE:* 280. *IB:* 25.
BTEC Dip: D*D*. *BTEC ExtDip:* DMM. *OCR NED:* M2 Interview required.

R72 ROYAL HOLLOWAY, UNIVERSITY OF LONDON
ROYAL HOLLOWAY, UNIVERSITY OF LONDON
EGHAM
SURREY TW20 0EX
t: 01784 414944 f: 01784 473662
e: Admissions@rhul.ac.uk
// www.rhul.ac.uk

B990 BSc Biomedical Sciences
Duration: 3FT Hon
Entry Requirements: *GCE:* ABB. *SQAH:* AABBB. *IB:* 34.

B908 BSc Science Foundation - Option: Biomedical Sciences
Duration: 4FT Hon
Entry Requirements: Contact the institution for details.

S03 THE UNIVERSITY OF SALFORD
SALFORD M5 4WT
t: 0161 295 4545 f: 0161 295 4646
e: ug-admissions@salford.ac.uk
// www.salford.ac.uk

B900 BSc Biomedical Science
Duration: 3FT/4SW Hon
Entry Requirements: *GCE:* 280. *IB:* 28.

B9C8 BSc Counselling and Psychotherapy (Professional Practice)
Duration: 3FT Hon
Entry Requirements: Contact the institution for details.

CB69 BSc Exercise, Physical Activity and Health
Duration: 3FT Hon   CRB Check: Required
Entry Requirements: *GCE:* 280. *IB:* 29. *OCR NED:* M2

B920 BSc Occupational Therapy
Duration: 3FT Hon   CRB Check: Required
Entry Requirements: *GCE:* 240. *SQAH:* BCCCC. *SQAAH:* CCC. *IB:* 24. Interview required.

BC96 BSc Sport Rehabilitation
Duration: 3FT Hon   CRB Check: Required
Entry Requirements: *GCE:* 300. *SQAH:* AABBB. *SQAAH:* BBB. *IB:* 29.

S18 THE UNIVERSITY OF SHEFFIELD
THE UNIVERSITY OF SHEFFIELD
LEVEL 2, ARTS TOWER
WESTERN BANK
SHEFFIELD S10 2TN
t: 0114 222 8030 f: 0114 222 8032
// www.sheffield.ac.uk

B991 BMedSci Health and Human Sciences
Duration: 3FT Hon   CRB Check: Required
Entry Requirements: *GCE:* BBC. *SQAH:* BBBBB. *IB:* 30. *BTEC ExtDip:* DMM.

B900 BSc Biomedical Science (3 years)
Duration: 3FT Hon
Entry Requirements: *GCE:* AAB. *SQAH:* AAAAB. *IB:* 35. *BTEC ExtDip:* DDD.

S21 SHEFFIELD HALLAM UNIVERSITY
CITY CAMPUS
HOWARD STREET
SHEFFIELD S1 1WB
t: 0114 225 5555 f: 0114 225 2167
e: admissions@shu.ac.uk
// www.shu.ac.uk

B940 BSc Biomedical Sciences
Duration: 4SW Hon
Entry Requirements: *GCE:* 260.

B920 BSc Occupational Therapy
Duration: 3FT Hon
Entry Requirements: *GCE:* 260.

B990 DipHE Operating Department Practice
Duration: 2FT Dip
Entry Requirements: *GCE:* 220.

B780 DipHE Paramedic Practice
Duration: 2FT Dip
Entry Requirements: *GCE:* 280. Interview required.

S27 UNIVERSITY OF SOUTHAMPTON
HIGHFIELD
SOUTHAMPTON SO17 1BJ
t: 023 8059 4732 f: 023 8059 3037
e: admissions@soton.ac.uk
// www.southampton.ac.uk

B940 BSc Biomedical Sciences
Duration: 3FT Hon
Entry Requirements: *GCE:* AAA-ABB. *SQAAH:* AAB-BBB. *IB:* 32.

B920 BSc Occupational Therapy
Duration: 3FT Hon   CRB Check: Required
Entry Requirements: *GCE:* BBB. *IB:* 28.

S30 SOUTHAMPTON SOLENT UNIVERSITY
EAST PARK TERRACE
SOUTHAMPTON
HAMPSHIRE SO14 0RT
t: +44 (0) 23 8031 9039 f: + 44 (0)23 8022 2259
e: admissions@solent.ac.uk
// www.solent.ac.uk/

BC96 BSc Health, Exercise and Physical Activity
Duration: 3FT Hon
Entry Requirements: *GCE:* 220.

C8B9 BSc Psychology (Counselling)
Duration: 3FT Hon
Entry Requirements: *Foundation:* Distinction. *GCE:* 240. *SQAAH:* AA-CCD. *IB:* 24. *BTEC ExtDip:* MMM. *OCR ND:* D *OCR NED:* M3

S32 SOUTH DEVON COLLEGE
LONG ROAD
PAIGNTON
DEVON TQ4 7EJ
t: 08000 213181 f: 01803 540541
e: university@southdevon.ac.uk
// www.southdevon.ac.uk/
welcome-to-university-level

CB69 FdSc Exercise Science and Fitness
Duration: 2FT Fdg
Entry Requirements: Contact the institution for details.

B900 FdSc Healthcare Practice
Duration: 2FT Fdg   CRB Check: Required
Entry Requirements: Interview required.

S36 UNIVERSITY OF ST ANDREWS
ST KATHARINE'S WEST
16 THE SCORES
ST ANDREWS
FIFE KY16 9AX
t: 01334 462150 f: 01334 463330
e: admissions@st-andrews.ac.uk
// www.st-andrews.ac.uk

B900 FYr International Foundation for Medicine
Duration: 1FT FYr
Entry Requirements: Contact the institution for details.

S41 SOUTH CHESHIRE COLLEGE
DANE BANK AVENUE
CREWE CW2 8AB
t: 01270 654654 f: 01270 651515
e: admissions@s-cheshire.ac.uk
// www.s-cheshire.ac.uk

B940 CertHE Counselling
Duration: 1FT Cer
Entry Requirements: Contact the institution for details.

S43 SOUTH ESSEX COLLEGE OF FURTHER & HIGHER EDUCATION
LUKER ROAD
SOUTHEND-ON-SEA
ESSEX SS1 1ND
t: 0845 52 12345 f: 01702 432320
e: Admissions@southessex.ac.uk
// www.southessex.ac.uk

B941 BA Counselling
Duration: 1FT Hon
Entry Requirements: Interview required.

B940 FdA Counselling
Duration: 2FT Fdg   CRB Check: Required
Entry Requirements: *GCE:* 60. *IB:* 24. Interview required.
Admissions Test required.

S49 ST GEORGE'S, UNIVERSITY OF LONDON
CRANMER TERRACE
LONDON SW17 0RE
t: +44 (0)20 8725 2333 f: +44 (0)20 8725 0841
e: enquiries@sgul.ac.uk
// www.sgul.ac.uk

B940 BSc Biomedical Science
Duration: 3FT Hon
Entry Requirements: *GCE:* 300. *IB:* 27.

B780 FdSc Paramedic Science
Duration: 2FT Fdg   CRB Check: Required
Entry Requirements: Interview required.

S64 ST MARY'S UNIVERSITY COLLEGE, TWICKENHAM
WALDEGRAVE ROAD
STRAWBERRY HILL
MIDDLESEX TW1 4SX
t: 020 8240 4029 f: 020 8240 2361
e: admit@smuc.ac.uk
// www.smuc.ac.uk

BXY3 BA Health Exercise & Physical Activity and Physical & Sport Education
Duration: 3FT Hon
Entry Requirements: *GCE:* 240. *SQAH:* BBBC. *IB:* 28. *OCR ND:* D *OCR NED:* M3 Interview required.

BNY2 BA/BSc Health, Exercise & Physical Activity and Management Studies
Duration: 3FT Hon
Entry Requirements: *GCE:* 220. *IB:* 28. *OCR ND:* M1 *OCR NED:* P1 Interview required.

BCY6 BSc Health, Exercise & Physical Activity and Sport Science
Duration: 3FT Hon
Entry Requirements: *GCE:* 240. *SQAH:* BBBC. *IB:* 28. *OCR ND:* D *OCR NED:* M3 Interview required.

B900 BSc Health, Exercise and Physical Activity
Duration: 3FT Hon
Entry Requirements: *GCE:* 220. *IB:* 28. *OCR ND:* M1 *OCR NED:* P1 Interview required.

CB6X FdA Sport, Health and Fitness
Duration: 2FT Fdg
Entry Requirements: *GCE:* 120. *SQAH:* BBBC. Interview required.

CB89 FdSc Psychology and Counselling
Duration: 2FT Fdg
Entry Requirements: *SQAH:* BBBC. Interview required.

S72 STAFFORDSHIRE UNIVERSITY
COLLEGE ROAD
STOKE ON TRENT ST4 2DE
t: 01782 292753 f: 01782 292740
e: admissions@staffs.ac.uk
// www.staffs.ac.uk

B900 BSc Biomedical Science
Duration: 3FT Hon
Entry Requirements: *GCE:* 200-260. *IB:* 24.

CB89 BSc Psychology and Counselling
Duration: 3FT Hon
Entry Requirements: *GCE:* 200-280. *IB:* 24.

BC96 BSc Sports Therapy
Duration: 3FT Hon   CRB Check: Required
Entry Requirements: *GCE:* 200-260. *IB:* 24. Interview required.

B902 DipHE Operating Department Practice (March intake)
Duration: 2FT Dip   CRB Check: Required
Entry Requirements: *GCE:* 160. *IB:* 24. Interview required.

B780 FdSc Paramedic Science
Duration: 2FT Fdg   CRB Check: Required
Entry Requirements: *GCE:* 160. Interview required.

S82 UNIVERSITY CAMPUS SUFFOLK (UCS)
WATERFRONT BUILDING
NEPTUNE QUAY
IPSWICH
SUFFOLK IP4 1QJ
t: 01473 338833 f: 01473 339900
e: info@ucs.ac.uk
// www.ucs.ac.uk

B944 BA Counselling (Level 3 entry only)
Duration: 1FT Hon
Entry Requirements: HND required.

B942 BA Person-centred Counselling
Duration: 3FT Hon
Entry Requirements: *GCE:* 280. *IB:* 28. *BTEC ExtDip:* DMM. Interview required.

BL9M BSc Health & Wellbeing
Duration: 3FT Hon
Entry Requirements: *GCE:* 240. *IB:* 28. *BTEC ExtDip:* DMM. Interview required. Admissions Test required.

B991 DipHE Operating Department Practice
Duration: 2FT Dip   CRB Check: Required
Entry Requirements: *GCE:* 200. *IB:* 28. *BTEC ExtDip:* DMM. Interview required. Admissions Test required.

B941 FdA Counselling
Duration: 2FT Fdg
Entry Requirements: *GCE:* 200. *IB:* 28. *BTEC ExtDip:* DMM. Interview required.

B930 FdA Health Care Practice (Rehabilitation)
Duration: 2FT Fdg
Entry Requirements: *GCE:* 200. *IB:* 28. *BTEC ExtDip:* DMM. Interview required.

S84 UNIVERSITY OF SUNDERLAND
STUDENT HELPLINE
THE STUDENT GATEWAY
CHESTER ROAD
SUNDERLAND SR1 3SD
t: 0191 515 3000 f: 0191 515 3805
e: student.helpline@sunderland.ac.uk
// www.sunderland.ac.uk

B940 BSc Biomedical Science
Duration: 3FT Hon
Entry Requirements: *GCE:* 260. *IB:* 36.

B948 BSc Biomedical Science (Foundation)
Duration: 4FT/5SW Hon
Entry Requirements: *GCE:* 100-360. *SQAH:* CC.

B901 BSc Biomedical Science Route P (Foundation)
Duration: 4FT Hon
Entry Requirements: Contact the institution for details.

B910 BSc Community & Public Health
Duration: 3FT Hon
Entry Requirements: *GCE:* 260-360. *OCR ND:* D *OCR NED:* M3

C8BX BSc Psychology with Counselling
Duration: 3FT Hon
Entry Requirements: *GCE:* 260-360. *IB:* 24. *OCR ND:* D

BL95 FdSc Health and Social Care
Duration: 2FT Fdg
Entry Requirements: *GCE:* 260-360. *OCR ND:* P3 *OCR NED:* P3

S85 UNIVERSITY OF SURREY
STAG HILL
GUILDFORD
SURREY GU2 7XH
t: +44(0)1483 689305 f: +44(0)1483 689388
e: ugteam@surrey.ac.uk
// www.surrey.ac.uk

B900 BSc Biomedical Sciences (3 or 4 years)
Duration: 3FT Hon
Entry Requirements: *GCE:* AAB-ABB. *SQAH:* AABBB-ABBBB. Interview required.

B780 BSc Paramedic Practice
Duration: 3FT Hon   CRB Check: Required
Entry Requirements: *GCE:* AAB-ABB. Interview required.

B990 DipHE Operating Department Practice
Duration: 2FT Dip   CRB Check: Required
Entry Requirements: *GCE:* BBB. Interview required.

S93 SWANSEA UNIVERSITY
SINGLETON PARK
SWANSEA SA2 8PP
t: 01792 295111 f: 01792 295110
e: admissions@swansea.ac.uk
// www.swansea.ac.uk

BV95 BSc Medical Sciences and Humanities
Duration: 3FT Hon
Entry Requirements: *GCE:* ABB. *IB:* 33.

S96 SWANSEA METROPOLITAN UNIVERSITY
MOUNT PLEASANT CAMPUS
SWANSEA SA1 6ED
t: 01792 481000 f: 01792 481061
e: gemma.green@smu.ac.uk
// www.smu.ac.uk

BW94 BA Counselling and Drama
Duration: 3FT Hon
Entry Requirements: *GCE:* 180-360. *IB:* 24. Interview required.

BX93 BA Counselling and Educational Studies
Duration: 3FT Hon   CRB Check: Required
Entry Requirements: *GCE:* 180-360. *IB:* 24. Interview required.

BC98 BA Counselling and Psychology
Duration: 3FT Hon
Entry Requirements: *GCE:* 180-360. *IB:* 24. Interview required.

T20 TEESSIDE UNIVERSITY
MIDDLESBROUGH TS1 3BA
t: 01642 218121 f: 01642 384201
e: registry@tees.ac.uk
// www.tees.ac.uk

B910 BSc Environmental Health
Duration: 3FT/4SW Hon
Entry Requirements: *GCE:* 280. *IB:* 30. *BTEC Dip:* D*D*. *BTEC ExtDip:* DDM. *OCR NED:* M2 Interview required.

B920 BSc Occupational Therapy
Duration: 3FT Hon   CRB Check: Required
Entry Requirements: *GCE:* 240. *IB:* 24. *BTEC Dip:* DD. *BTEC ExtDip:* MMM. Interview required.

L550 BSc Psychology and Counselling
Duration: 3FT Hon
Entry Requirements: *GCE:* 260.

B991 DipHE Operating Department Practice
Duration: 2FT Dip   CRB Check: Required
Entry Requirements: *Foundation:* Pass. *GCE:* 160-200. *IB:* 24. *BTEC Dip:* MM. *BTEC ExtDip:* MPP. *OCR ND:* M2 *OCR NED:* P2 Interview required.

T80 UNIVERSITY OF WALES TRINITY SAINT DAVID
COLLEGE ROAD
CARMARTHEN SA31 3EP
t: 01267 676767 f: 01267 676766
e: registry@trinitysaintdavid.ac.uk
// www.tsd.ac.uk

BC96 BSc Health & Exercise Referral
Duration: 3FT Hon
Entry Requirements: *GCE:* 180-360. *IB:* 26. Interview required.

T85 TRURO AND PENWITH COLLEGE
TRURO COLLEGE
COLLEGE ROAD
TRURO
CORNWALL TR1 3XX
t: 01872 267122 f: 01872 267526
e: heinfo@trurocollege.ac.uk
// www.truro-penwith.ac.uk

B940 FdA Counselling Studies
Duration: 2FT Fdg
Entry Requirements: *GCE:* 60. *IB:* 24. *BTEC Dip:* MP. *BTEC ExtDip:* PPP. Interview required.

B910 FdSc Environmental and Public Health
Duration: 2FT Fdg
Entry Requirements: *GCE:* 60. *IB:* 24. *BTEC Dip:* MP. *BTEC ExtDip:* PPP. Interview required.

U20 UNIVERSITY OF ULSTER
COLERAINE
CO. LONDONDERRY
NORTHERN IRELAND BT52 1SA
t: 028 7012 4221 f: 028 7012 4908
e: online@ulster.ac.uk
// www.ulster.ac.uk

B992 BSc Biomedical Sciences
Duration: 3FT Hon
Entry Requirements: *GCE:* 300. *IB:* 25.

P9B9 BSc Communication with Counselling
Duration: 3FT Hon
Entry Requirements: *GCE:* 260-280. *IB:* 24.

B911 BSc Environmental Health
Duration: 3FT Hon
Entry Requirements: *GCE:* 280. *SQAH:* AAAA. *SQAAH:* BBC.

B910 BSc Environmental Health with DPP
Duration: 4SW Hon
Entry Requirements: *GCE:* 300. *IB:* 25.

Q9B9 BSc Language & Linguistics with Counselling
Duration: 3FT Hon
Entry Requirements: *GCE:* 260-280. *IB:* 24.

B930 BSc Occupational Therapy
Duration: 3FT Hon **CRB Check:** Required
Entry Requirements: *GCE:* BBB. *SQAH:* AABCC. *SQAAH:* BBB. *IB:* 25. Admissions Test required.

B990 BSc Hons Biomedical Science Coterminous, with DPP (Pathology)
Duration: 4SW Hon **CRB Check:** Required
Entry Requirements: *GCE:* 300. *IB:* 25.

B991 BSc Hons Biomedical Sciences with DPP/DIAS
Duration: 4SW Hon
Entry Requirements: *GCE:* 300. *IB:* 25.

U40 UNIVERSITY OF THE WEST OF SCOTLAND
PAISLEY
RENFREWSHIRE
SCOTLAND PA1 2BE
t: 0141 848 3727 f: 0141 848 3623
e: admissions@uws.ac.uk
// www.uws.ac.uk

B940 BSc Biomedical Science
Duration: 4FT/5SW Hon
Entry Requirements: *GCE:* CCC. *SQAH:* BBC-BCCC.

B910 BSc Environmental Health
Duration: 4FT Hon
Entry Requirements: *GCE:* CCC. *SQAH:* BBC-BCCC.

B920 BSc Occupational Safety and Health
Duration: 3FT Ord
Entry Requirements: *GCE:* CCC. *SQAH:* BBC-BCCC.

U80 UNIVERSITY COLLEGE LONDON (UNIVERSITY OF LONDON)
GOWER STREET
LONDON WC1E 6BT
t: 020 7679 3000 f: 020 7679 3001
// www.ucl.ac.uk

B990 BSc Biomedical Sciences
Duration: 3FT Hon
Entry Requirements: *GCE:* AAAe. *SQAAH:* AAA. *IB:* 38. Interview required.

W05 THE UNIVERSITY OF WEST LONDON
ST MARY'S ROAD
EALING
LONDON W5 5RF
t: 0800 036 8888 f: 020 8566 1353
e: learning.advice@uwl.ac.uk
// www.uwl.ac.uk

C8B9 BSc Psychology with Counselling Theory
Duration: 3FT Hon
Entry Requirements: *GCE:* 200. *IB:* 28. Interview required.

B991 DipHE Operating Department Practice
Duration: 2FT Dip **CRB Check:** Required
Entry Requirements: *GCE:* 100. *IB:* 24. Interview required.

W08 WAKEFIELD COLLEGE
MARGARET STREET
WAKEFIELD
WEST YORKSHIRE WF1 2DH
t: 01924 789111 f: 01924 789281
e: courseinfo@wakefield.ac.uk
// www.wakefield.ac.uk

CB69 FdSc Health Related Exercise and Fitness
Duration: 2FT Fdg
Entry Requirements: *GCE:* 120.

W20 THE UNIVERSITY OF WARWICK
COVENTRY CV4 8UW
t: 024 7652 3723 f: 024 7652 4649
e: ugadmissions@warwick.ac.uk
// www.warwick.ac.uk

BF91 BSc Biomedical Chemistry
Duration: 3FT Hon
Entry Requirements: *GCE:* AAB. *SQAAH:* AA. *IB:* 36.

B900 BSc Biomedical Science
Duration: 3FT Hon
Entry Requirements: *GCE:* AAB. *SQAAH:* AA-AB. *IB:* 36.

W25 WARWICKSHIRE COLLEGE
WARWICK NEW ROAD
LEAMINGTON SPA
WARWICKSHIRE CV32 5JE
t: 01926 884223 f: 01926 318 111
e: kgooch@warkscol.ac.uk
// www.warwickshire.ac.uk

B940 FdSc Counselling (Cognitive Behavioural)
Duration: 2FT Fdg
Entry Requirements: Contact the institution for details.

B941 FdSc Counselling (Person Centred)
Duration: 2FT Fdg
Entry Requirements: Contact the institution for details.

W36 WEST CHESHIRE COLLEGE
EATON ROAD
HANDBRIDGE
CHESTER
CHESHIRE CH4 7ER
t: 01244 656555 f: 01244 670687
e: info@west-cheshire.ac.uk
// www.west-cheshire.ac.uk

CB69 FdSc Fitness and Health
Duration: 2FT Fdg
Entry Requirements: Contact the institution for details.

W50 UNIVERSITY OF WESTMINSTER
2ND FLOOR, CAVENDISH HOUSE
101 NEW CAVENDISH STREET,
LONDON W1W 6XH
t: 020 7915 5511
e: course-enquiries@westminster.ac.uk
// www.westminster.ac.uk

B900 BSc Biomedical Sciences
Duration: 4SW Hon
Entry Requirements: *GCE:* CCC. *SQAH:* CCCC. *IB:* 26. Interview required.

B940 BSc Biomedical Sciences
Duration: 3FT Hon
Entry Requirements: *GCE:* CCC. *SQAH:* CCCC. *IB:* 26. Interview required.

B903 BSc Biomedical Sciences with Foundation
Duration: 4FT Hon
Entry Requirements: *GCE:* CCD. *SQAH:* CCCC. *IB:* 26. Interview required.

WB69 BSc Clinical Photography
Duration: 3FT Hon
Entry Requirements: *GCE:* CC. *SQAH:* CCCC. *IB:* 26. Interview required.

B901 BSc Human and Medical Science
Duration: 3FT Hon
Entry Requirements: *GCE:* CCD. *SQAH:* CCCC. *IB:* 26. Interview required.

B902 BSc Human and Medical Science with Foundation
Duration: 4FT Hon
Entry Requirements: *GCE:* CCD. *SQAH:* CCCC. *IB:* 26. Interview required.

W51 CITY OF WESTMINSTER COLLEGE
CITY OF WESTMINSTER COLLEGE
PADDINGTON GREEN CAMPUS
25 PADDINGTON GREEN
LONDON W2 1NB
t: 020 7723 8826
e: customer.services@cwc.ac.uk
// www.cwc.ac.uk

B900 HNC Health and Social Care
Duration: 1FT HNC   CRB Check: Required
Entry Requirements: Contact the institution for details.

W65 WEST THAMES COLLEGE
LONDON ROAD
ISLEWORTH
MIDDLESEX TW7 4HS
t: 020 8326 2000 f: 020 8326 2001
e: info@west-thames.ac.uk
// www.west-thames.ac.uk/en/
higher-education/

B901 HND Biomedical Science
Duration: 2FT HND
Entry Requirements: Contact the institution for details.

W67 WIGAN AND LEIGH COLLEGE
PO BOX 53
PARSON'S WALK
WIGAN
GREATER MANCHESTER WN1 1RS
t: 01942 761605 f: 01942 761164
e: applications@wigan-leigh.ac.uk
// www.wigan-leigh.ac.uk

BC96 FdSc Health & Personal Training
Duration: 2FT Fdg
Entry Requirements: Interview required.

W75 UNIVERSITY OF WOLVERHAMPTON
ADMISSIONS UNIT
MX207, CAMP STREET
WOLVERHAMPTON
WEST MIDLANDS WV1 1AD
t: 01902 321000 f: 01902 321896
e: admissions@wlv.ac.uk
// www.wlv.ac.uk

B904 BMed Sci Medical Science
Duration: 3FT Hon
Entry Requirements: *GCE:* 280. *IB:* 25. *BTEC Dip:* D*D*. *BTEC ExtDip:* DMM. *OCR NED:* M2

LB27 BSc Armed Forces and Combat Medicine
Duration: 3FT Hon   CRB Check: Required
Entry Requirements: Contact the institution for details.

B990 BSc Biomedical Science
Duration: 3FT/4SW Hon
Entry Requirements: *GCE:* 260-320. *IB:* 24.

B912 BSc Environmental Health
Duration: 3FT/4SW Hon
Entry Requirements: *GCE:* 200. *IB:* 24. *BTEC Dip:* DM. *BTEC ExtDip:* MMP. *OCR ND:* M1 *OCR NED:* P1

B900 BSc Health Studies
Duration: 3FT Hon
Entry Requirements: *GCE:* 160-220. *IB:* 30.

B902 BSc Health Studies (Top-Up)
Duration: 1FT Hon
Entry Requirements: Contact the institution for details.

CB69 BSc Physical Activity, Exercise and Health
Duration: 3FT Hon   CRB Check: Required
Entry Requirements: *GCE:* 200. *IB:* 24. *BTEC Dip:* DM. *BTEC ExtDip:* MMP. *OCR ND:* M1 *OCR NED:* P1

B914 BSc Public Health
Duration: 3FT Hon
Entry Requirements: Contact the institution for details.

B930 BSc Rehabilitation Studies (Top Up)
Duration: 1FT Hon
Entry Requirements: Contact the institution for details.

BL95 BSc Social Care and Health Studies
Duration: 3FT Hon
Entry Requirements: *GCE:* 160-220.

W76 UNIVERSITY OF WINCHESTER
WINCHESTER
HANTS SO22 4NR
t: 01962 827234 f: 01962 827288
e: course.enquiries@winchester.ac.uk
// www.winchester.ac.uk

BL95 BSc Health, Community and Social Care Studies
Duration: 3FT Hon
Entry Requirements: *Foundation:* Pass. *GCE:* 260-300. *IB:* 24. *OCR ND:* D

W80 UNIVERSITY OF WORCESTER
HENWICK GROVE
WORCESTER WR2 6AJ
t: 01905 855111 f: 01905 855377
e: admissions@worc.ac.uk
// www.worcester.ac.uk

B940 BA Counselling
Duration: 1FT Hon
Entry Requirements: Contact the institution for details.

B990 BSc Health Sciences
Duration: 1FT Hon
Entry Requirements: Contact the institution for details.

B941 FdSc Counselling
Duration: 2FT Fdg   CRB Check: Required
Entry Requirements: Contact the institution for details.

Y75 YORK ST JOHN UNIVERSITY
LORD MAYOR'S WALK
YORK YO31 7EX
t: 01904 876598 f: 01904 876940/876921
e: admissions@yorksj.ac.uk
// w3.yorksj.ac.uk

BX91 BA Counselling, Coaching & Mentoring
Duration: 3FT Hon   CRB Check: Required
Entry Requirements: *GCE:* 220.

B930 BHSc Occupational Therapy
Duration: 3FT Hon   CRB Check: Required
Entry Requirements: *GCE:* 260. *IB:* 24. Interview required.

CB6X BSc Sports Science and Injury Management
Duration: 3FT Hon
Entry Requirements: *GCE:* 220-260. *IB:* 24.

CB69 BSc Sports Science: Exercise Practice
Duration: 3FT Hon
Entry Requirements: *GCE:* 220-260. *IB:* 24.

SOCIAL CARE AND SOCIAL WORK

A44 ACCRINGTON & ROSSENDALE COLLEGE
BROAD OAK ROAD,
ACCRINGTON,
LANCASHIRE, BB5 2AW.
t: 01254 389933 f: 01254 354001
e: info@accross.ac.uk
// www.accrosshighereducation.co.uk/

LL53 BA Health and Applied Social Studies
Duration: 3FT Hon
Entry Requirements: *GCE:* 160. Interview required.

L511 FdA Health and Social Care
Duration: 2FT Fdg   CRB Check: Required
Entry Requirements: Contact the institution for details.

A60 ANGLIA RUSKIN UNIVERSITY
BISHOP HALL LANE
CHELMSFORD
ESSEX CM1 1SQ
t: 0845 271 3333 f: 01245 251789
e: answers@anglia.ac.uk
// www.anglia.ac.uk

L520 BA Early Childhood Studies
Duration: 3FT Hon   CRB Check: Required
Entry Requirements: *GCE:* 200. *SQAH:* BBCC. *SQAAH:* CC. *IB:* 24.

L501 BA Social Work
Duration: 3FT Hon   CRB Check: Required
Entry Requirements: *GCE:* 240. *SQAH:* CCCC. *SQAAH:* CC. *IB:* 26.
Interview required.

L506 MA Social Work
Duration: 2FT PMD   CRB Check: Required
Entry Requirements: Interview required.

B06 BANGOR UNIVERSITY
BANGOR UNIVERSITY
BANGOR
GWYNEDD LL57 2DG
t: 01248 388484 f: 01248 370451
e: admissions@bangor.ac.uk
// www.bangor.ac.uk

LL3M BA Cymdeithaseg and Health & Social Care
Duration: 3FT Hon
Entry Requirements: Contact the institution for details.

L510 BA Health & Social Care
Duration: 3FT Hon
Entry Requirements: *GCE:* 220-260. *IB:* 28.

LM52 BA Health & Social Care and Criminology & Criminal Justice
Duration: 3FT Hon
Entry Requirements: *GCE:* 240-260. *IB:* 28.

LQ55 BA Health & Social Care/Cymraeg
Duration: 3FT Hon
Entry Requirements: *GCE:* 220-260. *IB:* 28.

LN52 BA Health & Social Care/Management
Duration: 3FT Hon
Entry Requirements: *GCE:* 240-280. *IB:* 28.

LL54 BA Health & Social Care/Social Policy
Duration: 3FT Hon
Entry Requirements: *GCE:* 220-260. *IB:* 28.

LL53 BA Health & Social Care/Sociology
Duration: 3FT Hon
Entry Requirements: *GCE:* 220-260. *IB:* 28.

LL5K BA Polisi Cymdeithasol and Health & Social Care
Duration: 3FT Hon
Entry Requirements: Contact the institution for details.

X312 FdA Early Childhood and Learning Support Studies
Duration: 2FT Fdg
Entry Requirements: *GCE:* 60-100. *IB:* 24.

B16 UNIVERSITY OF BATH
CLAVERTON DOWN
BATH BA2 7AY
t: 01225 383019 f: 01225 386366
e: admissions@bath.ac.uk
// www.bath.ac.uk

LX5H BA Childhood, Youth and Education Studies
Duration: 3FT Hon
Entry Requirements: *GCE:* ABB. *SQAAH:* ABB. *IB:* 35.

LXM3 BA Childhood, Youth and Education Studies
Duration: 4SW Hon
Entry Requirements: *GCE:* ABB. *SQAAH:* ABB. *IB:* 35.

L501 BSc Social Work and Applied Social Studies (including Placement)
Duration: 3FT Hon   CRB Check: Required
Entry Requirements: *GCE:* BBC. *SQAAH:* BBC. *IB:* 32. Interview required.

B940 FdSc Addictions Counselling
Duration: 2FT Fdg
Entry Requirements: Contact the institution for details.

B20 BATH SPA UNIVERSITY
NEWTON PARK
NEWTON ST LOE
BATH BA2 9BN
t: 01225 875875 f: 01225 875444
e: enquiries@bathspa.ac.uk
// www.bathspa.ac.uk/clearing

XL34 BA/BSc Education/Health Studies
Duration: 3FT Hon   CRB Check: Required
Entry Requirements: *GCE:* 220-280. *IB:* 24.

XL15 BSc Education/Health Studies
Duration: 3FT Hon   CRB Check: Required
Entry Requirements: *GCE:* 220-280. *IB:* 24.

B22 UNIVERSITY OF BEDFORDSHIRE
PARK SQUARE
LUTON
BEDS LU1 3JU
t: 0844 8482234 f: 01582 489323
e: admissions@beds.ac.uk
// www.beds.ac.uk

L550 BA Child and Adolescent Studies
Duration: 3FT Hon
Entry Requirements: *Foundation:* Pass. *GCE:* 200. *SQAH:* BCC. *SQAAH:* BCC. *IB:* 24. *OCR ND:* M1 *OCR NED:* P1

X310 BA Childhood and Youth Studies
Duration: 3FT Hon
Entry Requirements: *GCE:* 200-220. *OCR ND:* M1 *OCR NED:* P1

L590 BA Health and Social Care
Duration: 3FT Hon
Entry Requirements: *Foundation:* Pass. *GCE:* 200. *SQAH:* BCC. *SQAAH:* BCC. *IB:* 24. *OCR ND:* M1 *OCR NED:* P1

L592 BA Youth and Community Studies
Duration: 3FT Hon   CRB Check: Required
Entry Requirements: Interview required.

L501 BSc Social Work
Duration: 3FT Hon   CRB Check: Required
Entry Requirements: *Foundation:* Pass. *GCE:* 240. *SQAH:* BBBB-BBBC. *SQAAH:* BCC. *IB:* 24. *OCR ND:* D *OCR NED:* M3 Interview required.

LN52 FdA Care Management
Duration: 2FT Fdg
Entry Requirements: *GCE:* 120.

L591 FdA Child and Adolescent Studies
Duration: 2FT Fdg
Entry Requirements: Contact the institution for details.

L521 FdA Early Years Senior Practitioner
Duration: 2FT Fdg
Entry Requirements: Contact the institution for details.

L508 MSc Social Work (Postgraduate Entry)
Duration: 2FT PMD   CRB Check: Required
Entry Requirements: Interview required.

B25 BIRMINGHAM CITY UNIVERSITY
PERRY BARR
BIRMINGHAM B42 2SU
t: 0121 331 5595 f: 0121 331 7994
// www.bcu.ac.uk

L590 BA Children and Integrated Professional Care
Duration: 3FT Hon   CRB Check: Required
Entry Requirements: *GCE:* 200.

L501 BSc Social Work
Duration: 3FT Hon   CRB Check: Required
Entry Requirements: *GCE:* 260. *SQAAH:* CCCCC. *IB:* 32. Interview required. Portfolio required.

B32 THE UNIVERSITY OF BIRMINGHAM
EDGBASTON
BIRMINGHAM B15 2TT
t: 0121 415 8900 f: 0121 414 7159
e: admissions@bham.ac.uk
// www.birmingham.ac.uk

L4L5 BA Social Policy (Policing and Community Justice)
Duration: 3FT Hon
Entry Requirements: *GCE:* ABB. *SQAH:* ABBBB. *SQAAH:* AB.

L501 BA Social Work
Duration: 3FT Hon   CRB Check: Required
Entry Requirements: *GCE:* ABB. *SQAH:* ABBBB. *SQAAH:* AB.
Interview required. Admissions Test required.

L502 MA Social Work (Postgraduate Entry)
Duration: 2FT PMD   CRB Check: Required
Entry Requirements: Interview required.

B37 BISHOP BURTON COLLEGE
BISHOP BURTON
BEVERLEY
EAST YORKSHIRE HU17 8QG
t: 01964 553000 f: 01964 553101
e: enquiries@bishopburton.ac.uk
// www.bishopburton.ac.uk

LL4M BA Police and Community Studies (Top-up)
Duration: 1FT Hon
Entry Requirements: Contact the institution for details.

LL45 FdA Police and Community Studies
Duration: 2FT Fdg
Entry Requirements: *GCE:* 80.

B38 BISHOP GROSSETESTE UNIVERSITY COLLEGE LINCOLN
BISHOP GROSSETESTE UNIVERSITY COLLEGE
LINCOLN LN1 3DY
t: 01522 583658 f: 01522 530243
e: admissions@bishopg.ac.uk
// www.bishopg.ac.uk/courses

L591 BA Applied Studies in Children and Youth Work
Duration: 1FT Hon   CRB Check: Required
Entry Requirements: Interview required.

L520 BA Applied Studies in Early Childhood
Duration: 1FT Hon   CRB Check: Required
Entry Requirements: Interview required.

C8L5 BA Early Childhood Studies with Psychology
Duration: 3FT Hon   CRB Check: Required
Entry Requirements: Contact the institution for details.

L590 FdA Applied Studies (Children and Youth Work)
Duration: 2FT Fdg   CRB Check: Required
Entry Requirements: *GCE:* 40. Interview required.

LX53 FdA Applied Studies (Early Childhood)
Duration: 2FT Fdg   CRB Check: Required
Entry Requirements: *GCE:* 40. Interview required.

B40 BLACKBURN COLLEGE
FEILDEN STREET
BLACKBURN BB2 1LH
t: 01254 292594 f: 01254 679647
e: he-admissions@blackburn.ac.uk
// www.blackburn.ac.uk

L512 BA Care Practice (Top-Up)
Duration: 1FT Hon
Entry Requirements: Contact the institution for details.

LX5H BA Early Childhood Studies (Top-Up)
Duration: 1FT Hon
Entry Requirements: Contact the institution for details.

L590 BA Working with Children and Young People (Top-Up)
Duration: 1FT Hon
Entry Requirements: Contact the institution for details.

L540 FdA Community Policing and Justice Management
Duration: 2FT Fdg
Entry Requirements: Contact the institution for details.

L591 FdA Disability Studies (Inclusive Practice)
Duration: 2FT Fdg
Entry Requirements: *GCE:* 120.

LX53 FdA Early Childhood Studies
Duration: 2FT Fdg
Entry Requirements: *GCE:* 120.

L520 FdA Positive Practice with Children & Young People
Duration: 2FT Fdg
Entry Requirements: *GCE:* 120.

L510 FdA Social Care
Duration: 2FT Fdg
Entry Requirements: *GCE:* 80.

B41 BLACKPOOL AND THE FYLDE COLLEGE AN ASSOCIATE COLLEGE OF LANCASTER UNIVERSITY
ASHFIELD ROAD
BISPHAM
BLACKPOOL
LANCS FY2 0HB
t: 01253 504346 f: 01253 504198
e: admissions@blackpool.ac.uk
// www.blackpool.ac.uk

L590 BA Early Childhood Studies (Top-Up)
Duration: 1FT Hon
Entry Requirements: Contact the institution for details.

L511 BA Health and Social Care: Adult (Top-Up)
Duration: 1FT Hon
Entry Requirements: Contact the institution for details.

L512 BA Health and Social Care: Children and Young People (Top up)
Duration: 1FT Hon   CRB Check: Required
Entry Requirements: Contact the institution for details.

L510 FdA Professional Practice in Health and Social Care
Duration: 2FT Fdg   CRB Check: Required
Entry Requirements: *GCE:* 200-360. *IB:* 24. *OCR ND:* M1 *OCR NED:* P1

L540 FdA Working with Young People in the Community
Duration: 2FT Fdg   CRB Check: Required
Entry Requirements: *GCE:* 200-360. *OCR ND:* M1 *OCR NED:* P1

L520 FdSc Professional Practice - Early Years
Duration: 2FT Fdg   CRB Check: Required
Entry Requirements: *GCE:* 200-360. *IB:* 24. *OCR ND:* M1 *OCR NED:* P1

B44 UNIVERSITY OF BOLTON
DEANE ROAD
BOLTON BL3 5AB
t: 01204 903903 f: 01204 399074
e: enquiries@bolton.ac.uk
// www.bolton.ac.uk

L530 BA Community Studies
Duration: 3FT Hon   CRB Check: Required
Entry Requirements: *GCE:* 240. Interview required.

L591 BA Early Childhood Studies
Duration: 1FT Hon   CRB Check: Required
Entry Requirements: Interview required.

L590 BA Youth & Community Work
Duration: 3FT Hon   CRB Check: Required
Entry Requirements: *GCE:* 240. Interview required.

L592 FdA Early Years Childhood Studies
Duration: 2FT Fdg   CRB Check: Required
Entry Requirements: *GCE:* 100. Interview required.

L510 FdA Health and Social Care
Duration: 2FT Fdg   CRB Check: Required
Entry Requirements: *GCE:* 100. Interview required.

B50 BOURNEMOUTH UNIVERSITY
TALBOT CAMPUS
FERN BARROW
POOLE
DORSET BH12 5BB
t: 01202 524111
// www.bournemouth.ac.uk

LX53 BA Early Years Care and Education (Top-Up)
Duration: 1FT Hon   CRB Check: Required
Entry Requirements: HND required.

L500 BA Social Work
Duration: 3FT Hon   CRB Check: Required
Entry Requirements: *GCE:* 320. *IB:* 32. *BTEC Dip:* D*D*. *BTEC ExtDip:* DDM. Interview required.

L501 MA Social Work
Duration: 2FT PMD   CRB Check: Required
Entry Requirements: Interview required.

B56 THE UNIVERSITY OF BRADFORD
RICHMOND ROAD
BRADFORD
WEST YORKSHIRE BD7 1DP
t: 0800 073 1225 f: 01274 235585
e: course-enquiries@bradford.ac.uk
// www.bradford.ac.uk

L541 BA Community Justice
Duration: 1FT Hon
Entry Requirements: Contact the institution for details.

L500 BA Social Work
Duration: 3FT Hon   CRB Check: Required
Entry Requirements: *GCE:* 260. *IB:* 24. Interview required.

L590 BA Working with Children, Young People and Families
Duration: 3FT Hon   CRB Check: Required
Entry Requirements: *GCE:* 240. *IB:* 24. Interview required.

L501 MA Social Work (Postgraduate Entry)
Duration: 2FT PMD   CRB Check: Required
Entry Requirements: Interview required.

B60 BRADFORD COLLEGE: AN ASSOCIATE COLLEGE OF LEEDS METROPOLITAN UNIVERSITY

GREAT HORTON ROAD
BRADFORD
WEST YORKSHIRE BD7 1AY
t: 01274 433008 f: 01274 431652
e: heregistry@bradfordcollege.ac.uk
// www.bradfordcollege.ac.uk/
university-centre

CL85 BA Counselling and Psychology in Community Settings
Duration: 3FT Hon   CRB Check: Required
Entry Requirements: *GCE:* 200. Interview required.

L520 BA Early Years Practice
Duration: 3FT Hon   CRB Check: Required
Entry Requirements: *GCE:* 120-160. Interview required.

B900 BA Health and Social Welfare
Duration: 3FT Hon   CRB Check: Required
Entry Requirements: *GCE:* 100-140.

L500 BA Social Work
Duration: 3FT Hon   CRB Check: Required
Entry Requirements: *GCE:* 200. Interview required.

L522 BA Youth and Community Development
Duration: 3FT Hon   CRB Check: Required
Entry Requirements: *GCE:* 100-140. Interview required.

L591 BA Youth and Community Studies (Top-up)
Duration: 1FT Hon   CRB Check: Required
Entry Requirements: Contact the institution for details.

B72 UNIVERSITY OF BRIGHTON

MITHRAS HOUSE 211
LEWES ROAD
BRIGHTON BN2 4AT
t: 01273 644644 f: 01273 642607
e: admissions@brighton.ac.uk
// www.brighton.ac.uk

L541 BA Applied Social Science
Duration: 3FT Hon
Entry Requirements: *GCE:* BBC. *IB:* 28.

L511 BA Health Studies (Top-Up)
Duration: 1FT Hon
Entry Requirements: HND required.

L540 BA Social Science
Duration: 3FT Hon
Entry Requirements: *GCE:* BBB. *IB:* 30.

L500 BSc Social Work
Duration: 3FT Hon   CRB Check: Required
Entry Requirements: *GCE:* BBB. *IB:* 30.

L508 MSc Social Work (Postgraduate Entry)
Duration: 2FT PMD
Entry Requirements: Interview required.

B77 BRISTOL, CITY OF BRISTOL COLLEGE

SOUTH BRISTOL SKILLS ACADEMY
CITY OF BRISTOL COLLEGE
PO BOX 2887 BS2 2BB
t: 0117 312 5000
e: HEAdmissions@cityofbristol.ac.uk
// www.cityofbristol.ac.uk

015L HND Health and Social Care
Duration: 2FT HND   CRB Check: Required
Entry Requirements: *GCE:* 140. Interview required.

B78 UNIVERSITY OF BRISTOL

UNDERGRADUATE ADMISSIONS OFFICE
SENATE HOUSE
TYNDALL AVENUE
BRISTOL BS8 1TH
t: 0117 928 9000 f: 0117 331 7391
e: ug-admissions@bristol.ac.uk
// www.bristol.ac.uk

L520 BSc Childhood Studies
Duration: 3FT Hon
Entry Requirements: *GCE:* ABB. *SQAH:* AABBB. *SQAAH:* ABB. *IB:* 33.

B80 UNIVERSITY OF THE WEST OF ENGLAND, BRISTOL

FRENCHAY CAMPUS
COLDHARBOUR LANE
BRISTOL BS16 1QY
t: +44 (0)117 32 83333 f: +44 (0)117 32 82810
e: admissions@uwe.ac.uk
// www.uwe.ac.uk

L500 BSc Social Work
Duration: 3FT Hon   CRB Check: Required
Entry Requirements: *GCE:* 300. Interview required.

L510 FdSc Health and Social Care Practice
Duration: 2FT Fdg
Entry Requirements: *GCE:* 100.

B84 BRUNEL UNIVERSITY

UXBRIDGE
MIDDLESEX UB8 3PH
t: 01895 265265 f: 01895 269790
e: admissions@brunel.ac.uk
// www.brunel.ac.uk

L500 BA Social Work
Duration: 3FT Hon   CRB Check: Required
Entry Requirements: *GCE:* BBB. *SQAAH:* BBB. *IB:* 32. *BTEC ExtDip:* DDD. Interview required.

L508 MA Social Work (Postgraduate Entry)
Duration: 2FT PMD   CRB Check: Required
Entry Requirements: Interview required.

B94 BUCKINGHAMSHIRE NEW UNIVERSITY
QUEEN ALEXANDRA ROAD
HIGH WYCOMBE
BUCKINGHAMSHIRE HP11 2JZ
t: 0800 0565 660 f: 01494 605 023
e: admissions@bucks.ac.uk
// bucks.ac.uk

L504 BSc Social Work
Duration: 3FT Hon   CRB Check: Required
Entry Requirements: *GCE:* 240-280. *IB:* 25. *OCR ND:* D *OCR NED:* M2 Interview required.

L510 FdA Health and Social Care
Duration: 2FT Fdg
Entry Requirements: *GCE:* 100-140. *IB:* 24. *OCR ND:* P1 *OCR NED:* P2 Interview required.

L500 MSc Social Work (Postgraduate Entry)
Duration: 2FT PMD   CRB Check: Required
Entry Requirements: Interview required.

C10 CANTERBURY CHRIST CHURCH UNIVERSITY
NORTH HOLMES ROAD
CANTERBURY
KENT CT1 1QU
t: 01227 782900 f: 01227 782888
e: admissions@canterbury.ac.uk
// www.canterbury.ac.uk

LX53 BA Education and Learning (Youth Work and Community Learning and Development)
Duration: 3FT Hon
Entry Requirements: Contact the institution for details.

L590 BA Social Pedagogy (Youth Work and Community Learning and Development)
Duration: 3FT Hon
Entry Requirements: Contact the institution for details.

L500 BA Social Work
Duration: 3FT Hon   CRB Check: Required
Entry Requirements: *GCE:* 240. *IB:* 24. Interview required.

L591 BA Youth Work and Community Learning and Development
Duration: 3FT Hon
Entry Requirements: Contact the institution for details.

LT57 BA/BSc Health Studies and American Studies (With a Year in USA)
Duration: 4FT Hon
Entry Requirements: Contact the institution for details.

LT5T BA/BSc Health Studies with American Studies (With a Year in USA)
Duration: 4FT Hon
Entry Requirements: Contact the institution for details.

L508 MA Social Work (Postgraduate Entry)
Duration: 2FT PMD   CRB Check: Required
Entry Requirements: Interview required.

C15 CARDIFF UNIVERSITY
PO BOX 927
30-36 NEWPORT ROAD
CARDIFF CF24 0DE
t: 029 2087 9999 f: 029 2087 6138
e: admissions@cardiff.ac.uk
// www.cardiff.ac.uk

L508 MA Social Work (Postgraduate Entry)
Duration: 2FT PMD   CRB Check: Required
Entry Requirements: Interview required.

C20 CARDIFF METROPOLITAN UNIVERSITY (UWIC)
ADMISSIONS UNIT
LLANDAFF CAMPUS
WESTERN AVENUE
CARDIFF CF5 2YB
t: 029 2041 6070 f: 029 2041 6286
e: admissions@cardiffmet.ac.uk
// www.cardiffmet.ac.uk

L511 BSc Health and Social Care (3 years)
Duration: 3FT Hon   CRB Check: Required
Entry Requirements: *GCE:* 240. *IB:* 24. *BTEC Dip:* DD. *BTEC ExtDip:* MMM. *OCR ND:* D *OCR NED:* M3

L510 BSc Health and Social Care (4 years inc Foundation)
Duration: 4FT Hon
Entry Requirements: *Foundation:* Pass. *GCE:* 80. *IB:* 24. *BTEC Dip:* PP. *BTEC ExtDip:* PPP. *OCR ND:* P3 *OCR NED:* P3

L501 BSc Social Work
Duration: 3FT Hon   CRB Check: Required
Entry Requirements: *GCE:* 240. *IB:* 24. *BTEC Dip:* DD. *BTEC ExtDip:* MMM. *OCR ND:* D *OCR NED:* M3 Interview required.

015L HND Health and Social Care (2 years)
Duration: 2FT HND   CRB Check: Required
Entry Requirements: *GCE:* 120. *IB:* 24. *BTEC SubDip:* D. *BTEC Dip:* MP. *BTEC ExtDip:* PPP. *OCR ND:* P2 *OCR NED:* P3

115L HND Health and Social Care (3 years inc Foundation)
Duration: 3FT HND
Entry Requirements: *Foundation:* Pass. *GCE:* 80. *IB:* 24. *BTEC Dip:* PP. *BTEC ExtDip:* PPP. *OCR ND:* P3 *OCR NED:* P3

C22 COLEG SIR GAR / CARMARTHENSHIRE COLLEGE
SANDY ROAD
LLANELLI
CARMARTHENSHIRE SA15 4DN
t: 01554 748000 f: 01554 748170
e: admissions@colegsirgar.ac.uk
// www.colegsirgar.ac.uk

L500 FdSc Care Studies
Duration: 2FT Fdg   CRB Check: Required
Entry Requirements: Contact the institution for details.

C30 UNIVERSITY OF CENTRAL LANCASHIRE
PRESTON
LANCS PR1 2HE
t: 01772 201201 f: 01772 894954
e: uadmissions@uclan.ac.uk
// www.uclan.ac.uk

L590 BA Care, Community & Citizenship
Duration: 3FT Hon
Entry Requirements: *GCE:* 240. *SQAH:* BBBC. *IB:* 28. *OCR ND:* D *OCR NED:* M3

LLH5 BA Care, Community & Citizenship (Foundation entry)
Duration: 4FT Hon
Entry Requirements: Contact the institution for details.

L591 BA Children, Families and Schools (Top-Up)
Duration: 1FT Hon
Entry Requirements: Contact the institution for details.

L541 BA Children, Schools and Families
Duration: 3FT Hon
Entry Requirements: *GCE:* 240-280. *SQAH:* BBBC. *IB:* 28. *OCR ND:* D *OCR NED:* M3

L500 BA Social Work
Duration: 3FT Hon   CRB Check: Required
Entry Requirements: *GCE:* 240. *IB:* 26. Interview required.

CL65 BA Sports Development
Duration: 3FT/4SW Hon
Entry Requirements: *GCE:* 240-280. *SQAH:* AABB-BBBC. *IB:* 28. *OCR ND:* D

L512 BSc Health and Social Care (Top Up)
Duration: 1FT Hon
Entry Requirements: Contact the institution for details.

L690 FdA Children, Young People and their Services
Duration: 2FT Fdg
Entry Requirements: Contact the institution for details.

L511 FdA Health and Social Care
Duration: 2FT Fdg
Entry Requirements: *GCE:* 100. *OCR ND:* P3 *OCR NED:* P3

L540 FdA Volunteering & Community Action
Duration: 2FT Fdg   CRB Check: Required
Entry Requirements: *GCE:* 80.

L508 MA Social Work (Postgraduate Entry)
Duration: 2FT PMD   CRB Check: Required
Entry Requirements: Contact the institution for details.

C55 UNIVERSITY OF CHESTER
PARKGATE ROAD
CHESTER CH1 4BJ
t: 01244 511000 f: 01244 511300
e: enquiries@chester.ac.uk
// www.chester.ac.uk

LW54 BA Counselling Skills and Drama & Theatre Studies
Duration: 3FT Hon
Entry Requirements: *Foundation:* Pass. *GCE:* 260-300. *SQAH:* BBBB. *IB:* 28.

LL35 BA Counselling Skills and Sociology
Duration: 3FT Hon
Entry Requirements: *GCE:* 240-280. *SQAH:* BBBB. *IB:* 26.

LV56 BA Counselling Skills and Theology & Religious Studies
Duration: 3FT Hon
Entry Requirements: *GCE:* 240-280. *SQAH:* BBBB. *IB:* 26.

ML9N BA Criminology and Counselling Skills
Duration: 3FT Hon
Entry Requirements: *GCE:* 240-280. *SQAH:* BBBB. *IB:* 26.

L510 BA Health and Social Care
Duration: 3FT Hon
Entry Requirements: *GCE:* 240-280. *SQAH:* BBBB. *IB:* 24.

L505 BA Social Work
Duration: 3FT Hon   CRB Check: Required
Entry Requirements: *GCE:* 240-280. *SQAH:* BBBB. *IB:* 24. Interview required.

L531 BA Youth Work
Duration: 3FT Hon   CRB Check: Required
Entry Requirements: *GCE:* 240-280. *SQAH:* BBBB. *IB:* 26. Interview required.

C58 UNIVERSITY OF CHICHESTER
BISHOP OTTER CAMPUS
COLLEGE LANE
CHICHESTER
WEST SUSSEX PO19 6PE
t: 01243 816002 f: 01243 816161
e: admissions@chi.ac.uk
// www.chiuni.ac.uk

L500 BA Social Work
Duration: 3FT Hon   CRB Check: Required
Entry Requirements: *GCE:* BCC. *SQAH:* BBBCC-BBCCC. *SQAAH:* BCC. *IB:* 30. Interview required.

C62 CITY COLLEGE, BIRMINGHAM
FORDROUGH CAMPUS
300 BORDESLEY GREEN
BIRMINGHAM B9 5NA
t: 0845 5050 1144 f: 0121 204 0150
e: enquiries@citycol.ac.uk
// www.citycol.ac.uk

L520 HND Advanced Practice in Work with Children and Families
Duration: 2FT HND   CRB Check: Required
Entry Requirements: Contact the institution for details.

L510 HND Health & Social Care
Duration: 2FT HND   CRB Check: Required
Entry Requirements: Contact the institution for details.

C69 CITY OF SUNDERLAND COLLEGE
BEDE CENTRE
DURHAM ROAD
SUNDERLAND
TYNE AND WEAR SR3 4AH
t: 0191 511 6260
e: highered.admissions@citysun.ac.uk
// www.citysun.ac.uk

35XL HND Advanced Practice in Working with Children and Families
Duration: 2FT HND   CRB Check: Required
Entry Requirements: *GCE:* 100. Interview required.

L51A HND Health and Social Care
Duration: 2FT HND   CRB Check: Required
Entry Requirements: Interview required.

C75 COLCHESTER INSTITUTE
SHEEPEN ROAD
COLCHESTER
ESSEX CO3 3LL
t: 01206 712777 f: 01206 712800
e: info@colchester.ac.uk
// www.colchester.ac.uk

LX53 BA Early Years
Duration: 3FT Hon   CRB Check: Required
Entry Requirements: *GCE:* 160.

L511 BA Health and Social Care
Duration: 3FT Hon   CRB Check: Required
Entry Requirements: *GCE:* 120. Interview required.

L510 FdA Health and Social Care
Duration: 2FT Fdg   CRB Check: Required
Entry Requirements: *GCE:* 60-80.

C78 CORNWALL COLLEGE
POOL
REDRUTH
CORNWALL TR15 3RD
t: 01209 616161 f: 01209 611612
e: he.admissions@cornwall.ac.uk
// www.cornwall.ac.uk

LL45 BSc Health & Social Care (top up)
Duration: 1FT Hon
Entry Requirements: Interview required.

L592 FdA Children and Young People's Workforce
Duration: 2FT Fdg   CRB Check: Required
Entry Requirements: *GCE:* 120. *IB:* 24. Interview required. Portfolio required.

XL35 FdA Early Childhood Studies
Duration: 2FT Fdg   CRB Check: Required
Entry Requirements: *GCE:* 120. *IB:* 24. Interview required. Portfolio required.

L590 FdA Health & Community Studies
Duration: 2FT Fdg   CRB Check: Required
Entry Requirements: *GCE:* 120. *IB:* 24. Interview required. Portfolio required.

395L HNC Children & Young People's Workforce
Duration: 1FT HNC   CRB Check: Required
Entry Requirements: Contact the institution for details.

L510 HNC Health and Community Studies
Duration: 1FT HNC   CRB Check: Required
Entry Requirements: *GCE:* 120. *IB:* 24. Interview required. Portfolio required.

C85 COVENTRY UNIVERSITY
THE STUDENT CENTRE
COVENTRY UNIVERSITY
1 GULSON RD
COVENTRY CV1 2JH
t: 024 7615 2222 f: 024 7615 2223
e: studentenquiries@coventry.ac.uk
// www.coventry.ac.uk

L590 BA Applied Community and Social Studies
Duration: 3FT/4SW Hon
Entry Requirements: *GCE:* CCD. *SQAH:* CCCDD. *IB:* 26. *BTEC ExtDip:* MMM. *OCR NED:* M3

LL54 BA Applied Community and Social Studies
Duration: 2FT Hon
Entry Requirements: *GCE:* BBC. *SQAH:* BBCCC. *IB:* 26. *BTEC ExtDip:* DMM. *OCR NED:* M2

NL25 BA International Leadership and Management in Health and Social Care
Duration: 3FT Hon
Entry Requirements: *GCE:* CCC. *SQAH:* CCCCC. *IB:* 27. *BTEC ExtDip:* MMM. *OCR NED:* M3

L500 BA Social Work
Duration: 3FT Hon   CRB Check: Required
Entry Requirements: *GCE:* BBB. *SQAH:* BBBBC. *IB:* 30. *BTEC ExtDip:* DDM. *OCR NED:* M1 Interview required.

L530 BA Youth Work
Duration: 3FT/4SW Hon   CRB Check: Required
Entry Requirements: *GCE:* CCC. *SQAH:* CCCCC. *IB:* 27. *BTEC ExtDip:* MMM. *OCR NED:* M3 Interview required.

L592 FYr Health and Social Care (Foundation)
Duration: 1FT FYr
Entry Requirements: *GCE:* 100. *IB:* 24. *BTEC Dip:* MP. *BTEC ExtDip:* PPP. *OCR ND:* P2 *OCR NED:* P3

C88 CRAVEN COLLEGE
HIGH STREET
SKIPTON
NORTH YORKSHIRE BD23 1JY
t: 01756 791411 f: 01756 794872
e: enquiries@craven-college.ac.uk
// www.craven-college.ac.uk

L520 FdA Early Years
Duration: 2FT Fdg
Entry Requirements: Contact the institution for details.

C92 CROYDON COLLEGE
COLLEGE ROAD
CROYDON CR9 1DX
t: 020 8760 5934 f: 020 8760 5880
e: admissions@croydon.ac.uk
// www.croydon.ac.uk

L520 BA Early Childhood Studies with Practitioner Option
Duration: 3FT Hon   CRB Check: Required
Entry Requirements: Contact the institution for details.

LL45 FdA Public Health and Social Care
Duration: 2FT Fdg   CRB Check: Required
Entry Requirements: Contact the institution for details.

C99 UNIVERSITY OF CUMBRIA
FUSEHILL STREET
CARLISLE
CUMBRIA CA1 2HH
t: 01228 616234 f: 01228 616235
// www.cumbria.ac.uk

L521 BA Early Childhood Studies
Duration: 1FT Hon   CRB Check: Required
Entry Requirements: Contact the institution for details.

L501 BA Social Work
Duration: 3FT Hon   CRB Check: Required
Entry Requirements: *Foundation:* Pass. *GCE:* 200. *IB:* 30. *OCR ND:* D Interview required.

L502 BA Working with Children and Families
Duration: 3FT Hon   CRB Check: Required
Entry Requirements: Contact the institution for details.

L530 BA Youth and Community Work
Duration: 3FT Hon   CRB Check: Required
Entry Requirements: *Foundation:* Pass. *GCE:* 80. *IB:* 24. Interview required.

L53Y BA Youth and Community Work (Top-Up)
Duration: 1FT Hon
Entry Requirements: Contact the institution for details.

L598 BSc Child and Family Studies Top-Up
Duration: 1FT Hon
Entry Requirements: Contact the institution for details.

L52Y FdA Early Years Education and Care
Duration: 2FT Fdg   CRB Check: Required
Entry Requirements: Contact the institution for details.

L512 FdA Health & Social Care Management
Duration: 2FT Fdg
Entry Requirements: Contact the institution for details.

L510 FdSc Health and Social Care
Duration: 2FT Fdg   CRB Check: Required
Entry Requirements: *GCE:* 80. Interview required.

L500 MA Social Work
Duration: 2FT Deg   CRB Check: Required
Entry Requirements: Contact the institution for details.

D22 DEARNE VALLEY COLLEGE
MANVERS PARK
WATH-UPON-DEARNE
ROTHERHAM S63 7EW
t: 01709 513101 f: 01709 513110
e: learn@dearne-coll.ac.uk
// www.dearne-coll.ac.uk

L510 HND Health & Social Care
Duration: 2FT HND
Entry Requirements: Contact the institution for details.

D26 DE MONTFORT UNIVERSITY
THE GATEWAY
LEICESTER LE1 9BH
t: 0116 255 1551 f: 0116 250 6204
e: enquiries@dmu.ac.uk
// www.dmu.ac.uk

L520 BA Evaluating Practice (Working with Children, Top-Up)
Duration: 1FT Hon
Entry Requirements: Interview required.

L510 BA Health Studies (Top-Up)
Duration: 1FT Hon
Entry Requirements: Interview required.

L502 BA Social Work (Leicester)
Duration: 3FT Hon   CRB Check: Required
Entry Requirements: *GCE:* 300. *SQAH:* BBCC. *IB:* 30. *BTEC ExtDip:* DDM. *OCR NED:* D2 Interview required. Admissions Test required. Portfolio required.

L531 BA Working with Young People (Top-Up)
Duration: 1FT Hon
Entry Requirements: Interview required.

L530 BA Youth and Community Development
Duration: 3FT Hon   CRB Check: Required
Entry Requirements: *GCE:* 260. *IB:* 28. *BTEC Dip:* D*D. *BTEC ExtDip:* DMM. *OCR NED:* M2 Interview required. Admissions Test required. Portfolio required.

LL35 FdA Children, Families and Community Health
Duration: 2FT Fdg   CRB Check: Required
Entry Requirements: *GCE:* 180. *IB:* 26. *BTEC Dip:* DM. *BTEC ExtDip:* MMP. *OCR ND:* M1 *OCR NED:* P1 Interview required.

LL34 FdA Policing Studies, Criminology and Criminal Justice
Duration: 2FT Fdg   CRB Check: Required
Entry Requirements: *GCE:* 180. *IB:* 26. *BTEC Dip:* DM. *BTEC ExtDip:* MMP. *OCR ND:* M1 *OCR NED:* P1 Interview required.

L590 FdA Work with Communities and Young People
Duration: 2FT Fdg   CRB Check: Required
Entry Requirements: *GCE:* 180. *IB:* 26. *BTEC Dip:* DM. *BTEC ExtDip:* MMP. *OCR ND:* M1 *OCR NED:* P1 Interview required. Admissions Test required. Portfolio required.

D39 UNIVERSITY OF DERBY
KEDLESTON ROAD
DERBY DE22 1GB
t: 01332 591167 f: 01332 597724
e: askadmissions@derby.ac.uk
// www.derby.ac.uk

L530 BA Applied Community and Youth Work
Duration: 3FT Hon   CRB Check: Required
Entry Requirements: *Foundation:* Merit. *GCE:* 200. *IB:* 28. *BTEC Dip:* D*D. *BTEC ExtDip:* MMP. *OCR ND:* M1 *OCR NED:* P1 Interview required.

L510 BA Applied Social Work
Duration: 3FT Hon   CRB Check: Required
Entry Requirements: *Foundation:* Distinction. *GCE:* 260. *IB:* 28. *BTEC Dip:* D*D*. *BTEC ExtDip:* DMM. *OCR NED:* M2 Interview required.

L531 BA Child and Youth Studies
Duration: 3FT Hon   CRB Check: Required
Entry Requirements: *Foundation:* Distinction. *GCE:* 240. *IB:* 28. *BTEC Dip:* DD. *BTEC ExtDip:* MMM. *OCR ND:* D *OCR NED:* M3 Interview required.

L5T7 BA Early Childhood Studies and American Studies
Duration: 3FT Hon
Entry Requirements: *Foundation:* Distinction. *GCE:* 260-300. *IB:* 28. *BTEC Dip:* D*D*. *BTEC ExtDip:* DMM. *OCR NED:* M2

L5W8 BA Early Childhood Studies and Creative Writing
Duration: 3FT Hon
Entry Requirements: *Foundation:* Distinction. *GCE:* 260-300. *IB:* 28. *BTEC Dip:* D*D*. *BTEC ExtDip:* DMM. *OCR NED:* M2

LX53 BA Early Childhood Studies and Education Studies
Duration: 3FT Hon
Entry Requirements: *Foundation:* Distinction. *GCE:* 260-300. *IB:* 28. *BTEC Dip:* D*D*. *BTEC ExtDip:* DMM. *OCR NED:* M2

LQ53 BA Early Childhood Studies and English
Duration: 3FT Hon
Entry Requirements: *Foundation:* Distinction. *GCE:* 260-300. *IB:* 28. *BTEC Dip:* D*D*. *BTEC ExtDip:* DMM. *OCR NED:* M2

L590 BA Health and Social Care
Duration: 3FT Hon   CRB Check: Required
Entry Requirements: *Foundation:* Distinction. *GCE:* 260. *IB:* 26. *BTEC Dip:* D*D*. *BTEC ExtDip:* DMM. *OCR NED:* M2 Interview required.

LL56 BA/BSc Early Childhood Studies and Applied Criminology
Duration: 3FT Hon
Entry Requirements: *Foundation:* Distinction. *GCE:* 260-300. *IB:* 28. *BTEC Dip:* D*D*. *BTEC ExtDip:* DMM. *OCR NED:* M2

L5C1 BA/BSc Early Childhood Studies and Biology
Duration: 3FT Hon
Entry Requirements: *Foundation:* Distinction. *GCE:* 260-300. *IB:* 28. *BTEC Dip:* D*D*. *BTEC ExtDip:* DMM. *OCR NED:* M2

LF58 BA/BSc Early Childhood Studies and Geography
Duration: 3FT Hon
Entry Requirements: *Foundation:* Distinction. *GCE:* 260-300. *IB:* 28. *BTEC Dip:* D*D*. *BTEC ExtDip:* DMM. *OCR NED:* M2

LG51 BA/BSc Early Childhood Studies and Mathematics
Duration: 3FT Hon
Entry Requirements: *Foundation:* Distinction. *GCE:* 260-300. *IB:* 28. *BTEC Dip:* D*D*. *BTEC ExtDip:* DMM. *OCR NED:* M2

LC58 BA/BSc Early Childhood Studies and Psychology
Duration: 3FT Hon
Entry Requirements: *Foundation:* Distinction. *GCE:* 260-300. *IB:* 28. *BTEC Dip:* D*D*. *BTEC ExtDip:* DMM. *OCR NED:* M2

L5C3 BA/BSc Early Childhood Studies and Zoology
Duration: 3FT Hon
Entry Requirements: *Foundation:* Distinction. *GCE:* 260-300. *IB:* 28. *BTEC Dip:* D*D*. *BTEC ExtDip:* DMM. *OCR NED:* M2

D52 DONCASTER COLLEGE
THE HUB
CHAPPELL DRIVE
SOUTH YORKSHIRE DN1 2RF
t: 01302 553610
e: he@don.ac.uk
// www.don.ac.uk

L510 BA Applied Social Science
Duration: 3FT Hon
Entry Requirements: *GCE:* 160.

D65 UNIVERSITY OF DUNDEE
NETHERGATE
DUNDEE DD1 4HN
t: 01382 383838 f: 01382 388150
e: contactus@dundee.ac.uk
// www.dundee.ac.uk/admissions/undergraduate/

L500 BA Social Work
Duration: 4FT Hon   CRB Check: Required
Entry Requirements: *GCE:* AB-CCC. *SQAH:* ABB-BBBC. *IB:* 29. Interview required.

L508 MSc Social Work - Postgraduate Entry
Duration: 2FT PMD   CRB Check: Required
Entry Requirements: Portfolio required.

D86 DURHAM UNIVERSITY
DURHAM UNIVERSITY
UNIVERSITY OFFICE
DURHAM DH1 3HP
t: 0191 334 2000 f: 0191 334 6055
e: admissions@durham.ac.uk
// www.durham.ac.uk

L508 MA Social Work (Postgraduate Entry)
Duration: 2FT PMD   CRB Check: Required
Entry Requirements: Contact the institution for details.

E10 EALING, HAMMERSMITH AND WEST LONDON COLLEGE
GLIDDON ROAD
BARONS COURT
LONDON W14 9BL
t: 020 7565 1234 f: 020 8563 8247
e: admissions@wlc.ac.uk
// www.wlc.ac.uk

L510 FdA Social Care
Duration: 2FT Fdg
Entry Requirements: Contact the institution for details.

E14 UNIVERSITY OF EAST ANGLIA
NORWICH NR4 7TJ
t: 01603 591515 f: 01603 591523
e: admissions@uea.ac.uk
// www.uea.ac.uk

L501 BA Social Work
Duration: 3FT Hon   CRB Check: Required
Entry Requirements: *GCE:* BBB. *SQAH:* AABBB. *SQAAH:* BBB. *IB:* 31. *BTEC SubDip:* D. *BTEC Dip:* DM. *BTEC ExtDip:* DDM. *OCR ND:* M1 *OCR NED:* M1 Interview required.

L508 MA Social Work (Postgraduate Entry)
Duration: 2FT PMD   CRB Check: Required
Entry Requirements: Interview required.

E28 UNIVERSITY OF EAST LONDON
DOCKLANDS CAMPUS
UNIVERSITY WAY
LONDON E16 2RD
t: 020 8223 3333 f: 020 8223 2978
e: study@uel.ac.uk
// www.uel.ac.uk

L592 BA Community Services and Enterprise - Extended
Duration: 4FT Hon
Entry Requirements: *GCE:* 80. *IB:* 24.

L591 BA Community Services and Enterprises
Duration: 3FT Hon
Entry Requirements: *GCE:* 240. *IB:* 24.

ML95 BA Criminology and Youth & Community Work
Duration: 3FT Hon
Entry Requirements: *GCE:* 240.

M9L5 BA Criminology with Youth & Community Work
Duration: 3FT Hon
Entry Requirements: *GCE:* 240. *IB:* 24.

L501 BA Social Work
Duration: 3FT Hon
Entry Requirements: *GCE:* 280. Interview required.

L9L5 BA Third World Development with Youth & Community Work
Duration: 3FT Hon
Entry Requirements: *GCE:* 240. *IB:* 24.

L5X3 BA Youth & Community Work with Early Childhood Studies
Duration: 3FT Hon
Entry Requirements: *GCE:* 240. *IB:* 24.

L5N2 BA Youth & Community Work with Health Services Management
Duration: 3FT Hon
Entry Requirements: *GCE:* 240. *IB:* 24.

L5P3 BA Youth & Community Work with Media Studies
Duration: 3FT Hon
Entry Requirements: *GCE:* 240. *IB:* 24.

L5C8 BA Youth & Community Work with Psychology
Duration: 3FT Hon
Entry Requirements: *GCE:* 240. *IB:* 24.

L5C6 BA Youth & Community Work with Sports Development
Duration: 3FT Hon
Entry Requirements: *GCE:* 240. *IB:* 24.

L533 BA Youth Studies
Duration: 3FT Hon
Entry Requirements: *GCE:* 240.

L530 BA Youth and Community Work
Duration: 3FT Hon
Entry Requirements: *GCE:* 240. *IB:* 24.

X1L5 BSc Sports Coaching with Youth & Community Work
Duration: 3FT Hon
Entry Requirements: *GCE:* 240. *IB:* 24.

C6L5 BSc Sports Development with Youth & Community Work
Duration: 3FT Hon
Entry Requirements: *GCE:* 240. *IB:* 24.

LX5H FdA Childcare and Education
Duration: 2FT Fdg
Entry Requirements: *GCE:* 120. Interview required.

E29 EAST RIDING COLLEGE
LONGCROFT HALL
GALLOWS LANE
BEVERLEY
EAST YORKSHIRE HU17 7DT
t: 0845 120 0037
e: info@eastridingcollege.ac.uk
// www.eastridingcollege.ac.uk/

XL35 FdEd Early Childhood Policy and Practice
Duration: 2FT Fdg   CRB Check: Required
Entry Requirements: Contact the institution for details.

E42 EDGE HILL UNIVERSITY
ORMSKIRK
LANCASHIRE L39 4QP
t: 01695 657000 f: 01695 584355
e: study@edgehill.ac.uk
// www.edgehill.ac.uk

L5L1 BA Child Health and Wellbeing
Duration: 3FT Hon   CRB Check: Required
Entry Requirements: *GCE:* 280. *IB:* 26. *OCR ND:* D *OCR NED:* M2 Interview required.

L590 BA Childhood & Youth Studies
Duration: 3FT Hon
Entry Requirements: *GCE:* 280. *IB:* 26. *OCR ND:* D *OCR NED:* M2

XL25 BA Children and Young People's Learning and Development
Duration: 3FT Hon   CRB Check: Required
Entry Requirements: *GCE:* 280. *IB:* 26. *OCR ND:* D *OCR NED:* M2 Interview required.

L520 BA Early Childhood Studies
Duration: 3FT Hon
Entry Requirements: *GCE:* 280. *IB:* 26. *OCR ND:* D *OCR NED:* M2

LL53 BA Early Childhood Studies and Sociology
Duration: 3FT Hon
Entry Requirements: *GCE:* 280. *IB:* 26. *OCR ND:* D *OCR NED:* M2

L511 BA Health and Social Wellbeing
Duration: 3FT Hon
Entry Requirements: *GCE:* 280. *IB:* 26. *OCR ND:* D *OCR NED:* M2

L500 BA Social Work
Duration: 3FT Hon   CRB Check: Required
Entry Requirements: *GCE:* 280. *IB:* 26. *OCR ND:* D *OCR NED:* M2
Interview required.

L512 FdA Health and Social Care (Assistant Practitioner)
Duration: 2FT Fdg
Entry Requirements: *GCE:* 40. *OCR ND:* P3 *OCR NED:* P3 Interview required.

E56 THE UNIVERSITY OF EDINBURGH
STUDENT RECRUITMENT & ADMISSIONS
57 GEORGE SQUARE
EDINBURGH EH8 9JU
t: 0131 650 4360 f: 0131 651 1236
e: sra.enquiries@ed.ac.uk
// www.ed.ac.uk/studying/undergraduate/

L500 BSc Social Work
Duration: 4FT Hon   CRB Check: Required
Entry Requirements: *GCE:* AAA-BBB. *SQAH:* AAAA-BBBB. *IB:* 34.

L508 MSW Master of Social Work (MSW) [Postgraduate Entry]
Duration: 2FT PMD   CRB Check: Required
Entry Requirements: Contact the institution for details.

E81 EXETER COLLEGE
HELE ROAD
EXETER
DEVON EX4 4JS
t: 0845 111 6000
e: info@exe-coll.ac.uk
// www.exe-coll.ac.uk/he

L510 FdA Health and Social Care Studies
Duration: 2FT Fdg
Entry Requirements: *GCE:* 160.

G14 UNIVERSITY OF GLAMORGAN, CARDIFF AND PONTYPRIDD
ENQUIRIES AND ADMISSIONS UNIT
PONTYPRIDD CF37 1DL
t: 08456 434030 f: 01443 654050
e: enquiries@glam.ac.uk
// www.glam.ac.uk

L531 BSc Childhood Studies (Top-Up)
Duration: 1FT Hon
Entry Requirements: Contact the institution for details.

L590 BSc Childhood and Youth
Duration: 3FT Hon
Entry Requirements: *GCE:* BBC. *IB:* 25. *BTEC SubDip:* M. *BTEC Dip:* D*D*. *BTEC ExtDip:* DMM.

L510 BSc Health and Social Care
Duration: 3FT Hon   CRB Check: Required
Entry Requirements: *GCE:* BBC. *BTEC Dip:* D*D*. *BTEC ExtDip:* DMM.

L500 BSc Social Work
Duration: 3FT Hon   CRB Check: Required
Entry Requirements: *GCE:* BCC. *BTEC Dip:* D*D. *BTEC ExtDip:* DMM. Interview required.

LL45 FdSc Care Studies
Duration: 2FT Fdg
Entry Requirements: *IB:* 24.

LX53 FdSc Childhood Studies
Duration: 2FT Fdg
Entry Requirements: *IB:* 24.

G28 UNIVERSITY OF GLASGOW
71 SOUTHPARK AVENUE
UNIVERSITY OF GLASGOW
GLASGOW G12 8QQ
t: 0141 330 6062 f: 0141 330 2961
e: student.recruitment@glasgow.ac.uk
// www.glasgow.ac.uk

XL35 BA Community Development
Duration: 3FT Ord
Entry Requirements: *GCE:* BBB. *SQAH:* BBBB. *IB:* 30. Interview required.

G42 GLASGOW CALEDONIAN UNIVERSITY
STUDENT RECRUITMENT & ADMISSIONS SERVICE
CITY CAMPUS
COWCADDENS ROAD
GLASGOW G4 0BA
t: 0141 331 3000 f: 0141 331 8676
e: undergraduate@gcu.ac.uk
// www.gcu.ac.uk

L500 BA Social Work
Duration: 4FT Hon   CRB Check: Required
Entry Requirements: *GCE:* CCC. *SQAH:* BBCC. *IB:* 24. Interview required.

L510 BSc Health Studies
Duration: 4FT Hon
Entry Requirements: Contact the institution for details.

L508 MSc Social Work (Postgraduate Entry)
Duration: 2FT PMD   CRB Check: Required
Entry Requirements: Interview required.

G50 THE UNIVERSITY OF GLOUCESTERSHIRE
PARK CAMPUS
THE PARK
CHELTENHAM GL50 2RH
t: 01242 714501 f: 01242 714869
e: admissions@glos.ac.uk
// www.glos.ac.uk

L52A BA Childhood Studies
Duration: 3FT Hon   CRB Check: Required
Entry Requirements: Contact the institution for details.

L530 BA Integrated Youth Practice
Duration: 3FT Hon   CRB Check: Required
Entry Requirements: *GCE:* 280-300. Interview required.

VL65 BA Youth & Community Work and Practical Theology
Duration: 3FT Hon
Entry Requirements: *GCE:* 280-300.

L532 BA Youth Work
Duration: 3FT Hon   CRB Check: Required
Entry Requirements: *GCE:* 280-300. Interview required.

L511 BSc Health, Community and Social Care
Duration: 3FT Hon   CRB Check: Required
Entry Requirements: *GCE:* 220. Interview required.

L502 BSc Social Work
Duration: 3FT Hon   CRB Check: Required
Entry Requirements: *GCE:* 280-300. Interview required.

L531 FdA Supporting Youth Practice
Duration: 2FT Fdg   CRB Check: Required
Entry Requirements: *GCE:* 120. Interview required.

L520 FdSc Children and Young People's Practice
Duration: 2FT Fdg   CRB Check: Required
Entry Requirements: *GCE:* 120. Interview required.

L510 FdSc Health and Social Care Practice
Duration: 2FT Fdg   CRB Check: Required
Entry Requirements: *GCE:* 120. Interview required.

L512 FdSc Mental Health Practice
Duration: 2FT Fdg   CRB Check: Required
Entry Requirements: *GCE:* 120. Interview required.

G53 GLYNDWR UNIVERSITY
PLAS COCH
MOLD ROAD
WREXHAM LL11 2AW
t: 01978 293439 f: 01978 290008
e: sid@glyndwr.ac.uk
// www.glyndwr.ac.uk

L500 BA Social Work (Qualified Status)
Duration: 3FT Hon   CRB Check: Required
Entry Requirements: *GCE:* 260.

L593 BA Youth and Community Work
Duration: 3FT Hon   CRB Check: Required
Entry Requirements: *GCE:* 240. Interview required.

G56 GOLDSMITHS, UNIVERSITY OF LONDON
GOLDSMITHS, UNIVERSITY OF LONDON
NEW CROSS
LONDON SE14 6NW
t: 020 7048 5300 f: 020 7919 7509
e: admissions@gold.ac.uk
// www.gold.ac.uk

L530 BA Applied Social Science, Community Development and Youth Work
Duration: 3FT Hon   CRB Check: Required
Entry Requirements: *GCE:* CC. *SQAH:* CCCC. *SQAAH:* CC. Interview required. Portfolio required.

L500 BA Social Work
Duration: 3FT Hon   CRB Check: Required
Entry Requirements: *GCE:* BBC. *SQAH:* BBBCC. *SQAAH:* BBC. *IB:* 30. Interview required.

L508 MA Social Work (Postgraduate Entry)
Duration: 2FT PMD   CRB Check: Required
Entry Requirements: Interview required.

G70 UNIVERSITY OF GREENWICH
GREENWICH CAMPUS
OLD ROYAL NAVAL COLLEGE
PARK ROW
LONDON SE10 9LS
t: 020 8331 9000 f: 020 8331 8145
e: courseinfo@gre.ac.uk
// www.gre.ac.uk

X302 BA Education and Child Development
Duration: 3FT Hon
Entry Requirements: *GCE:* 280.

X3L5 BA Education with Child Development
Duration: 3FT Hon
Entry Requirements: *GCE:* 280. *IB:* 24.

L501 BA Social Care (Top-Up)
Duration: 1FT Hon
Entry Requirements: HND required.

L500 BA Social Work
Duration: 3FT Hon
Entry Requirements: *GCE:* 180. Interview required.

L530 BA (Hons) Youth and Community Work
Duration: 3FT Hon
Entry Requirements: *GCE:* 240.

L590 FdA Every Child Matters
Duration: 2FT Fdg
Entry Requirements: Contact the institution for details.

L510 FdSc Health and Social Care (Care)
Duration: 2FT Fdg
Entry Requirements: Contact the institution for details.

L511 FdSc Health and Social Care (Early Years Care)
Duration: 2FT Fdg
Entry Requirements: *IB:* 24.

L502 PGDip/MA Social Work
Duration: 2FT PMD   **CRB Check:** Required
Entry Requirements: Interview required.

G80 GRIMSBY INSTITUTE OF FURTHER AND HIGHER EDUCATION
NUNS CORNER
GRIMSBY
NE LINCOLNSHIRE DN34 5BQ
t: 0800 328 3631
e: headmissions@grimsby.ac.uk
// www.grimsby.ac.uk

L541 BA Community Development (Top-Up)
Duration: 1FT Hon
Entry Requirements: Interview required.

L591 BA Community and Youth Work Studies
Duration: 3FT Hon
Entry Requirements: *GCE:* 120-240. Interview required.

L513 BA Health and Social Care (Top-up)
Duration: 1FT Hon
Entry Requirements: Interview required. HND required.

L540 FdA Children, Parenting & Communities
Duration: 2FT Fdg
Entry Requirements: Interview required.

L510 FdA Social Care
Duration: 2FT Fdg
Entry Requirements: *GCE:* 40-120. Interview required.

L512 FdSc Mental Health Studies
Duration: 2FT Fdg
Entry Requirements: *GCE:* 120. Interview required.

L520 Fded Early Childhood Studies
Duration: 2FT Fdg
Entry Requirements: *GCE:* 40-120. Interview required.

H14 HAVERING COLLEGE OF FURTHER AND HIGHER EDUCATION
ARDLEIGH GREEN ROAD
HORNCHURCH
ESSEX RM11 2LL
t: 01708 462793 f: 01708 462736
e: HE@havering-college.ac.uk
// www.havering-college.ac.uk

L500 BA Social Work
Duration: 3FT Hon   **CRB Check:** Required
Entry Requirements: Interview required.

LX53 FdA Early Years, Childcare and Education
Duration: 2FT Fdg   **CRB Check:** Required
Entry Requirements: Interview required.

015L HNC Health and Social Care
Duration: 1FT HNC
Entry Requirements: Contact the institution for details.

H36 UNIVERSITY OF HERTFORDSHIRE
UNIVERSITY ADMISSIONS SERVICE
COLLEGE LANE
HATFIELD
HERTS AL10 9AB
t: 01707 284800
// www.herts.ac.uk

L500 BSc Social Work
Duration: 3FT Hon   **CRB Check:** Required
Entry Requirements: *GCE:* 240. Interview required. Admissions Test required.

H39 HIGHBURY COLLEGE
TUDOR CRESCENT
PORTSMOUTH
HAMPSHIRE PO6 2SA
t: 023 9238 3131
e: info@highbury.ac.uk
// www.highbury.ac.uk

L510 HND Health and Social Care
Duration: 2FT HND
Entry Requirements: *GCE:* 120. Interview required.

H49 UNIVERSITY OF THE HIGHLANDS AND ISLANDS
UHI EXECUTIVE OFFICE
NESS WALK
INVERNESS
SCOTLAND IV3 5SQ
t: 01463 279000 f: 01463 279001
e: info@uhi.ac.uk
// www.uhi.ac.uk

L530 BA Child & Youth Studies
Duration: 4FT Hon
Entry Requirements: *GCE:* CC. *SQAH:* CCC. Interview required.

L510 BA Health Studies (Health and Welfare)
Duration: 4FT Hon
Entry Requirements: *GCE:* CC. *SQAH:* CCC.

L511 BA Health Studies (Rural Health)
Duration: 4FT Hon
Entry Requirements: *GCE:* CC. *SQAH:* CCC.

015L HNC Health Care
Duration: 1FT HNC
Entry Requirements: *GCE:* C. *SQAH:* CC.

045L HNC Social Care
Duration: 1FT HNC
Entry Requirements: *GCE:* D. *SQAH:* C.

H60 THE UNIVERSITY OF HUDDERSFIELD
QUEENSGATE
HUDDERSFIELD HD1 3DH
t: 01484 473969 f: 01484 472765
e: admissionsandrecords@hud.ac.uk
// www.hud.ac.uk

LX53 BA Early Years (Top-Up)
Duration: 1FT Hon CRB Check: Required
Entry Requirements: Interview required.

L530 BA Youth and Community Work
Duration: 3FT Hon CRB Check: Required
Entry Requirements: *GCE:* 280. Interview required.

L540 BSc Health and Community Studies
Duration: 3FT Hon
Entry Requirements: *GCE:* 280. Interview required.

L500 BSc Social Work
Duration: 3FT Hon CRB Check: Required
Entry Requirements: *GCE:* 320. Interview required.

H72 THE UNIVERSITY OF HULL
THE UNIVERSITY OF HULL
COTTINGHAM ROAD
HULL HU6 7RX
t: 01482 466100 f: 01482 442290
e: admissions@hull.ac.uk
// www.hull.ac.uk

LX53 BA Children's Inter-professional Studies
Duration: 3FT Hon CRB Check: Required
Entry Requirements: *GCE:* 260. *IB:* 28. *BTEC ExtDip:* MMM.

L531 BA Community and Youth Work Studies
Duration: 3FT Hon CRB Check: Required
Entry Requirements: *GCE:* 280-320. *IB:* 28. Interview required. Portfolio required.

L50A BA Social Care Practice (Top-Up)
Duration: 1FT Hon CRB Check: Required
Entry Requirements: Contact the institution for details.

L500 BA Social Work (including professional qualification)
Duration: 3FT Hon CRB Check: Required
Entry Requirements: *GCE:* 280. *IB:* 28. *BTEC ExtDip:* DMM. Interview required. Admissions Test required.

L510 FdA Health and Social Care of Adults
Duration: 2FT Fdg CRB Check: Required
Entry Requirements: Contact the institution for details.

L590 FdA Working with Children, Young People and Families
Duration: 2FT Fdg CRB Check: Required
Entry Requirements: Interview required.

XL35 FdEd Early Childhood Policy and Practice
Duration: 2FT Fdg CRB Check: Required
Entry Requirements: Interview required.

L540 FdSc Community Care
Duration: 2FT Fdg CRB Check: Required
Entry Requirements: Contact the institution for details.

L508 MA Social Work (Postgraduate)
Duration: 2FT PMD CRB Check: Required
Entry Requirements: Interview required. Admissions Test required.

H73 HULL COLLEGE
QUEEN'S GARDENS
HULL HU1 3DG
t: 01482 329943 f: 01482 598733
e: info@hull-college.ac.uk
// www.hull-college.ac.uk/higher-education

LL53 FdA Crime and Community Safety
Duration: 2FT Fdg   CRB Check: Required
Entry Requirements: *GCE:* 120. Interview required. Admissions Test required.

K12 KEELE UNIVERSITY
KEELE UNIVERSITY
STAFFORDSHIRE ST5 5BG
t: 01782 734005 f: 01782 632343
e: undergraduate@keele.ac.uk
// www.keele.ac.uk

L500 BA Social Work
Duration: 3FT Hon   CRB Check: Required
Entry Requirements: *GCE:* 280. Interview required.

L501 MA Social Work (Postgraduate Entry)
Duration: 2FT PMD   CRB Check: Required
Entry Requirements: Interview required.

K24 THE UNIVERSITY OF KENT
RECRUITMENT & ADMISSIONS OFFICE
REGISTRY
UNIVERSITY OF KENT
CANTERBURY, KENT CT2 7NZ
t: 01227 827272 f: 01227 827077
e: information@kent.ac.uk
// www.kent.ac.uk

LL45 BA Health and Social Care
Duration: 3FT Hon
Entry Requirements: *GCE:* BBC. *SQAH:* BBBBB. *SQAAH:* BBC. *IB:* 33. *OCR ND:* D *OCR NED:* M2

L590 BA Social Sciences International Foundation Programme
Duration: 1FT FYr
Entry Requirements: *IB:* 28.

L508 BA Social Work
Duration: 3SW Hon   CRB Check: Required
Entry Requirements: *GCE:* BBC. *SQAH:* BBBBC. *SQAAH:* BBC. *IB:* 33. *OCR ND:* D *OCR NED:* M2 Interview required. Admissions Test required.

L514 BSc Autism Studies
Duration: 3FT Hon
Entry Requirements: Contact the institution for details.

L512 BSc Intellectual and Developmental Disabilities
Duration: 3FT Hon
Entry Requirements: *GCE:* 200. *IB:* 27.

L515 FdSc Autism Studies
Duration: 2FT Hon
Entry Requirements: Contact the institution for details.

L513 FdSc Intellectual and Developmental Disabilities
Duration: 2FT Fdg
Entry Requirements: *GCE:* 200. *IB:* 27.

K84 KINGSTON UNIVERSITY
STUDENT INFORMATION & ADVICE CENTRE
COOPER HOUSE
40-46 SURBITON ROAD
KINGSTON UPON THAMES KT1 2HX
t: 0844 8552177 f: 020 8547 7080
e: aps@kingston.ac.uk
// www.kingston.ac.uk

L953 BA Child Centred Interprofessional Practice (Top-Up)
Duration: 1FT Hon
Entry Requirements: Contact the institution for details.

L501 BA Social Work
Duration: 3FT Hon   CRB Check: Required
Entry Requirements: *GCE:* 280. *IB:* 27. Interview required. Admissions Test required.

LX53 FdA Child Centred Interprofessional Practice FdA CCIP
Duration: 2FT Fdg
Entry Requirements: Contact the institution for details.

L508 MSW Social Work Masters (Postgraduate)
Duration: 2FT PMD   CRB Check: Required
Entry Requirements: Interview required. Admissions Test required.

K90 KIRKLEES COLLEGE
HALIFAX ROAD
DEWSBURY
WEST YORKSHIRE WF13 2AS
t: 01924 436221 f: 01924 457047
e: admissionsdc@kirkleescollege.ac.uk
// www.kirkleescollege.ac.uk

XL35 FdA Early Years
Duration: 2FT Fdg
Entry Requirements: Interview required.

L05 LAKES COLLEGE - WEST CUMBRIA
HALLWOOD ROAD
LILLYHALL
WORKINGTON CA14 4JN
t: 01946 839300 f: 01946 839302
e: student.services@lcwc.ac.uk
// www.lcwc.ac.uk

L520 FdA Integrated Education and Care of Children and Young People
Duration: 2FT Fdg
Entry Requirements: *GCE:* 40-120. Interview required.

L511 HND Health and Social Care
Duration: 2FT HND   CRB Check: Required
Entry Requirements: Contact the institution for details.

L14 LANCASTER UNIVERSITY
THE UNIVERSITY
LANCASTER
LANCASHIRE LA1 4YW
t: 01524 592029 f: 01524 846243
e: ugadmissions@lancaster.ac.uk
// www.lancs.ac.uk

L500 BA Social Work
Duration: 3FT Hon   CRB Check: Required
Entry Requirements: *GCE:* ABB. *SQAH:* BBBBB. *SQAAH:* BBB. *IB:* 32. Interview required.

L508 PGDip Social Work (Postgraduate Entry)
Duration: 2FT PMD
Entry Requirements: Interview required.

L21 LEEDS CITY COLLEGE
TECHNOLOGY CAMPUS
COOKRIDGE STREET
LEEDS LS2 8BL
t: 0113 216 2406 f: 0113 216 2401
e: helen.middleton@leedscitycollege.ac.uk
// www.leedscitycollege.ac.uk

L521 FdA Childrens Care Learning and Development
Duration: 2FT Fdg   CRB Check: Required
Entry Requirements: Contact the institution for details.

L23 UNIVERSITY OF LEEDS
THE UNIVERSITY OF LEEDS
WOODHOUSE LANE
LEEDS LS2 9JT
t: 0113 343 3999
e: admissions@leeds.ac.uk
// www.leeds.ac.uk

L500 BA Social Work
Duration: 3FT Hon   CRB Check: Required
Entry Requirements: *GCE:* BBB. *SQAAH:* BBB. *BTEC ExtDip:* DDD.

L24 LEEDS TRINITY UNIVERSITY COLLEGE
BROWNBERRIE LANE
HORSFORTH
LEEDS LS18 5HD
t: 0113 283 7150 f: 0113 283 7222
e: enquiries@leedstrinity.ac.uk
// www.leedstrinity.ac.uk

XL35 BA Early Years and Education Studies
Duration: 3FT Hon
Entry Requirements: *GCE:* 240. *IB:* 24.

L540 BA Working with Children, Young People and Families
Duration: 3FT Hon
Entry Requirements: *GCE:* 240. *IB:* 24.

L27 LEEDS METROPOLITAN UNIVERSITY
COURSE ENQUIRIES OFFICE
CITY CAMPUS
LEEDS LS1 3HE
t: 0113 81 23113 f: 0113 81 23129
// www.leedsmet.ac.uk

L512 BA Health and Social Care
Duration: 1FT Hon
Entry Requirements: HND required.

L520 BA Playwork
Duration: 3FT Hon   CRB Check: Required
Entry Requirements: *Foundation:* Pass. *GCE:* 120. *IB:* 24. *OCR ND:* P2 *OCR NED:* P3

L500 BA Social Work
Duration: 3FT Hon   CRB Check: Required
Entry Requirements: *GCE:* 200. *IB:* 28. Interview required.

LMLM BA Youth Work and Community Development (JNC)
Duration: 3FT Hon   CRB Check: Required
Entry Requirements: *GCE:* 200. *IB:* 24. Interview required.

L508 MA Social Work (Postgraduate Entry)
Duration: 2FT PMD   CRB Check: Required
Entry Requirements: Interview required.

L34 UNIVERSITY OF LEICESTER
UNIVERSITY ROAD
LEICESTER LE1 7RH
t: 0116 252 5281 f: 0116 252 2447
e: admissions@le.ac.uk
// www.le.ac.uk

L500 MA Social Work (Postgraduate Entry)
Duration: 2FT PMD   CRB Check: Required
Entry Requirements: Interview required.

L39 UNIVERSITY OF LINCOLN
ADMISSIONS
BRAYFORD POOL
LINCOLN LN6 7TS
t: 01522 886097 f: 01522 886146
e: admissions@lincoln.ac.uk
// www.lincoln.ac.uk

L510 BSc Health & Social Care
Duration: 3FT Hon
Entry Requirements: *GCE:* 260.

L500 BSc Social Work
Duration: 3FT Hon   CRB Check: Required
Entry Requirements: *GCE:* 260. Interview required.

L502 MSc Social Work
Duration: 2FT PMD   CRB Check: Required
Entry Requirements: Interview required.

L43 LIVERPOOL COMMUNITY COLLEGE
LIVERPOOL COMMUNITY COLLEGE
CLARENCE STREET
LIVERPOOL L3 5TP
t: 0151 252 3352 f: 0151 252 3351
e: enquiry@liv-coll.ac.uk
// www.liv-coll.ac.uk

L500 BA Social Work
Duration: 3FT Hon   CRB Check: Required
Entry Requirements: Contact the institution for details.

L46 LIVERPOOL HOPE UNIVERSITY
HOPE PARK
LIVERPOOL L16 9JD
t: 0151 291 3331 f: 0151 291 3434
e: administration@hope.ac.uk
// www.hope.ac.uk

L500 BA Social Work
Duration: 3FT Hon   CRB Check: Required
Entry Requirements: *GCE:* 300-320. *IB:* 25.

LG51 BSc Health and Mathematics
Duration: 3FT Hon
Entry Requirements: *GCE:* 300-320. *IB:* 25.

LC65 BSc Health and Sport & Exercise Science
Duration: 3FT Hon
Entry Requirements: *GCE:* 300-320. *IB:* 25.

L501 MA Social Work
Duration: 2FT PMD   CRB Check: Required
Entry Requirements: *GCE:* 300-320. Interview required.

L51 LIVERPOOL JOHN MOORES UNIVERSITY
KINGSWAY HOUSE
HATTON GARDEN
LIVERPOOL L3 2AJ
t: 0151 231 5090 f: 0151 904 6368
e: courses@ljmu.ac.uk
// www.ljmu.ac.uk

XL35 BA Early Childhood Studies
Duration: 3FT Hon   CRB Check: Required
Entry Requirements: *GCE:* 260.

L512 BA Health and Social Care for Individuals, Families and Communities
Duration: 3FT Hon
Entry Requirements: *GCE:* 260. *IB:* 24.

L500 BA Social Work
Duration: 3FT Hon   CRB Check: Required
Entry Requirements: *GCE:* 280. Interview required.

L508 MA Social Work (Postgraduate Entry)
Duration: 2FT PMD   CRB Check: Required
Entry Requirements: Interview required.

L53 COLEG LLANDRILLO CYMRU
LLANDUDNO ROAD
RHOS-ON-SEA
COLWYN BAY
NORTH WALES LL28 4HZ
t: 01492 542338/339 f: 01492 543052
e: degrees@llandrillo.ac.uk
// www.llandrillo.ac.uk

L510 BA Childhood and Learning Support Studies
Duration: 1FT Hon
Entry Requirements: Contact the institution for details.

XL35 FdA Childhood and Learning Support Studies
Duration: 2FT Fdg
Entry Requirements: Interview required.

LN52 FdA Health and Social Care Management (Adult)
Duration: 2FT Fdg
Entry Requirements: *GCE:* 200.

LN53 FdA Health and Social Care Management (Adult) (bilingual Welsh/English)
Duration: 2FT Fdg
Entry Requirements: *GCE:* 200.

L62 THE LONDON COLLEGE, UCK
VICTORIA GARDENS
NOTTING HILL GATE
LONDON W11 3PE
t: 020 7243 4000 f: 020 7243 1484
e: admissions@lcuck.ac.uk
// www.lcuck.ac.uk

115L HNC Health and Social Care
Duration: 1FT HNC
Entry Requirements: Contact the institution for details.

215L HNC Health and Social Care (Applied Social Studies)
Duration: 1FT HNC
Entry Requirements: Contact the institution for details.

25LN HNC Health and Social Care (Management)
Duration: 1FT HNC
Entry Requirements: Contact the institution for details.

015L HND Health and Social Care
Duration: 2FT HND
Entry Requirements: Interview required.

415L HND Health and Social Care (Applied Social Studies)
Duration: 2FT HND
Entry Requirements: Contact the institution for details.

315L HND Health and Social Care (Management)
Duration: 2FT HND
Entry Requirements: Contact the institution for details.

L68 LONDON METROPOLITAN UNIVERSITY
166-220 HOLLOWAY ROAD
LONDON N7 8DB
t: 020 7133 4200
e: admissions@londonmet.ac.uk
// www.londonmet.ac.uk

ML95 BSc Criminology and Youth Studies
Duration: 3FT Hon
Entry Requirements: GCE: 280. IB: 28. Interview required.

L590 BSc Health and Social Care
Duration: 3FT Hon
Entry Requirements: Contact the institution for details.

L500 BSc Social Work
Duration: 3FT Hon   CRB Check: Required
Entry Requirements: GCE: 280. IB: 28. Interview required.

L531 BSc Youth Studies
Duration: 3FT Hon
Entry Requirements: GCE: 280. IB: 28. Interview required.

L530 BSc Youth Work
Duration: 3FT Hon   CRB Check: Required
Entry Requirements: GCE: 260. IB: 28. Interview required.

L540 FdA Community Work
Duration: 2FT Fdg
Entry Requirements: Contact the institution for details.

LL45 FdA Public Health and Social Care
Duration: 2FT Fdg
Entry Requirements: GCE: 200. IB: 28. Interview required.

L508 MSc Social Work (Postgraduate Entry)
Duration: 2FT PMD   CRB Check: Required
Entry Requirements: Interview required.

L75 LONDON SOUTH BANK UNIVERSITY
ADMISSIONS AND RECRUITMENT CENTRE
90 LONDON ROAD
LONDON SE1 6LN
t: 0800 923 8888 f: 020 7815 8273
e: course.enquiry@lsbu.ac.uk
// www.lsbu.ac.uk

L500 BA Social Work
Duration: 3FT Hon   CRB Check: Required
Entry Requirements: GCE: 260. IB: 24. BTEC ExtDip: DMM. OCR NED: M2 Interview required. Admissions Test required.

L508 MA Social Work (Postgraduate Entry)
Duration: 2FT PMD   CRB Check: Required
Entry Requirements: Interview required.

M20 THE UNIVERSITY OF MANCHESTER
RUTHERFORD BUILDING
OXFORD ROAD
MANCHESTER M13 9PL
t: 0161 275 2077 f: 0161 275 2106
e: ug-admissions@manchester.ac.uk
// www.manchester.ac.uk

L590 BA Applied Community and Youth Work Studies
Duration: 3FT Hon   CRB Check: Required
Entry Requirements: GCE: ABB-BBB. SQAH: ABBBB-BBBBB. SQAAH: BBB. Interview required.

L508 MA Social Work (Postgraduate Entry)
Duration: 2FT PMD
Entry Requirements: Interview required.

M40 THE MANCHESTER METROPOLITAN UNIVERSITY
ADMISSIONS OFFICE
ALL SAINTS (GMS)
ALL SAINTS
MANCHESTER M15 6BH
t: 0161 247 2000
// www.mmu.ac.uk

L590 BA Abuse Studies
Duration: 3FT Hon
Entry Requirements: *GCE:* 280. *IB:* 28. *BTEC Dip:* D*D*. *BTEC ExtDip:* DMM.

LX5J BA Abuse Studies/Childhood & Youth Studies
Duration: 3FT Hon
Entry Requirements: *GCE:* 280. *IB:* 28. *BTEC Dip:* D*D*. *BTEC ExtDip:* DMM.

LL53 BA Abuse Studies/Crime Studies
Duration: 3FT Hon
Entry Requirements: *GCE:* 280. *IB:* 28. *BTEC Dip:* D*D*. *BTEC ExtDip:* DMM.

LW55 BA Abuse Studies/Dance
Duration: 3FT Hon
Entry Requirements: *GCE:* 280. *IB:* 28. *BTEC Dip:* D*D*. *BTEC ExtDip:* DMM.

LW54 BA Abuse Studies/Drama
Duration: 3FT Hon
Entry Requirements: *GCE:* 280. *IB:* 28. *BTEC Dip:* D*D*. *BTEC ExtDip:* DMM.

LXM3 BA Abuse Studies/Education Studies
Duration: 3FT Hon
Entry Requirements: *GCE:* 280. *IB:* 28. *BTEC Dip:* D*D*. *BTEC ExtDip:* DMM.

LM52 BA Abuse Studies/Legal Studies
Duration: 3FT Hon
Entry Requirements: *GCE:* 280. *IB:* 28. *BTEC Dip:* D*D*. *BTEC ExtDip:* DMM.

LV55 BA Abuse Studies/Philosophy
Duration: 3FT Hon
Entry Requirements: *GCE:* 280. *IB:* 28. *BTEC Dip:* D*D*. *BTEC ExtDip:* DMM.

LL5H BA Abuse Studies/Sociology
Duration: 3FT Hon
Entry Requirements: *GCE:* 280. *IB:* 28. *BTEC Dip:* D*D*. *BTEC ExtDip:* DMM.

XW35 BA Childhood & Youth Studies/Dance
Duration: 3FT Hon
Entry Requirements: *GCE:* 280. *IB:* 28. *BTEC Dip:* D*D*. *BTEC ExtDip:* DMM. Interview required.

X350 BA Childhood & Youth Studies/Early Years
Duration: 3FT Hon   CRB Check: Required
Entry Requirements: *GCE:* 280. *IB:* 28. *BTEC Dip:* D*D*. *BTEC ExtDip:* DMM.

LX5H BA Childhood & Youth Studies/Education Studies
Duration: 3FT Hon
Entry Requirements: *GCE:* 280. *IB:* 28. *BTEC Dip:* D*D*. *BTEC ExtDip:* DMM.

ML25 BA Childhood & Youth Studies/Legal Studies
Duration: 3FT Hon
Entry Requirements: *GCE:* 280. *IB:* 28. *BTEC Dip:* D*D*. *BTEC ExtDip:* DMM.

XLH3 BA Childhood & Youth Studies/Sociology
Duration: 3FT Hon
Entry Requirements: *GCE:* 280. *IB:* 28. *BTEC Dip:* D*D*. *BTEC ExtDip:* DMM.

LC5P BA Childhood & Youth Studies/Sport Development
Duration: 3FT Hon
Entry Requirements: *GCE:* 280. *IB:* 28. *BTEC Dip:* D*D*. *BTEC ExtDip:* DMM.

L591 BA Childhood and Youth Studies
Duration: 3FT Hon
Entry Requirements: *GCE:* 280. *IB:* 28. *BTEC Dip:* D*D*. *BTEC ExtDip:* DMM.

LXN3 BA Childhood and Youth Studies (with Foundation)
Duration: 4FT Hon
Entry Requirements: *GCE:* 160. *IB:* 24. *BTEC Dip:* MM. *BTEC ExtDip:* MPP.

L500 BA Social Work/Diploma in Social Work
Duration: 3FT Hon   CRB Check: Required
Entry Requirements: *GCE:* 280. Interview required. Admissions Test required.

L523 BA Youth and Community Work
Duration: 3FT Hon   CRB Check: Required
Entry Requirements: *GCE:* 280. *OCR ND:* D *OCR NED:* M2 Interview required.

L3L4 BA Youth and Community Work (Foundation)
Duration: 4FT Hon   CRB Check: Required
Entry Requirements: Contact the institution for details.

L522 BA Youth and Community Work Studies (top-up)
Duration: 1FT Hon
Entry Requirements: Contact the institution for details.

LC58 BA/BSc Abuse Studies/Psychology
Duration: 3FT Hon
Entry Requirements: *GCE:* 280. *IB:* 28. *BTEC Dip:* D*D*. *BTEC ExtDip:* DMM.

X301 BA/BSc Childhood & Youth Studies/Outdoor Studies
Duration: 3FT Hon
Entry Requirements: *GCE:* 280. *IB:* 28. *BTEC Dip:* D*D*. *BTEC ExtDip:* DMM.

CL85 BA/BSc Childhood & Youth Studies/Psychology
Duration: 3FT Hon
Entry Requirements: *GCE:* 280. *IB:* 28. *BTEC Dip:* D*D*. *BTEC ExtDip:* DMM.

L510 FdA Health & Social Care
Duration: 2FT Fdg   CRB Check: Required
Entry Requirements: *GCE:* 180. Interview required.

L508 PGDip Social Work (PGDip/MA)
Duration: 2FT PMD   CRB Check: Required
Entry Requirements: Interview required. Admissions Test required.

M77 MID CHESHIRE COLLEGE
HARTFORD CAMPUS
NORTHWICH
CHESHIRE CW8 1LJ
t: 01606 74444 f: 01606 720700
e: eandrews@midchesh.ac.uk
// www.midchesh.ac.uk

L540 FdA Public Community Services
Duration: 2FT Fdg
Entry Requirements: Contact the institution for details.

M80 MIDDLESEX UNIVERSITY
MIDDLESEX UNIVERSITY
THE BURROUGHS
LONDON NW4 4BT
t: 020 8411 5555 f: 020 8411 5649
e: enquiries@mdx.ac.uk
// www.mdx.ac.uk

L535 BA Integrated Youth Work and Support
Duration: 3FT Hon
Entry Requirements: Contact the institution for details.

L501 BA Social Work
Duration: 3FT Hon
Entry Requirements: *GCE:* 200-300. *IB:* 28.

L500 MA Social Work (Postgraduate Entry)
Duration: 2FT PMD
Entry Requirements: Contact the institution for details.

N11 NAZARENE THEOLOGICAL COLLEGE
DENE ROAD
DIDSBURY
MANCHESTER M20 2GU
t: 0161 445 3063
e: enquiries@nazarene.ac.uk
// www.nazarene.ac.uk

LV56 BA Theology: Youth Work and Ministry
Duration: 3FT Hon   CRB Check: Required
Entry Requirements: Interview required.

VL65 DipHE Theology and Youth Ministry
Duration: 2FT Dip   CRB Check: Required
Entry Requirements: Interview required.

N13 NEATH PORT TALBOT COLLEGE
NEATH CAMPUS
DWR-Y-FELIN ROAD
NEATH
NEATH PORT TALBOT BOROUGH SA10 7RF
t: 01639 648000 f: 01639 648077
e: admissions@nptc.ac.uk
// www.nptc.ac.uk

L512 BSc Care Studies
Duration: 1FT Deg
Entry Requirements: Interview required. HND required.

L522 BSc Childhood Studies
Duration: 1FT Deg
Entry Requirements: Interview required. HND required.

L591 CertHE Substance Misuse
Duration: 1FT Cer
Entry Requirements: Contact the institution for details.

L590 CertHE Working with Vulnerable Adults
Duration: 1FT Cer
Entry Requirements: Contact the institution for details.

L511 DipHE Health Promotion
Duration: 1FT Dip
Entry Requirements: Contact the institution for details.

L510 FdA Care Practice
Duration: 2FT Fdg
Entry Requirements: Contact the institution for details.

L520 FdA Childhood Studies
Duration: 2FT Fdg
Entry Requirements: Contact the institution for details.

N23 NEWCASTLE COLLEGE
STUDENT SERVICES
RYE HILL CAMPUS
SCOTSWOOD ROAD
NEWCASTLE UPON TYNE NE4 7SA
t: 0191 200 4110 f: 0191 200 4349
e: enquiries@ncl-coll.ac.uk
// www.newcastlecollege.co.uk

L591 BA Children and Young Persons (Top-up)
Duration: 1FT Hon   CRB Check: Required
Entry Requirements: Contact the institution for details.

L510 BSc Social Care (Top-up)
Duration: 1FT Hon
Entry Requirements: Contact the institution for details.

L590 FdA Children and Young Persons
Duration: 2FT Fdg
Entry Requirements: *GCE:* 160-200. *OCR ND:* P1 *OCR NED:* P2
Interview required.

L540 FdA Social Care
Duration: 2FT Fdg   CRB Check: Required
Entry Requirements: *GCE:* 160-200. *OCR ND:* P1 *OCR NED:* P2
Interview required.

N28 NEW COLLEGE DURHAM
FRAMWELLGATE MOOR CAMPUS
DURHAM DH1 5ES
t: 0191 375 4210/4211 f: 0191 375 4222
e: admissions@newdur.ac.uk
// www.newcollegedurham.ac.uk

L500 BA Social Work
Duration: 3FT Hon
Entry Requirements: *GCE:* 160. Interview required. Admissions Test required.

L510 FdSc Applied Health and Social Care
Duration: 2FT Fdg   CRB Check: Required
Entry Requirements: Contact the institution for details.

N33 NEW COLLEGE STAMFORD
DRIFT ROAD
STAMFORD
LINCOLNSHIRE PE9 1XA
t: 01780 484300 f: 01780 484301
e: enquiries@stamford.ac.uk
// www.stamford.ac.uk

L521 FdA Applied Studies (Early Childhood)
Duration: 2FT Fdg
Entry Requirements: Interview required.

L522 FdA Applied Studies (Learning Support)
Duration: 2FT Fdg   CRB Check: Required
Entry Requirements: Contact the institution for details.

N36 NEWMAN UNIVERSITY COLLEGE, BIRMINGHAM
GENNERS LANE
BARTLEY GREEN
BIRMINGHAM B32 3NT
t: 0121 476 1181 f: 0121 476 1196
e: Admissions@newman.ac.uk
// www.newman.ac.uk

QL35 BA English and Working with Children Young People and Families
Duration: 3FT Hon
Entry Requirements: *Foundation:* Distinction. *GCE:* 260. *IB:* 24. *BTEC ExtDip:* DMM. *OCR ND:* M2 *OCR NED:* M2

NL25 BA Management & Business and Working with Children, Young People & Families
Duration: 3FT Hon
Entry Requirements: *Foundation:* Distinction. *GCE:* 260. *IB:* 24. *BTEC ExtDip:* DMM. *OCR ND:* M2 *OCR NED:* M2

PL35 BA Media & Communication and Working with Children, Young People & Families
Duration: 3FT Hon
Entry Requirements: *Foundation:* Distinction. *GCE:* 260. *IB:* 24. *BTEC ExtDip:* DMM. *OCR ND:* M2 *OCR NED:* M2

LC58 BA Working with Children Young People & Families and Applied Psychology
Duration: 3FT Hon
Entry Requirements: *Foundation:* Distinction. *GCE:* 260. *IB:* 24. *BTEC ExtDip:* DMM. *OCR ND:* M2 *OCR NED:* M2

LX53 BA Working with Children Young People & Families and Education Studies
Duration: 3FT Hon
Entry Requirements: *Foundation:* Distinction. *GCE:* 260. *IB:* 24. *BTEC ExtDip:* DMM. *OCR ND:* M2 *OCR NED:* M2

LV51 BA Working with Children Young People & Families and History
Duration: 3FT Hon
Entry Requirements: *Foundation:* Distinction. *GCE:* 260. *IB:* 24. *BTEC ExtDip:* DMM. *OCR ND:* M2 *OCR NED:* M2

LC56 BA Working with Children Young People & Families and Sports Studies
Duration: 3FT Hon
Entry Requirements: *Foundation:* Distinction. *GCE:* 260. *IB:* 24. *BTEC ExtDip:* DMM. *OCR ND:* M2 *OCR NED:* M2

L5C8 BA Working with Children Young People & Families with Applied Psychology
Duration: 3FT Hon
Entry Requirements: *Foundation:* Distinction. *GCE:* 260. *IB:* 24. *BTEC ExtDip:* DMM. *OCR ND:* M2 *OCR NED:* M2

L5W8 BA Working with Children Young People & Families with Creative Writing
Duration: 3FT Hon
Entry Requirements: *Foundation:* Distinction. *GCE:* 260. *IB:* 24.
BTEC ExtDip: DMM. *OCR ND:* M2 *OCR NED:* M2

L5X3 BA Working with Children Young People & Families with Education Studies
Duration: 3FT Hon
Entry Requirements: *Foundation:* Distinction. *GCE:* 260. *IB:* 24.
BTEC ExtDip: DMM. *OCR ND:* M2 *OCR NED:* M2

L5Q3 BA Working with Children Young People & Families with English Literature
Duration: 3FT Hon
Entry Requirements: Contact the institution for details.

L5N2 BA Working with Children Young People & Families with Management & Business
Duration: 3FT Hon
Entry Requirements: *Foundation:* Distinction. *GCE:* 260. *IB:* 24.
BTEC ExtDip: DMM. *OCR ND:* M2 *OCR NED:* M2

L5C6 BA Working with Children Young People & Families with Sports Studies
Duration: 3FT Hon
Entry Requirements: *Foundation:* Distinction. *GCE:* 260. *IB:* 24.
BTEC ExtDip: DMM. *OCR ND:* M2 *OCR NED:* M2

LMP3 BA Working with Children Young People and Families with Media and Communication
Duration: 3FT Hon
Entry Requirements: *Foundation:* Distinction. *GCE:* 260. *IB:* 24.
BTEC ExtDip: DMM. *OCR ND:* M2 *OCR NED:* M2

L5VC BA Working with Children, Young People & Families with Ancient History
Duration: 3FT Hon
Entry Requirements: *Foundation:* Merit. *GCE:* 260. *IB:* 24. *OCR ND:* M1 *OCR NED:* P1

L590 BA Working with Children, Young People and Families
Duration: 3FT Hon   CRB Check: Required
Entry Requirements: *Foundation:* Merit. *GCE:* 260. *IB:* 24. *OCR ND:* M1 *OCR NED:* P1

LMQ3 BA Working with Children, Young People and Families with English Language
Duration: 3FT Hon
Entry Requirements: *Foundation:* Merit. *GCE:* 260. *IB:* 24. *OCR ND:* M1 *OCR NED:* P1

L530 BA Youth and Community Work
Duration: 3FT Hon   CRB Check: Required
Entry Requirements: *Foundation:* Distinction. *GCE:* 260. *IB:* 24.
BTEC ExtDip: DMM. *OCR ND:* M2 *OCR NED:* M2

N37 UNIVERSITY OF WALES, NEWPORT
ADMISSIONS
LODGE ROAD
CAERLEON
NEWPORT NP18 3QT
t: 01633 432030 f: 01633 432850
e: admissions@newport.ac.uk
// www.newport.ac.uk

L520 BA Childhood Studies Foundation Year
Duration: 4FT Hon
Entry Requirements: Interview required.

L500 BA Social Work
Duration: 3FT Hon   CRB Check: Required
Entry Requirements: *GCE:* 240. *IB:* 24. Interview required.

L521 BA Youth and Community Work
Duration: 3FT Hon   CRB Check: Required
Entry Requirements: *GCE:* 240. *IB:* 24. Interview required.

L593 BA Youth and Community Work (Sport)
Duration: 3FT Hon   CRB Check: Required
Entry Requirements: *GCE:* 240. *IB:* 24. Interview required.

L594 BA Youth and Communtiy Work (Youth Justice)
Duration: 3FT Hon   CRB Check: Required
Entry Requirements: *GCE:* 240. *IB:* 24. Interview required.

L511 FdSc Community Health and Well Being
Duration: 2FT Fdg   CRB Check: Required
Entry Requirements: *GCE:* 120. *IB:* 24. Interview required.

N38 UNIVERSITY OF NORTHAMPTON
PARK CAMPUS
BOUGHTON GREEN ROAD
NORTHAMPTON NN2 7AL
t: 0800 358 2232 f: 01604 722083
e: admissions@northampton.ac.uk
// www.northampton.ac.uk

N5LM BA Advertising/Social Care
Duration: 3FT Hon
Entry Requirements: *GCE:* 260-280. *SQAH:* AAA-BBBB. *IB:* 24.
BTEC Dip: DD. *BTEC ExtDip:* DMM. *OCR ND:* D *OCR NED:* M2

N1L5 BA Business/Social Care
Duration: 3FT Hon
Entry Requirements: *GCE:* 260-280. *SQAH:* AAA-BBBB. *IB:* 24.
BTEC Dip: DD. *BTEC ExtDip:* DMM. *OCR ND:* D *OCR NED:* M2

L590 BA Childhood and Youth
Duration: 3FT Hon   CRB Check: Required
Entry Requirements: *GCE:* 260-280. *SQAH:* AAA-BBBB. *IB:* 24.
BTEC Dip: DD. *BTEC ExtDip:* DMM. *OCR ND:* D *OCR NED:* M2
Interview required.

W8L5 BA Creative Writing/Social Care
Duration: 3FT Hon
Entry Requirements: *GCE:* 260-280. *SQAH:* AAA-BBBB. *IB:* 24.
BTEC Dip: DD. *BTEC ExtDip:* DMM. *OCR ND:* D *OCR NED:* M2

W4L5 BA Drama/Social Care
Duration: 3FT Hon
Entry Requirements: *GCE:* 260-280. *SQAH:* AAA-BBBB. *IB:* 24.
BTEC Dip: DD. *BTEC ExtDip:* DMM. *OCR ND:* D *OCR NED:* M2
Interview required.

L1L5 BA Economics/Social Care
Duration: 3FT Hon
Entry Requirements: *GCE:* 260-280. *SQAH:* AAA-BBBB. *IB:* 24.
BTEC Dip: DD. *BTEC ExtDip:* DMM. *OCR ND:* D *OCR NED:* M2

X3L5 BA Education Studies/Social Care
Duration: 3FT Hon
Entry Requirements: *GCE:* 260-280. *SQAH:* AAA-BBBB. *IB:* 24.
BTEC Dip: DD. *BTEC ExtDip:* DMM. *OCR ND:* D *OCR NED:* M2

Q3L5 BA English/Social Care
Duration: 3FT Hon
Entry Requirements: *GCE:* 260-280. *SQAH:* AAA-BBBB. *IB:* 24.
BTEC Dip: DD. *BTEC ExtDip:* DMM. *OCR ND:* D *OCR NED:* M2

N8LM BA Events Management/Social Care
Duration: 3FT Hon
Entry Requirements: *GCE:* 260-280. *SQAH:* AAA-BBBB. *IB:* 24.
BTEC Dip: DD. *BTEC ExtDip:* DMM. *OCR ND:* D *OCR NED:* M2

W6L5 BA Film & Television Studies/Social Care
Duration: 3FT Hon
Entry Requirements: *GCE:* 260-280. *SQAH:* AAA-BBBB. *IB:* 24.
BTEC Dip: DD. *BTEC ExtDip:* DMM. *OCR ND:* D *OCR NED:* M2

L4L5 BA Health Studies/Social Care
Duration: 3FT Hon
Entry Requirements: *GCE:* 260-280. *SQAH:* AAA-BBBB. *IB:* 24.
BTEC Dip: DD. *BTEC ExtDip:* DMM. *OCR ND:* D *OCR NED:* M2

L9LM BA International Development/Social Care
Duration: 3FT Hon
Entry Requirements: *GCE:* 260-280. *SQAH:* AAA-BBBB. *IB:* 24.
BTEC Dip: DD. *BTEC ExtDip:* DMM. *OCR ND:* D *OCR NED:* M2

M1L5 BA Law/Social Care
Duration: 3FT Hon
Entry Requirements: *GCE:* 260-280. *SQAH:* AAA-BBBB. *IB:* 24.
BTEC Dip: DD. *BTEC ExtDip:* DMM. *OCR ND:* D *OCR NED:* M2

N2L5 BA Management/Social Care
Duration: 3FT Hon
Entry Requirements: *GCE:* 260-280. *SQAH:* AAA-BBBB. *IB:* 24.
BTEC Dip: DD. *BTEC ExtDip:* DMM. *OCR ND:* D *OCR NED:* M2

N5L5 BA Marketing/Social Care
Duration: 3FT Hon
Entry Requirements: *GCE:* 260-280. *SQAH:* AAA-BBBB. *IB:* 24.
BTEC Dip: DD. *BTEC ExtDip:* DMM. *OCR ND:* D *OCR NED:* M2

P3L5 BA Media Production/Social Care
Duration: 3FT Hon
Entry Requirements: *GCE:* 260-280. *SQAH:* AAA-BBBB. *IB:* 24.
BTEC Dip: DD. *BTEC ExtDip:* DMM. *OCR ND:* D *OCR NED:* M2

L2L5 BA Politics/Social Care
Duration: 3FT Hon
Entry Requirements: *GCE:* 260-280. *SQAH:* AAA-BBBB. *IB:* 24.
BTEC Dip: DD. *BTEC ExtDip:* DMM. *OCR ND:* D *OCR NED:* M2

W3L5 BA Popular Music/Social Care
Duration: 3FT Hon
Entry Requirements: *GCE:* 260-280. *SQAH:* AAA-BBBB. *IB:* 24.
BTEC Dip: DD. *BTEC ExtDip:* DMM. *OCR ND:* D *OCR NED:* M2

C8L5 BA Psychology/Social Care
Duration: 3FT Hon
Entry Requirements: *GCE:* 260-280. *SQAH:* AAA-BBBB. *IB:* 24.
BTEC Dip: DD. *BTEC ExtDip:* DMM. *OCR ND:* D *OCR NED:* M2

L5D4 BA Social Care with Applied Equine Studies
Duration: 3FT Hon
Entry Requirements: *GCE:* 260-280. *SQAH:* AAA-BBBB. *IB:* 24.
BTEC Dip: DD. *BTEC ExtDip:* DMM. *OCR ND:* D *OCR NED:* M2

L5NG BA Social Care with Applied Management
Duration: 3FT Hon
Entry Requirements: *GCE:* 260-280. *SQAH:* AAA-BBBB. *IB:* 24.
BTEC Dip: DD. *BTEC ExtDip:* DMM. *OCR ND:* D *OCR NED:* M2

L5NM BA Social Care/Advertising
Duration: 3FT Hon
Entry Requirements: *GCE:* 260-280. *SQAH:* AAA-BBBB. *IB:* 24.
BTEC Dip: DD. *BTEC ExtDip:* DMM. *OCR ND:* D *OCR NED:* M2

L5C1 BA Social Care/Biological Conservation
Duration: 3FT Hon
Entry Requirements: *GCE:* 260-280. *SQAH:* AAA-BBBB. *IB:* 24.
BTEC Dip: DD. *BTEC ExtDip:* DMM. *OCR ND:* D *OCR NED:* M2

L5N1 BA Social Care/Business
Duration: 3FT Hon
Entry Requirements: *GCE:* 260-280. *SQAH:* AAA-BBBB. *IB:* 24.
BTEC Dip: DD. *BTEC ExtDip:* DMM. *OCR ND:* D *OCR NED:* M2

L5G5 BA Social Care/Business Computing Systems
Duration: 3FT Hon
Entry Requirements: *GCE:* 260-280. *SQAH:* AAA-BBBB. *IB:* 24.
BTEC Dip: DD. *BTEC ExtDip:* DMM. *OCR ND:* D *OCR NED:* M2

L5G4 BA Social Care/Computing
Duration: 3FT Hon
Entry Requirements: *GCE:* 260-280. *SQAH:* AAA-BBBB. *IB:* 24.
BTEC Dip: DD. *BTEC ExtDip:* DMM. *OCR ND:* D *OCR NED:* M2

L5W8 BA Social Care/Creative Writing
Duration: 3FT Hon
Entry Requirements: *GCE:* 260-280. *SQAH:* AAA-BBBB. *IB:* 24.
BTEC Dip: DD. *BTEC ExtDip:* DMM. *OCR ND:* D *OCR NED:* M2

L5W4 BA Social Care/Drama
Duration: 3FT Hon
Entry Requirements: *GCE:* 260-280. *SQAH:* AAA-BBBB. *IB:* 24.
BTEC Dip: DD. *BTEC ExtDip:* DMM. *OCR ND:* D *OCR NED:* M2
Interview required.

L5L1 BA Social Care/Economics
Duration: 3FT Hon
Entry Requirements: *GCE:* 260-280. *SQAH:* AAA-BBBB. *IB:* 24.
BTEC Dip: DD. *BTEC ExtDip:* DMM. *OCR ND:* D *OCR NED:* M2

L5X3 BA Social Care/Education Studies
Duration: 3FT Hon
Entry Requirements: *GCE:* 260-280. *SQAH:* AAA-BBBB. *IB:* 24.
BTEC Dip: DD. *BTEC ExtDip:* DMM. *OCR ND:* D *OCR NED:* M2

L5Q3 BA Social Care/English
Duration: 3FT Hon
Entry Requirements: *GCE:* 260-280. *SQAH:* AAA-BBBB. *IB:* 24.
BTEC Dip: DD. *BTEC ExtDip:* DMM. *OCR ND:* D *OCR NED:* M2

L5NV BA Social Care/Events Management
Duration: 3FT Hon
Entry Requirements: *GCE:* 260-280. *SQAH:* AAA-BBBB. *IB:* 24.
BTEC Dip: DD. *BTEC ExtDip:* DMM. *OCR ND:* D *OCR NED:* M2

L5W6 BA Social Care/Film & Television Studies
Duration: 3FT Hon
Entry Requirements: *GCE:* 260-280. *SQAH:* AAA-BBBB. *IB:* 24.
BTEC Dip: DD. *BTEC ExtDip:* DMM. *OCR ND:* D *OCR NED:* M2

L5L4 BA Social Care/Health Studies
Duration: 3FT Hon
Entry Requirements: *GCE:* 260-280. *SQAH:* AAA-BBBB. *IB:* 24.
BTEC Dip: DD. *BTEC ExtDip:* DMM. *OCR ND:* D *OCR NED:* M2

L5L9 BA Social Care/International Development
Duration: 3FT Hon
Entry Requirements: *GCE:* 260-280. *SQAH:* AAA-BBBB. *IB:* 24.
BTEC Dip: DD. *BTEC ExtDip:* DMM. *OCR ND:* D *OCR NED:* M2

L5M1 BA Social Care/Law
Duration: 3FT Hon
Entry Requirements: *GCE:* 260-280. *SQAH:* AAA-BBBB. *IB:* 24.
BTEC Dip: DD. *BTEC ExtDip:* DMM. *OCR ND:* D *OCR NED:* M2

L5N2 BA Social Care/Management
Duration: 3FT Hon
Entry Requirements: *GCE:* 260-280. *SQAH:* AAA-BBBB. *IB:* 24.
BTEC Dip: DD. *BTEC ExtDip:* DMM. *OCR ND:* D *OCR NED:* M2

L5N5 BA Social Care/Marketing
Duration: 3FT Hon
Entry Requirements: *GCE:* 260-280. *SQAH:* AAA-BBBB. *IB:* 24.
BTEC Dip: DD. *BTEC ExtDip:* DMM. *OCR ND:* D *OCR NED:* M2

L5P3 BA Social Care/Media Production
Duration: 3FT Hon
Entry Requirements: *GCE:* 260-280. *SQAH:* AAA-BBBB. *IB:* 24.
BTEC Dip: DD. *BTEC ExtDip:* DMM. *OCR ND:* D *OCR NED:* M2

L5F8 BA Social Care/Physical Geography
Duration: 3FT Hon
Entry Requirements: *GCE:* 260-280. *SQAH:* AAA-BBBB. *IB:* 24.
BTEC Dip: DD. *BTEC ExtDip:* DMM. *OCR ND:* D *OCR NED:* M2

L5L2 BA Social Care/Politics
Duration: 3FT Hon
Entry Requirements: *GCE:* 260-280. *SQAH:* AAA-BBBB. *IB:* 24.
BTEC Dip: DD. *BTEC ExtDip:* DMM. *OCR ND:* D *OCR NED:* M2

L5W3 BA Social Care/Popular Music
Duration: 3FT Hon
Entry Requirements: *GCE:* 260-280. *SQAH:* AAA-BBBB. *IB:* 24.
BTEC Dip: DD. *BTEC ExtDip:* DMM. *OCR ND:* D *OCR NED:* M2

L5C8 BA Social Care/Psychology
Duration: 3FT Hon
Entry Requirements: *GCE:* 260-280. *SQAH:* AAA-BBBB. *IB:* 24.
BTEC Dip: DD. *BTEC ExtDip:* DMM. *OCR ND:* D *OCR NED:* M2

L5L3 BA Social Care/Sociology
Duration: 3FT Hon
Entry Requirements: *GCE:* 260-280. *SQAH:* AAA-BBBB. *IB:* 24.
BTEC Dip: DD. *BTEC ExtDip:* DMM. *OCR ND:* D *OCR NED:* M2

L5C6 BA Social Care/Sport Studies
Duration: 3FT Hon
Entry Requirements: *GCE:* 260-280. *SQAH:* AAA-BBBB. *IB:* 24.
BTEC Dip: DD. *BTEC ExtDip:* DMM. *OCR ND:* D *OCR NED:* M2

L5N8 BA Social Care/Tourism
Duration: 3FT Hon
Entry Requirements: *GCE:* 260-280. *SQAH:* AAA-BBBB. *IB:* 24.
BTEC Dip: DD. *BTEC ExtDip:* DMM. *OCR ND:* D *OCR NED:* M2

L5GK BA Social Care/Web Design
Duration: 3FT Hon
Entry Requirements: *GCE:* 260-280. *SQAH:* AAA-BBBB. *IB:* 24.
BTEC Dip: DD. *BTEC ExtDip:* DMM. *OCR ND:* D *OCR NED:* M2

L500 BA Social Work
Duration: 3FT Hon   CRB Check: Required
Entry Requirements: *GCE:* 260-280. *SQAH:* AAA-BBBB. *IB:* 24.
BTEC Dip: DD. *BTEC ExtDip:* DMM. *OCR ND:* D *OCR NED:* M2
Interview required.

L510 BA Social and Community Development
Duration: 3FT/4SW Hon
Entry Requirements: *GCE:* 260-280. *SQAH:* AAA-BBBB. *IB:* 24.
BTEC Dip: DD. *BTEC ExtDip:* DMM. *OCR ND:* D *OCR NED:* M2

L3L5 BA Sociology/Social Care
Duration: 3FT Hon
Entry Requirements: *GCE:* 260-280. *SQAH:* AAA-BBBB. *IB:* 24.
BTEC Dip: DD. *BTEC ExtDip:* DMM. *OCR ND:* D *OCR NED:* M2

XL35 BA Special Educational Needs & Inclusion/Social Care
Duration: 3FT Hon
Entry Requirements: *GCE:* 260-280. *SQAH:* AAA-BBBB. *IB:* 24.
BTEC Dip: DD. *BTEC ExtDip:* DMM. *OCR ND:* D *OCR NED:* M2

C6L5 BA Sport Studies/Social Care
Duration: 3FT Hon
Entry Requirements: *GCE:* 260-280. *SQAH:* AAA-BBBB. *IB:* 24.
BTEC Dip: DD. *BTEC ExtDip:* DMM. *OCR ND:* D *OCR NED:* M2

N8L5 BA Tourism/Social Care
Duration: 3FT Hon
Entry Requirements: *GCE:* 260-280. *SQAH:* AAA-BBBB. *IB:* 24.
BTEC Dip: DD. *BTEC ExtDip:* DMM. *OCR ND:* D *OCR NED:* M2

C1L5 BSc Biological Conservation/Social Care
Duration: 3FT Hon
Entry Requirements: *GCE:* 260-280. *SQAH:* AAA-BBBB. *IB:* 24.
BTEC Dip: DD. *BTEC ExtDip:* DMM. *OCR ND:* D *OCR NED:* M2

G5L5 BSc Business Computing Systems/Social Care
Duration: 3FT Hon
Entry Requirements: *GCE:* 260-280. *SQAH:* AAA-BBBB. *IB:* 24.
BTEC Dip: DD. *BTEC ExtDip:* DMM. *OCR ND:* D *OCR NED:* M2

G4L5 BSc Computing/Social Care
Duration: 3FT Hon
Entry Requirements: *GCE:* 260-280. *SQAH:* AAA-BBBB. *IB:* 24.
BTEC Dip: DD. *BTEC ExtDip:* DMM. *OCR ND:* D *OCR NED:* M2

L512 BSc Health and Social Care (Top-Up)
Duration: 1FT Hon **CRB Check:** Required
Entry Requirements: Interview required. HND required.

F8L5 BSc Physical Geography/Social Care
Duration: 3FT Hon
Entry Requirements: *GCE:* 260-280. *SQAH:* AAA-BBBB. *IB:* 24.
BTEC Dip: DD. *BTEC ExtDip:* DMM. *OCR ND:* D *OCR NED:* M2

G4LM BSc Web Design/Social Care
Duration: 3FT Hon
Entry Requirements: *GCE:* 260-280. *SQAH:* AAA-BBBB. *IB:* 24.
BTEC Dip: DD. *BTEC ExtDip:* DMM. *OCR ND:* D *OCR NED:* M2

L561 FdA Offender Management
Duration: 2FT Fdg **CRB Check:** Required
Entry Requirements: *GCE:* 220-260. *SQAH:* BC-CCC. *IB:* 24.
BTEC Dip: DD. *BTEC ExtDip:* DMM. *OCR ND:* D *OCR NED:* M2
Interview required.

L511 FdSc Health and Social Care
Duration: 2FT Fdg **CRB Check:** Required
Entry Requirements: *GCE:* 140-160. *SQAH:* BC-CCC. *IB:* 24.
BTEC Dip: MP. *BTEC ExtDip:* MPP. *OCR ND:* P1 *OCR NED:* P2
Interview required.

N58 NORTH EAST WORCESTERSHIRE COLLEGE
PEAKMAN STREET
REDDITCH
WORCESTERSHIRE B98 8DW
t: 01527 570020 f: 01527 572901
e: admissions@ne-worcs.ac.uk
// www.ne-worcs.ac.uk

L500 BA Social Work
Duration: 3FT Hon **CRB Check:** Required
Entry Requirements: *GCE:* 240. Interview required. Admissions Test required.

005L HNC Health and Social Care
Duration: 1FT HNC
Entry Requirements: Contact the institution for details.

N64 NORTH LINDSEY COLLEGE
KINGSWAY
SCUNTHORPE
NORTH LINCS DN17 1AJ
t: 01724 294125 f: 01724 295378
e: he@northlindsey.ac.uk
// www.northlindsey.ac.uk

L530 FdA Applied Studies (Children and Youth Work)
Duration: 2FT Fdg **CRB Check:** Required
Entry Requirements: Contact the institution for details.

N77 NORTHUMBRIA UNIVERSITY
TRINITY BUILDING
NORTHUMBERLAND ROAD
NEWCASTLE UPON TYNE NE1 8ST
t: 0191 243 7420 f: 0191 227 4561
e: er.admissions@northumbria.ac.uk
// www.northumbria.ac.uk

LXN3 BA Childhood Studies and Disability Studies
Duration: 3FT Hon **CRB Check:** Required
Entry Requirements: *SQAH:* BBCCC. *SQAAH:* BCC. *IB:* 25.

LXMH BA Childhood Studies and Health in Contemporary Society
Duration: 3FT Hon **CRB Check:** Required
Entry Requirements: *SQAH:* BBCCC. *SQAAH:* BCC. *IB:* 25.

L590 BA Disability Studies and Health in Contemporary Society
Duration: 3FT Hon **CRB Check:** Required
Entry Requirements: *SQAH:* BBCCC. *SQAAH:* BCC. *IB:* 25.

LXM3 BA Early Years and Disability Studies
Duration: 3FT Hon   CRB Check: Required
Entry Requirements: *SQAH:* BBCCC. *SQAAH:* BCC. *IB:* 25.

LX5J BA Early Years and Health in Contemporary Society
Duration: 3FT Hon   CRB Check: Required
Entry Requirements: *SQAH:* BBCCC. *SQAAH:* BCC. *IB:* 25.

L502 BSc Social Work
Duration: 3FT Hon   CRB Check: Required
Entry Requirements: *SQAH:* BBCCC. *SQAAH:* BCC. *IB:* 25.
Interview required.

L501 BSc Social Work, AWBL Route
Duration: 3FT Hon   CRB Check: Required
Entry Requirements: *SQAH:* BBCCC. *SQAAH:* BCC. *IB:* 25.
Interview required.

N82 NORWICH CITY COLLEGE OF FURTHER AND HIGHER EDUCATION (AN ASSOCIATE COLLEGE OF UEA)
IPSWICH ROAD
NORWICH
NORFOLK NR2 2LJ
t: 01603 773012 f: 01603 773301
e: he_office@ccn.ac.uk
// www.ccn.ac.uk

L501 BA Applied Social Work
Duration: 3FT Hon
Entry Requirements: *GCE:* 120. *SQAH:* A-C. *SQAAH:* C.

XL35 BA Early Childhood Studies
Duration: 3FT Hon
Entry Requirements: Contact the institution for details.

LX53 FdA Early Years Childcare and Education
Duration: 2FT Fdg
Entry Requirements: *GCE:* 80-180.

N84 THE UNIVERSITY OF NOTTINGHAM
THE ADMISSIONS OFFICE
THE UNIVERSITY OF NOTTINGHAM
UNIVERSITY PARK
NOTTINGHAM NG7 2RD
t: 0115 951 5151 f: 0115 951 4668
// www.nottingham.ac.uk

LL54 BA Social Work and Social Policy
Duration: 3FT Hon   CRB Check: Required
Entry Requirements: *GCE:* BBB. *SQAAH:* BBB. *IB:* 30. Interview required.

L508 MA Social Work (postgraduate entry)
Duration: 2FT PMD   CRB Check: Required
Entry Requirements: Interview required.

N91 NOTTINGHAM TRENT UNIVERSITY
DRYDEN BUILDING
BURTON STREET
NOTTINGHAM NG1 4BU
t: +44 (0) 115 848 4200 f: +44 (0) 115 848 8869
e: applications@ntu.ac.uk
// www.ntu.ac.uk

L510 BA Health and Social Care
Duration: 3FT Hon
Entry Requirements: *GCE:* 280. *OCR NED:* M2

L500 BA Social Work
Duration: 3FT Hon   CRB Check: Required
Entry Requirements: *GCE:* 300. *OCR NED:* D2

O66 OXFORD BROOKES UNIVERSITY
ADMISSIONS OFFICE
HEADINGTON CAMPUS
GIPSY LANE
OXFORD OX3 0BP
t: 01865 483040 f: 01865 483983
e: admissions@brookes.ac.uk
// www.brookes.ac.uk

L500 BA Social Work
Duration: 3FT Hon   CRB Check: Required
Entry Requirements: *GCE:* BBC.

L520 FdA Early Years Sector Endorsed (Solihull)
Duration: 2FT Fdg
Entry Requirements: Contact the institution for details.

P51 PETROC
OLD STICKLEPATH HILL
BARNSTAPLE
NORTH DEVON EX31 2BQ
t: 01271 852365 f: 01271 338121
e: he@petroc.ac.uk
// www.petroc.ac.uk

BL95 FdSc Health and Social Care
Duration: 2FT Fdg   CRB Check: Required
Entry Requirements: *GCE:* 80. Interview required.

P56 UNIVERSITY CENTRE PETERBOROUGH
PARK CRESCENT
PETERBOROUGH PE1 4DZ
t: 0845 1965750 f: 01733 767986
e: UCPenquiries@anglia.ac.uk
// www.anglia.ac.uk/ucp

LXM3 FdA Early Years Childcare and Education
Duration: 2FT Fdg
Entry Requirements: *GCE:* 120-300. Interview required.

P60 PLYMOUTH UNIVERSITY
DRAKE CIRCUS
PLYMOUTH PL4 8AA
t: 01752 585858 f: 01752 588055
e: admissions@plymouth.ac.uk
// www.plymouth.ac.uk

L501 BA Social Work
Duration: 3FT Hon **CRB Check:** Required
Entry Requirements: *GCE:* 230. *IB:* 27. *OCR ND:* D *OCR NED:* M3

L512 BSc Health and Social Care
Duration: 3FT Hon
Entry Requirements: *GCE:* 240. *IB:* 24.

L508 MA Social Work (Postgraduate Entry)
Duration: 2FT PMD **CRB Check:** Required
Entry Requirements: Interview required.

P63 UCP MARJON - UNIVERSITY COLLEGE PLYMOUTH ST MARK & ST JOHN
DERRIFORD ROAD
PLYMOUTH PL6 8BH
t: 01752 636890 f: 01752 636819
e: admissions@marjon.ac.uk
// www.ucpmarjon.ac.uk

L521 BA Children and Young People
Duration: 3FT Hon
Entry Requirements: *GCE:* 180.

L541 BA Community Development
Duration: 3FT Hon
Entry Requirements: *GCE:* 180.

L542 BA Community and Society
Duration: 3FT Hon
Entry Requirements: *GCE:* 180.

L510 BA Health & Social Welfare
Duration: 3FT Hon
Entry Requirements: *GCE:* 180.

L530 BA Youth and Community Work
Duration: 3FT Hon **CRB Check:** Required
Entry Requirements: *GCE:* 180. Interview required.

L520 FdA Child Centred and Therapeutic Practice
Duration: 2FT Fdg
Entry Requirements: *GCE:* 180.

L501 FdA Children, Parenting and Communities
Duration: 2FT Fdg
Entry Requirements: Contact the institution for details.

L511 FdA Health and Social Care
Duration: 2FT Fdg
Entry Requirements: Contact the institution for details.

L590 FdA Learning Support
Duration: 2FT Fdg
Entry Requirements: Contact the institution for details.

P80 UNIVERSITY OF PORTSMOUTH
ACADEMIC REGISTRY
UNIVERSITY HOUSE
WINSTON CHURCHILL AVENUE
PORTSMOUTH PO1 2UP
t: 023 9284 8484 f: 023 9284 3082
e: admissions@port.ac.uk
// www.port.ac.uk

L590 BA Childhood and Youth Studies
Duration: 3FT Hon
Entry Requirements: *GCE:* 240-300. *BTEC Dip:* DD. *BTEC ExtDip:* MMM.

L5C8 BA Childhood and Youth Studies with Psychology
Duration: 3FT Hon
Entry Requirements: *GCE:* 240-300. *BTEC Dip:* DD. *BTEC ExtDip:* MMM.

L500 BSc Social Work
Duration: 3FT Hon **CRB Check:** Required
Entry Requirements: *GCE:* 300. *IB:* 29. *BTEC ExtDip:* DMM. Interview required.

L508 MSc Social Work (Postgraduate Entry)
Duration: 2FT PMD **CRB Check:** Required
Entry Requirements: Interview required.

Q75 QUEEN'S UNIVERSITY BELFAST
UNIVERSITY ROAD
BELFAST BT7 1NN
t: 028 9097 3838 f: 028 9097 5151
e: admissions@qub.ac.uk
// www.qub.ac.uk

L500 BSW Social Work
Duration: 3FT Hon **CRB Check:** Required
Entry Requirements: *GCE:* ABB-BBBb. *SQAH:* ABBBB. *SQAAH:* ABB. Interview required.

L501 BSW Social Work (Relevant Graduate Route)
Duration: 2FT PMD **CRB Check:** Required
Entry Requirements: Interview required.

R36 ROBERT GORDON UNIVERSITY
ROBERT GORDON UNIVERSITY
SCHOOLHILL
ABERDEEN
SCOTLAND AB10 1FR
t: 01224 26 27 28 f: 01224 26 21 47
e: UGOffice@rgu.ac.uk
// www.rgu.ac.uk

L500 BA Social Work
Duration: 4FT Hon   CRB Check: Required
Entry Requirements: *GCE:* 240. *SQAH:* BBCC. *IB:* 26. Interview required.

L508 MSc Social Work (Postgraduate Entry)
Duration: 2FT PMD   CRB Check: Required
Entry Requirements: Interview required.

R52 ROTHERHAM COLLEGE OF ARTS AND TECHNOLOGY
EASTWOOD LANE
ROTHERHAM
SOUTH YORKSHIRE S65 1EG
t: 08080 722777 f: 01709 373053
e: info@rotherham.ac.uk
// www.rotherham.ac.uk

L510 HNC Health and Social Care (Health)
Duration: 1FT HNC   CRB Check: Required
Entry Requirements: *GCE:* 120. *OCR NED:* M3 Interview required.

R72 ROYAL HOLLOWAY, UNIVERSITY OF LONDON
ROYAL HOLLOWAY, UNIVERSITY OF LONDON
EGHAM
SURREY TW20 0EX
t: 01784 414944 f: 01784 473662
e: Admissions@rhul.ac.uk
// www.rhul.ac.uk

L508 MSc Social Work (Postgraduate Entry)
Duration: 2FT PMD
Entry Requirements: Contact the institution for details.

R90 RUSKIN COLLEGE OXFORD
WALTON STREET
OXFORD OX1 2HE
t: 01865 759604 f: 01865 759640
e: admissions@ruskin.ac.uk
// www.ruskin.ac.uk

L500 BA Social Work
Duration: 3FT Hon   CRB Check: Required
Entry Requirements: Interview required. Admissions Test required.

L590 BA Youth and Community Work
Duration: 1FT Hon
Entry Requirements: Contact the institution for details.

L592 BA Youth and Community Work
Duration: 3FT Hon   CRB Check: Required
Entry Requirements: Contact the institution for details.

S03 THE UNIVERSITY OF SALFORD
SALFORD M5 4WT
t: 0161 295 4545 f: 0161 295 4646
e: ug-admissions@salford.ac.uk
// www.salford.ac.uk

L500 BA Social Work Studies
Duration: 3FT Hon   CRB Check: Required
Entry Requirements: *GCE:* 280. *IB:* 27. Interview required.

CL85 BSc Psychology Studies and Counselling Studies
Duration: 3FT Hon
Entry Requirements: *GCE:* 300. *IB:* 27. *OCR NED:* M1

L508 MA Social Work Studies (Postgraduate Entry)
Duration: 2FT PMD   CRB Check: Required
Entry Requirements: Interview required. Admissions Test required.

S18 THE UNIVERSITY OF SHEFFIELD
THE UNIVERSITY OF SHEFFIELD
LEVEL 2, ARTS TOWER
WESTERN BANK
SHEFFIELD S10 2TN
t: 0114 222 8030 f: 0114 222 8032
// www.sheffield.ac.uk

L508 MA Social Work (Postgraduate Entry)
Duration: 2FT PMD   CRB Check: Required
Entry Requirements: Interview required.

S21 SHEFFIELD HALLAM UNIVERSITY
CITY CAMPUS
HOWARD STREET
SHEFFIELD S1 1WB
t: 0114 225 5555 f: 0114 225 2167
e: admissions@shu.ac.uk
// www.shu.ac.uk

L520 BA Children and Playwork
Duration: 3FT Hon
Entry Requirements: *GCE:* 240.

L500 BA Social Work Studies
Duration: 3FT Hon
Entry Requirements: *GCE:* 200.

CL65 BA Sport & Community Development
Duration: 3FT Hon
Entry Requirements: *GCE:* 240.

L990 BA Youth and Community Studies (Top-Up)
Duration: 1FT Hon
Entry Requirements: Contact the institution for details.

L590 BA Youth and Community Work
Duration: 3FT Hon
Entry Requirements: *GCE:* 180.

L535 BSc Nutrition, Health and Lifestyles
Duration: 3FT Hon
Entry Requirements: *GCE:* 280.

LX53 FdA Working with Children, Young People and Families
Duration: 2FT Fdg
Entry Requirements: *GCE:* 120.

L508 MA Social Work (Postgraduate Entry)
Duration: 2FT PMD
Entry Requirements: Contact the institution for details.

S27 UNIVERSITY OF SOUTHAMPTON
HIGHFIELD
SOUTHAMPTON SO17 1BJ
t: 023 8059 4732 f: 023 8059 3037
e: admissions@soton.ac.uk
// www.southampton.ac.uk

L510 BSc Health and Social Care (Top-Up)
Duration: 1FT Hon **CRB Check:** Required
Entry Requirements: Contact the institution for details.

S28 SOMERSET COLLEGE OF ARTS AND TECHNOLOGY
WELLINGTON ROAD
TAUNTON
SOMERSET TA1 5AX
t: 01823 366331 f: 01823 366418
e: enquiries@somerset.ac.uk
// www.somerset.ac.uk/student-area/
considering-a-degree.html

LL45 BSc Health and Social Care Management (Top-Up)
Duration: 1FT Hon
Entry Requirements: HND required.

L520 FdA Early Childhood Studies
Duration: 2FT Fdg
Entry Requirements: *GCE:* 60-150. *IB:* 24. Interview required.

L510 FdA Health & Social Care - Health & Social Care Studies
Duration: 2FT Fdg
Entry Requirements: *GCE:* 60-150. *IB:* 24. Interview required.

S30 SOUTHAMPTON SOLENT UNIVERSITY
EAST PARK TERRACE
SOUTHAMPTON
HAMPSHIRE SO14 0RT
t: +44 (0) 23 8031 9039 f: + 44 (0)23 8022 2259
e: admissions@solent.ac.uk
// www.solent.ac.uk/

L501 BA Social Work
Duration: 3FT Hon **CRB Check:** Required
Entry Requirements: *Foundation:* Distinction. *GCE:* 240. *SQAAH:* AA-CCD. *IB:* 24. *BTEC ExtDip:* MMM. *OCR ND:* D *OCR NED:* M3
Interview required.

S35 SOUTHPORT COLLEGE
MORNINGTON ROAD
SOUTHPORT
MERSEYSIDE PR9 0TT
t: 08450066236 f: 01704 392610
e: guidance@southport-college.ac.uk
// www.southport-college.ac.uk

L5L2 FdA Children, Young People and their Services
Duration: 2FT Fdg
Entry Requirements: Contact the institution for details.

L510 HND Health & Social Care
Duration: 2FT HND **CRB Check:** Required
Entry Requirements: Contact the institution for details.

S41 SOUTH CHESHIRE COLLEGE
DANE BANK AVENUE
CREWE CW2 8AB
t: 01270 654654 f: 01270 651515
e: admissions@s-cheshire.ac.uk
// www.s-cheshire.ac.uk

L590 FdA Public and Community Services
Duration: 2FT Fdg **CRB Check:** Required
Entry Requirements: *GCE:* 100. Interview required.

S43 SOUTH ESSEX COLLEGE OF FURTHER & HIGHER EDUCATION
LUKER ROAD
SOUTHEND-ON-SEA
ESSEX SS1 1ND
t: 0845 52 12345 f: 01702 432320
e: Admissions@southessex.ac.uk
// www.southessex.ac.uk

L500 BA Social Work
Duration: 3FT Hon **CRB Check:** Required
Entry Requirements: *GCE:* 160. *IB:* 24. Interview required.
Admissions Test required.

S72 STAFFORDSHIRE UNIVERSITY
COLLEGE ROAD
STOKE ON TRENT ST4 2DE
t: 01782 292753 f: 01782 292740
e: admissions@staffs.ac.uk
// www.staffs.ac.uk

LL45 BA Advice Work
Duration: 3FT Hon
Entry Requirements: *GCE:* 160-200. *IB:* 24.

LVM6 BA Children & Family Work and Practical Theology
Duration: 3FT Hon   CRB Check: Required
Entry Requirements: Interview required.

LV5P BA Children's Work and Ministry
Duration: 3FT Hon   CRB Check: Required
Entry Requirements: *GCE:* 180. *IB:* 24. Interview required.

L590 BA Early Childhood Studies
Duration: 3FT Hon   CRB Check: Required
Entry Requirements: *GCE:* 180-240. *IB:* 24. Interview required.

LV5Q BA Family Support Work and Ministry
Duration: 3FT Hon   CRB Check: Required
Entry Requirements: *GCE:* 180. *IB:* 24. Interview required.

VLQ5 BA School, Youth and Community Work and Practical Theology
Duration: 3FT Hon   CRB Check: Required
Entry Requirements: Interview required.

L500 BA Social Work
Duration: 3FT Hon   CRB Check: Required
Entry Requirements: *GCE:* 180-240. *IB:* 24. Interview required.

L540 BA Young People, Communities and Practical Theology
Duration: 3FT Hon
Entry Requirements: Contact the institution for details.

LV56 BA Youth Work and Ministry
Duration: 3FT Hon   CRB Check: Required
Entry Requirements: *GCE:* 180. *IB:* 24. Interview required.

L510 BSc Health Studies with a Foundation Year
Duration: 4FT Hon
Entry Requirements: Interview required.

LV65 FdA Children's Work and Ministry
Duration: 2FT Hon
Entry Requirements: Contact the institution for details.

VL65 FdA Family Support Work and Ministry
Duration: 2FT Hon
Entry Requirements: Contact the institution for details.

L501 FdA Social Care (Adult)
Duration: 2FT Hon
Entry Requirements: *GCE:* 60. Interview required.

LV6N FdA Youth Work and Ministry
Duration: 2FT Fdg
Entry Requirements: Contact the institution for details.

L513 HND Health and Social Care
Duration: 2FT HND   CRB Check: Required
Entry Requirements: Contact the institution for details.

S75 THE UNIVERSITY OF STIRLING
STUDENT RECRUITMENT & ADMISSIONS SERVICE
UNIVERSITY OF STIRLING
STIRLING
SCOTLAND FK9 4LA
t: 01786 467044 f: 01786 466800
e: admissions@stir.ac.uk
// www.stir.ac.uk

L500 BA Social Work
Duration: 4FT Hon   CRB Check: Required
Entry Requirements: *GCE:* BBC. *SQAH:* BBBB. *SQAAH:* AAA-CCC. *IB:* 32. *BTEC ExtDip:* DMM.

L508 PGDip Social Work Studies (Postgraduate Entry)
Duration: 2FT PMD   CRB Check: Required
Entry Requirements: Contact the institution for details.

S76 STOCKPORT COLLEGE
WELLINGTON ROAD SOUTH
STOCKPORT SK1 3UQ
t: 0161 958 3143 f: 0161 958 3663
e: susan.kelly@stockport.ac.uk
// www.stockport.ac.uk

L510 BA Health and Social Care
Duration: 3FT Hon   CRB Check: Required
Entry Requirements: Interview required.

L501 BA Social Work
Duration: 3FT Hon   CRB Check: Required
Entry Requirements: Interview required.

XL3M FdA Early Years Practice [Sector Endorsed]
Duration: 2FT Fdg   CRB Check: Required
Entry Requirements: Interview required.

XL35 FdA Working with Children and Young People
Duration: 2FT Fdg   CRB Check: Required
Entry Requirements: Interview required.

S77 STOURBRIDGE COLLEGE
HAGLEY ROAD
STOURBRIDGE
WEST MIDLANDS DY8 1QU
t: 01384 344344 f: 01384 344600
e: info@stourbridge.ac.uk
// www.stourbridge.ac.uk

099L HND Health and Social Care
Duration: 2FT HND
Entry Requirements: Contact the institution for details.

S78 THE UNIVERSITY OF STRATHCLYDE
GLASGOW G1 1XQ
t: 0141 552 4400 f: 0141 552 0775
// www.strath.ac.uk

L501 BA Social Work
Duration: 4FT Hon   CRB Check: Required
Entry Requirements: GCE: BBB. SQAAH: BBBB-BBBCC. Portfolio required.

L508 MSW Social Work (Postgraduate Entry)
Duration: 2FT PMD   CRB Check: Required
Entry Requirements: Contact the institution for details.

S79 STRANMILLIS UNIVERSITY COLLEGE: A COLLEGE OF QUEEN'S UNIVERSITY BELFAST
STRANMILLIS ROAD
BELFAST BT9 5DY
t: 028 9038 1271 f: 028 9038 4444
e: Registry@stran.ac.uk
// www.stran.ac.uk

LX53 FdA Early Childhood Studies
Duration: 2FT Fdg   CRB Check: Required
Entry Requirements: GCE: BC.

S82 UNIVERSITY CAMPUS SUFFOLK (UCS)
WATERFRONT BUILDING
NEPTUNE QUAY
IPSWICH
SUFFOLK IP4 1QJ
t: 01473 338833 f: 01473 339900
e: info@ucs.ac.uk
// www.ucs.ac.uk

LL54 BA Children, Young People and Policy
Duration: 3FT Hon
Entry Requirements: GCE: 240-280. IB: 28. BTEC ExtDip: DMM.

LX53 BA Early Childhood Studies and Youth Studies
Duration: 3FT Hon
Entry Requirements: GCE: 280. IB: 28. BTEC ExtDip: DMM.
Interview required.

L501 BA Social Work
Duration: 3FT Hon   CRB Check: Required
Entry Requirements: GCE: 280. IB: 28. BTEC ExtDip: DMM.
Interview required.

LL3M BA Sociology and Youth Studies
Duration: 3FT Hon
Entry Requirements: GCE: 240-280. IB: 28. BTEC ExtDip: DMM.

ML95 BSc Criminology and Youth Studies
Duration: 3FT Hon
Entry Requirements: GCE: 240-280. IB: 28. BTEC ExtDip: DMM.

CL85 BSc Psychology and Youth Studies
Duration: 3FT Hon
Entry Requirements: GCE: 240-280. IB: 28. BTEC ExtDip: DMM.

CL65 FdSc Sport, Health & Exercise
Duration: 2FT Fdg
Entry Requirements: GCE: 200. IB: 28. BTEC ExtDip: DMM.

S84 UNIVERSITY OF SUNDERLAND
STUDENT HELPLINE
THE STUDENT GATEWAY
CHESTER ROAD
SUNDERLAND SR1 3SD
t: 0191 515 3000 f: 0191 515 3805
e: student.helpline@sunderland.ac.uk
// www.sunderland.ac.uk

N1L5 BA Business Management with Health & Social Care
Duration: 3FT Hon
Entry Requirements: GCE: 260-360.

XLH5 BA Childhood Studies and Health & Social Care
Duration: 3FT Hon
Entry Requirements: GCE: 260-360.

L3X5 BA Childhood Studies with Education
Duration: 3FT Hon
Entry Requirements: GCE: 260-360.

X3LM BA Childhood Studies with Health & Social Care
Duration: 3FT Hon
Entry Requirements: GCE: 260-360.

L522 BA Community and Youth Work
Duration: 3FT Hon
Entry Requirements: GCE: 260-360. SQAH: AAAA-CCCC. OCR ND: D OCR NED: M3 Interview required.

W5L5 BA Dance with Health & Social Care
Duration: 3FT Hon
Entry Requirements: GCE: 260-360.

W4L5 BA Drama with Health & Social Care
Duration: 3FT Hon
Entry Requirements: GCE: 260-360.

Q1L5 BA English Language & Linguistics with Health & Social Care
Duration: 3FT Hon
Entry Requirements: *GCE:* 260-360.

Q3L5 BA English with Health & Social Care
Duration: 3FT Hon
Entry Requirements: *GCE:* 260-360.

NL25 BA Health & Social Care and Business Management
Duration: 3FT Hon
Entry Requirements: *GCE:* 260-360.

ML95 BA Health & Social Care and Criminology
Duration: 3FT Hon
Entry Requirements: *GCE:* 260-360.

WL55 BA Health & Social Care and Dance
Duration: 3FT Hon
Entry Requirements: *GCE:* 260-360.

WL45 BA Health & Social Care and Drama
Duration: 3FT Hon
Entry Requirements: *GCE:* 260-360.

XL35 BA Health & Social Care and Education
Duration: 3FT Hon
Entry Requirements: *GCE:* 260-360.

QL35 BA Health & Social Care and English
Duration: 3FT Hon
Entry Requirements: *GCE:* 260-360.

QL15 BA Health & Social Care and English Language & Linguistics
Duration: 3FT Hon
Entry Requirements: *GCE:* 260-360.

LV51 BA Health & Social Care and History
Duration: 3FT Hon
Entry Requirements: *GCE:* 260-360.

LM51 BA Health & Social Care and Law
Duration: 3FT Hon
Entry Requirements: *GCE:* 260-360.

LR51 BA Health & Social Care and MFL French
Duration: 3FT Hon
Entry Requirements: *GCE:* 260-360.

LP53 BA Health & Social Care and Media Studies
Duration: 3FT Hon
Entry Requirements: *GCE:* 260-360.

LR52 BA Health & Social Care and Modern Foreign Languages German
Duration: 3FT Hon
Entry Requirements: *GCE:* 260-360.

LR54 BA Health & Social Care and Modern Foreign Languages Spanish
Duration: 3FT Hon
Entry Requirements: *GCE:* 260-360.

LW56 BA Health & Social Care and Photography
Duration: 3FT Hon
Entry Requirements: *GCE:* 260-360.

LL52 BA Health & Social Care and Politics
Duration: 3FT Hon
Entry Requirements: *GCE:* 260-360.

LP52 BA Health & Social Care and Public Relations
Duration: 3FT Hon
Entry Requirements: *GCE:* 260-360.

LL53 BA Health & Social Care and Sociology
Duration: 3FT Hon
Entry Requirements: *GCE:* 260-360.

LX51 BA Health & Social Care and TESOL
Duration: 3FT Hon
Entry Requirements: *GCE:* 260-360.

LN58 BA Health & Social Care and Tourism
Duration: 3FT Hon
Entry Requirements: *GCE:* 260-360.

L5N2 BA Health & Social Care with Business Management
Duration: 3FT Hon
Entry Requirements: *GCE:* 260-360.

L5XH BA Health & Social Care with Childhood Studies
Duration: 3FT Hon
Entry Requirements: *GCE:* 260-360.

L5M9 BA Health & Social Care with Criminology
Duration: 3FT Hon
Entry Requirements: *GCE:* 260-360.

L5W5 BA Health & Social Care with Dance
Duration: 3FT Hon
Entry Requirements: *GCE:* 260-360.

L5W4 BA Health & Social Care with Drama
Duration: 3FT Hon
Entry Requirements: *GCE:* 260-360.

L5X3 BA Health & Social Care with Education
Duration: 3FT Hon
Entry Requirements: *GCE:* 260-360.

L5Q3 BA Health & Social Care with English
Duration: 3FT Hon
Entry Requirements: *GCE:* 260-360.

L5Q1 BA Health & Social Care with English Language/Linguistics
Duration: 3FT Hon
Entry Requirements: *GCE:* 260-360.

L5V1 BA Health & Social Care with History
Duration: 3FT Hon
Entry Requirements: *GCE:* 260-360.

L5P5 BA Health & Social Care with Journalism
Duration: 3FT Hon
Entry Requirements: *GCE:* 260-360.

L5P3 BA Health & Social Care with Media Studies
Duration: 3FT Hon
Entry Requirements: *GCE:* 260-360.

L5P2 BA Health & Social Care with Public Relations
Duration: 3FT Hon
Entry Requirements: Contact the institution for details.

L5L3 BA Health & Social Care with Sociology
Duration: 3FT Hon
Entry Requirements: *GCE:* 260-360.

L5X1 BA Health & Social Care with TESOL
Duration: 3FT Hon
Entry Requirements: *GCE:* 260-360.

L5N8 BA Health & Social Care with Tourism
Duration: 3FT Hon
Entry Requirements: *GCE:* 260-360.

L5L2 BA Health and Social Care with Politics
Duration: 3FT Hon
Entry Requirements: *GCE:* 260-360.

V1L5 BA History with Health & Social Care
Duration: 3FT Hon
Entry Requirements: *GCE:* 260-360.

P5L5 BA Journalism with Health & Social Care
Duration: 3FT Hon
Entry Requirements: *GCE:* 260-360.

P3L5 BA Media Studies with Health & Social Care
Duration: 3FT Hon
Entry Requirements: *GCE:* 260-360.

R1L5 BA Modern Foreign Languages French with Health & Social Care
Duration: 3FT Hon
Entry Requirements: *GCE:* 260-360.

R2L5 BA Modern Foreign Languages German with Health & Social Care
Duration: 3FT Hon
Entry Requirements: *GCE:* 260-360.

R4L5 BA Modern Foreign Languages Spanish with Health & Social Care
Duration: 3FT Hon
Entry Requirements: *GCE:* 260-360.

W6L5 BA Photography with Health & Social Care
Duration: 3FT Hon
Entry Requirements: *GCE:* 260-360.

L2L5 BA Politics with Health & Social Care
Duration: 3FT Hon
Entry Requirements: *GCE:* 260-360.

P2L5 BA Public Relations with Health & Social Care
Duration: 3FT Hon
Entry Requirements: *GCE:* 260-360.

L500 BA Social Work
Duration: 3FT Hon
Entry Requirements: *GCE:* 260-360. *OCR ND:* D *OCR NED:* M3 Interview required.

L3L5 BA Sociology with Health & Social Care
Duration: 3FT Hon
Entry Requirements: *GCE:* 260-360.

C6L5 BA Sport with Health & Social Care
Duration: 3FT Hon
Entry Requirements: *GCE:* 260-360.

X1L5 BA TESOL with Health & Social Care
Duration: 3FT Hon
Entry Requirements: *GCE:* 260-360.

N8L5 BA Tourism with Health & Social Care
Duration: 3FT Hon
Entry Requirements: *GCE:* 260-360.

LC58 BA/BSc Health & Social Care and Psychology
Duration: 3FT Hon
Entry Requirements: *GCE:* 260-360.

LC56 BA/BSc Health & Social Care and Sport
Duration: 3FT Hon
Entry Requirements: *GCE:* 260-360.

L5C8 BA/BSc Health & Social Care with Psychology
Duration: 3FT Hon
Entry Requirements: *GCE:* 260-360.

L5C6 BA/BSc Health & Social Care with Sport
Duration: 3FT Hon
Entry Requirements: *GCE:* 260-360.

C8L5 BA/BSc Psychology with Health & Social Care
Duration: 3FT Hon
Entry Requirements: *GCE:* 260-360.

L510 BSc Health and Social Care
Duration: 3FT Hon
Entry Requirements: *GCE:* 260-360. *SQAH:* AAAA-CCCC.

S90 UNIVERSITY OF SUSSEX
UNDERGRADUATE ADMISSIONS
SUSSEX HOUSE
UNIVERSITY OF SUSSEX
BRIGHTON BN1 9RH
t: 01273 678416 f: 01273 678545
e: ug.applicants@sussex.ac.uk
// www.sussex.ac.uk

L500 BA Social Work
Duration: 3FT Hon   CRB Check: Required
Entry Requirements: *GCE:* ABB. *SQAH:* AABBB. *IB:* 34. *BTEC SubDip:* D. *BTEC Dip:* DM. *BTEC ExtDip:* DDM. *OCR ND:* M1 *OCR NED:* D2 Interview required.

L520 BA Working with Children and Young People
Duration: 3FT Hon   CRB Check: Required
Entry Requirements: *GCE:* ABB. *SQAH:* AABBB. *IB:* 34. *BTEC SubDip:* D. *BTEC Dip:* DM. *BTEC ExtDip:* DDM. *OCR ND:* M1 *OCR NED:* D2

L508 MA Social Work (Postgraduate Entry)
Duration: 2FT PMD   CRB Check: Required
Entry Requirements: *BTEC SubDip:* D. *BTEC Dip:* DD. *BTEC ExtDip:* DDD. Interview required.

S93 SWANSEA UNIVERSITY
SINGLETON PARK
SWANSEA SA2 8PP
t: 01792 295111 f: 01792 295110
e: admissions@swansea.ac.uk
// www.swansea.ac.uk

LX53 BSc Childhood and Youth
Duration: 3FT Hon
Entry Requirements: *GCE:* 260.

L510 BSc Health and Social Care
Duration: 3FT Hon
Entry Requirements: Contact the institution for details.

L500 BSc Social Work
Duration: 3FT Hon   CRB Check: Required
Entry Requirements: *GCE:* BCC. Interview required.

S96 SWANSEA METROPOLITAN UNIVERSITY
MOUNT PLEASANT CAMPUS
SWANSEA SA1 6ED
t: 01792 481000 f: 01792 481061
e: gemma.green@smu.ac.uk
// www.smu.ac.uk

L510 BSc Health and Social Care
Duration: 1FT Hon
Entry Requirements: Interview required. HND required.

015L HND Health and Social Care
Duration: 2FT HND
Entry Requirements: *GCE:* 80-360. *IB:* 24. Interview required.

T20 TEESSIDE UNIVERSITY
MIDDLESBROUGH TS1 3BA
t: 01642 218121 f: 01642 384201
e: registry@tees.ac.uk
// www.tees.ac.uk

L501 BA Social Work
Duration: 3FT Hon   CRB Check: Required
Entry Requirements: *GCE:* 240. *IB:* 24. *BTEC ExtDip:* MMM. Interview required.

LX53 BSc Childhood and Youth Studies
Duration: 3FT Hon
Entry Requirements: *GCE:* 220.

M9L5 BSc Criminology with Youth Studies
Duration: 3FT Hon
Entry Requirements: *GCE:* 240.

015L HND Health and Social Care
Duration: 2FT HND   CRB Check: Required
Entry Requirements: *GCE:* 40-80.

T80 UNIVERSITY OF WALES TRINITY SAINT DAVID
COLLEGE ROAD
CARMARTHEN SA31 3EP
t: 01267 676767 f: 01267 676766
e: registry@trinitysaintdavid.ac.uk
// www.tsd.ac.uk

VLPN BA Crefydd a Chymdeithas
Duration: 3FT Hon
Entry Requirements: Contact the institution for details.

L521 BA Early Childhood
Duration: 3FT Hon   CRB Check: Required
Entry Requirements: Contact the institution for details.

L591 BA Gwaith Ieuenctid & Chymuned
Duration: 3FT Hon   CRB Check: Required
Entry Requirements: *GCE:* 140-360. *IB:* 26. Interview required.

L522 BA Plentyndod Cynnar
Duration: 3FT Hon   CRB Check: Required
Entry Requirements: Contact the institution for details.

L592 BA Youth & Community Work
Duration: 3FT Hon   **CRB Check:** Required
Entry Requirements: *GCE:* 140-360. Interview required.

T85 TRURO AND PENWITH COLLEGE
TRURO COLLEGE
COLLEGE ROAD
TRURO
CORNWALL TR1 3XX
t: 01872 267122 f: 01872 267526
e: heinfo@trurocollege.ac.uk
// www.truro-penwith.ac.uk

LX53 FdA Children and Young People's Workforce
Duration: 2FT Fdg
Entry Requirements: *GCE:* 60. *IB:* 24. *BTEC Dip:* MP. *BTEC ExtDip:* PPP. Interview required.

L530 FdSc Community Studies (Development and Youth Work)
Duration: 2FT Fdg
Entry Requirements: *GCE:* 80. *IB:* 24. *BTEC Dip:* MP. *BTEC ExtDip:* PPP. Interview required.

U20 UNIVERSITY OF ULSTER
COLERAINE
CO. LONDONDERRY
NORTHERN IRELAND BT52 1SA
t: 028 7012 4221 f: 028 7012 4908
e: online@ulster.ac.uk
// www.ulster.ac.uk

L521 BSc Community Youth Work
Duration: 3FT Hon   **CRB Check:** Required
Entry Requirements: *GCE:* 200. *IB:* 24. Interview required.

L510 BSc Health and Social Care Policy
Duration: 3FT Hon   **CRB Check:** Required
Entry Requirements: *GCE:* 280. *IB:* 24.

L500 BSc Social Work
Duration: 3FT Hon   **CRB Check:** Required
Entry Requirements: *GCE:* 300. *IB:* 25. Interview required.

L505 BSc Social Work (BMC)
Duration: 3FT Hon   **CRB Check:** Required
Entry Requirements: *GCE:* 300. *IB:* 25. Interview required.

L501 BSc Social Work (Graduate Entry)
Duration: 2FT PMD   **CRB Check:** Required
Entry Requirements: Interview required.

L506 BSc Social Work (SWC)
Duration: 3FT Hon   **CRB Check:** Required
Entry Requirements: *GCE:* 300. *IB:* 25. Interview required.

U40 UNIVERSITY OF THE WEST OF SCOTLAND
PAISLEY
RENFREWSHIRE
SCOTLAND PA1 2BE
t: 0141 848 3727 f: 0141 848 3623
e: admissions@uws.ac.uk
// www.uws.ac.uk

L560 BA Childhood Studies
Duration: 2FT Ord   **CRB Check:** Required
Entry Requirements: Interview required.

L540 BA Community Learning and Participation
Duration: 3FT/4FT Ord/Hon   **CRB Check:** Required
Entry Requirements: Contact the institution for details.

L500 BA Social Work
Duration: 4FT Hon   **CRB Check:** Required
Entry Requirements: *GCE:* CCD. *SQAH:* BBBC.

W05 THE UNIVERSITY OF WEST LONDON
ST MARY'S ROAD
EALING
LONDON W5 5RF
t: 0800 036 8888 f: 020 8566 1353
e: learning.advice@uwl.ac.uk
// www.uwl.ac.uk

L500 BSc Social Work
Duration: 3FT Hon   **CRB Check:** Required
Entry Requirements: *GCE:* 200. *IB:* 28. Interview required.

W25 WARWICKSHIRE COLLEGE
WARWICK NEW ROAD
LEAMINGTON SPA
WARWICKSHIRE CV32 5JE
t: 01926 884223 f: 01926 318 111
e: kgooch@warkscol.ac.uk
// www.warwickshire.ac.uk

XL35 BA Early Years Care and Education
Duration: 1FT Hon   **CRB Check:** Required
Entry Requirements: Contact the institution for details.

L540 FdA Social Care and Community Studies
Duration: 2FT Fdg
Entry Requirements: Contact the institution for details.

35XL HND Advanced Practice in Work w/ Children & Families
Duration: 2FT HND
Entry Requirements: *GCE:* 40.

W35 COLLEGE OF WEST ANGLIA
MAIN CAMPUS
TENNYSON AVENUE
KING'S LYNN
NORFOLK PE30 2QW
t: 01553 761144 f: 01553 770115
e: enquiries@col-westanglia.ac.uk
// www.col-westanglia.ac.uk

XL35 BA Early Childhood Studies
Duration: 1FT Hon
Entry Requirements: Contact the institution for details.

LX5H FdA Early Years Childcare and Education
Duration: 2FT Fdg
Entry Requirements: *GCE:* 80-160.

W51 CITY OF WESTMINSTER COLLEGE
CITY OF WESTMINSTER COLLEGE
PADDINGTON GREEN CAMPUS
25 PADDINGTON GREEN
LONDON W2 1NB
t: 020 7723 8826
e: customer.services@cwc.ac.uk
// www.cwc.ac.uk

095L HND Health and Social Care
Duration: 2FT HND   CRB Check: Required
Entry Requirements: Contact the institution for details.

W67 WIGAN AND LEIGH COLLEGE
PO BOX 53
PARSON'S WALK
WIGAN
GREATER MANCHESTER WN1 1RS
t: 01942 761605 f: 01942 761164
e: applications@wigan-leigh.ac.uk
// www.wigan-leigh.ac.uk

L520 FdSc Children, Young People and their Services
Duration: 2FT Fdg   CRB Check: Required
Entry Requirements: Interview required.

L511 FdSc Health and Social Care
Duration: 2FT Fdg   CRB Check: Required
Entry Requirements: Interview required.

W73 WIRRAL METROPOLITAN COLLEGE
CONWAY PARK CAMPUS
EUROPA BOULEVARD
BIRKENHEAD, WIRRAL
MERSEYSIDE CH41 4NT
t: 0151 551 7777 f: 0151 551 7001
// www.wmc.ac.uk

L590 FdA Early Years Practice (Sector Endorsed)
Duration: 2FT Fdg
Entry Requirements: Interview required.

W74 WILTSHIRE COLLEGE
WILTSHIRE COLLEGE LACKHAM
LACOCK
CHIPPENHAM
WILTSHIRE SN15 2NY
t: 01249 466806 f: 01249 444474
e: HEAdmissions@wiltshire.ac.uk
// www.wiltshire.ac.uk

L500 BSc Social Work
Duration: 3FT Hon   CRB Check: Required
Entry Requirements: *GCE:* 260. *OCR NED:* M2 Interview required.

XL15 FdA Early Childhood Studies
Duration: 2FT Fdg   CRB Check: Required
Entry Requirements: Contact the institution for details.

W75 UNIVERSITY OF WOLVERHAMPTON
ADMISSIONS UNIT
MX207, CAMP STREET
WOLVERHAMPTON
WEST MIDLANDS WV1 1AD
t: 01902 321000 f: 01902 321896
e: admissions@wlv.ac.uk
// www.wlv.ac.uk

L592 BA Childhood & Family Studies
Duration: 3FT Hon   CRB Check: Required
Entry Requirements: *GCE:* 200. *IB:* 24. *BTEC Dip:* DM. *BTEC ExtDip:* MMP. *OCR ND:* M1 *OCR NED:* P1

XXH3 BA Childhood & Family Studies and Education Studies
Duration: 3FT Hon   CRB Check: Required
Entry Requirements: *GCE:* 200. *IB:* 24. *BTEC Dip:* DM. *BTEC ExtDip:* MMP. *OCR ND:* M1 *OCR NED:* P1

LL5K BA Childhood & Family Studies and Social Policy
Duration: 3FT Hon   CRB Check: Required
Entry Requirements: *GCE:* 200. *IB:* 24. *BTEC Dip:* DM. *BTEC ExtDip:* MMP. *OCR ND:* M1 *OCR NED:* P1

XL35 BA Childhood & Family Studies and Special Needs & Inclusion Studies
Duration: 3FT Hon   CRB Check: Required
Entry Requirements: *GCE:* 200. *IB:* 24. *BTEC Dip:* DM. *BTEC ExtDip:* MMP. *OCR ND:* M1 *OCR NED:* P1

LM59 BA Social Care and Criminology & Criminal Justice
Duration: 3FT Hon
Entry Requirements: *GCE:* 160-220. *IB:* 26.

LL45 BA Social Care and Social Policy
Duration: 3FT Hon
Entry Requirements: *GCE:* 160-220. *IB:* 24.

L500 BA Social Work
Duration: 3FT Hon   CRB Check: Required
Entry Requirements: *GCE:* 160-220. *IB:* 24. Interview required.

LB55 BA Special Needs & Inclusion Studies and Deaf Studies
Duration: 3FT Hon
Entry Requirements: *GCE:* 160-220. *IB:* 24.

LXM3 BA Special Needs & Inclusion Studies and Education Studies
Duration: 3FT Hon   CRB Check: Required
Entry Requirements: *GCE:* 180. *IB:* 24. *BTEC Dip:* DM. *BTEC ExtDip:* MMP. *OCR ND:* M1 *OCR NED:* P1

LX53 BA Special Needs and Inclusion Studies
Duration: 3FT Hon   CRB Check: Required
Entry Requirements: *GCE:* 180. *IB:* 24. *BTEC Dip:* DM. *BTEC ExtDip:* MMP. *OCR ND:* M1 *OCR NED:* P1

LL35 BSc Social Care and Sociology
Duration: 3FT Hon
Entry Requirements: Contact the institution for details.

L511 FdA Health and Social Care
Duration: 2FT Fdg
Entry Requirements: *GCE:* 60-120. *IB:* 24.

L508 MA Social Work
Duration: 2FT PMD   CRB Check: Required
Entry Requirements: Interview required.

W76 UNIVERSITY OF WINCHESTER
WINCHESTER
HANTS SO22 4NR
t: 01962 827234 f: 01962 827288
e: course.enquiries@winchester.ac.uk
// www.winchester.ac.uk

TLR5 BA American Studies and Health, Community & Social Care Studies
Duration: 3FT Hon
Entry Requirements: Contact the institution for details.

VLKN BA Archaeology and Health, Community & Social Care Studies
Duration: 3FT Hon
Entry Requirements: Contact the institution for details.

NL25 BA Business Management and Health, Community & Social Care Studies
Duration: 3FT Hon
Entry Requirements: Contact the institution for details.

LXMH BA Childhood Youth & Community Studies and Education Studies (Modern Liberal Arts)
Duration: 3FT Hon
Entry Requirements: *Foundation:* Distinction. *GCE:* 260-300. *IB:* 24. *OCR ND:* D *OCR NED:* M2

L594 BA Childhood, Youth & Community Studies and Health, Community & Social Care Studies
Duration: 3FT Hon
Entry Requirements: Contact the institution for details.

LL35 BA Criminology and Health, Community & Social Care Studies
Duration: 3FT Hon
Entry Requirements: Contact the institution for details.

WL45 BA Drama and Health, Community & Social Care Studies
Duration: 3FT Hon
Entry Requirements: Contact the institution for details.

XL35 BA Education Studies (Early Childhood) and Health, Community & Social Care Studies
Duration: 3FT Hon
Entry Requirements: Contact the institution for details.

LX35 BA Education Studies (Modern Liberal Arts) and Health, Community & Social Care Stud
Duration: 3FT Hon
Entry Requirements: Contact the institution for details.

XL3M BA Education Studies and Health, Community & Social Care Studies
Duration: 3FT Hon
Entry Requirements: Contact the institution for details.

QL53 BA English Language Studies and Health, Community and Social Care Studies
Duration: 3FT Hon
Entry Requirements: Contact the institution for details.

QL35 BA English and Health, Community & Social Care Studies
Duration: 3FT Hon
Entry Requirements: Contact the institution for details.

PL53 BA Film & Cinema Technologies and Health, Community & Social Care Studies
Duration: 3FT Hon
Entry Requirements: Contact the institution for details.

PL5H BA Film Studies and Health, Community & Social Care Studies
Duration: 3FT Hon
Entry Requirements: Contact the institution for details.

LV51 BA Health, Community & Social Care Studies and History
Duration: 3FT Hon
Entry Requirements: Contact the institution for details.

LP55 BA Health, Community & Social Care Studies and Journalism Studies
Duration: 3FT Hon
Entry Requirements: Contact the institution for details.

LM15 BA Health, Community & Social Care Studies and Law
Duration: 3FT Hon
Entry Requirements: Contact the institution for details.

PL5J BA Health, Community & Social Care Studies and Media Production
Duration: 3FT Hon
Entry Requirements: Contact the institution for details.

PL3N BA Health, Community & Social Care Studies and Media Studies
Duration: 3FT Hon
Entry Requirements: Contact the institution for details.

LV55 BA Health, Community & Social Care Studies and Modern Liberal Arts
Duration: 3FT Hon
Entry Requirements: Contact the institution for details.

LL2N BA Health, Community & Social Care Studies and Politics & Global Studies
Duration: 3FT Hon
Entry Requirements: Contact the institution for details.

LL3N BA Health, Community & Social Care Studies and Sociology
Duration: 3FT Hon
Entry Requirements: Contact the institution for details.

LN85 BA Health, Community & Social Care Studies and Sports Management
Duration: 3FT Hon
Entry Requirements: Contact the institution for details.

LC65 BA Health, Community & Social Care Studies and Sports Studies
Duration: 3FT Hon
Entry Requirements: Contact the institution for details.

LV65 BA Health, Community & Social Care Studies and Theology & Religious Studies
Duration: 3FT Hon
Entry Requirements: Contact the institution for details.

WL35 BA Health, Community & Social Care and Performing Arts (Contemporary Performance)
Duration: 3FT Hon
Entry Requirements: Contact the institution for details.

LL3M BA (Hons) Childhood, Youth & Community Studies and Sociology
Duration: 3FT Hon
Entry Requirements: Contact the institution for details.

L500 BSc Social Work
Duration: 3FT Hon   CRB Check: Required
Entry Requirements: *Foundation:* Distinction. *GCE:* 260-300. *IB:* 25. *OCR ND:* D *OCR NED:* M2 Interview required.

W80 UNIVERSITY OF WORCESTER
HENWICK GROVE
WORCESTER WR2 6AJ
t: 01905 855111 f: 01905 855377
e: admissions@worc.ac.uk
// www.worcester.ac.uk

XL35 BA Education Studies and Social Welfare
Duration: 3FT Hon
Entry Requirements: *GCE:* 220-260. *IB:* 24. *OCR ND:* D *OCR NED:* M3

LX53 BA Integrated Working with Children and Families
Duration: 1FT Hon
Entry Requirements: HND required.

LL25 BA Politics: People & Power and Social Welfare
Duration: 3FT Hon
Entry Requirements: *GCE:* 240-300. *IB:* 24. *OCR ND:* D *OCR NED:* M3

L510 BA Social Welfare
Duration: 3FT Hon
Entry Requirements: *GCE:* 200. *IB:* 24. *OCR ND:* D *OCR NED:* M3

L540 BA Social Welfare (Top-Up)
Duration: 1FT Hon
Entry Requirements: HND required.

LL53 BA Social Welfare and Sociology
Duration: 3FT Hon
Entry Requirements: *GCE:* 240-300. *IB:* 24. *OCR ND:* D *OCR NED:* M3

L590 BA Youth and Community
Duration: 3FT Hon   CRB Check: Required
Entry Requirements: *GCE:* 220. *IB:* 24. *OCR ND:* D *OCR NED:* M3

CL85 BA/BSc Psychology and Social Welfare
Duration: 3FT Hon
Entry Requirements: *GCE:* 280. *IB:* 25. *OCR ND:* D *OCR NED:* M3

L52A CertHE Birth and Beyond Practitioner
Duration: 1FT Cer
Entry Requirements: Contact the institution for details.

L511 FdA Health & Social Care
Duration: 2FT Fdg   CRB Check: Required
Entry Requirements: *GCE:* 60. *IB:* 24.

L514 FdA Health & Social Care (Child & Adolescent Mental Health)
Duration: 2FT Fdg   CRB Check: Required
Entry Requirements: *GCE:* 60. *IB:* 24.

L520 FdA Integrated Children's Services
Duration: 2FT Fdg
Entry Requirements: *GCE:* 60. *IB:* 24.

LL45 FdA Young Peoples Services
Duration: 2FT Fdg   CRB Check: Required
Entry Requirements: *GCE:* 60. *IB:* 24.

L512 FdSc Health & Social Care (Learning Disabilities and Autism)
Duration: 2FT Fdg   CRB Check: Required
Entry Requirements: *GCE:* 60. *IB:* 24.

L515 FdSc Mental Health
Duration: 2FT Fdg   CRB Check: Required
Entry Requirements: *GCE:* 60. *IB:* 24.

L508 MA Social Work (Postgraduate Entry)
Duration: 2FT PMD   CRB Check: Required
Entry Requirements: Interview required.

W81 WORCESTER COLLEGE OF TECHNOLOGY
DEANSWAY
WORCESTER WR1 2JF
t: 01905 725555 f: 01905 28906
// www.wortech.ac.uk

L520 FdA Early Years
Duration: 2FT Fdg
Entry Requirements: *GCE:* 100.

005L HND Advanced Practice Work with Children and Families
Duration: 2FT HND   CRB Check: Required
Entry Requirements: *GCE:* 120. Interview required.

Y50 THE UNIVERSITY OF YORK
STUDENT RECRUITMENT AND ADMISSIONS
UNIVERSITY OF YORK
HESLINGTON
YORK YO10 5DD
t: 01904 324000 f: 01904 323538
e: ug-admissions@york.ac.uk
// www.york.ac.uk

L500 BA Social Work
Duration: 3FT Hon
Entry Requirements: *GCE:* BBB. *SQAH:* AABBB. *IB:* 31. *BTEC ExtDip:* DDM.

L508 MA Social Work (Postgraduate entry)
Duration: 2FT PMD   CRB Check: Required
Entry Requirements: Contact the institution for details.

Y75 YORK ST JOHN UNIVERSITY
LORD MAYOR'S WALK
YORK YO31 7EX
t: 01904 876598 f: 01904 876940/876921
e: admissions@yorksj.ac.uk
// w3.yorksj.ac.uk

L541 BA Children, Young People & Families
Duration: 3FT Hon
Entry Requirements: *GCE:* 200-240.

LXM3 BA Children, Young People & Families and Education Studies
Duration: 3FT Hon
Entry Requirements: *GCE:* 200-220.

PS